Lecture Notes in Computer Science 5000

Commenced Publication in 1973
Founding and Former Series Editors:
Gerhard Goos, Juris Hartmanis, and Jan van Leeuwen

T0222761

Orna Grumberg   Helmut Veith (Eds.)

25 Years
of Model Checking

History, Achievements, Perspectives

 Springer

Volume Editors

Orna Grumberg
Technion - Israel Institute of Technology
Computer Science Department
Technion City, Haifa 32000, Israel
E-mail: orna@cs.technion.ac.il

Helmut Veith
Technische Universität Darmstadt, Fachbereich Informatik
Hochschulstr. 10, 64289 Darmstadt, Germany
E-mail: veith@forsyte.cs.tu-darmstadt.de

Cover illustration: taken from
"Das große Rasenstück" by Albrecht Dürer (1471-1528)
Current location of the original painting: Albertina, Vienna

Library of Congress Control Number: 2008929605

CR Subject Classification (1998): F.3, D.2.4, D.3.1, D.2, F.4.1, I.2.3

LNCS Sublibrary: SL 1 – Theoretical Computer Science and General Issues

ISSN   0302-9743
ISBN-10   3-540-69849-3 Springer Berlin Heidelberg New York
ISBN-13   978-3-540-69849-4 Springer Berlin Heidelberg New York

Springer is a part of Springer Science+Business Media

springer.com

© Springer-Verlag Berlin Heidelberg 2008
Printed in Germany

Typesetting: Camera-ready by author, data conversion by Scientific Publishing Services, Chennai, India
Printed on acid-free paper   SPIN: 12326419   06/3180   5 4 3 2 1 0

Preface

As this volume is going to print, model checking is attracting worldwide media attention, and we are celebrating the ACM Turing Award 2007 for the paradigm-shifting work initiated a quarter century ago. Today, model checking technology evidently ranges among the foremost applications of logic to computer science and computer engineering. The model checking community has achieved multiple breakthroughs, bridging the gap between theoretical computer science, hardware and software engineering, and is reaching out to new challenging areas such as systems biology and hybrid systems. Model checking is extensively used in the hardware industry, and has become feasible for verifying many types of software as well. Model checking has been introduced into computer science and electrical engineering curricula at universities worldwide, and has become a universal tool for the analysis of systems.

This volume presents a collection of invited papers based on talks at the symposium "25 Years of Model Checking (25MC)." In addition, we have included facsimile reprints of the two visionary papers on model checking by Edmund Clarke, Allen Emerson, Jean-Pierre Queille, and Joseph Sifakis. The 25MC symposium was part of the 18th International Conference on Computer Aided Verification (CAV), which in turn was part of the Federated Logic Conference (FLOC) 2006 in Seattle. The program was complemented by a panel on "Verification in the Next 25 Years" organized by Limor Fix.

In organizing 25MC, we aimed to encourage a sense of common achievement in the model checking community, and also to give students and young researchers a global perspective on the field. As the number of research groups and conferences in model checking is steadily increasing, the 25MC symposium focused on the state of the art and the future challenges, seen through the eyes of the researchers who have shaped the field during the last decades. The invited speakers were encouraged to reflect on historical perspectives as well as exciting future research directions. Consequently, the present volume contains recollections and surveys as well as original technical contributions.

As the 25MC symposium replaced traditional tutorials in CAV 2006, our program was confined to a single day with a limited number of slots. In selecting the invited speakers and the sessions, our main goal was to reflect the diversity of schools and topics in the community, and to make the event exciting and enjoyable. Given the size and success of our community, our selection of speakers, alas, was inevitably contingent. Nevertheless, we are somewhat proud that 25MC brought together three Turing award winners, and, with an overlap of two at the time of writing, seven Kannelakis award winners.

We are grateful to many people who helped make this enterprise a success, in particular to Ed Clarke, Allen Emerson, Joseph Sifakis (who unfortunately was unable to attend FLOC 2006), and Jean-Pierre Queille for agreeing to reprint their papers in this volume; to Alfred Hofmann of Springer and his colleagues Ronan Nugent and Ursula Barth for their enthusiasm and support in this project; to the CAV 2006 Chairs Tom Ball and Robert Jones for making 25MC possible, as well as the CAV 2008 Chairs Aarti Gupta and Sharad Malik for presenting this volume at the 20th anniversary CAV in Princeton 2008. We also thank Mohammad Khaleghi and Stefan Kugele for Web design and editorial help with the proceedings. The panel and the lunch were sponsored by the ACM Distinguished Lectureship Program – a program that encourages technical education and dissemination of technical information.

The cover painting of this volume evokes a period when art and science came together. Completed by Albrecht Dürer 505 years ago, *Das große Rasenstück* is both a celebrated Renaissance masterpiece, and an accurate model of a bug-free piece of nature. *Ad multos annos !*

April 2008   Orna Grumberg
                                                                              Helmut Veith

From left to right: Amir Pnueli, Gerard Holzmann, Moshe Vardi, Bob Kurshan, David Dill, Ken McMillan, Edmund Clarke, Tom Henzinger, Limor Fix, Randy Bryant, Rajeev Alur, Allen Emerson.   (Photography by Robert Jones)

Table of Contents

The Birth of Model Checking*

Edmund M. Clarke

Department of Computer Science
Carnegie Mellon University
Pittsburgh, PA, USA
emc@cs.cmu.edu

"When the time is ripe for certain things, these things appear in different places in the manner of violets coming to light in early spring." (Wolfgang Bolyai to his son Johann in urging him to claim the invention of non-Euclidean geometry without delay [Vit88]).

1 Model Checking

Model Checking did not arise in a historical vacuum. There was an important problem that needed to be solved, namely Concurrent Program Verification. Concurrency errors are particularly difficult to find by program testing, since they are often hard to reproduce. Most of the formal research on this topic involved constructing proofs by hand using a Floyd-Hoare style logic. Probably, the best known formal system was the one proposed by Owicki and Gries [OG76] for reasoning about Conditional Critical Regions. Although I had written my thesis on the meta-theory of Hoare Logic [Cla77a, Cla77b, Cla78, Cla79a, Cla79c, Cla80] and was very familiar with the Owick-Gries proof methodology, I was quite skeptical about the scalability of hand constructed proofs. There had been some practical research on state exploration methods for communication protocols by Gregor Bochmann and others, but it was largely ignored by the "Formal Verification Community". Also, in the late 1970's, Pnueli [Pnu77] and Owicki and Lamport [OL82] had proposed the use of Temporal Logic for specifying concurrent programs. Although they still advocated hand constructed proofs, their work demonstrated convincingly that Temporal Logic was ideal for expressing concepts like mutual exclusion, absence of deadlock, and absence of starvation.

Allen Emerson and I combined the state-exploration approach with Temporal Logic in an efficient manner and showed that the result could be used to solve non-trivial problems. Here is a quote from our original 1981 paper [CE81]:

---

* This research was sponsored by the National Science Foundation under grant nos. CNS- 0411152, CCF-0429120, CCR-0121547, and CCR-0098072, the US Army Research Office under grant no. DAAD19-01-1-0485, and the Office of Naval Research under grant no. N00014-01-1-0796. The views and conclusions contained in this document are those of the author and should not be interpreted as representing the official policies, either expressed or implied, of any sponsoring institution, the U.S. government or any other entity.

O. Grumberg and H. Veith (Eds.): 25MC Festschrift, LNCS 5000, pp. 1–26, 2008.
© Springer-Verlag Berlin Heidelberg 2008

"The task of proof construction is in general quite tedious and a good deal of ingenuity may be required to organize the proof in a manageable fashion. We argue that proof construction is unnecessary in the case of finite state concurrent systems and can be replaced by a model-theoretic approach which will mechanically determine if the system meets a specification expressed in propositional temporal logic. The global state graph of the concurrent systems can be viewed as a finite Kripke structure and an efficient algorithm can be given to determine whether a structure is a model of a particular formula (i.e. to determine if the program meets its specification)."

1.1   What Is Model Checking?

The Model Checking problem is easy to state:

Let M be a Kripke structure (i.e., state-transition graph). Let f be a formula of temporal logic (i.e., the specification). Find all states s of M such that $M, s \models f$.

We used the term *Model Checking* because we wanted to determine if the temporal formula f was true in the Kripke structure M, i.e., whether the structure M was a *model* for the formula f. Some people believe erroneously that the use of the term "model" refers to the dictionary meaning of this word (e.g., a miniature representation of something or a pattern of something to be made) and indicates that we are dealing with an abstraction of the actual system under study.

Emerson and I gave a polynomial algorithm for solving the Model Checking Problem for the logic CTL. The figure below shows the structure of a typical Model Checking system. A preprocessor extracts a state transition graph from a program or circuit. The Model Checking engine takes the state transition graph and a temporal formula and determines whether the formula is true or not (Figure 1).

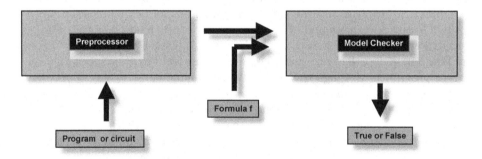

Fig. 1. Model Checker Structure

1.2   Advantages of Model Checking

Model Checking has a number of advantages compared to other verification techniques such as automated theorem proving or proof checking. A partial list of some of these advantages is given below:

- No proofs! The user of a Model Checker does not need to construct a correctness proof. In principle, all that is necessary is for the user to enter a description of the circuit or program to be verified and the specification to be checked and press the "return" key. The checking process is automatic.
- Fast. In practice, Model checking is fast compared to other rigorous methods such as the use of a proof checker, which may require months of the user's time working in interactive mode.
- Diagnostic counterexamples. If the specification is not satisfied, the Model Checker will produce a counterexample execution trace that shows why the specification does not hold (Figure 2). It is impossible to overestimate the importance of the counterexample feature. The counterexamples are invaluable in debugging complex systems. Some people use Model Checking just for this feature.
- No problem with partial specifications. It is unnecessary to completely specify the program or circuit before beginning to Model Check properties. Thus, Model Checking can be used during the design of a complex system. The user does not have to wait until the design phase is complete.
- Temporal Logics can easily express many of the properties that are needed for reasoning about concurrent systems. This is important because the reason some concurrency property holds is often quite subtle, and it is difficult to verify all possible cases manually.

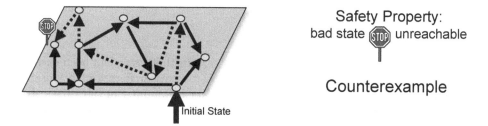

Fig. 2. Diagnostic Counterexample

1.3   Disadvantages of Model Checking

Over the last twenty-five years I have heard many objections to the use of Model Checking. I discuss some of these objections below:

- Proving a program helps you understand it. I do not believe that this is a valid objection. In my opinion it is somewhat like the saying that "Suffering makes us stronger". It is possible to understand a program just as well, if not better, by checking properties and examining the counterexamples when they are false.
- Temporal logic specifications are ugly. I think this depends on who is writing the specifications. I have seen very complicated and unreadable specifications in languages designed for formal specification based on Z (Zed) notation [ASM80]. A good rule of thumb is to keep the specifications as short as

possible. Some model checkers have a macro facility that allows the user to encapsulate sub-expressions of formulas that would otherwise make it complicated. Temporal logics like PSL [EF06] have very expressive sets of operators that facilitate writing specifications.

- Writing specifications is hard. This is true. But it is also true of other verification techniques like automated theorem proving. Certainly, part of the solution is better education. Very few computer science and electrical engineering departments currently offer courses on formal verification. (Electrical engineers in the U.S. often spend more time learning about the Laplace transform than writing formal specifications for circuits!)
- State explosion is a major problem. This is absolutely true. The number of global system states of a concurrent system with many processes or complicated data structures can be enormous. All Model Checkers suffer from this problem. In fact, the state explosion problem has been the driving force behind much of the research in Model Checking and the development of new Model Checkers.

2 Verification Tools Before 1981

Automated verification tools in use before 1981 were either based on theorem proving or exhaustive state exploration. I will focus on the state exploration techniques since they are more closely related to Model Checking.

2.1 Petri Net Tools

When I started research on this paper, I was certain that there had been earlier work on tools for verifying Petri Nets. I contacted two researchers, Tadao Murata and Kurt Jensen, who were active in the Petri Net community in the 1970's. To my surprise, I quickly discovered that there had been little serious work on verification tools for Petri Nets before 1981. I include brief quotes from Murata and Jensen below.

Murata:

"I started working on Petri nets from mid-1970, and attended the First International Workshop on Petri Nets held in 1980 and thereafter. But I do not recall any papers discussing formal verification using Petri Nets (PNs) BEFORE 1981. Also, I doubt there were any PN reachability tools before 1981. MetaSoft Company was selling earlier PN drawing tools and may have had a primitive one before 1981."

Jensen:

"Like Tad, I do not think there is any work on Petri net tools prior to 1981.The first Meta Software tool was made in the mid 80's and was merely a drawing tool for low level Petri nets. High-level Petri nets were invented in the late 70's. The first two publications appeared in TCS in 1979 and 1980. It is only after this that people really started the construction of tools. The first simulator for high-level nets and the first state space tools for these were made in the late 80's."

2.2   Bochmann and Protocol Verification

Around 1980, I became aware of the use of automatic verification techniques based on exhaustive state exploration by researchers in communication protocol verification. In particular, I read several very interesting papers by Gregor Bochmann. While researching my 25MC presentation, I contacted Bochmann and asked him to comment about his work on this topic. I enclose below a quote from his email message:

Bochmann:

"For a workshop organized by Andre Danthine, I prepared the paper **Finite State Description of Protocols** in which I presented a method for the verification of communication protocols using the systematic exploration of the global state space of the system (sometimes called reachability analysis). This paper was later published in Computer Networks (1978) and was much cited. At the same time, Colin West had developed some automated tools for doing essentially the same as what I was proposing, but I learned about his activities only later."

In the same message Bochmann commented about the importance of Model Checking.

"The need for exploring the reachable state space of the global system is the basic requirement in protocol verification. Here model checking has not provided anything new. However, temporal logic has brought a more elegant way to talk about liveness and eventuality; in the protocol verification community we were talking about reachable deadlock states (easy to characterize) or undesirable loops (difficult to characterize)."

I believe that Bochmann's comment is very perceptive, although I disagree with his statement that Model Checking has not contributed to the task of computing the reachable state space of a protocol. Indeed, much of the research in Model Checking has focused on finding efficient techniques computing and representing the set of reachable states. Symbolic Model Checking [BCM$^+$90], for example, was a major breakthrough because it enabled much larger state spaces to be searched than was possible using explicit state space traversal.

2.3   Holzmann and Protocol Verification

I was not aware of Gerard Holzmann's work on protocol verification until the late 1980's. In preparing for my 25MC presentation, I contacted him to find out about his early work on automatic techniques for protocol verification.

Holzmann:

> "My first paper-method (never implemented) was from 1978-1979 – as part of my PhD thesis work in Delft. My first fully implemented system was indeed the *Pan* verifier (a first on-the-fly verification system), which found its first real bug in switching software (based on a model that I built in the predecessor language to Spin's *Promela*) at AT&T on November 21, 1980."

Spin did not use temporal logic for specifications until 1987 or 1988 and thus was not a true Model Checker in the sense that Emerson and I used the term until the late 1980's.

Holzmann continued:

> "Things changed quite a bit towards the late eighties, with machines getting faster and RAM memory larger. I implemented a small set of temporal properties (inspired by Pnueli's **Tools and Rules for the Practicing Verifier**) that expressed liveness in my verification system for SDL (the first such system built) in 1987/1988. That led to Spin in 1989 which generalized the method and allowed correctness properties to be expressed as unrestricted omega-regular properties (i.e., as never claims). The first full Spin version is from 1989. The converter from LTL to never claims was later designed by Doron, I think around 95, to make it easier for users to express LTL formulae directly."

Holzmann argues that a Model Checker need not provide a logic for writing specifications.

> "When do we call an efficient checker that uses models a Model Checker though? I sometimes use the distinction between Model Checker and Logic Model Checker" – where to qualify for the latter term you need to support a logic."

I believe that Holzmann does have a valid point. Verification tools that compute some representation for the set of reachable states are often called Model Checkers as are sequential equivalence checkers in hardware verification. This is reasonable to me, although the term is not used in the spirit that Emerson and I originally intended.

3   Fixpoint Theory, Hoare Logic, and Concurrency

There is a close relationship between fixpoint theory and Model Checking algorithms for Branching-Time Logics. I read many papers on this topic as background research for my Ph.D. thesis. Perhaps the two most important results for my subsequent research on Model Checking were Tarski's Fixpoint Lemma [Tar55] and Kleene's First Recursion Theorem [Kle71]. Most Symbolic Model Checkers exploit Tarski's Lemma [Tar55] that every monotonic functional on a complete lattice has a fixpoint. A paper by David Park **Finiteness is Mu-Ineffable** [Par74] gives a first-order version of the Mu-calculus that I suggested as the logical basis for the first paper on Symbolic Model Checking that Burch, Dill, McMillan and I published in the 1990 LICS conference [BCM+90, BCM+92].

My first paper with Emerson [EC80] made the connection between Branching-Time Logics and the Mu-calculus. Kozen references the 1980 paper that Emerson and I wrote in his influential paper on the propositional Mu-calculus [Koz83].

Because of the close connection between the Mu-Calculus and Branching-time Temporal Logics, I believe it was inevitable that Model Checking algorithms were developed for Branching-time Logics before Linear-time Logics.

3.1   Thesis Research on Hoare Logic

My thesis dealt with the *Soundness* and *Completeness* of *Hoare Logic*. The two papers that influenced me most were:

- J. deBakker and L. Meertens, **On the Completeness of the Inductive Assertion Method**, [dBM75].
- S. Cook, **Soundness and Completeness of an Axiom System for Program Verification**, [Coo78].

Cook's paper introduced the notion of *Relative Completeness* of Hoare Logics.

I started on my thesis, entitled **Completeness and Incompleteness Theorems For Hoare Logics**, in July 1975 and finished it a year later in August 1976. Robert Constable was my advisor at Cornell. I waited until I had completed my thesis before publishing any papers on my research. I wrote three papers based on my thesis:

- E. Clarke, **Programming Language Constructs for which it is impossible to obtain Good Hoare-like Axiom Systems**, [Cla77b, Cla79c].
- E. Clarke, **Program Invariants as Fixedpoints**, [Cla77a, Cla79a].
- E. Clarke, **Proving Correctness of Coroutines Without History Variables**, [Cla78, Cla80].

In later research, I addressed the question of what programming language constructs could have *good* Hoare axiomatizations, i.e., sound and relatively complete axiomatizations.

- E. Clarke, S. German, J. Halpern, **Effective Axiomatizations of Hoare Logic**, [CGH83].
- E. Clarke, **Characterization Problem for Hoare Logics**, [Cla85].

The paper with German and Halpern gives a necessary and sufficient condition for the existence of a sound and relatively complete Hoare axiomatization. The 1985 paper gives a unified account of my research on Hoare logic and extends the results to *total correctness*.

3.2   Program Invariants as Fixed Points

In my thesis I showed that soundness and relative completeness results are really fixed point theorems. I gave a characterization of program invariants as fixed points of functionals obtained from the program text. For example, let $b * A$ denote **while b do A**. Let $wp[S](P)$ be the *weakest precondition for partial correctness* of the Predicate P and the programming language statement S. Thus, $wp[S](P)$ satisfies two properties:

1. The Hoare triple $\{\, wp[S](P)\,\}\ S\ \{\, P\,\}$ is true in the logical structure under consideration, and
2. If the triple $\{\, P\,\}\ S\ \{\, Q\,\}$ is true, then $P \to wp[S](Q)$ is true.

It is not difficult to prove

$$wp[b * A](Q) = (\neg b \wedge Q) \vee (b \wedge wp[A](wp[b * A](Q)))$$

Thus, $wp[b * A](Q)$ is a fixpoint of the functional

$$\tau(U) = (\neg b \wedge Q) \vee (b \wedge wp[A](U)).$$

In fact, $wp[b * A](Q)$ is the greatest fixpoint of the functional τ. The fixpoint characterizations are more complicated for programming language constructs that are not tail recursive.[1]

I showed that Relative Completeness is logically equivalent to the *existence* of a fixed point for an appropriate functional, and that Relative Soundness follows from the *maximality* of the fixed point.

For finite interpretations, the results give a decision procedure for partial correctness, i.e., a primitive Model Checker for partial correctness! When I originally proved these results, this idea occurred to me, but I thought it would not be practical and did not pursue the idea further at the time.

3.3   Data-Flow Analysis

In 1978, I moved to Harvard. At Harvard, I taught the undergraduate course on Compilers. In preparing for this course, I read a number of papers on *data-flow analysis* including:

– G. Killdall, **A Unified Approach to Global Program Optimization**, [Kil73].

---

[1] I was unaware of the work by Basu and Yeh [BY75] until I saw it cited in Emerson's paper in this volume. The paper shows that the weakest precondition for total correctness is the least fixed point of a functional obtained from the body of a while loop. The theory in my thesis and the papers mentioned above applies to partial correctness as well as total correctness and handles general loops (regular recursions) and non-regular recursions as well. I also relate my fixpoint theory to relative soundness and completeness proofs of Cook and others.

- J. B. Kam and J. D. Ullmann, **Monotone Data-flow Analysis Frameworks**, [KU77].
- Richard N. Taylor and Leon J. Osterweil, **Anomaly Detection in Concurrent Software by Static Data Flow Analysis**, [TO80].
- P. Cousot and R. Cousot, **Abstract Interpretation: A Unified Lattice Model for Static Analysis of Programs by Construction or Approximation of Fixpoints**, [CC77].

The paper by Taylor and Osterweil was definitely ahead of its time. Although it was written thirty years ago, the title sounds surprisingly modern. In fact, several papers with similar sounding titles have been published in recent CAV and TACAS conferences.

Data-flow analysis can be considered to be an instance of Model Checking as the 1998 paper by David Schmidt demonstrates:

- D. Schmidt, **Data-flow Analysis is Model Checking of Abstract Interpretations**, [Sch98].

3.4 My Early Research on Concurrency

In 1977 I read the classic paper by Owicki and Gries [OG76] on methods for reasoning about concurrent systems using *conditional critical regions* for synchronization. My research focussed on fixpoint equations, abstract interpretation, and widening for concurrent programs. This research led to three papers:

- E. M. Clarke, **Synthesis of Resource Invariants for Concurrent Programs**, [Cla79b].
- E. Clarke and L. Liu, **Approximate Algorithms for Optimization of Busy Waiting in Parallel Programs**, [CL79].
- L. Liu and E. Clarke, **Optimization of Busy Waiting in Conditional Critical Regions**, [LC80].

4 Temporal Logic

Temporal logics describe the ordering of events in time without introducing time explicitly. They were developed by philosophers and linguists for investigating how time is used in natural language arguments. Most temporal logics have an operator like Gf that is true in the present if f is always true in the future. To assert that two events e_1 and e_2 never occur at the same time, one would write $G(\neg e_1 \vee \neg e_2)$. Temporal logics are often classified according to whether time is assumed to have a linear or a branching structure. The meaning of a temporal logic formula is determined with respect to a labeled state-transition graph or *Kripke structure.*

4.1 Temporal Logic and Program Verification

Burstall [Bur74], Kröger [Krö77], and Pnueli [Pnu77], all proposed using temporal logic for reasoning about computer programs. Pnueli was the first to use temporal logic for reasoning about concurrency. He proved program properties from a set of axioms that described the behavior of the individual statements. The method was extended to sequential circuits by Bochmann [Boc82] and Malachi and Owicki [MO81]. Since proofs were constructed by hand, the technique was often difficult to use in practice.

4.2   Pnueli's 1977 Paper and Model Checking

I reread Pnueli's 1977 paper [Pnu77] in preparing for my 25MC lecture. The section entitled Finite State Systems is extremely interesting, although I do not remember reading it before Emerson and I wrote our 1981 paper [CE81]. After rereading this section, an obvious question is whether Pnueli should be credited with inventing Model Checking in 1977. Theorems 4 and 5 in his paper are particularly noteworthy.

> **Theorem 4:** The validity of an arbitrary eventuality $G(A \to FB)$ is decidable for any finite state system.

The proof of this theorem uses strongly connected components and is very similar to the technique used for EG(P) in CES 83/86 [CES83, CES86]. Theorem 5 is quite general.

> **Theorem 5:** The validity of an arbitrary tense formula on a finite state system is decidable and the extended system Kb is adequate for proving all valid (propositional) tense formulas.

The proof of Theorem 5 is briefly discussed in an appendix to Pnueli's paper.

> Theorem 5 may be proved by reduction of the problem of validity of a propositional tense formula on a finite state system to that of the validity of a formula in the Monadic Second Order Theory of Successor.

> We show that for each propositional tense formula formula W, we can construct an ω-regular language $L(W)$ which describes all those S^ω sequences on which W is true.

> Our decision problem reduces to the question is $L(A_\Sigma) \subseteq L(W)$, i.e. do all proper execution sequences of A_Σ satisfy W.

The reference that Pnueli [Pnu77] gives for checking containment of ω-regular languages does not indicate how an efficient algorithm could be constructed for this purpose. Clearly, if Pnueli did discover Model Checking in 1977, he also discovered *Automata Theoretic Model Checking* at the same time.

4.3   Branching-Time Logics

Emerson and I [EC80] proposed a very general branching-time temporal logic based on *Computation Trees* (Figure 3) and made the connection with the mu-calculus. Ben-Ari, Manna, and Pnueli (81 / 83) [BAMP83] gave an elegant syntax

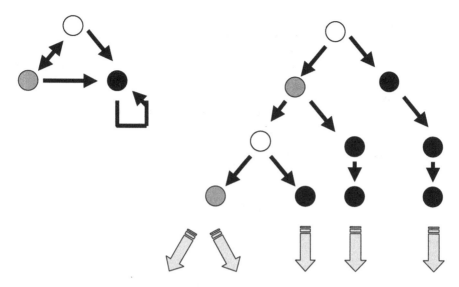

Fig. 3. Kripke Structure and Computation Tree

for a branching time logic called UB. Here is how *inevitably p* would be expressed in both logics. In EC 80, we wrote ∀ path ∃ node p. The notation in BMP 81 was much more concise. They simply wrote AF p. In [CE81] we adopted the UB notation and introduced two versions of the until operator (AU and EU).

4.4 Expressive Power of Temporal Logic

Lamport was the first to investigate the expressive power of various temporal logics for verification. His 1980 POPL paper [Lam80] discusses two logics: a simple linear-time logic and a simple branching-time logic. He showed that each logic could express certain properties that could not be expressed in the other. Branching-time logic cannot express certain natural fairness properties that can be easily expressed in the linear-time logic. Linear-time logic cannot express the possibility of an event occurring sometime in the future along some computation path. Technical difficulties made Lamport's result somewhat like comparing "apples and oranges".

Emerson and Halpern [EH86] provided a uniform framework for investigating this question. They formulated the problem in terms of a single logic called CTL*, which combines both linear-time and branching-time operators. A state formula may be obtained from a path formula by prefixing it with a path quantifier, either be an A (for every path) or an E (there exists a path). Linear-time logic (LTL) is identified with the set of CTL* state formulas Af where f is a path formula not containing any state sub-formulas. The branching-time part (CTL) consists of all state formulas in which every linear-time operator is immediately preceded by a path quantifier. Since both LTL and CTL consist entirely of state formulas, they were able to avoid the uniform framework problem in Lamport's paper.

They showed that there exists a formula of LTL that cannot be expressed in CTL and vice versa. In general, the proofs of their inexpressibility results are quite long and tedious. For example, the proof that the linear-time formula $A(FGp)$ is not expressible in CTL uses a complicated inductive argument that requires 3.5 journal pages to present. Furthermore, the technique that they use does not easily generalize to other examples.

In [CD88], Anca Dragahicescu (now Browne) proved the following theorem:

> **Theorem:** Let $M = (S, R, L, F)$ be a Kripke Structure with Müller Fairness Constraints, and let $M' = (S, R, L, F')$ where the set of constraints F' extends F. Then for all CTL formulas f and all states $s \in S$, $M, s \models f$ if and only if $M', s \models f$.

We used the theorem to give a short proof that no CTL formula can express $A(FG\,p)$ for the special case of Kripke structures with Müller fairness constraints.

5   Temporal Logic Model Checking

The basic papers on the use of Temporal Logic Model Checking were written in the early 1980's. I describe what was done and comment on similarities and differences between various approaches.

5.1   Clarke and Emerson 1981

My work with Emerson came first in the spring of 1981 [CE81]. It was presented in a predecessor conference of LICS organized by Dexter Kozen.

- Edmund M. Clarke and E. Allen Emerson,
- Design and Synthesis of Synchronization Skeletons Using Branching-Time Temporal Logic.
- Presented at the Logics of Programs Workshop at Yorktown Heights, New York in May 1981.
- The proceedings were published in LNCS 131.
- Also in Emerson's 1981 Ph.D. Thesis.

The temporal logic model checking algorithms that Emerson and I developed allowed this type of reasoning to be automated. Checking that a single structure satisfies a formula is much easier than proving the validity of a formula for all structures. Our algorithm for CTL was polynomial in the product of $|M|$ and $|f|$. We also showed how fairness could be handled without changing the complexity of the algorithm.

Emerson and I had a Harvard undergraduate (Marshall Brin) implement the fixpoint algorithm for Model Checking. Unfortunately, the implementation was incorrect. There was a problem with fairness constraints. To our embarrassment, we discovered this when we demonstrated the Model Checker to Bochmann when he gave a lecture at Harvard.

5.2   My Eureka Moment

In the fall of 1980 and the spring of 1981, Emerson was writing his Ph.D. thesis on the synthesis of finite state concurrent programs from CTL specifications. The idea was to use a decision procedure for satisfiability of CTL formulas to extract a finite model from a specification in CTL. The concurrent program could then be extracted from the finite model. There were two disadvantages to this approach: the exponential complexity of the decision procedure (in practice as well as theory) and the need to completely specify the concurrent program in temporal logic.

In January of 1981, I attended POPL where the paper by Ben-Ari, Manna, and Pnueli [BAMP83] on "The Temporal Logic of Branching Time" was originally presented. I had trouble understanding non-trivial formulas of the logic. I spent several hours drawing Kripke Structures and checking to see if various formulas were true or not. If the structures had many states and the formulas were complicated, this turned out to be more complicated than I expected, and my first guess was often wrong. I tried to find an algorithm to automate this process. For some operators like AF p, the algorithm was obvious–just perform a depth-first search starting from the initial state of the structure and see if there was a path ending in a cycle along which $\neg p$ always held. I suspected that there was a linear algorithm for the problem, but getting it correct for all of CTL was tricky.

After trying several examples, it occurred to me that often complex communication and synchronization protocols were specified by state machines and that an efficient algorithm for checking formulas on models could be used to see if the state machines satisfied their specifications. This was my "Eureka moment"! I realized that the important problem for verification was not the synthesis problem but the problem of checking formulas on finite models. I began to work on a depth-first search algorithm for the Model Checking problem. When I told Emerson about my conclusion, he saw how fixpoint techniques could be used to obtain an algorithm for the complete logic that was quadratic in the size of the model. Of course, the quadratic complexity of the algorithm meant that it did not scale to large models. I doubt if it would have been able to handle a model with a 1000 states.

In the fall of 1982 after my move to Carnegie Mellon, I developed a strictly graph theoretic algorithm for CTL Model Checking with Fairness Constraints. My algorithm had linear complexity in the size of the model. I implemented the algorithm myself in the EMC Model Checker. I wrote the program in a language called "Franz Lisp" and still have the original code! The new implementation is described in my 1983 POPL paper with Emerson and Sistla [CES83, CES86].

5.3   Queille and Sifakis 1982

The work of Queille and Sifakis was presented at a conference in the Spring of 1982 [QS82], although a technical report version appeared in June of 1981. I learned about their research when I was working on CES 83 / 86 probably late in the fall of 1982. Their work was certainly independent of ours. I regard this as a case of essentially simultaneous discovery of an idea whose time was ripe.

- J.P. Queille and J. Sifakis
- Specification and Verification of Concurrent Systems in CESAR
- Technical Report 254 June 1981
- International Symposium on Programming, Turin, April, 1982
- Springer Lecture Notes in Computer Science 137, published in 1982

There are a number of similarities between the work that Emerson and I did and the work of Quielle and Sifakis:

- Both used a branching-time temporal logic related to [BAMP83]. (**POT** is like **EF** and **INEV** is like our **AF**.)
- Formula evaluation in [QS82] is by computing fixpoints as in [CE81]. In [CES83, CES86] more efficient graph algorithms are used.
- The programming language CSP [Hoa85] is used for describing models in both [QS82] and [CES83, CES86]. The Alternating Bit Protocol [BSW69] is also used for illustration in both [QS82] and [CES83, CES86].
- There is a clear distinction between the model and the formula to be checked in both (the term "Model Checking" originates with [CE81], however).

There are also a number of important differences:

- The logic used in [QS82] does not have an *until* operator **U** (trivial).
- Queille and Sifakis do not analyze the complexity of their algorithm.
- Finally, they did not implement *fairness constraints*.

Their paper references Clarke [Cla77a, Cla79a] and Cousot [CC77] for computing fixed points of monotonic operators on a lattice [2].

5.4   The EMC Model Checker

My paper with Emerson and Sistla [CES83, CES86] gave an improved algorithm that was linear in the product of $|M|$ and $|f|$. The algorithm was implemented in the EMC Model Checker and used to check a number of network protocols and sequential circuits (EMC stands for *Extended Model Checker*. At the risk of being obvious, note the similarity to my initials). It could check state transition graphs with between 10^4 and 10^5 states at a rate of about 100 states per second for typical formulas. In spite of these limitations, EMC was used successfully to find previously unknown errors in several published circuit designs.

The EMC Model Checker was the first Model Checker to implement *Fairness Constraints*. Fairness Constraints are formulas that must hold infinitely often

---

[2] I sent a draft of this paper to Sifakis. He replied that they had another paper in FOCS 1982 and Acta Inf. 1983 [QS83] that included the *until* operator and could express a particular class of fairness properties. However, this paper references [CE81], and after 25 years, Sifakis was unable to explain how it differed from our first paper.

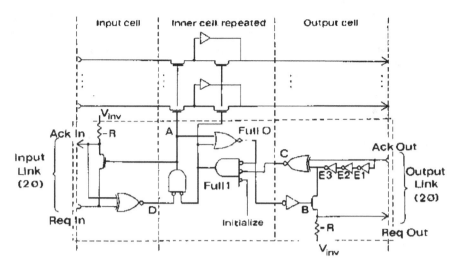

Fig. 4. Self-Timed FIFO Queue from Mead and Conway

on each fair path. This feature made it possible to check some important properties that could not be expressed in CTL. An example of such a property is $A(GF\,enabled \rightarrow GF\,executed)$, which expresses the property that a process that is enabled for execution infinitely often must actually be executed infinitely often. Because of this feature, the EMC algorithm was able to solve the *Emptiness Problem for Non-deterministic Büchi Automata* in time linear in the size of the automaton.

Hardware Verification. My student, Bud Mishra, was the first to use Model Checking for Hardware Verification [MC85]. He found a bug in the Sietz FIFO Queue (Figure 4) from Mead and Conway's book, Introduction to VLSI Systems [MC79]. David Dill and Mike Browne also started working on hardware verification. The four of us wrote several papers on applying Model Checking to hardware verification [MC85, BCD85, BCD86, BCDM86, DC86]

Witnesses and Counterexamples. EMC did not give counterexamples for universal CTL properties that were false or witnesses for existential properties that were true. I asked my student, Michael C. Browne, to add this feature to the MCB model Checker in 1984 (MCB stands for *Model Checker B*. However, note the similarity to Browne's initials). It has been an important feature of Model Checkers ever since (Figure 5).

5.5   LTL and CTL*

Complexity of LTL. Sistla and I [SC86] analyzed the model checking problem for LTL and showed that the problem was PSPACE-complete. Pnueli and Lichtenstein [LP85] gave an algorithm that is exponential in the length of the

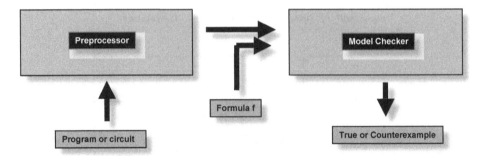

Fig. 5. A Model Checker that supports Counterexamples

formula, but linear in the size of the Model. Based on this observation, they argued that LTL model checking is feasible for short formulas.

CTL* Model Checking. CTL* is a very expressive logic that combines both branching-time and linear-time operators. Model checking for this logic was first considered in [CES83, CES86] where it was shown to be PSPACE-complete. Emerson and Lei [EL85] showed that CTL* and LTL Model Checking have the same complexity in $|M|$ and $|f|$. Thus, for purposes of Model Checking, there is no practical complexity advantage to restricting oneself to a linear temporal logic.

5.6   Automata Theoretic Techniques and Process Algebra

Using Automata for Both Models and Specifications. Alternative techniques for verifying concurrent systems have been proposed by a number of other researchers. Some approaches use automata for specifications as well as for implementations. The implementation is checked to see whether its behavior conforms to that of the specification. Thus, an implementation at one level can be used as a specification for the next level. The use of language containment is implicit in the work of Kurshan, which ultimately resulted in the development of the COSPAN verifier [AKS83, HK87, Dil89].

Automata Theoretic Model Checking with LTL. Vardi and Wolper [VW86] first proposed the use of ω-automata (automata over infinite words) for automated verification. They showed how linear temporal logic Model Checking could be formulated in terms of language containment. Many explicit state LTL Model Checkers (e.g., Spin) use a variant of this construction. It can also be used with Symbolic and Bounded Model Checkers as well.

Links to Process Algebra. If two finite Kripke Structures can be distinguished by some CTL* formula, then they can be distinguished by a CTL formula. In [BCG88] we showed that for any finite Kripke structure M, it is possible to construct a CTL formula F_M that uniquely characterizes M. We use a notion of equivalence between Kripke Structures, similar to the notion of bisimulation studied by Milner [Mil71] and Park [Par81]. The first construction of F_M uses of the next-time operator X. We also considered the case in which the next-time operator is disallowed. The proof, in this case, required another notion of equivalence, *equivalence with respect to stuttering*. We gave a polynomial algorithm for determining if two structures are stuttering equivalent.

6 Dealing with Very Complex Systems

Significant progress was made on the State Explosion Problem around 1990. Both Symbolic Model Checking and the Partial Order Reduction were developed about this time.

6.1 Symbolic Model Checking

In the original implementation of the Model Checking algorithm, transition relations were represented explicitly by adjacency lists. For concurrent systems with small numbers of processes, the number of states was usually fairly small, and the approach was often quite practical. In systems with many concurrent parts the number of states in the global state transition graph was too large to handle. In the fall of 1987, McMillan, then a graduate student of mine at Carnegie Mellon, realized that by using a symbolic representation for the state transition graphs, much larger systems could be verified. The new symbolic representation was based on *ordered binary decision diagrams* (OBDDs) [BCM+90, McM93]. OBDDs provide a canonical form for boolean formulas that is often substantially more compact than conjunctive or disjunctive normal form, and very efficient algorithms have been developed for manipulating them. Because the symbolic representation captures some of the regularity in the state space determined by circuits and protocols, it is possible to verify systems with an extremely large number of states—many orders of magnitude larger than could be handled by the explicit-state algorithms. By using the original CTL Model Checking algorithm of Clarke and Emerson with the new representation for state transition graphs, it became possible to verify some examples that had more than 10^{20} states. Since then, various refinements of the OBDD-based techniques by other researchers have pushed the state count up to more than 10^{120}.

The SMV Model Checker. The Model Checking system that McMillan developed as part of his Ph.D. thesis is called SMV [McM93]. It is based on a language for describing hierarchical finite-state concurrent systems. Programs in the language can be annotated by specifications expressed in temporal logic. The Model Checker extracts a transition system represented as an OBDD from a program in the SMV language and uses an OBDD-based search algorithm to determine whether the system satisfies its specification. If the transition system does not satisfy some specification, the verifier will produce an execution trace that shows why the specification is false. The SMV system has been widely distributed, and a large number of examples have now been verified with it. These examples provide convincing evidence that SMV can be used to debug real industrial designs. Now there are two widely used versions of SMV: Cadence SMV released by Cadence Berkeley Labs and an open source version, called *NuSMV* [CCGR00], released by IRST in Trento, Italy.

Verification of the cache coherence protocol in the IEEE Futurebus+ standard illustrates the power of the SMV Model Checker. Development of the protocol began in 1988, but all previous attempts to validate it were based on informal techniques. In the summer of 1992 my group at Carnegie Mellon constructed a precise model of the protocol. Using SMV we were able to find several previously undetected errors and potential errors in the design of the protocol. This was the first time that an automatic verification tool had been used to find errors in an IEEE standard [CGH+93, Lon93].

Other Work on Symbolic Model Checking. Several other researchers independently discovered that OBDDs can be used to represent state-transition systems. Coudert, et al. [CBM89] gave an algorithm for sequential equivalence checking that used OBDDs for the transition functions. Bose and Fisher [BF89], Pixley [Pix90], and Coudert et al. [CBM90] also experimented with symbolic Model Checking algorithms.

6.2   Partial Order Reduction

Verifying software causes some problems for Model Checking. Software tends to be less structured than hardware. In addition, concurrent software is usually *asynchronous*, i.e., most of the activities taken by different processes are performed independently, without a global synchronizing clock. For these reasons, the state explosion phenomenon is a particularly serious problem for software. Consequently, Model Checking has been used less frequently for software verification than for hardware verification. The most successful techniques for dealing with asynchronous systems are based on the *partial order reduction*. These techniques exploit the independence of concurrently executed events. Two events are *independent* of each other when executing them in either order results in the same global state.

Model Checking algorithms that incorporate the partial order reduction are described in several different papers. The *stubborn sets* of Valmari [Val90], the *persistent sets* of Godefroid [God90] and the *ample sets* of Peled [Pel94] differ on the actual details, but contain many similar ideas. Other methods that exploit similar observations about the relation between the partial and total order models of execution are McMillan's *unfolding technique* [McM93] and Godefroid's *sleep sets* [God90].

6.3   Special Purpose Techniques

Special techniques are needed when symbolic methods and the partial order reduction don't work. Four basic techniques are

- Compositional Reasoning,
- Abstraction,
- Symmetry Reduction,
- Induction and Parameterized Verification.

Compositional Reasoning. This technique exploits the modular structure of complex circuits and protocols. Many finite state systems are composed of multiple processes running in parallel. The specifications for such systems can often be decomposed into properties that describe the behavior of small parts of the system. An obvious strategy is to check each of the local properties using only the part of the system that it describes. If the system satisfies each local property, and if the conjunction of the local properties implies the overall specification, then the complete system must satisfy this specification as well.

The naive form of compositional reasoning may not be feasible because of mutual dependencies between the components. When verifying a property of one component assumptions are needed about the behavior of the other components. The assumptions must later be discharged when the correctness of the other components is established. This strategy is called *assume-guarantee reasoning* [MC81, Jon83, Pnu84, GL94].

The main problem in employing assume-guarantee style reasoning in verification relates to effectively computing environment assumptions for each component. Initial attempts to perform such reasoning focused on hardware systems [McM97, AH99] and the assumptions were provided manually. Recently, a method for automatically generating these assumptions has been proposed [CGP03]. Here, the task of computing an assumption is posed as a machine learning problem, where a learning algorithm for regular languages L^* [Ang87, RS93] is used to generate a finite-state assumption in an iterative fashion by making queries to a *teacher* entity. A model checker plays the role of the teacher and assists the learner by answering queries and providing counterexamples. Extensions of this approach have been used to solve the *Component Substitutability Problem* [CCSS05, CCST05]. A symbolic extension of this approach using BDDs has also been proposed [AMN05].

Abstraction. Abstraction is essential for reasoning about reactive systems that involve data. It is based on the observation that specifications of systems usually involve simple relationships among data values. For example, verifying a program may depend on simple arithmetical relationships (predicate abstraction). In such situations abstraction can be used to reduce the complexity of Model Checking. The abstraction is usually specified by a mapping between data values in the system and a small set of abstract data values. By extending the mapping to states and transitions, it is possible to produce a much smaller, abstract version [CGL92, BBLS92, CGL94].

Symmetry Reduction. Symmetry [ID93, CFJ93, ES93] can be used to reduce the state explosion problem. Finite state concurrent systems often contain replicated components, e.g., a network of identical processes communicating in some fashion. This information can be used to obtain reduced models. Having physical symmetry in a system often implies existence of a non-trivial permutation group that preserves the transition graph. The permutation group can be used to define an equivalence relation on the state space. The resulting reduced model can be used to simplify verification of Temporal logic properties.

Parameterized Systems. Induction involves reasoning automatically about entire families of finite state systems. Typically, circuit and protocol designs are parameterized, that is, they define an infinite family of systems. For example, a bus protocol may be designed for an arbitrary number of processors. Ideally, one would like to be able to check that every system in a given family satisfies some temporal logic property. In general, the problem is undecidable [AK86]. Often it is possible to provide an invariant process that represents the behavior of an arbitrary member of the family. Using the invariant, one can check the property for all members of the family at once [CGB86, KM89, WL89].

7   Big Events Since 1990 and Future Challenges

The pace of research in Model Checking has accelerated since 1990. Below I list several of the most important breakthroughs during this period. I only cite the initial paper (or papers) that led to the breakthrough, although each of the seminal papers led to many papers often containing significant extensions of the original work.

- Timed and Hybrid Automata [ACD90, HKPV95]
- Model Checking for Security Protocols [Ros94, MCJ97]
- Bounded Model Checking [BCCY99, BCC+03]
- Localization Reduction and CEGAR [Kur94, CGJ+00]
- Compositional Model Checking and Learning [MC81, Jon83, Pnu84, GL94]
- Predicate Abstraction [GS97, BMMR01]
- Infinite State Systems (e.g., pushdown systems) [BEM97]

I conclude with a list of challenges for the future. I believe that all of the problems in the list are important and that all require major breakthroughs in order to become sufficiently practical for widespread use in industry.

- Software Model Checking, Model Checking and Static Analysis
- Model Checking and Theorem Proving
- Exploiting the Power of SAT, Satisfiability Modulo Theories (SMT)
- Probabilistic Model Checking
- Efficient Model Checking for Timed and Hybrid Automata
- Interpreting Counterexamples
- Coverage (incomplete Model Checking, have I checked enough properties?)
- Scaling up even more!!

I expect the next twenty-five years will hold many surprises and be at least as exciting as the past twenty-five. I look forward with great enthusiasm to participating in at least some of this research.

Acknowledgements. The author wishes to thank Nishant Sinha for his help in preparing this document. Martha Clarke, Jonathan Clarke, and Katie Clarke read early versions of this document and gave useful comments.

References

[ACD90]   Alur, R., Courcourbetis, C., Dill, D.: Model-checking for real-time systems. In: Proceedings of the 5th Symp. on Logic in Computer Science, pp. 414–425 (1990)

[AH99]   Alur, R., Henzinger, T.A.: Reactive modules. Formal Methods in System Design: An International Journal 15(1), 7–48 (1999)

[AK86]   Apt, K., Kozen, D.: Limits for automatic verification of finite-state systems. IPL 15, 307–309 (1986)

[AKS83]   Aggarwal, S., Kurshan, R.P., Sabnani, K.: A calculus for protocol specification and validation. In: Rudin, H., West, C.H. (eds.) Protocol Specification, Testing and Verification, pp. 19–34. North-Holland (1983)

[AMN05]   Alur, R., Madhusudan, P., Nam, W.: Symbolic Compositional Verification by Learning Assumptions. In: Etessami, K., Rajamani, S.K. (eds.) CAV 2005. LNCS, vol. 3576, pp. 548–562. Springer, Heidelberg (2005)

[Ang87]   Angluin, D.: Learning regular sets from queries and counterexamples. Information and Computation 75(2), 87–106 (1987)

[ASM80]   Abrial, J.-R., Schuman, S.A., Meyer, B.: Specification language. In: McKeag, R.M., Macnaughten, A.M. (eds.) On the Construction of Programs, pp. 343–410. Cambridge University Press (1980)

[BAMP83]   Ben-Ari, M., Manna, Z., Pnueli, A.: The temporal logic of branching time. Acta Informatica 20, 207–226 (1983)

[BBLS92]   Bensalem, S., Bouajjani, A., Loiseaux, C., Sifakis, J.: Property preserving simulations. In: Probst, D.K., von Bochmann, G. (eds.) CAV 1992. LNCS, vol. 663, pp. 260–273. Springer, Heidelberg (1992)

[BCC+03]   Biere, A., Cimatti, A., Clarke, E.M., Strichman, O., Zhu, Y.: Bounded Model Checking. Advances in computers, vol. 58. Academic Press (2003)

[BCCY99]   Clarke, E., Biere, A., Cimatti, A., Zhu, Y.: Symbolic Model Checking without BDDs. In: Cleaveland, W.R. (ed.) ETAPS 1999 and TACAS 1999. LNCS, vol. 1579, pp. 193–207. Springer, Heidelberg (1999)

[BCD85]   Browne, M.C., Clarke, E.M., Dill, D.: Checking the correctness of sequential circuits. In: Proceedings of the 1985 International Conference on Computer Design, Port Chester, New York, October 1985, pp. 545–548. IEEE (1985)

[BCD86]   Browne, M.C., Clarke, E.M., Dill, D.L.: Automatic circuit verification using temporal logic: Two new examples. In: Formal Aspects of VLSI Design. Elsevier Science Publishers, North Holland (1986)

[BCDM86]   Browne, M.C., Clarke, E.M., Dill, D.L., Mishra, B.: Automatic verification of sequential circuits using temporal logic. IEEE Transactions on Computers C-35(12), 1035–1044 (1986)

[BCG88]   Browne, M.C., Clarke, E.M., Grumberg, O.: Characterizing finite Kripke structures in propositional temporal logic. Theoretical Computer Science 59(1–2), 115–131 (1988)

[BCM+90]   Burch, J.R., Clarke, E.M., McMillan, K.L., Dill, D.L., Hwang, J.: Symbolic model checking: 10^{20} states and beyond. In: Proc. 5th Ann. Symp. on Logic in Comput. Sci., IEEE Comp. Soc. Press (June 1990)

[BCM⁺92]   Burch, J.R., Clarke, E.M., McMillan, K.L., Dill, D.L., Hwang, L.J.: Symbolic model checking: 10^{20} states and beyond. Information and Computation 98(2), 142–170 (1992)

[BEM97]   Bouajjani, A., Esparza, J., Maler, O.: Reachability analysis of pushdown automata: Application to model-checking. In: International Conference on Concurrency Theory, pp. 135–150 (1997)

[BF89]   Bose, S., Fisher, A.: Verifying pipelined hardware using symbolic logic simulation. In: IEEE International Conference on Computer Design (October 1989)

[BMMR01]   Ball, T., Majumdar, R., Millstein, T.D., Rajamani, S.K.: Automatic predicate abstraction of C programs 36(5), 203–213 (June 2001)

[Boc82]   Bochmann, G.V.: Hardware specification with temporal logic: An example. IEEE Transactions on Computers C-31(3) (March 1982)

[BSW69]   Bartlett, K.A., Scantlebury, R.A., Wilkinson, P.T.: A note on reliable full-duplex transmission over half-duplex links. Commun. ACM 12(5), 260–261 (1969)

[Bur74]   Burstall, R.M.: Program proving as hand simulation with a little induction. In: IFIP congress 1974, pp. 308–312. North Holland (1974)

[BY75]   Basu, S.K., Yeh, R.T.: Strong verification of programs. IEEE Trans. Software Eng. 1(3), 339–346 (1975)

[CBM89]   Coudert, O., Berthet, C., Madre, J.C.: Verification of synchronous sequential machines based on symbolic execution. In: Sifakis [Sif89], pp. 365–373.

[CBM90]   Coudert, O., Berthet, C., Madre, J.C.: Verifying temporal properties of sequential machines without building their state diagrams. In: Kurshan, Clarke [KC90], pp. 23–32

[CC77]   Cousot, P., Cousot, R.: Abstract interpretation: A unified lattice model for static analysis of programs by construction or approximation of fixpoints. In: Proc. 4th Ann. ACM Symp. on Principles of Prog. Lang., pp. 238–252 (January 1977)

[CCGR00]   Cimatti, A., Clarke, E.M., Giunchiglia, F., Roveri, M.: Nusmv: A new symbolic model checker. STTT 2(4), 410–425 (2000)

[CCSS05]   Chaki, S., Clarke, E., Sharygina, N., Sinha, N.: Dynamic component substitutability analysis. In: Proc. of Conf. on Formal Methods (2005)

[CCST05]   Chaki, S., Clarke, E., Sinha, N., Thati, P.: Automated assume-guarantee reasoning for simulation conformance. In: Proc. of Computer-Aided Verification (2005)

[CD88]   Clarke, E.M., Draghicescu, I.A.: Expressibility results for linear time and branching time logics. In: de Bakker, J.W., de Roever, W.-P., Rozenberg, G. (eds.) Linear Time, Branching Time and Partial Order in Logics and Models for Concurrency. LNCS, vol. 354, pp. 428–437. Springer, Heidelberg (1989)

[CE81]   Clarke, E.M., Emerson, E.A.: Design and synthesis of synchronization skeletons using branching time temporal logic. In: Kozen, D. (ed.) Logic of Programs 1981. LNCS, vol. 131. Springer, Heidelberg (1982)

[CES83]   Clarke, E.M., Emerson, E.A., Sistla, A.P.: Automatic verification of finite-state concurrent systems using temporal logic specifications. In: Proc. 10th Ann. ACM Symp. on Principles of Prog. Lang. (January 1983)

[CES86]   Clarke, E.M., Emerson, E.A., Sistla, A.P.: Automatic verification of finite-state concurrent systems using temporal logic specifications. ACM Transactions on Programming Languages and Systems 8(2), 244–263 (1986)

[CFJ93]   Clarke, E.M., Filkorn, T., Jha, S.: Exploiting symmetry in temporal logic
            model checking. In: Courcoubetis [Cou93], pp.450–462
[CGB86]   Clarke, E.M., Grumberg, O., Browne, M.C.: Reasoning about networks
            with many identical finite-state processes. In: Proceedings of the Fifth
            Annual ACM Symposium on Principles of Distributed Computing, pp.
            240–248. ACM (August 1986)
[CGH83]   Clarke, E.M., German, S.M., Halpern, J.Y.: Effective axiomatizations of
            Hoare logics. J. ACM 30(3), 612–636 (1983)
[CGH⁺93]   Clarke, E.M., Grumberg, O., Hiraishi, H., Jha, S., Long, D.E., McMillan,
            K.L., Ness, L.A.: Verification of the Futurebus+ cache coherence protocol.
            In: Claesen [Cla93]
[CGJ⁺00]   Clarke, E.M., Grumberg, O., Jha, S., Lu, Y., Veith, H.: Counterexample-
            guided abstraction refinement. In: Computer Aided Verification (CAV),
            pp. 154–169 (2000)
[CGL92]   Clarke, E.M., Grumberg, O., Long, D.E.: Model checking and abstraction.
            In: POPL, pp. 342–354 (1992)
[CGL94]   Clarke, E.M., Grumberg, O., Long, D.E.: Model checking and abstraction.
            ACM Transactions on Programming Languages and Systems 16(5), 1512–
            1542 (1994)
[CGP03]   Cobleigh, J., Giannakopoulou, D., Păsăreanu, C.S.: Learning Assumptions
            for Compositional Verification. In: Garavel, H., Hatcliff, J. (eds.) ETAPS
            2003 and TACAS 2003. LNCS, vol. 2619, pp. 331–346. Springer, Heidelberg
            (2003)
[CL79]   Clarke, E.M., Liu, L.: Approximate algorithms for optimization of busy
            waiting in parallel programs (preliminary report). In: 20th Annual Sympo-
            sium on Foundations of Computer Science, pp. 255–266. IEEE Computer
            Society (1979)
[Cla77a]   Clarke, E.M.: Program invariants as fixed points (preliminary reports). In:
            18th Annual Symposium on Foundations of Computer Science, pp. 18–29.
            IEEE Computer Society (November 1977)
[Cla77b]   Clarke, E.M.: Programming language constructs for which it is impossible
            to obtain good hoare-like axiom systems. In: Fourth ACM Symposium on
            Principles of Programming Languages, pp. 10–20. ACM Press, New York
            (1977)
[Cla78]   Clarke, E.M.: Proving the correctness of coroutines without history vari-
            ables. In: ACM-SE 16: Proceedings of the 16th annual Southeast regional
            conference, pp. 160–167. ACM Press, New York (1978)
[Cla79a]   Clarke, E.: Program invariants as fixed points. Computing 21(4), 273–294
            (1979)
[Cla79b]   Clarke, E.M.: Synthesis of resource invariants for concurrent programs. In:
            POPL, pp. 211–221 (1979)
[Cla79c]   Clarke, E.M.: Programming language constructs for which it is impossible
            to obtain good Hoare axiom systems. J. ACM 26(1), 129–147 (1979)
[Cla80]   Clarke, E.: Proving correctness of coroutines without history variables.
            Acta Inf. 13, 169–188 (1980)
[Cla85]   Clarke, E.M.: The characterization problem for hoare logics. In: Proc. of a
            discussion meeting of the Royal Society of London on Mathematical logic
            and programming languages, Upper Saddle River, NJ, USA, pp. 89–106.
            Prentice-Hall, Inc (1985)
[Cla93]   Claesen, L. (ed.): Proc. 11th Int. Symp. on Comput. Hardware Description
            Lang. and their Applications. North-Holland (April 1993)

[Coo78]   Cook, S.A.: Soundness and completeness of an axiom system for program verification. SIAM Journal on Computing 7(1), 70–90 (1978)

[Cou93]   Courcoubetis, C. (ed.): CAV 1993. LNCS, vol. 697. Springer, Heidelberg (1993)

[dBM75]   de Bakker, J.W., Meertens, L.: On the completeness of the inductive assertion method. Journal of Computer and System Sciences 11, 323–357 (1975)

[DC86]   Dill, D.L., Clarke, E.M.: Automatic verification of asynchronous circuits using temporal logic. IEE Proceedings, Part E 133(5) (1986)

[Dil89]   Dill, D.L.: Trace Theory for Automatic Hierarchical Verification of Speed-Independent Circuits. In: ACM Distinguished Dissertations. MIT Press (1989)

[EC80]   Emerson, E.A., Clarke, E.M.: Characterizing correctness properties of parallel programs using fixpoints. In: de Bakker, J.W., van Leeuwen, J. (eds.) ICALP 1980. LNCS, vol. 85, pp. 169–181. Springer, Heidelberg (1980)

[EF06]   Eisner, C., Fisman, D.: A Practical Introduction to PSL (Series on Integrated Circuits and Systems). Springer, New York (2006)

[EH86]   Emerson, E.A., Halpern, J.Y.: "Sometimes" and "Not Never" revisited: On branching time versus linear time. Journal of the ACM 33, 151–178 (1986)

[EL85]   Emerson, E.A., Lei, C.-L.: Modalities for model checking: Branching time strikes back. In: Twelfth Symposium on Principles of Programming Languages, New Orleans, La, pp. 84–96 (January 1985)

[ES93]   Emerson, E.A., Sistla, A.P.: Symmetry and model checking. In: Courcoubetis [Cou93], pp. 463–478

[GL94]   Grumberg, O., Long, D.E.: Model checking and modular verification. ACM Transactions on Programming Languages and Systems 16, 843–872 (1994)

[God90]   Godefroid, P.: Using partial orders to improve automatic verification methods. In: Kurshan, Clarke [KC90]

[GS97]   Graf, S., Saïdi, H.: Construction of abstract state graphs with PVS. In: Grumberg, O. (ed.) CAV 1997. LNCS, vol. 1254, pp. 72–83. Springer, Heidelberg (1997)

[HK87]   Har'El, Z., Kurshan, R.P.: The COSPAN user's guide. Technical Report 11211-871009-21TM, AT&T Bell Labs (1987)

[HKPV95]   Henzinger, T.A., Kopke, P.W., Puri, A., Varaiya, P.: What's decidable about hybrid automata? In: Proceedings of the 27th Annual Symposium on Theory of Computing, pp. 373–382. ACM Press (1995)

[Hoa85]   Hoare, C.A.R.: Communicating Sequential Processes. Prentice Hall (1985)

[ID93]   Ip, C.W., Dill, D.L.: Better verification through symmetry. In: Claesen [Cla93]

[Jon83]   Jones, C.B.: Specification and design of (parallel) programs. In: Proceedings of IFIP 1983, pp. 321–332. North-Holland (1983)

[KC90]   Kurshan, R.P., Clarke, E.M.: Proc. 1990 Workshop on Comput.-Aided Verification (June 1990)

[Kil73]   Kildall, G.A.: A unified approach to global program optimization. In: POPL, pp. 194–206 (1973)

[Kle71]   Kleene, S.C.: Introduction to Metamathematics, Wolters-Noordhoff, Groningen (1971)

[KM89]   Kurshan, R.P., McMillan, K.L.: A structural induction theorem for processes. In: Proc. 8th Ann. ACM Symp. on Principles of Distributed Computing, pp. 239–247. ACM Press (August 1989)

[Koz83]   Kozen, D.: Results on the propositional mu-calculus. Theoretical Computer Science 27, 333–354 (1983)

[Krö77]   Kröger, F.: Lar: A logic of algorithmic reasoning. Acta Inf. 8, 243–266 (1977)

[KU77]   Kam, J.B., Ullman, J.D.: Monotone data flow analysis frameworks. Acta Inf. 7, 305–317 (1977)

[Kur94]   Kurshan, R.P.: Computer-aided verification of coordinating processes: the automata-theoretic approach. Princeton University Press (1994)

[Lam80]   Lamport, L.: "Sometimes" is sometimes "Not Never". In: Ann. ACM Symp. on Principles of Prog. Lang., pp. 174–185 (1980)

[LC80]   Liu, L., Clarke, E.: Optimization of busy waiting in conditional critical regions. In: 13th Hawaii International Conference on System Sciences (January 1980)

[Lon93]   Long, D.E.: Model Checking, Abstraction, and Compositional Reasoning. PhD thesis, Carnegie Mellon Univ. (1993)

[LP85]   Lichtenstein, O., Pnueli, A.: Checking that finite state concurrent programs satisfy their linear specification. In: Proc. 12th Ann. ACM Symp. on Principles of Prog. Lang., pp. 97–107 (January 1985)

[MC79]   Mead, C., Conway, L.: Introduction to VLSI Systems. Addison-Wesley Longman Publishing Co., Inc., Boston (1979)

[MC81]   Misra, J., Chandy, K.M.: Proofs of networks of processes. IEEE Transactions on Software Engineering SE-7(4), 417–426 (1981)

[MC85]   Mishra, B., Clarke, E.M.: Hierarchical verification of asynchronous circuits using temporal logic. Theoretical Computer Science 38, 269–291 (1985)

[MCJ97]   Marrero, W., Clarke, E., Jha, S.: Model checking for security protocols (1997)

[McM93]   McMillan, K.L.: Symbolic Model Checking: An Approach to the State Explosion Problem. Kluwer Academic Publishers (1993)

[McM97]   McMillan, K.L.: A compositional rule for hardware design refinement. In: Grumberg, O. (ed.) CAV 1997. LNCS, vol. 1254, pp. 24–35. Springer, Heidelberg (1997)

[Mil71]   Milner, R.: An algebraic definition of simulation between programs. In: Proc. 2nd Int. Joint Conf. on Artificial Intelligence, pp. 481–489 (September 1971)

[MO81]   Malachi, Y., Owicki, S.S.: Temporal specifications of self-timed systems. In: Kung, H.T., Sproull, B., Steele, G. (eds.) VLSI Systems and Computations, Comp. Sci. Press (1981)

[OG76]   Owicki, S., Gries, D.: Verifying properties of parallel programs: an axiomatic approach. Commun. ACM 19(5), 279–285 (1976)

[OL82]   Owicki, S., Lamport, L.: Proving liveness properties of concurrent programs. ACM Trans. Program. Lang. Syst. 4(3), 455–495 (1982)

[Par74]   Park, D.M.R.: Finiteness is mu-ineffable. Theory of Computation Report No. 3, Warwick (1974)

[Par81]   Park, D.: Concurrency and automata on infinite sequences. In: Deussen, P. (ed.) GI-TCS 1981. LNCS, vol. 104, pp. 167–183. Springer, Heidelberg (1981)

[Pel94]   Peled, D.: Combining partial order reductions with on-the-fly model-checking. In: Dill, D.L. (ed.) CAV 1994. LNCS, vol. 818, pp. 377–390. Springer, Heidelberg (1994)

[Pix90]   Pixley, C.: Introduction to a computational theory and implementation of sequential hardware equivalence. In: Kurshan, Clarke [KC90], pp. 54–64

[Pnu77]   Pnueli, A.: The temporal semantics of concurrent programs. In: 18th Annual Symposium on Foundations of Computer Science (1977)

[Pnu84]   Pnueli, A.: In transition for global to modular temporal reasoning about programs. In: Apt, K.R. (ed.) Logics and Models of Concurrent Systems, NATO ASI series F, vol. 13. Springer (1984)

[QS82]   Quielle, J.P., Sifakis, J.: Specification and verification of concurrent systems in CESAR. In: Proceedings of the 5th International Symposium on Programming, pp. 337–350 (1982)

[QS83]   Queille, J.P., Sifakis, J.: Fairness and related properties in transition systems - a temporal logic to deal with fairness. Acta Inf. 19, 195–220 (1982) (presented originally in FOCS 1982)

[Ros94]   Roscoe, A.W.: Model-checking CSP. In: Roscoe, A.W. (ed.) A Classical Mind: Essays in Honour of C. A. R. Hoare, pp. 353–378. Prentice-Hall (1994)

[RS93]   Rivest, R.L., Schapire, R.E.: Inference of finite automata using homing sequences. Inf. Comp. 103(2), 299–347 (1993)

[SC86]   Sistla, A.P., Clarke, E.M.: Complexity of propositional temporal logics. Journal of the ACM 32(3), 733–749 (1986)

[Sch98]   David, A.: Schmidt. Data flow analysis is model checking of abstract interpretations. In: POPL, pp. 38–48 (1998)

[Sif89]   Sifakis, J. (ed.): Automatic Verification Methods for Finite State Systems. LNCS, vol. 407. Springer, Heidelberg (1989)

[Tar55]   Tarski, A.: A lattice-theoretical fixpoint theorem and its applications. Pacific J. Math. 5, 285–309 (1955)

[TO80]   Taylor, R.N., Osterweil, L.J.: Anomaly detection in concurrent software by static data flow analysis. IEEE Trans. Software Eng. 6(3), 265–278 (1980)

[Val90]   Valmari, A.: A stubborn attack on the state explosion problem. In: Kurshan, Clarke [KC90]

[Vit88]   Vitanyi, P.M.B.: Andrei nikolaevich kolmogorov. 1, 3–18 (1988)

[VW86]   Vardi, M.Y., Wolper, P.: An automata-theoretic approach to automatic program verification. In: Proc. 1st Ann. Symp. on Logic in Comput. Sci. IEEE Computer Society Press, Los Alamitos (1986)

[WL89]   Wolper, P., Lovinfosse, V.: Verifying properties of large sets of processes with network invariants. In: Sifakis [Sif89]

The Beginning of Model Checking: A Personal Perspective*

E. Allen Emerson[1,2]

[1]Department of Computer Sciences
[2]Computer Engineering Research Center
The University of Texas at Austin,
Austin TX 78712, USA
emerson@cs.utexas.edu
www.cs.utexas.edu/∼emerson/

Abstract. Model checking provides an automated method for verifying concurrent systems. Correctness specifications are given in temporal logic. The method hinges on an efficient and flexible graph-theoretic reachability algorithm. At the time of its introduction in the early 1980's, the prevailing paradigm for verification was a manual one of proof-theoretic reasoning using formal axioms and inference rules oriented towards sequential programs. The need to encompass concurrent programs, the desire to avoid the difficulties with manual deductive proofs, and the small model theorem for temporal logic motivated the development of model checking.

Keywords: model checking, model-theoretic, synthesis, history, origins.

1 Introduction

It has long been known that computer software programs, computer hardware designs, and computer systems in general exhibit errors. Working programmers may devote more than half of their time on testing and debugging in order to increase reliability. A great deal of research effort has been and is devoted to developing improved testing methods. Testing successfully identifies many significant errors. Yet, serious errors still afflict many computer systems including systems that are safety critical, mission critical, or economically vital. The US National Institute of Standards and Technology has estimated that programming errors cost the US economy $60B annually [Ni02].

Given the incomplete coverage of testing, alternative approaches have been sought. The most promising approach depends on the fact that programs and more generally computer systems may be viewed as mathematical objects with behavior that is in principle well-determined. This makes it possible to specify using mathematical logic what constitutes the intended (correct) behavior. Then

---

* This work was supported in part by National Science Foundation grants CCR-009-8141 & CCR-020-5483 and funding from Fujitsu Labs of America.

O. Grumberg and H. Veith (Eds.): 25MC Festschrift, LNCS 5000, pp. 27–45, 2008.

one can try to give a formal proof or otherwise establish that the program meets its specification. This line of study has been active for about four decades now. It is often referred to as *formal methods*.

The *verification problem* is: Given program M and specification h determine whether or not the behavior of M meets the specification h. Formulated in terms of Turing Machines, the verification problem was considered by Turing [Tu36]. Given a Turing Machine M and the specification h that it should eventually halt (say on blank input tape), one has the halting problem which is algorithmically unsolvable. In a later paper [Tu49] Turing argued for the need to give a (manual) proof of termination using ordinals, thereby presaging work by Floyd [Fl67] and others.

The model checking problem is an instance of the verification problem. Model checking provides an automated method for verifying concurrent (nominally) finite state systems that uses an efficient and flexible graph search, to determine whether or not the ongoing behavior described by a temporal property holds of the system's state graph. The method is algorithmic and often efficient because the system is finite state, despite reasoning about infinite behavior. If the answer is *yes* then the system meets its specification. If the answer is *no* then the system violates its specification; in practice, the model checker can usually produce a counterexample for debugging purposes.

At this point it should be emphasized that the verification problem and the model checking problem are mathematical problems. The specification is formulated in mathematical logic. The verification problem is distinct from the pleasantness problem [Di89] which concerns having a specification capturing a system that is truly needed and wanted. The pleasantness problem is inherently pre-formal. Nonetheless, it has been found that carefully writing a formal specification (which may be the conjunction of many sub-specifications) is an excellent way to illuminate the murk associated with the pleasantness problem.

At the time of its introduction in the early 1980's, the prevailing paradigm for verification was a manual one of proof-theoretic reasoning using formal axioms and inference rules oriented towards sequential programs. The need to encompass concurrent programs, and the desire to avoid the difficulties with manual deductive proofs, motivated the development of model checking.

In my experience, constructing proofs was sufficiently difficult that it did seem there ought to be an easier alternative. The alternative was suggested by temporal logic. Temporal logic possessed a nice combination of expressiveness and decidability. It could naturally capture a variety of correctness properties, yet was decidable on account of the "Small" Finite Model Theorem which ensured that any satisfiable formula was true in some finite model that was small. It should be stressed that the Small Finite Model Theorem concerns the satisfiability problem of propositional temporal logic, i.e., truth in *some* state graph. This ultimately lead to model checking, i.e., truth in a *given* state graph.

The origin and development of model checking will be described below. Despite being hampered by state explosion, over the past 25 years model checking has had a substantive impact on program verification efforts. Formal verification has progressed from discussions of how to manually prove programs correct to the routine, algorithmic, model-theoretic verification of many programs.

The remainder of the paper is organized as follows. Historical background is discussed in section 2 largely related to verification in the Floyd-Hoare paradigm; protocol verification is also considered. Section 3 describes temporal logic. A very general type of temporal logic, the mu-calculus, that defines correctness in terms of fixpoint expressions is described in section 4. The origin of model checking is described in section 5 along with some relevant personal influences on me. A discussion of model checking today is given in section 6. Some concluding remarks are made in section 7.

2   Background of Model Checking

At the time of the introduction of model checking in the early 1980's, axiomatic verification was the prevailing verification paradigm. The orientation of this paradigm was manual proofs of correctness for (deterministic) sequential programs, that nominally started with their input and terminated with their output. The work of Floyd [Fl67] established basic principles for proving *partial correctness*, a type of safety property, as well as *termination* and *total correctness*, forms of liveness properties. Hoare [Ho69] proposed an axiomatic basis for verification of partial correctness using axioms and inference rules in a formal deductive system. An important advantage of Hoare's approach is that it was *compositional* so that the proof a program was obtained from the proofs of its constituent subprograms.

The Floyd-Hoare framework was a tremendous success intellectually. It engendered great interest among researchers. Relevant notions from logic such as soundness and (relative) completeness as well as compositionality were investigated. Proof systems were proposed for new programming languages and constructs. Examples of proofs of correctness were given for small programs.

However, this framework turned out to be of limited use in practice. It did not scale up to "industrial strength" programs, despite its merits. Problems start with the approach being one of manual proof construction. These are formal proofs that can involve the manipulations of extremely long logical formulae. This can be inordinately tedious and error-prone work for a human. In practice, it may be wholly infeasible. Even if strict formal reasoning were used throughout, the plethora of technical detail could be overwhelming. By analogy, consider the task of a human adding 100,000 decimal numbers of 1,000 digits each. This is rudimentary in principle, but likely impossible in practice for any human to perform reliably. Similarly, the manual verification of 100,000 or 10,000 or even 1,000 line programs by hand is not feasible. Transcription errors alone would be prohibitive. Furthermore, substantial ingenuity may also be required on the part of the human to devise suitable assertions for loop invariants.

One can attempt to partially automate the process of proof construction using an interactive theorem prover. This can relieve much of the clerical burden.

However, human ingenuity is still required for invariants and various lemmas. Theorem provers may also require an expert operator to be used effectively.

Moreover, the proof-theoretic framework is one-sided. It focuses on providing a way to (syntactically) prove correct programs that are genuinely (semantically) correct. If one falters or fails in the laborious process of constructing a proof of a program, what then? Perhaps the program is really correct but one has not been clever enough to prove it so. On the other hand, if the program is really incorrect, the proof systems do not cater for proving incorrectness. Since in practice programs contain bugs in the overwhelming majority of the cases, the inability to identify errors is a serious drawback of the proof-theoretic approach.

It seemed there ought to be a better way. It would be suggested by temporal logic as discussed below.

Remark. We mention that the term *verification* is sometimes used in a specific sense meaning to establish correctness, while the term *refutation* (or *falsification*) is used meaning to detect an error. More generally, *verification* refers to the two-sided process of determining whether the system is correct or erroneous.

Lastly, we should also mention in this section the important and useful area of protocol validation. Network protocols are commonly finite state. This makes it possible to do simple graph reachability analysis to determine if a *bad* state is accessible (cf. [vB78], [Su78]). What was lacking here was a flexible and expressive means to specify a richer class of properties.

3   Temporal Logic

Modal and temporal logics provided key inspiration for model checking. Originally developed by philosophers, modal logic deals with different *modalities* of truth, distinguishing between P being true in the present circumstances, *possibly* P holding under some circumstances, and *necessarily* P holding under all circumstances. When the circumstances are points in time, we have a modal tense logic or *temporal logic*. Basic temporal modalities include *sometimes* P and *always* P.

Several writers including Prior [Pr67] and Burstall [Bu74] suggested that temporal logic might be useful in reasoning about computer programs. For instance, Prior suggested that it could be used to describe the "workings of a digital computer". But it was the seminal paper of Pnueli [Pn77] that made the critical suggestion of using temporal logic for reasoning about ongoing concurrent programs which are often characterized as *reactive systems*.

Reactive systems typically exhibit ideally nonterminating behavior so that they do not conform to the Floyd-Hoare paradigm. They are also typically non-deterministic so that their non-repeatable behavior was not amenable to testing. Their semantics can be given as infinite sequences of computation states (*paths*) or as computation *trees*. Examples of reactive systems include microprocessors, operating systems, banking networks, communication protocols, on-board avionics systems, automotive electronics, and many modern medical devices.

Pnueli used a temporal logic with basic temporal operators F (*sometimes*) and G (*always*); augmented with X (*next-time*) and U (*until*) this is today known as

LTL (Linear Time Logic). Besides the basic temporal operators applied to propositional arguments, LTL permitted formulae to be built up by forming nestings and boolean combinations of subformulae. For example, $G\neg(C_1 \wedge C_2)$ expresses mutual exclusion of critical sections C_1 and C_2; formula $G(T_1 \Rightarrow (T_1 \ U \ C_1))$ specifies that if process 1 is in its trying region it remains there until it eventually enters its critical section.

The advantages of such a logic include a high degree of expressiveness permitting the ready capture of a wide range of correctness properties of concurrent programs, and a great deal of flexibility. Pnueli focussed on a proof-theoretic approach, giving a proof in a deductive system for temporal logic of a small example program. Pnueli does sketch a decision procedure for truth over finite state graphs. However, the complexity would be nonelementary, growing faster than any fixed composition of exponential functions, as it entails a reduction to S1S, the monadic Second order theory of 1 Successor, (or SOLLO; see below). In his second paper [Pn79] on temporal logic the focus is again on the proof-theoretic approach.

I would claim that temporal logic has been a crucial factor in the success of model checking. We have one logical framework with a few basic temporal operators permitting the expression of limitless specifications. The connection with natural language is often significant as well. Temporal logic made it possible, by and large, to express the correctness properties that needed to be expressed. Without that ability, there would be no reason to use model checking. Alternative temporal formalisms in some cases may be used as they can be more expressive or succinct than temporal logic. But historically it was temporal logic that was the driving force.

These alternative temporal formalisms include: (finite state) automata (on infinite strings) which accept infinite inputs by infinitely often entering a designated set of automaton states [Bu62]. An expressively equivalent but less succinct formalism is that of ω-regular expressions; for example, $ab^\star c^\omega$ denotes strings of the form: one a, 0 or more bs, and infinitely many copies of c; and a property not expressible in LTL $(true \ P)^\omega$ ensuring that at every even moment P holds. FOLLO (First Order Language of Linear Order) which allows quantification over individual times, for example, $\forall i \geq 0 \ Q(i)$; and SOLLO (Second Order Language of Linear Order) which also allows quantification over sets of times corresponding to monadic predicates such as $\exists Q(Q(0) \wedge \forall i \geq 0(Q(i) \Rightarrow Q(i+1)))$.[1] These alternatives are sometimes used for reasons of familiarity, expressiveness or succinctness. LTL is expressively equivalent to FOLLO, but FOLLO can be nonelementarily more succinct. This succinctness is generally found to offer no significant practical advantage. Moreover, model checking is intractably (nonelementarily) hard for FOLLO. Similarly, SOLLO is expressively equivalent to ω−regular expressions but nonelementarily more succinct. See [Em90] for further discussion.

Temporal logic comes in two broad styles. A *linear time* LTL assertion h is interpreted with respect to a single path. When interpreted over a program there

---

[1] Technically, the latter abbreviates $\exists Q(Q(0) \wedge \forall i, j \geq 0(i < j \wedge \neg\exists k(i < k < j)) \Rightarrow (Q(i) \Rightarrow Q(j)))$.

is an implicit universal quantifications over all paths of the program. An assertion of a *branching time* logic is interpreted over computation trees. The universal A (for all futures) and existential E (for some future) *path quantifiers* are important in this context. We can distinguish between AFP (along all futures, P eventually holds and is thus inevitable)) and EFP (along some future, P eventually holds and is thus possible).

One widely used branching time logic is CTL (Computation Tree Logic) (cf. [CE81]). Its basic temporal modalities are A (for all futures) or E (for some future) followed by one of F (sometime), G (always), X (next-time), and U (until); compound formulae are built up from nestings and propositional combinations of CTL subformulae. CTL derives from [EC80]. There we defined the precursor branching time logic CTF which has path quantifiers $\forall fullpath$ and $\exists fullpath$, and is very similar to CTL. In CTF we could write $\forall fullpath \exists state P$ as well as $\exists fullpath \exists state P$ These would be rendered in CTL as AFP and EFP, respectively. The streamlined notation was derived from [BMP81]. We also defined a modal mu-calculus FPF, and then showed how to translate CTF into FPF. The heart of the translation was characterizing the temporal modalities such as AFP and EFP as fixpoints. Once we had the fixpoint characterizations of these temporal operators, we were close to having model checking.

CTL and LTL are of incomparable expressive power. CTL can assert the existence of behaviors, e.g., $AGEF start$ asserts that it is always possible to re-initialize a circuit. LTL can assert certain more complex behaviors along a computation, such as $GF en \Rightarrow F ex$ relating to fairness. (It turns out this formula is not expressible in CTL, but it is in "FairCTL" [EL87]) The branching time logic CTL* [EH86] provides a uniform framework that subsumes both LTL and CTL, but at the higher cost of deciding satisfiability. There has been an ongoing debate as to whether linear time logic or branching time logic is better for program reasoning (cf. [La80], [EH86], [Va01]).

Remark. The formal semantics of temporal logic formulae are defined with respect to a *(Kripke) structure* $M = (S, S_0, R, L)$ where S is a set of states, S_0 comprises the initial states, $R \subseteq S \times S$ is a total binary relation, and L is a labelling of states with atomic facts (propositions) true there. An LTL formula h such as FP is defined over path $x = t_0, t_1, t_2 \ldots$ through M by the rule $M, x \models FP$ iff $\exists i \geq 0\ P \in L(t_i)$. Similarly a CTL formula f such as EGP holds of a state t_0, denoted $M, t_0 \models EGP$, iff there exists a path $x = t_0, t_1, t_2, \ldots$ in M such that $\forall i \geq 0\ P \in L(t_i)$. For LTL h, we define $M \models h$ iff for all paths x starting in S_0, $M, x \models h$. For CTL formula f we define $M \models f$ iff for each $s \in S_0$, $M, s \models f$. A structure is also known as a *state graph* or *state transition graph* or *transition system*. See [Em90] for details.

4   The Mu-calculus

The mu-calculus may be viewed as a particular but very general temporal logic. Some formulations go back to the work of de Bakker and Scott [deBS69]; we deal specifically with the (propositional or) modal mu-calculus (cf. [EC80], [Ko83]).

The mu-calculus provides operators for defining correctness properties using recursive definitions plus least fixpoint and greatest fixpoint operators. Least fixpoints correspond to well-founded or terminating recursion, and are used to capture liveness or progress properties asserting that something does happen. Greatest fixpoints permit infinite recursion. They can be used to capture safety or invariance properties. The mu-calculus is very expressive and very flexible. It has been referred to as a "Theory of Everything".

The formulae of the mu-calculus are built up from atomic proposition constants $P, Q, \ldots$, atomic proposition variables $Y, Z, \ldots$, propositional connectives $\vee, \wedge, \neg$, and the least fixpoint operator, μ as well as the greatest fixpoint operator, ν. Each fixpoint formula such as $\mu Z.\tau(Z)$ should be syntactically monotone meaning Z occurs under an even number of negations, and similarly for ν.

The mu-calculus is interpreted with respect to a structure $M = (S, R, L)$. The power set of S, 2^S, may be viewed as the complete lattice $(2^S, S, \emptyset, \subseteq, \cup, \cap)$. Intuitively, each (closed) formula may be identified with the set of states of S where it is true. Thus, *false* which corresponds to the empty set is the bottom element, *true* which corresponds to S is the top element, and implication $(\forall s \in S[P(s) \Rightarrow Q(s)])$ which corresponds to simple set-theoretic containment $(P \subseteq Q)$ provides the partial ordering on the lattice. An open formula $\tau(Z)$ defines a mapping from $2^S \to 2^S$ whose value varies as Z varies. A given $\tau : 2^S \to 2^S$ is *monotone* provided that $P \subseteq Q$ implies $\tau(P) \subseteq \tau(Q)$.

Tarski-Knaster Theorem. (cf. [Ta55], [Kn28])
Let $\tau : 2^S \to 2^S$ be a monotone functional. Then

(a) $\mu Y.\tau(Y) = \cap \{Y : \tau(Y) = Y\} = \cap \{Y : \tau(Y) \subseteq Y\}$,
(b) $\nu Y.\tau(Y) = \cup \{Y : \tau(Y) = Y\} = \cup \{Y : \tau(Y) \supseteq Y\}$,
(c) $\mu Y.\tau(Y) = \cup_i \tau^i(false)$ where i ranges over all ordinals of cardinality at most that of the state space S, so that when S is finite i ranges over $[0:|S|]$, and
(d) $\nu Y.\tau(Y) = \cap_i \tau^i(true)$ where i ranges over all ordinals of cardinality at most that of the state space S, so that when S is finite i ranges over $[0:|S|]$.

Consider the CTL property AFP. Note that it is a fixed point or fixpoint of the functional $\tau(Z) = P \vee AXZ$. That is, as the value of the input Z varies, the value of the output $\tau(Z)$ varies, and we have $AFP = \tau(AFP) = P \vee AXAFP$. It can be shown that AFP is the least fixpoint of $\tau(Z)$, meaning the set of states associated with AFP is a subset of the set of states associated with Z, for any fixpoint $Z = \tau(Z)$. This might be denoted $\mu Z.Z = \tau(Z)$. More succinctly, we normally write just $\mu Z.\tau(Z)$. In this case we have $AFP = \mu Z.P \vee AXZ$.

We can get some intuition for the the mu-calculus by noting the following fixpoint characterizations for CTL properties:

$EFP = \mu Z.P \vee EXZ$
$AGP = \nu Z.P \wedge AXZ$
$AFP = \mu Z.P \vee AXZ$
$EGP = \nu Z.P \wedge EXZ$
$A(P\ U\ Q) = \mu Z.Q \vee (P \wedge AXZ)$
$E(P\ U\ Q) = \mu Z.Q \vee (P \wedge EXZ)$

For all these properties, as we see, the fixpoint characterizations are simple and plausible. It is not too difficult to give rigorous proofs of their correctness (cf. [EC80], [EL86]). We emphasize that the mu-calculus is a rich and powerful formalism; its formulae are really representations of alternating finite state automata on infinite trees [EJ91]. Since even such basic automata as deterministic finite state automata on finite strings can form quite complex "cans of worms", we should not be so surprised that it is possible to write down highly inscrutable mu-calculus formulae for which there is no readily apparent intuition regarding their intended meaning. The mu-calculus has also been referred to as the "assembly language of program logics" reflecting both its comprehensiveness and potentially intricate syntax. On the other hand, many mu-calculus characterizations of correctness properties are elegant due to its simple underlying mathematical organization.

In [EL86] we introduced the idea of model checking for the mu-calculus instead of testing satisfiability. We catered for efficient model checking in fragments of the the mu-calculus. This provides a basis for practical (symbolic) model checking algorithms. We gave an algorithm essentially of complexity n^d, where d is the alternation depth reflecting the number of significantly nested least and greatest fixpoint operators. We showed that common logics such as CTL, LTL, and CTL* were of low alternation depth $d = 1$ or $d = 2$. We also provided succinct fixpoint characterizations for various natural fair scheduling criteria. A symbolic fair cycle detection method, known as the "Emerson-Lei" algorithm, is comprised of a simple fixpoint characterization plus the Tarski-Knaster theorem. It is widely used in practice even though it has worst case quadratic cost. Empirically, it usually outperforms alternatives.

5   The Origin of Model Checking

There were several influences in my personal background that facilitated the development of model checking. In 1975 Zohar Manna gave a talk at the University of Texas on fixpoints and the Tarski-Knaster Theorem. I was familiar with Dijkstra's book [Di76] extending the Floyd-Hoare framework with *wlp* the *weakest liberal precondition* for partial correctness and *wp* the *weakest precondition* for total correctness. It turns out that *wlp* and *wp* may be viewed as modal operators, for which Dijkstra implicitly gave fixpoint characterizations, although Dijkstra did not favor this viewpoint. Basu and Yeh [BY75] at Texas gave fixpoint characterizations of weakest preconditions for while loops. Ed Clarke [Cl79] gave similar fixpoint characterizations for both *wp* and *wlp* for a variety of control structures.

I will now describe how model checking originated at Harvard University. In prior work [EC80] we gave fixpoint characterizations for the main modalities of a logic that was essentially CTL. These would ultimately provide the first key ingredient of model checking.

Incidentally, [EC80] is a paper that could very well not have appeared. Somehow the courier service delivering the hard-copies of the submission to

Amsterdam for the program chair at CWI (Dutch for "Center for Mathematics and Computer Science") sent the package in bill-the-recipient mode. Fortunately, CWI was gracious and accepted the package. All that remained to undo this small misfortune was to get an overseas bank draft to reimburse them.

The next work, entitled "Design and Synthesis of Synchronization Skeletons using Branching Time Logic", was devoted to program synthesis and model checking. I suggested to Ed Clarke that we present the paper, which would be known as [CE81], at the IBM Logics of Programs workshop, since he had an invitation to participate.

Both the idea and the term *model checking* were introduced by Clarke and Emerson in [CE81]. Intuitively, this is a method to establish that a given program meets a given specification where:

- The program defines a finite state graph M.
- M is searched for elaborate *patterns* to determine if the specification f holds.
- Pattern specification is *flexible*.
- The method is *efficient* in the sizes of M and, ideally, f.
- The method is *algorithmic*.
- The method is *practical*.

The conception of model checking was inspired by program synthesis. I was interested in verification, but struck by the difficulties associated with manual proof-theoretic verification as noted above. It seemed that it might be possible to avoid verification altogether and mechanically synthesize a correct program directly from its CTL specification. The idea was to exploit the small model property possessed by certain decidable temporal logics: any satisfiable formula must have a "small" finite model of size that is a function of the formula size. The synthesis method would be *sound*: if the input specification was satisfiable, it built a finite global state graph that was a model of the specification, from which individual processes could be extracted The synthesis method should also be *complete*: If the specification was unsatisfiable, it should say so.

Initially, it seemed to me technically problematic to develop a sound and complete synthesis method for CTL. However, it could always be ensured that an alleged synthesis method was at least sound. This was clear because *given any finite* **model** M *and CTL specification* f *one can algorithmically* **check** *that M is a genuine model of f by evaluating (verifying) the basic temporal modalities over M based on the Tarski-Knaster theorem.* This was the second key ingredient of model checking. Composite temporal formulae comprised of nested subformulae and boolean combinations of subformulae could be verified by recursive descent. Thus, fixpoint characterizations, the Tarski-Knaster theorem, and recursion yielded *model checking*.

Thus, we obtained the model checking framework. A model checker could be quite useful in practice, given the prevalence of finite state concurrent systems. The temporal logic CTL had the flexibility and expressiveness to capture many important correctness properties. In addition the CTL model checking algorithm was of reasonable efficiency, polynomial in the structure and specification sizes. Incidentally, in later years we sometimes referred to *temporal logic model checking*.

The crucial roles of abstraction, synchronization skeletons, and finite state spaces were discussed in [CE81]:

> The synchronization skeleton is an abstraction where detail irrelevant to synchronization is suppressed. *Most solutions to synchronization problems are in fact given as synchronization skeletons.*

> Because synchronization skeletons are in general finite state ... *propositional temporal logic can be used to specify their properties.*

> The finite model property ensures that any program whose synchronization properties can be expressed in propositional temporal logic *can be realized by a finite state machine.*

Conclusions of [CE81] included the following prognostications, which seem to have been on target:

> [Program Synthesis] may in the long run be quite practical. Much additional research will be needed, however, to make it feasible in practice. ... We believe that practical [model checking] tools could be developed in the near future.

To sum up, [CE81] made several contributions. It introduced model checking, giving an algorithm of quadratic complexity $O(|f||M|^2)$. It introduced the logic CTL. It gave an algorithmic method for concurrent program synthesis (that was both sound and complete). It argued that most concurrent systems can be abstracted to finite state synchronization skeletons. It described a method for efficiently model checking basic fairness using strongly connected components. An NP-hardness result was established for checking certain assertions in a richer logic than CTL. A prototype (and non-robust) model checking tool BMoC was developed, primarily by a Harvard undergraduate, to permit verification of synchronization protocols.

A later paper [CES86] improved the complexity of CTL model checking to linear $O(|f||M|)$. It showed how to efficiently model check relative to unconditional and weak fairness. The EMC model checking tool was described, and a version of the alternating bit protocol verified. A general framework for efficiently model checking fairness properties was given in [EL87], along with a reduction showing that CTL* model checking could be done as efficiently as LTL model checking.

Independently, a similar method was developed in France by Sifakis and his student [QS82]. Programs were interpreted over transition systems. A branching time logic with operators *POT* (*EF*) and *INEV* (*AF*) and their duals was used; omitted were the *X* (*next-time*) and *U* (*until*) operators available in CTL. Interestingly, there was no emphasis on the role of finiteness, no complexity analysis, and no proof of termination. However, the central role of fixpoint computation was identified. (The follow-on paper [FSS83] does emphasize the importance of finiteness.) A tool CESAR is described and the verification of an alternating bit protocol discussed.

Remark. The study of program synthesis together with analysis of programs (or verification) has a long history. In 1956 Kleene [Kl56] proposes (i) the *synthesis problem*: from a given regular expression h, construct an equivalent finite state automaton M; and (ii) the *analysis problem*: given a finite automaton M construct an equivalent regular expression h, i.e., in other words the strongest specification h such that M verifies h. Strictly speaking, Kleene dealt with machinery suitable for reasoning about ongoing but finite behavior; however, the results generalize to infinite behavior.

6 Model Checking Today

The fundamental accomplishment of model checking is enabling broad scale formal verification. Twenty five years ago our community mostly just talked about verification. Today we do verification: many industrial-strength systems have been verified using model checking. More are being verified on a routine basis. Formal verification is becoming a staple of CS and EE education. At the same time there is ever growing research interest in model checking.

How and why did this come about? I would argue that it is due to the following. In [CE81] a feasible framework including a usefully expressive branching time temporal logic (CTL) and a reasonably efficient model checking algorithm was introduced. Its utility was clear for small examples. Plainly one could model check many interesting programs because they could be represented at a meaningful level of abstraction by a finite state system with dozens to hundreds or thousands of states. Protocols provide many examples of this. Yet there was doubtless a need to be able to handle larger programs. This garnered the attention of a sizable and still growing number of researchers in both academia and industry.

The most serious (and obvious) drawback of model checking is the *state explosion problem*. The size of the global state graph can be (at least) exponential in the size of the program text. A concurrent program with k processes can have a state graph of size $exp(k)$. For instance in a banking network with 100 automatic teller machines each controlled by a finite state machine with 10 states, we can have 10^{100} global states. Systems with infinite state spaces, in general, cannot be handled.

To reduce the state explosion problem, methods based on abstraction, symbolic representation, and compositional reasoning are used. These are discussed in more detail subsequently.

Today, model checkers are able to verify protocols with millions of states and many hardware circuits with 10^{50} or more states. Even some systems with an infinite number of states can be amenable to model checking, if we have a suitable finite representation of infinite sets of states in terms of symbolic constraints.

Model checking has made verification commonplace in many industrial settings where applications are safety critical or economically vital. These include hardware and CAD companies such as IBM, Intel, Cadence, and Synopsys, software companies such as Microsoft, and government agencies such as NASA.

Today there are many logics and methods for model checking. CTL and the mu-calculus with associated fixpoint-based model checking algorithms are still in widespread use. There is also linear temporal logic LTL model checking. It was considered in a tableaux-theoretic approach by Lichtenstein and Pnueli [LP85]. More generally, LTL model checking can be done through reduction to automaton nonemptiness as shown by Vardi and Wolper [VW86], and independently by Kurshan (cf. [Ku94]). The automata-theoretic approach readily generalizes to a broader class of linear formalisms than just LTL. Interestingly, it is often implemented on top of a mu-calculus or (fair) CTL model checking algorithm (cf. [EL86], [EL87]), where linear temporal model checking over one structure is transformed to checking fairness over another structure.

A crucial factor is the formulation and application of abstractions. Given original system M an abstraction is obtained by suppressing detail yielding a simpler and likely smaller system $\overline{M}$ that is, ideally, equivalent to M for purposes of verification. The precise nature of the abstraction and the correspondence between M and $\overline{M}$ can vary considerably.

An *exact* abstraction guarantees that M is correct if and only if $\overline{M}$ is correct. A *bisimulation* is a technical concept [Pa81] associating M and $\overline{M}$ that guarantees an exact abstraction, and such that the original and the abstraction cannot be distinguished by any "reasonable" temporal logic.

Systems M comprised of multiple, interchangeable subcomponents typically exhibit symmetry which may be thought of as a form of redundancy. This can be abstracted out by identifying symmetric states to get abstraction $\overline{M}$ that is bisimilar to M. The symmetry abstraction can be exponentially smaller than the original, yielding a dramatic speedup in model checking. A resource controller with 150 homogeneous processes and a global state graph M of size about 10^{47} states[2] can be model checked over the abstract $\overline{M}$ in a few tens of minutes [ES97].

A related problem is *parameterized* model checking. Given a family of n similar processes, establish correctness for systems of all sizes n. (Note that collectively this amounts to an infinite state program.) While in general an undecidable problem, various restricted cases can be solved. In [EN96] we developed a mathematical theory for a restricted but still useful framework. In [EN98] we showed how to use this theory to verify parameterized correctness of the Society of Automotive Engineers SAE-J1850 automotive bus protocol. This solved a problem relating to the use of multiple embedded Motorola micro-controllers in Ford automobiles.

A *conservative* abstraction ensures that correctness of $\overline{M}$ implies correctness of M. An abstraction obtained from M by partitioning and clustering states in the natural way will be conservative. A *simulation* from M to $\overline{M}$ yields a

---

[2] It should be emphasized that the original state graph of size 10^{47} is not and cannot be constructed by the model checker. A smaller abstract graph representing the essential information is built instead.

conservative abstraction, preserving correctness in $\overline{M}$ to M. On the other hand, if $\overline{M}$ is incorrect the error may be bogus and the abstraction too coarse. Repeatedly refining it as needed and as resources permit typically leads to determination of correctness vs. incorrectness for M. (cf. [Ku94]).

For hardware verification a basic aid is symbolic representation of the program's states and state transitions using data structures called Reduced Ordered Binary Decision Diagrams (ROBDDs) [Br86] often called BDDs for short (cf. [Le59], [Ak78]). A BDD is essentially an acyclic deterministic finite state automaton. Given a set P of system states, each a string of bits $b_1 b_2 \ldots b_n$, the BDD for P accepts exactly those states in P. Note that a BDD with a polynomial number of nodes may have an exponential number of paths. In this way, a BDD may represent a vastly larger set of states.

Symbolic model checking [B+90] is based on the original CTL logic and fixpoint based model checking algorithm [CE81] plus BDDs to represent sets of states and transitions. It is routinely able to verify hardware designs modeled with 100 to 300 or more state variables and having about 10^{30} to 10^{90} or more global states. This corresponds to a large enough chunk of real estate on a chip to be extremely valuable. Larger components are often amenable to verification through decomposition and compositional reasoning.

BDDs tend to blow up in size for large designs. Conventional BDDs have topped out for systems with a few hundred state variables. SAT-based bounded model checking is an alternative approach [B+99]. The SAT approach can accommodate larger designs than the BDD approach. However it only explores for "close" errors at depth bounded by k where typically k ranges from a few tens to hundreds of steps. In general it cannot find "deep" errors and provide verification of correctness.

Remark. It should be emphasized that not all systems with, say, 10^{90} states can be handled, since there are relatively few succinct representations and they are insufficient to cover all such astronomically large systems. The pertinent fact is that the method works routinely on the large systems encountered in practice. On the other hand, there are some relatively small hardware systems for which BDDs are too big, while a conventional explicit state representation is workable.

In software model checking, Microsoft has routinely verified device drivers with 100,000 lines of code. The task is made easier by the fact that drivers are more or less sequential code. Therefore state explosion is less of an issue. However, software is usually more difficult to verify than hardware. It typically has less of a regular organization. It may involve significant use of recursion, and complex, dynamic data structures on the heap. It can also be extremely large.

A remaining significant factor in ameliorating state explosion is the exponential growth in computer power, speed and especially memory size, expressed in Moore's law which has obtained over the past quarter century. For example, in 1981 the IBM PC had less than 1M (random access) memory while today many PC's have 1G or more memory. Such a 1000-fold or larger increase in memory permits significantly larger programs to be handled.

There are numerous model checking tools. They typically include a modeling language for representing the program corresponding to the structure M, a specification logic such as CTL or LTL for capturing correctness properties f, a model checking algorithm that is often fixpoint based, and perhaps special data structures such as BDDs for symbolic model checking or for incrementally building the state graph for explicit state model checking. Some of these are academic tools, others are industrial internal tools, and some are for sale by CAD vendors.

7   Conclusions and Future Trends

The fundamental accomplishment of model checking is enabling broad scale formal verification. Twenty five years ago our community mostly just talked about verification. Today we do verification: many industrial-strength systems have been verified using model checking. More are being verified on a routine basis. Model checking thus has produced an era of feasible, automatic, model-theoretic verification. It should be emphasized that a model checker decides correctness: yes or no. Thus it caters for both verification and refutation of correctness properties. Since most programs do contain errors, an important strength of model checkers is that they can readily provide a counter-example for most errors.

Model checking realizes in small part the Dream of Leibniz (1646 – 1716) to permit calculation of the truth status of formalized assertions. The Dream of Leibniz was comprised of two parts: *lingua characteristica universalis*, a language in which all knowledge could be formally expressed; and *calculus ratiocinator*, a method of calculating the truth value of such an assertion. Leibniz's original Dream was unworkable because its scope was too vast and the level of available precision too low.

Model checking is feasible because its domain is both well-defined and much more narrow. Temporal logic is also precisely defined while limited in expressive power especially in comparison to formalisms such as First Order Arithmetic plus Monadic Predicates; yet, temporal logic and related formalisms seem ideally suited to describing synchronization and coordination behavior of concurrent systems; the restriction to finite state systems means that model checking procedures are in principle algorithmic and in practice efficient for many systems of considerable size. It is in just these coordination aspects that errors are most prone to occur for concurrent programs.

Beyond the Dream of Leibniz, model checking also validates in small part the seemingly naive expectation during the early days of computing that large problems could be solved by brute force computation including the technique of exhaustive search. Model checking algorithms are typically efficient in the size of the state graph. The difficulty is that the state graph can be immense. Abstraction can be helpful because it in effect replaces the original state graph by a much smaller one verifying the same formulae.

Model checking has been an enabling technology facilitating cross disciplinary work. Problems from diverse areas distinct from formal methods can with some frequency be handled with existing model checking tools and possibly without a deep understanding of model checking per se.

It is worth mentioning some of the applications of model checking elsewhere. These include understanding and analyzing legal contracts, which are after all prescriptions for behavior [Da00]; analyzing processes in living organisms for systems biology [H+06]; e-business processes such as accounting and workflow systems [Wa+00]. Model checking has also been employed for tasks in artificial intelligence such as planning [GT99]. Conversely, techniques from artificial intelligence related to SAT-based planning [KS92] are relevant to (bounded) model checking.

In the present formal methods research milieu, the ideal paper contributes both new theory and practical experimental evidence of the merits of the theory. A significant benefit of this tight coupling is that it promotes the development of concretely applicable theory. On the other hand, such a synchronous organization may risk slowing down the rate of advance on the theoretical track as well as on the practice track. It will be interesting to see if as the field develops in the future it might adopt something of the more specialized organization of older disciplines. For instance, one has the broad divisions of theoretical physics and experimental physics, which are more loosely coupled.

Model checking would benefit from future theoretical advances. This is especially important in view of the fact that many model checking methods are in principle algorithmic but of high theoretical, worst case complexity. Their good performance in practice has a heuristic character and is not well-understood on a mathematical basis. Many efficiency enhancement techniques produce an unpredictable gain in efficiency. To gain a better theoretical understanding of when good efficiency obtains would be a very desirable goal for the future.

It is thus especially important to obtain convincing empirical documentation of a verification method's effectiveness and efficiency. One way to do this might be to establish a broad set of benchmarks. A major obstacle, however, is that proprietary hardware designs and software code are virtually never available in an open fashion because they are patented, or trade secrets, etc. This means that, to the extent that success at verifying industrial systems is the yardstick of merit, we have lost the critical standard of repeatability normally associated with experimental sciences.

Various interesting remarks have been made concerning model checking. Edsger W. Dijkstra commented to me that it was an "acceptable crutch" if one was going to do after-the-fact verification. When I had the pleasure of meeting Saul Kripke and explaining model checking over Kripke structures to him, he commented that he never thought of that. Daniel Jackson has remarked that model checking has "saved the reputation" of formal methods [Ja97].

In summary, model checking today provides automatic verification that is applicable to a broad range of sizable systems including many that are industrial strength. At the same time the verification problem is not solved. We still have quite a way to go.

Grand Challenge for Hardware. Hardware designs with a few hundreds to thousands of state variables can be model checked in some fashion; but not an entire microprocessor. It would be a Grand Challenge to verify an entire microprocessor with one hundred thousand state variables.

Grand Challenge for Software. Software device drivers have been shown amenable to software model checking. These are mostly sequential software with up to one hundred thousand lines of code. Of course, there is software with millions of lines of code. Windows Vista contains somewhat over 50 million lines of code, and entails concurrency as well. It would be a Grand Challenge to to verify software with millions to tens of millions lines of code.

In the future, we should see progress on the key topics of limiting state explosion, improved abstractions, better symbolic representations, broader parameterized reasoning techniques, and the development of temporal formalisms specialized to particular application domains (cf. [IEEE05]). It seems likely that parallel and distributed model checking will grow in importance (cf. [HvdP06]). In any case, I expect that model checking will become yet more useful.

References

[Ak78]   Akers, S.B.: Binary Decision Diagrams. IEEE Trans. on Computers C-27(6), 509–516 (1978)

[AENT01] Amla, N., Emerson, E.A., Namjoshi, K.S., Trefler, R.J.: Assume-Guarantee Based Compositional Reasoning for Synchronous Timing Diagrams. In: Margaria, T., Yi, W. (eds.) ETAPS 2001 and TACAS 2001. LNCS, vol. 2031, pp. 465–479. Springer, Heidelberg (2001)

[B+90]   Birch, J., Clarke, E., MacMillan, K., Dill, D., Hwang, L.: Symbolic Model Checking: 10^{20} States and Beyond. In: Logic in Computer Science. LICS, pp. 428–439 (1990)

[B+99]   Clarke, E., Biere, A., Cimatti, A., Zhu, Y.: Symbolic Model Checking without BDDs. In: Cleaveland, W.R. (ed.) ETAPS 1999 and TACAS 1999. LNCS, vol. 1579, pp. 193–207. Springer, Heidelberg (1999)

[BMP81]   Ben-Ari, M., Manna, Z., Pnueli, A.: The Temporal Logic of Branching Time. In: Principles of Programming Languages, POPL 1981, pp. 164–176 (1981)

[Br86]   Bryant, R.: Graph-Based Algorithms for Boolean Function Manipulation. IEEE Trans. Computers 35(8), 677–691 (1986)

[BY75]   Basu, S.K., Yeh, R.T.: Strong Verification of Programs. IEEE Trans. on Software Engineering SE-1(3), 339–345 (1975)

[Bu62]   Buchi, J.R.: On a Decision Method in Restricted Second Order Arithmetic. In: Proc. of Int'l. Congress on Logic Method, and Philosophy of Science 1960, pp. 1–12. Stanford Univ. Press (1962)

[Bu74]   Burstall, R.M.: Program Proving as Hand Simulation with a Little Induction. In: IFIP Congress, pp. 308–312 (1974)

[CE81]   Clarke, E.M., Emerson, E.A.: The Design and Synthesis of Synchronization Skeletons Using Temporal Logic. In: Proceedings of the Workshop on Logics of Programs, IBM Watson Research Center, Yorktown Heights, May 1981. LNCS, vol. 131, pp. 52–71. Springer, New York (1981)

[CES86]   Clarke, E.M., Emerson, E.A., Sistla, A.P.: Automatic Verification of Finite State Concurrent Systems Using Temporal Logic Specifications. ACM Trans. Prog. Lang. and Sys. 2(8), 244–263 (1986)

[Cl79]   Clarke, E.M.: Program Invariants as Fixpoints. Computing 21(4), 3–294 (1979)

[Da00]   Daskalopulu, A.: Model Checking Contractual Protocols. In: Breuker, Leenes, Winkels (eds.) Legal Knowledge and Information Systems. JURIX 2000: The 13th Annual Conference, pp. 35–47. IOS Press, Breuker (2000)

[DEG06] Deshmukh, J., Emerson, E.A., Gupta, P.: Automatic Verification of Parameterized Data Structures. In: Hermanns, H., Palsberg, J. (eds.) TACAS 2006 and ETAPS 2006. LNCS, vol. 3920, pp. 27–41. Springer, Heidelberg (2006)

[deBS69] de Bakker, J.W., Scott, D.: A Theory of Programs (unpublished manuscript, 1969)

[Di76]   Dijkstra, E.W.: Discipline of Programming. Prentice-Hall (1976)

[Di89]   Dijkstra, E.W.: In Reply to Comments. EWD1058 (1989)

[EC80]   Emerson, E.A., Clarke, E.M.: Characterizing Correctness Properties of Parallel Programs Using Fixpoints. In: de Bakker, J.W., van Leeuwen, J. (eds.) ICALP 1980. LNCS, vol. 85, pp. 169–181. Springer, Heidelberg (1980)

[EH86]   Emerson, E.A., Halpern, J.Y.: Sometimes and Not Never revisited: on branching versus linear time temporal logic. J. ACM 33(1), 151–178 (1986)

[EJ91]   Emerson, E.A., Jutla, C.S.: Tree Automata, Mu-calculus, and Determinacy. In: FOCS 1991, pp. 368–377 (1991)

[EL86]   Emerson, E.A., Lei, C.-L.: Efficient Model Checking in Fragments of the Propositional Mu-Calculus. In: Logic in Computer Science, LICS 1986, pp. 267–278 (1986)

[EL87]   Emerson, E.A., Lei, C.-L.: Modalities for Model Checking: Branching Time Strikes Back. Sci. of Comp. Prog. 8(3), 275–306 (1987)

[Em90]   Emerson, E.A.: Temporal and Modal Logic. In: Handbook of Theoretical Computer Science, vol. B. North-Holland (1990)

[EN96]   Emerson, E.A., Namjoshi, K.S.: Automatic Verification of Parameterized Synchronous Systems. In: Alur, R., Henzinger, T.A. (eds.) CAV 1996. LNCS, vol. 1102, pp. 87–98. Springer, Heidelberg (1996)

[EN98]   Emerson, E.A., Namjoshi, K.S.: Verification of a Parameterized Bus Arbitration Protocol. In: Y. Vardi, M. (ed.) CAV 1998. LNCS, vol. 1427, pp. 452–463. Springer, Heidelberg (1998)

[ES97]   Allen Emerson, E., Prasad Sistla, A.: Utilizing Symmetry when Model-Checking under Fairness Assumptions: An Automata-Theoretic Approach. ACM Trans. Program. Lang. Syst. 19(4), 617–638 (1997)

[FG99]   Giunchiglia, F., Traverso, P.: Planning as Model Checking. In: ECP 1999, pp. 1–20 (1999)

[Fl67]   Floyd, R.W.: Assigning meanings to programs. In: Schwartz, J.T. (ed.) Proceedings of a Symposium in Applied Mathematics. Mathematical Aspects of Computer Science, vol. 19, pp. 19–32 (1967)

[FSS83]   Jean-Claude Fernandez, J., Schwartz, P., Sifakis, J.: An Example of Specification and Verification in Cesar. The Analysis of Concurrent Systems, 199–210 (1983)

[GT99]   Giunchiglia, F., Traverso, P.: Planning as Model Checking. In: ECP 1999. LNCS (LNAI), Springer (1999)

[H+06]   Heath, J., Kwiatkowska, M., Norman, G., Parker, D., Tymchysyn, O.: Probabilistic Model Checking of Complex Biological Pathways. In: Priami, C. (ed.) CMSB 2006. LNCS (LNBI), vol. 4210, pp. 32–47. Springer (October 2006)

[HvdP06] Brim, L., Haverkort, B.R., Leucker, M., van de Pol, J. (eds.): FMICS 2006 and PDMC 2006. LNCS, vol. 4346. Springer, Heidelberg (2006)

[Ho69]   Hoare, C.A.R.: An Axiomatic Basis for Computer Programming. Commun. ACM 12(10), 576–580 (1969)

[Ho96]   Holzmann, G.J.: On-The-Fly Model Checking. ACM Comput. Surv. 28(4es), 120 (1996)

[IEEE05] IEEE-P1850-2005 Standard for Property Specification Language (PSL).

[Ja97]   Jackson, D.: Mini-tutorial on Model Checking. In: Third IEEE Intl. Symp. on Requirements Engineering, Annapolis, Maryland, January 6-10 (1997)

[JPZ06]   Jurdenski, M., Paterson, M., Zwick, U.: A Deterministic Subexponential Algorithm for Parity Games. In: ACM-SIAM Symp. on Algorithms for Discrete Systems, pp. 117–123 (January 2006)

[Ko83]   Kozen, D.: Results on the Propositional Mu-Calculus. Theor. Comput. Sci. 27, 333–354 (1983)

[Kl56]   Kleene, S.C.: Representation of Events in Nerve Nets and Finite Automata. In: McCarthy, J., Shannon, C. (eds.) Automata Studies, pp. 3–42. Princeton Univ. Press (1956)

[Kn28]   Knaster, B.: Un théorème sur les fonctions d'ensembles. Ann. Soc. Polon. Math. 6, 133̌2013134 (1928)

[KS92]   Kautz, H., Selman, B.: Planning as Satisfiability. In: Proceedings European Conference on Artificial Intelligence. ECAI (1992)

[Ku94]   Kurshan, R.P.: Computer Aided Verification of Coordinating Processes: An Automata-theoretic Approach. Princeton University Press (1994)

[La80]   Lamport, L.: "Sometimes" is Sometimes 'Not Never' - On the Temporal Logic of Programs. In: Principles of Programming Languages, POPL 1980, pp. 174–185 (1980)

[Le59]   Lee, C.Y.: Representation of Switching Circuits by Binary-Decision Programs. Bell Systems Technical Journal 38, 985–999 (1959)

[LP85]   Lichtenstein, O., Pnueli, A.: Checking that Finite State Programs meet their Linear Specification. In: Principles of Programming Languages, POPL, pp. 97–107 (1985)

[Lo+94]   Long, D.E., Browne, A., Clarke, E.M., Jha, S., Marero, W.: An improved Algorithm for the Evaluation of Fixpoint Expressions. In: Dill, D.L. (ed.) CAV 1994. LNCS, vol. 818, pp. 338–350. Springer, Heidelberg (1994)

[NASA97] Formal Methods Specification and Analysis Guidebook for the Verification of Software and Computer Systems, vol. II, A Practioners Companion, p.245 (1997) [NASA-GB-01-97]

[NK00]   Kedar, S., Namjoshi, R.P.: Syntactic Program Transformations for Automatic Abstraction. In: Emerson, E.A., Sistla, A.P. (eds.) CAV 2000. LNCS, vol. 1855, pp. 435–449. Springer, Heidelberg (2000)

[Ni02]   National Institute of Standards and Technology, US Department of Commerce, Software Errors Cost U.S. Economy $59.5 Billion Annually, NIST News Release (June 28, 2002), http://www.nist.gov/public_affairs/releases/n02-10.htm

[Pa69]   Park, D.: Fixpoint induction and proofs of program properties. In: Meltzer, B., Michie, D. (eds.) Machine Intelligence, Scotland, vol. 5, Edinburgh University Press, Edinburgh (1969)

[Pa81]   Park, D.: Concurrency and Automata on Infinite Sequences. Theoretical Computer Science, pp. 167–183 (1981)

[Pn77]   Pnueli, A.: The Temporal Logic of Programs. Foundations of Computer Science, FOCS, pp. 46–57 (1977)

[Pn79]   Pnueli, A.: The Temporal Semantics of Concurrent Programs. Semantics of Concurrent Computation, pp 1–20 (1979)

[Pr67]   Prior, A.: Past, Present, and Future. Oxford University Press (1967)

[QS82]   Queille, J.-P., Sifakis, J.: Specification and verification of concurrent systems
           in CESAR. In: Symposium on Programming. LNCS, vol. 137, pp. 337–351.
           Springer (1982)

[Su78]   Sunshine, C.A.: Survey of protocol definition and verification techniques.
           ACM SIGCOMM Computer Communication Review 8(3), 35–41 (1978)

[Ta55]   Tarski, A.: A lattice-theoretical fixpoint theorem and its applications. Pac.
           J. Math. 5, 285–309 (1955)

[Tu36]   Turing, A.M.: On Computable Numbers, with an Application to the
           Entscheidungproblem. Proc. London Math. Society 2(42), 230–265 (1936);
           A Correction, ibid 43, 544–546

[Tu49]   Turing, A.M.: Checking a Large Routine. In: EDSAC Inaugural Conference,
           Typescript published in Report of a Conference on High Speed Automatic
           Calculating Machines, pp. 67–69 (June 24, 1949)

[Va01]   Vardi, M.Y.: Branching vs. Linear Time: Final Showdown. In: Margaria, T.,
           Yi, W. (eds.) ETAPS 2001 and TACAS 2001. LNCS, vol. 2031, pp. 1–22.
           Springer, Heidelberg (2001)

[VW86]   Vardi, M.Y., Wolper, P.: An Automata-Theoretic Approach to Automatic
           Program Verification (Preliminary Report). In: Logic in Computer Science.
           LICS, pp. 332–344 (1986)

[vB78]   von Bochmann, G.: Finite State Description of Communication Protocols.
           Computer Networks 2, 361–372 (1978)

[Wa+00]   Wang, W., Hidvegi, Z., Bailey, A., Whinston, A.: E-Process Design and
           Assurance Using Model Checking. IEEE Computer 33(10), 48–53 (2000)

Verification Technology Transfer

R. P. Kurshan

Cadence Design Systems, Inc., New Providence, NJ 07974

Abstract. In the last quarter century computer-aided verification – especially in the form of model checking – has evolved from a research concept to a commercial product. While the pace of this technology transfer was anything but rapid, the new technology had almost insuperable hurdles to jump on its way to the market place. Hurdle number one was a required significant change in methodology. On account of its limited capacity, model checking must be applied only to design components (RTL blocks in the case of hardware) instead of the whole design as with simulation test. Thus, the functional behavior of these design components must be specified. Since component level functionality is often revealed at best obscurely in the design's functional specification, either designers must convey component functionality to those doing the testing or else testers must somehow fathom it on their own. The former was considered an unacceptable diversion of vaunted designer resources while the latter was often undoable. A second hurdle was uncertainty surrounding the quality of the new tools. Initially the tools were incomparable and required the user to create considerable tool-specific infrastructure to specify properties before a tool could be evaluated. Recreating the required infrastructure for several tools was infeasible. This meant choosing a tool without a head-to-head evaluation against other tools. With the high cost and uncertain outcome afforded by these hurdles, no circuit manufacturer was willing even to consider seriously this new technology. Not, that is, until the cost of testing-as-usual became higher than the cost of jumping these formidable hurdles. This essay is the saga of the transfer of computer-aided verification technology from research to the market place.

1 Introduction

Computer-aided verification could be said to derive from Russell-Whitehead's *Principia Mathematica* (1910-1913) [WR13], which laid a foundation for axiomatic reasoning. More germane was Alan Turing's model of computation [Tur36]. The Turing Machine led to automata theory developed by Rabin and Scott [RS59] for languages of strings and then by Büchi [Büc62] for languages of sequences. The latter provided the basis for automata-theoretic verification [Kur94, VW86] on which model checking can be founded. Model checking *per se* was developed in 1980 by Clarke and Emerson [CE82] and Queille and Sifakis [QS82] independently. Earlier, around 1960, computer-aided verification was introduced in the form of automated theorem proving. Theorem proving derived especially from

O. Grumberg and H. Veith (Eds.): 25MC Festschrift, LNCS 5000, pp. 46–64, 2008.

the resolution method of Robinson [Rob65], which evolved into other more practical non-resolution methods by Bledsoe and others, leading to the UT Austin school of automated theorem proving that featured Gypsy (by Ron Goode and J. C. Browne) and then the famous Boyer-Moore theorem prover – see [BL84]. Until 1990, most of the investment in computer-aided verification went to automated theorem proving. This was especially true for U. S. government support, which was lavished on automated theorem proving during this period.

For all its expressiveness and proving potential, automated theorem proving has not quite yet made it into main-stream commercial use for computer-aided verification. One important reason is scalability of use: using an automated theorem prover requires specialized expertise that precludes its broad use in industry. Moreover, even in the hands of experts, using an automated theorem prover tends to take more time than would allow it to be applied broadly and still track the development of a large design project. Therefore, to the extent that automated theorem proving is used on commercial projects, it tends to be used for niche applications like verification of numerical algorithms (hardware multipliers and dividers, for example). Although one company in particular, AMD, has made extensive practical use of theorem proving for such applications, utilization is presently too narrow and specialized to attract much attention in the Electronic Design Automation (EDA) marketplace, where vendors such as Cadence, Synopsys, Mentor Graphics and others sell software tools for industrial development of integrated circuits. A brief exception was the failed attempt by Abstract Hardware Ltd. of Scotland to market the LAMBDA theorem prover based on HOL [GMW79]. Based on Milner's ML, HOL had been developed originally for hardware verification. Its commercialization was led by M. Fourman and R. Harris.

Perhaps it was the inherent difficulties in applying automated theorem proving that led Amir Pnueli to envision a more restricted but potentially simpler approach to verifying concurrent programs for properties expressed in Temporal Logic [Pnu77]. Although he too was focused on deductive reasoning, he noted (in passing) that Temporal Logic formulas could be checked algorithmically. In this incidental observation, commercial computer-aided verification could be said to have been conceived. Its birth would come three years later as model checking.

Analyzing a finite state coordinating system through an exploration of its composite state space was actually proposed by Rudin and West [RW82, Wes78] around 1980 too. However, it was model checking that formalized the process in terms of checking a model for a property defined in a temporal logic. This difference was very germane to practicality, as it led to decision procedures. Moreover, only with model checking could properties cast as assertions to be checked be reused as constraints to define the environment of an adjoining block. These two: formalization of assertions and algorithmic verification paved the path to the broad success of model checking. In fact, the gating issues for technology transfer were procedural, not technical. Model checking technology has continuously far out-stripped its pace of adoption.

1.1 First Projects

Although the theory spoke of *verification*, anyone who applied the theory soon realized that its real value lay in *falsification*. Go to a designer with the the claim "I verified that your design is correct" and you get a muffled yawn – of course her design is correct, she thinks, why wouldn't it be? (And who knows what "verified" means anyway.) But, show her a bug in a form she can readily comprehend (a simulation error trace) and she immediately recognizes the value: you found a bug that she did not know was there. From the first applications of model checking, it was clear that the real value of model checking was that it was an uncommonly good debugger – *reductio ad bug*. It is more effective to find a bug by trying to prove that there is none, than to go looking for it directly – the bug is always where you didn't think to look. As a debugger, the model checker is forgiven for any black magic that went into its application (like abstractions, restrictions, unsoundness) since it's only the bug that matters; no need to understand the means. "I don't need to understand what model checking is, because I know a bug when I see it (and 'verified' only means 'failed to find a bug')."

In 1983 I applied an early version of the COSPAN [HHK96] model checker to a model that I created by hand. The model was a very high level abstraction of an implementation developed in AT&T of the link-level protocol of the X.25 standard. Through this process I found 2 bugs that were manifest in their implementation (among about a dozen artifactual failures manifest by my abstraction, but not reflecting design errors). Although before this event my "verification" work was viewed with jaundiced suspicion at Bell Labs Research, my "practical contribution" lent me some (begrudged) breathing room. (Begrudged, because my work was hard to categorize among recognized fields of research that were supported at Bell Labs.) With this breathing room I found another similar application that was credited with saving AT&T a half-million dollars. This earned me the resources to re-write and develop COSPAN, which I then started with Zvi Har'el in 1985. During this process, I began to understand what I was doing (having been embarrassingly ignorant of the entire relevant literature). COSPAN was based on ω-automata, which I then learned were classical objects in computer science. In 1986 I proposed a development methodology based on automata-theoretic verification, in which design testing (*via* verification) could be started earlier in the development flow than previously possible and this I claimed would accelerate the design development process [KH90].

As I found others working in this area, especially Ed Clarke whom I met in 1985, I learned that my application experiences were common and shared by most who tried to apply algorithmic verification. In fact Ed and his students had made interesting and relevant advances that I could use, as had others. Ed was impressed that COSPAN (*circa* 1986) could explore as many as a million states (!), and did much to encourage me to continue my work.

In 1987-89 COSPAN was applied to an ambitious hardware development project: a packet layer controller chip (PLC). With an anticipated layout of 200,000 transistors, it was medium-sized at the time. The project was spec'd but rejected by Marketing based on its projected development cost – 30 staff years. The disgruntled project manager had read an early draft (internal TM) of [KH90] and invited me to try my method on his design, which we would run as a "black bag" job – off the record. I agreed to contribute 100% of my time and he would contribute his architect for the project. Together (in the end, he contributed 2 more people), we completed the project in 6 staff years, 2 calendar years. We had succeeded to verify over 200 properties (well, more or less), drawn from a list of what the test group would test for. The design was developed through a 4-level abstraction hierarchy, wherein each subsequent refinement was correct by construction. The bottom level was synthesized automatically, from C code generated by COSPAN. Although the performance of the design was only half as fast as expected – on account of some architectural decisions we had made to simplify verification – the design passed system integration test with flying colors. It was said to have the level of reliability of a second generic release. The low development cost (20% of what had been projected) and speed to market was said to out-weigh its somewhat poor performance.

The PLC project created a stir in AT&T MicroElectronics, as the TM that documented the project was circulated. By this time both myself and the project manager were vindicated and rewarded. It was 1989, and I was confident that the last six years of wandering had finally reached a conclusion and all that remained was to help shepherd this new and obviously valuable technology into general use. Little could I imagine that I had another 15 years of shepherding ahead of me.

1.2   The Catch 22 of Technology Transfer

Post-PLC, I was certain that my new technology would be in great demand. I worked out a *triage* plan to deal with the anticipated requests for my time, to avoid dilution of effort and remain effective. I would demand assistants, carefully select which projects I would handle.

But after a few days, my phone had registered nary a ring. Was my name misspelled in the TM? Where are all my anticipated fans? What's going on?

Swallowing my pride, I went back to the same development group that had the success with the PLC and asked about their next project. Were they planning to use the PLC methodology? (A rhetorical politeness for "why haven't you called me for the next project?") To my astonishment, the answer was "no" – no future anticipated application of the PLC methodology! Amazing! What's going on? "Well," they said, "the PLC was a great project, but we could never implement your methodology ourselves, you may be the only one in the world who can do this for all we know, and anyway we could never rely on 'Research software' for a 'real' (*i.e.*, non-black-bag) project – who would maintain the software? Next month you may be working on something else, and then who do we go to when your software breaks?". "No, go to our CAD group", they counseled, "convince them to support your software and then we will eagerly use it".

Ah, so reasonable! How could I have been so naive? Off to the CAD group. "Had they heard about the PLC project?" "Well, here's who to speak to." "What do you mean, 'no point'? This is a proven productivity enhancer! You must support it! Ask them."

The answer remained "No". They said "We cannot support a complex piece of software embedded in a revolutionary new methodology just because one development team asks us to – we would never make back our investment. Come back to us when you have *20* development teams asking us to support this. Then we will consider it."

"Hmm.. At 2 years per project, I could reach 20 successes in 40 years. Would the first project still be around to remember?" To be broadly used it must be supported; to be supported, it must already be broadly used. The inescapable vicious circle!

Utterly depressed, I accepted an invitation to give a course on this technology, first at UC Berkeley, then at the Technion in Israel. (My book [Kur94] came directly from my Berkeley course notes.) Attending my Technion course were four designers from Intel. They invited me down to Intel to give a mini-course there. It was 1990. From the mini-course came a challenge: verify this P5 cache protocol. It had been simulated for 13 months with billions of vectors, and had no known problems, but they were still worried about it. They drew some diagrams on the board, I translated them into a model, tried to verify the model, found a "bug" and they explained to me, based on the bug, what was wrong with my model. This process repeated for ten days, generating about two revisions per day. In fact, I wasn't allowed to use the Intel computers (nor was I authorized to download COSPAN there), so all my runs were at the Technion where a university licensed COSPAN was installed. The explanations for revisions came by email. By the afternoon of the tenth day, I still had not received an explanation of what was wrong with model version 19. I called – had they received my latest error track? "Come down to Intel" was the answer. When I arrived, I was greeting by a small reception committee of designers: they had been studying my last bug all morning and had just demonstrated that it was a real bug in their P5 design.

The next day the head of Intel-Israel, Dov Fromann came up from Jerusalem to meet me: "I don't know what this COSPAN is, but whatever it is, we want it!" Thus ensued a year-long haggling match between AT&T and Intel. Intel offered $.25M, AT&T demanded $2.5M. (AT&T had no idea of the value of COSPAN, but they figured 10x was a good negotiating position.) It turned ugly, Intel threatened that it would just take CMU software for free (SMV had just become available), while AT&T decided that Intel was wasting their time for too little money and the negotiations were broken off. However, back at AT&T, the head of AT&T MicroElectronics was alerted to the situation and called me in to ask "If this is so valuable to Intel, why isn't it of value to us?"

Well, I commended his excellent question (in fact, her question, as it was asked by a consultant who had been brought in to figure out why AT&T MicroElectronics was losing money – she saw the Intel contract drafts and called me in). Thus I got to relate the "Alice's Restaurant" saga with its Catch 22 to the head of AT&T MicroElectronics. He set up a meeting with the CAD head whom he proceeded to chastise in an unseemly fashion in front of me. (I could guess from this why MicroElectronics was losing money, and it had nothing to do with COSPAN.) From this day, COSPAN would be developed and officially supported by the MicroElectronics CAD group.

I knew that a shotgun wedding was not a union made in heaven, and indeed, for the first three years, very little happened. Arno Penzias, the head of Bell Labs Research (and a Nobel Laureate) asked me to keep quiet: he would make it work. And indeed, he used \$.5M of his discretionary funds to pay the MicroElectronics CAD group to seed their support for COSPAN. At the time I thought this was bizarre and outrageous – that we should pay MicroElectronics to allow us to help them – but in the end, this made it work. By 1993, MicroElectronics support for COSPAN was begun in earnest and it was released internally as the CAD tool FormalCheck. The first internal users were in the misbegotten AT&T acquisition NCR. But internal use was slack, and after a huge fight, it was decided to market FormalCheck externally. The basis of the fight was fear of "back-bite": "what if our competitors figure out how to use FormalCheck more effectively than we have (because we never like to change our methodology and never learned how to be really competitive)? It is better to kill it than expose it to our competitors!" The fight was resolved by the transfer of the CAD group from MicroElectronics to Advanced Technologies, from where they were free to market FormalCheck externally.

The decision to market FormalCheck was fortuitous, as in 1995 AT&T was broken up, Lucent Technologies was formed out of Bell Labs, NCR was regurgitated (to their great joy) and MicroElectronics was spun off as Agere. Thus, the FormalCheck internal user base evaporated and product development could be justified only by anticipated external users. By then the FormalCheck development team had grown to 30 and it had gotten far enough along that it was decided to complete its development for the external market – the only remaining potential user base. In 1998, FormalCheck was released into the EDA marketplace. In 9 months it generated a stunning \$4.5M, after which it was "sold" (actually, licensed exclusively) to Cadence Design Systems. FormalCheck continued to be supported by Cadence until 2005 when it was replaced by a new model checking tool – IFV – that integrated COSPAN with new SAT-based technology from Cadence Berkeley Labs.

What does this say about technology transfer? Was COSPAN a successful technology transfer? In 1990, my Executive Director Sandy Fraser suggested (facetiously?) that the "Intel Model" for technology transfer may be the best way: get an outside organization to ask for the technology, so that we know it is useful and then we will develop it. I always considered the experience as a demonstration that technology transfer of "disruptive" technologies was next to impossible. That the COSPAN transfer succeeded was a fluke.

With more hindsight, however, I see another view of this saga as a blundering into a process whereby a disruptive technology can be effectively transferred from research to commerce. A discussion of this forms the sequel.

2   Impediments to Change

In retrospect it is crystal clear what were the impediments to the COSPAN technology transfer: the required methodology change and the lack of interchangeability of tools.

Anything new is suspect – and for good reason. Just think of all the questionable ideas that are eagerly advanced by the research community. Industry has neither the bandwidth nor expertise to evaluate them (and engineers eventually tire of hearing about yet another great idea that will save the day).

Acceptability of a new technology is inversely proportional to the required change in the user interface. A faster compiler that plugs in transparently is an immediate win, because the users see no change (beyond improved performance). Model checking intrudes into the entire development flow. It requires developers to become part of the verification process (by specifying properties). It requires the test team to learn a completely new tool with new concepts and new considerations. The concept of model checking is not transparent to someone who understands testing in terms of executing the design through scenarios. Even today it is sometimes a challenge to wean testers from their tendency to write properties that look like scenarios instead of global properties. *E.g.*, instead of writing a property that enumerates the various steps of packet-handling under a variety of contingencies – that will invariably be incomplete on account of the combinatorial explosion of possibilities – instead write the simple high-level property "Every packet is received within two clock cycles after it is sent".

Properties that are successfully model-checked need not be simulated. Since model checking can be started before a simulation test bench is available, the flow should be changed to accommodate the introduction of model checking before simulation test would normally start. (Doing so is one of the big productivity enhancers afforded by model checking – finding bugs earlier in the design flow can greatly decrease the cost of development, of which 50%–80% is allocated to test.)

Capacity (the size model that can be checked) has always been (and still is) an issue. The smaller the capacity, the more partitioning is required for verification. Partitioning at RTL block boundaries is natural (given that partitioning is necessary). If capacity is below the size of a typical RTL block, then the block itself must be partitioned. Typically, partitioning a single block would be considered too much effort and too fraught with the risk of introducing errors to be seriously supported in a real development flow. Therefore, block-level capacity is an essential ingredient for technology transfer. The advent of BDD-based algorithms to support symbolic model checking [McM93] elevated model checking capacity above block level, thus eliminating capacity as a show-stopper in many cases. Since then capacity has steadily improved, especially with the introduction of SAT-based symbolic model checking [CBRZ01, McM03], which has afforded as much as two orders of magnitude increase in capacity over BDDs. Nonetheless, while necessary, thus improving capacity was not sufficient for technology transfer.

Considerations driven by capacity limitations require the user to understand abstraction, partitioning, compositional verification and restriction. Even when these are automated in the tool, the boundaries of the automation can be reached and then must be addressed. Since performance is critical, the user often must become familiar with a variety of "engines" like BDD-based algorithms and SAT-based algorithms, or complete algorithms for verification *vs* incomplete falsification engines such as bounded model checking [CBRZ01]. These have different sweet-spots that may be hard to identify automatically.

A design factory cannot risk a major disruptive process change that could destroy a thin margin of profitability, even as the change promises to improve profitability. Therefore, a major methodology change is almost always a killer for technology transfer.

Of course, no industry would consider turning a major development process upside-down over night. A potentially valuable change is carefully evaluated, first in a dark corner by a summer intern, then if that shows promise, by the CAD group in their spare time on an old design. Only after a succession of promising evaluations might the new process be evaluated tentatively (in parallel with the old process) on a real design. Only when all these evaluation hurdles are passed might the new technology begin to be fully integrated into the design flow.

To facilitate this evaluation process, a variety of products are compared head-to-head. Competition among vendors breeds confidence. Several vendors advancing similar products lends verisimilitude to the field, whereas a unique product without competition is suspect.

If each product requires substantial unique infrastructure – like properties specified in an manner that is compatible with that product alone – then it may be too costly to perform such an evaluation at all. This was a severely limiting factor when each model checking product had its own proprietary specification language.

In summary, it takes much time and thus cost to generate confidence in a new disruptive technology. In view of the high cost of change, it requires a compelling need.

2.1   Pain and Gain

For the industry the tradeoff is simple: the pain of doing nothing in the face of deteriorating test coverage *vs* the gain and associated cost of improving reliability via model checking.

Here's a "theorem":

Theorem 1. *Commercial Electronic Design Automation will inevitably be based on Formal Methods.*

Proof

Functional complexity grows exponentially with IC size. Therefore, adequate simulation test analysis will soon (if not already) become intractable. The only known way to deal with intractability is divide-and-conquer. That is, analyze components then "stitch" together component solutions into a virtual global solution. This cannot be done without mathematical precision, *i.e.*, Formal Methods.

Around 1990, major IC designers like Intel and IBM began to understand that the increasing functional complexity of designs was rendering them untestable. Without a dramatic change, decreasing reliability would become the gating factor in design complexity. The new circuits could be built, but they would malfunction. There is nothing like a half-billion dollar bug [Coe95] to drive this message home.

Today, there is a rapidly growing sector of the IC design community that has come to the realization that maintaining testing-as-usual would drive them out of business on account of the rapidly degraded quality that accompanies increasing functional complexity. They are driven to seek almost any promising remedy – even one so disruptive as model checking – in view of the fatal alternative. This is what the academic community had been predicting for decades; over the last decade, it finally has become a reality.

3   False Starts

In 1993, FormalCheck was at the "cutting edge" – meaning, it was ahead of its time. Only a very few companies had started to feel enough pain to seriously consider formal verification. A few more were looking to the future, but would not yet be serious customers. These included TI, Motorola, Cray/SGI and a few others. Today that has all changed, but back then it was hard to get a good sense of direction from prospective customers.

One of the first – classical – mistakes made in the architecture of FormalCheck concerned the issue of power *vs* automation. Coming from a research background, it was all too tempting to convince oneself that all the current knowledge and power of model checking must be supported and used. How else could one expect to verify global properties? FormalCheck came with 150 pages of painstakingly drawn documentation, plus a two-day lab course. It was more than many could handle. Only a decade later did we understand that "less is more": at Cadence, the new goal was to do the most that is possible fully automatically, not more than that. (Today, 13 years later, customers are starting to request more power through user control, but this is now the second generation of users that has gained considerable sophistication in the interim.) In 1993, it seemed inconceivable to manage with less than what was needed for hierarchical and compositional verification, as all the important design properties needed that. Ten years later we learned that users were more than content to check "unimportant" local properties, as long as it could be done fully automatically, without "education". That is, take a small step before taking a larger step.

A beautiful case in point here was equivalence checking. Equivalence checking grew quitely in the 90s before it burst forth as a very successful product that is used extensively and broadly in the design development flow. The ideas of equivalence checking had been simmering quietly since around 1980. Then the problem was capacity, but the main ideas – mapping states to convert sequential equivalence checking into combinational equivalence checking and then further mapping nets via names and topology – were already established. With the advent of BDDs, the capacity issue ameliorated and products emerged. The research community took little note, as the great challenges were in model checking. But suddenly, by the turn of the century, equivalence checking was fully established as a main-stream product. A small step. But one of great significance and value.

Perhaps the grand-daddy of classical mistakes was around *verification vs falsification*. We wanted things that worked. Broken things were shameful and hidden. No one was proud of finding a bug. The only means that was (potentially) powerful enough to prove that a program was correct was automated theorem proving. Hence the enormous early investment in automated theorem proving. However, somewhere along the line bugs became beautiful. Remember the designer: she doesn't even *believe* "verified", but knows a bug when she sees one. This is when model checking began to leave theorem proving in the dust: go for the bugs. Model checking is an uncommonly useful debugging tool. Dijkstra's dream of verified software would have to wait.

Since the name of the game became *falsification*, completeness was less of an issue. This opened the door for under-approximations such as restrictions on inputs (for example, setting some data paths to near-constants) and restriction of the depth of search as with bounded model checking. Less is more.

Even soundness became expendable to some extent. This sounds horrific, but even in the early days, soundness was discarded when error tracks from abstractions were admitted. The user would need to try to simulate the error track. As long as there were not too many false fails, the user was content. At no time would a false *pass* be considered acceptable, and yet almost no product is without bugs, so there may well be some false passes out there – if only as an artifact of faulty book-keeping. But this is the real world: you do your best, but keep moving. A Herculean effort to verify the correctness of a model checker would not be a welcome diversion of resources. Early focus on proving the soundness of the model checker was misplaced. More important than soundness is coverage: instead of worrying about correctness, worry about writing more properties to check more of the design. That's the value assessment. After all, simulation test has known semantic faults, and these are tolerated. Only academics worry about them.

As a last "false start" I'll mention interoperability. In the early days, model checking was an alternative to simulation test. The two at best were disdaining neighbors: model checking could not put simulation out of business, although the secret wish was there. Simulation was the work-horse of the test community; model checking by comparison seemed a toy. As a result, the two efforts evolved in different groups. The company 0-In (recently acquired by Mentor Graphics) may have been the first to establish peace between the two in the form of an alliance aptly called *hybrid* verification (not to be confused with "hybrid systems"). The idea was to use a simulator to quickly drive the design to "deep" states unreachable with a model checker. From those deep states, model checking (perhaps on an abstraction) could be started. Synopsys has perfected the idea with their tool Magellan^{TM}, and today others are finding other useful ways to combine simulation test and model checking. A big virtue of this hybrid is that it moves model checking into more familiar territory for the vast majority of the testing community who practice simulation test. Through this connection lies the best chance to put a model checker on the desk of everyone who today runs a simulator. The idea of hybrid was overlooked (or passed by) because it seemed to those working in model checking like a meager contribution. In retrospect, it was a important early opportunity that was overlooked. A small but valuable step.

4   A Framework for Technology Transfer

So what then was the grand technology transfer lesson learned here? What in 1995 seemed like a blundering into a fluke technology transfer, in retrospect points to a process whereby a disruptive technology can be effectively transferred from research to commerce.

The key method inferred here is a process based upon *small steps*. Each step entails only a small change for the user, thus avoiding excessive disruption. Each step produces *some* positive benefit, thus demonstrating efficacy and justifying the next (small) step.

One starts with a *roadmap* with two points: where we are now, and where we want to reach, technologically. Then one fills in the middle with a succession of small steps, each of which will show some positive benefit and is small enough to avoid excessive disruption.

This is not a brilliant strategy, but only a simple observation of how things are. Disruptive technologies get adopted incrementally. The increments are sustained by successive benefits – even small benefits are good enough to show "promise" and keep the process going.

As simple and natural an observation as this is, it provides a cautionary note to the over-eager: dig in for the long slog; get a hobby that will compensate for the frustration; be prepared for many false starts and keep adjusting the roadmap.

The real art here is filling in the roadmap – solving the "getting from here to there" problem. That takes great vision or many course changes.

5   Formal Functional Verification in Commercial Use Today

Automated theorem proving is used today in a few niche applications, primarily for data-path verification of numerical algorithms such as multipliers. AMD is one of the primary companies that has found a way to use this effectively in their development flow. Today it is not supported commercially by the Electronic Design Automation (EDA) industry (although a decade ago it briefly was, in the UK). The reasons for this have already been discussed.

Equivalence checking is broadly used and of all formal methods is the one that has most pervasively penetrated the IC industry development flow. It is a central product in EDA. Presently, the focus is on combinational equivalence checking – checking the equivalence of stateless boolean functions. However, there is presently an important push towards sequential equivalence checking: checking the equivalence of full circuit designs with latches (states) that cannot readily be mapped from one design to the hopefully equivalent one. In the limit, sequential equivalence checking reduces to model checking. While organizationally, equivalence checking and model checking have developed separately in the EDA industry, the advent of sequential equivalence checking will inevitably bring them together.

While not yet commercially supported by the EDA industry, model checking high-level (abstract) models of complex protocols such as cache protocols is routine in the processor design industry. This application of model checking is less main-stream than checking local properties of RTL blocks, so the EDA industry has not gotten here yet, in spite of its importance and perfect fit with model checking technology. Meanwhile, the tool of preference for those who design cache protocols is MurPhi [DDHY92] designed by David Dill and his students. While David has moved on to other interests, MurPhi is actively maintained by Ganesh Gopalakrishnan at the University of Utah, thus providing an important service to this segment of the industry.

The application of formal methods to software design and development has proved much harder than for hardware[1]. There are numerous reasons for this. First is the relative lack of semantics for C code. Hardware specification languages were no better, but had a semantics forced on them by the need to automatically synthesize a program into a circuit. It is precisely this imputed semantics that provides the hooks for model checking. Formal analysis of software entails assigning a semantics that in some cases may be arbitrary and fail to match the semantics imputed in other contexts.

Moreover, the performance of synthesis for hardware is intimately tied to an efficient assignment of sequential elements (states) to the design. Optimizing which program variables are "state" variables has been the object of enormous effort in the EDA industry for the purpose of efficient synthesis. Model checking capitalizes on this effort by using the synthesis assignment.

Since software has no such concern for synthesis, model checking for software must incorporate a step wherein sequentiality is imputed to the program: which actions happen simultaneously, which occur sequentially. Again, doing this efficiently is very important for the performance of the model checking, but in the case of software, there are no years of effort in this direction to stand upon. The general solution for software has been to assume that actions are sequential, and that actions in different "processes" interleave. This is satisfactory for small software models, but does not come close to passing the component capacity threshold discussed earlier. Interleaving also tends to be more efficiently implemented by explicit state analysis, further limiting capacity.

There are still other impediments to software verification. Since C is the language of choice for designs, pointers, memory handling and the general infinite state of the system all must be handled. While there has been some impressive progress in this area [CKL04], it has some distance to go before it can be picked up for commercial use.

Nonetheless, there has been one important achievement in commercial software verification: at Microsoft, SLAM [BR02] has penetrated main-stream driver development. It uses a software model based on a driver program's control flow graph to overcome all the problems cited above. Its verification is based on a push-down automaton associated with the control flow graph. While SLAM has been fanned out into the design development process in Microsoft and is an important example of model checking technology transfer, its very particular

---

[1] In our context, "hardware" means HDL, *e.g.*, verilog code, whereas "software" means primarily C or C++ code. Of course, pedantically speaking they are both "software", whereas "hardware" is something attached with a soldering iron.

application must be understood as brushing the boundary of what is currently possible for model checking software in an industrial setting.

Europe has recently taken a more "progressive" attitude toward technology than the US or the Far East. (I attribute this to the pervasive availability of government and now EU funding for new technology, allowing many ideas to flourish without passing the acid test of the free market, as required elsewhere. This atmosphere is reminiscent of the lavish post-Sputnik funding in the US, fueled by freely flowing government grants in the sciences, defining a period that coincided with the "golden age" of research in the US, but also with a level of "dead-end" research that would no longer be tolerated). Be that as it may, there are a number of commercial formal verification successes in the EU, for example, Esterel Technologies whose web site has many pointers to its industrial applications. Although model checking was not a key to its success, the ability to analyze formal models may have been. The background technology was developed over more than a decade by Girard Berry [BG92]. Esterel Technologies has applied formal analysis to high-level models of critical applications, prominently aerospace and automotive, thereby circumventing the obstacles of C code verification.

Likewise, iLogix has seen commercial success with its implementations of StateCharts. Driven by David Harel and Amir Pnueli, the basic ideas have evolved in the literature over decades. Again, the object is analysis of high-level models. iLogix has had successful use in the telephony industry. Again, while based on a formal semantics that is important for the analysis they do, formal verification may have been peripheral to the company's success.

Finally we come to hardware model checking. This – at long last – is now a success story of technology transfer of computer-aided verification. As recently as five years ago, the jury was still out on whether the then nascent commercial hardware model checking would gain traction in the EDA industry. The barriers to technology transfer were primarily procedural, as already explained, and the technology has far outstripped its supported level in EDA. Today, commercially supported EDA model checking is only for local (RTL block-level) properties. These include properties such as arbitration, resource allocation (request/grant properties), flow control (underflow/overflow), local message delivery, local serialization as well as an endless list of hardware particulars (often of questionable value, having been derived from a simulation mind-set rather than the mind-set of correct design functional behavior).

The final great enabler to commercial hardware model checking was the introduction in 2003 of the Accellera Standard for property specification. The impetus was support for "Assertion-Based Verification" (ABV), meaning a more standard means for writing monitors for simulation. Simulation monitors evolved into "assertions" under the influence of model checking, but the driving motive was to simplify the creation of simulation test benches. The salutary effect on model checking was serendipitous. (Thus, two great enablers of model checking technology transfer were provided by established technologies: capitalizing on synthesis for state-efficient models, and capitalizing on ABV for standardized property specification. The importance of these for technology transfer – and the good luck of the synergies for model checking – are often overlooked. Software model checking will need both of these: efficient state models and a standardized property specification language before it can become a broadly supported commercial technology, it would seem.)

Originally chartered to establish a single property specification language, commercial politics drove the Accellera Committee to settle on three. (Remember the joke, "A camel is a horse designed by a committee"?) The first, OVL, is a very simple template language with severely limited expressiveness whose advantage is its nominal learning curve. The other two, PSL and SVA, are sufficiently (or even overly) expressive, and suffer from numerous "camelisms".

But all is forgiven, even the drudgery of having to support three (instead of one) property specification language. All is forgiven because it was only with a standard property specification language that the EDA industry could finally create products that could be effectively run interchangeably. Relieved from the requirement to create a tool-specific infrastructure for defining properties, all available tools could be run on the same design.

In particular, CAD groups could build their flow for model checking without being tied to a specific product. This liberation was a prime enabler for the acceptance of model checking in mainstream design flows. The interoperability afforded by the standards bred competition among the vendors, predictably increasing the quality of the the model checking products. It also liberated start-ups from the need to create a property specification infrastructure, allowing them to focus on the core technology. This in turn bred more competition.

Competition breeds confidence: confidence for the consumer that they can switch to the best available product without disturbing their flow; confidence for the vendor that this is a real product, not a "hair-brained" idea. No mainstream EDA vendor has the guts to to supply a product that no other vendor is supplying. One of the best arguments to vendor management to invest in a product is to point to the competition and show that if we don't invest in this product, the competition will pull ahead. With few exceptions (FormalCheck was one), completely new products enter the marketplace though start-ups, not the main-stream vendors.

Today there is an impressive array of EDA vendors competing in the model checking arena, including the big three: Cadence, Synopsys and Mentor Graphics, as well as a heady swell of start-ups with impressive model checking products, including Jasper, Calypto, Prover, Averant, RealIntent, @HDL, and others. Although not really an EDA vendor, IBM has nonetheless made impressive headway marketing their RuleBase model checker as well.

6   Algorithms

Until the advent of symbolic model checking based on BDDs [McM93] model checking was based on explicit state enumeration. This allowed searching a few million states typically, a bit more today with bigger and faster computers, but not enough to provide the capacity required to break through the RTL block threshold discussed above. With BDDs, blocks with 10^{50} states or more could be checked. This corresponds to 100–200 state bits, in contrast to around 20 state bits for explicit search.

However, BDDs have their own problems, mainly their chaotic thus unpredictable performance. In the late 90s Ed Clarke suggested using SAT as an alternative for model checking [BCC$^+$99, CBRZ01]. (Some, including this writer, voiced skepticism regarding the value of this approach, and in time were proved wrong. Ed deserves great credit for his insight.)

Today, model checking can be based on explicit state enumeration or symbolic state enumeration based on BDDs or SAT, as well as ATPG. McMillan's interpolation method [McM03] was the first complete SAT-based model checking algorithm and in our benchmark tests in Cadence, this generally out-performs all the others.

Unfortunately, there are a sufficient number of cases when each of the other algorithms does best that it is not feasible to rely only on interpolation. Therefore, all the above are supported. The best result comes from running several algorithms in parallel and killing the others as soon as the first finishes. Experience has shown a super-linear speed-up using this method when checking many properties, over running only the over-all single best algorithm.

Superimposed on top of the basic model checking algorithms are a variety of proof strategies. Many of these are based on abstraction, the most important lever for lifting large state spaces. One is localization wherein portions of the design that are irrelevant to checking a given property are eliminated through abstraction. In its original formulation [Kur94, Kur00] the algorithm iterates over abstractions determined by successive counterexamples on the abstractions. Ed Clarke *et al* refined this algorithm with a SAT-based decision procedure [CGJ$^+$00]. In a significant SAT-based improvement [MA03], the successive abstractions are determined not by the counterexamples but by the SAT clauses used to refute the property on the original model at the depth of the last counterexample. This "Abstraction-Refinement" loop has led to many further improvements of this basic idea, driven by the strength of the SAT solver in finding efficient refutations. Recently, Ranjit Jhala and Ken McMillan have extended the method using interpolation [JM05]. Through the successive improvements, the SAT solver is brought into play more and and more as a deductive reasoning engine. Will quantifiers be supported next? One may speculate if automated theorem proving will re-emerge through this thrust as truly automated deduction inspired by DPLL-style deductive procedures.

Other proof strategies in commercial play today include predicate abstraction, induction, symmetry reduction and (automatic) assume-guarantee reasoning. Assume-guarantee reasoning can be flat or can follow the design hierarchy.

The same core algorithms used for model checking are used for synthesis optimizations and automatic test bench synthesis for simulation. For the latter, BDDs or SAT are used for constraint-solving. Alternatively, properties viewed as constraints are converted to generators that generate only legal inputs. All of these are in main-stream product use today.

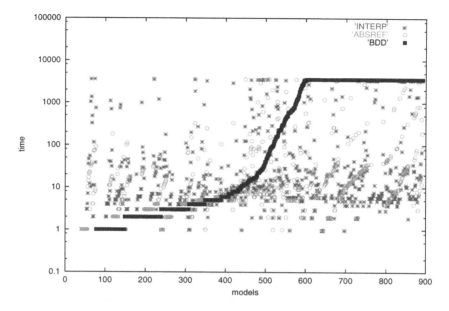

Fig. 1. BDD vs SAT (Interpolation, Abstraction-Refinement)

For falsification, various restrictions are used. The depth of search can be restricted with bounded model checking. The input space can be restricted as well, especially by restricting the range of data-path inputs.

In order to tune the choice of algorithms, extensive data bases of "typical" customer models are required. At Cadence, we tune and select algorithms using a data base of 1000 such models (*cf.* Figure 1). Relying on the results of such performance testing, heuristics and new algorithms are developed. Figure 1 shows the relative performance on 900 models of three algorithms: BDD-based symbolic model checking, interpolation-based symbolic model checking (using SAT) and abstraction-refinement (using SAT and BDDs). Each point gives the time for the model indexed on the X-axis using the designated algorithm. The models are ordered in increasing BDD time. The data suggest that when BDD is fast, it wins, but as it slows, the others are better, and of the other two, neither dominates.

7   Future

The easiest prediction for the future of commercial computer-aided verification is that today's technology will catch up with that future. This means that model checking will arrive to general software development – after the synthesis problem is solved for efficiency, and a standardized property language is adopted (perhaps they will simply adopt one of the hardware camels – why not).

For hardware (first) we are headed strongly to the support of hierarchical verification for top-down/bottom-up design. Languages such as SystemC and System Verilog are first attempts in this direction, but they do not address how to relate successive levels of abstraction. We need to be able to write a high-level design, verify it and then refine it to a low-level implementation target in a manner that guarantees that each successive refinement is consistent with its abstraction. In this way, properties verified at one level of abstraction are guaranteed to hold at all successive levels of refinement. This is a divide-and-conquer method that (potentially) supports the verification of global properties (beyond the reach of today's commercial model checkers). Global properties are verified once and for all in high-level abstractions, and then are guaranteed to hold in all refinements. A promising way to construct refinements is in a manner that guarantees that its is correct by construction. This saves the overhead of additional verification, but places restrictions on the structure of refinements. However, refinements must be guided by the low-level architecture in any case, so this restriction may be acceptable. In effect it leads to a dual top-down/bottom-up design methodology. With hierarchical verification the emphasis shifts from falsification to verification, as the correctness of the implementation depends upon verifying the correctness of the high-level abstractions.

The next easy prediction – because it is already happening – is integration of model checking with simulation for "hybrid" algorithms (*cf.* above) and integration of model checking with sequential equivalence checking. The latter is natural because in the worst case (when states and nets cannot be mapped) sequential equivalence checking *is* model checking. Sequential equivalence checking may also be used to check the correctness of refinements, if they are not already correct by construction.

With hierarchical verification comes the integration of model checking with design: since a high-level model will be verified before refinements are even designed, model checking becomes a design tool in which the correctness of architectures and algorithms are checked. In the course of checking algorithms, theorem proving may be brought into play, and in the future, a theorem prover may be an accessory to every model checker. While this requires expertise, by this time a new generation of designers hopefully will be ready for the challenge. Note that as an accessory, theorem proving can add its power without delaying the design process.

Theorem proving may re-emerge as a fully automatic DPLL-style deductive engine. There already is a trend in this direction (see above).

Finally, there will undoubtedly be ever greater use of pre-verified components ("IP"). This "reuse", a very important productivity enhancer, can fit in with hierarchical verification and top-down design. Moreover, when designs are outsourced, a more reliable contract than one that describes the design through discourse is one that specifies the design formally, requiring contractually that the completed design will pass a list of formally verified properties.

8   Conclusion

Computer-aided verification technology has finally – after 25 years – been transferred to the EDA industry in the form of equivalence checking and model checking. Equivalence checking was a fairly easy transfer because it was not impeded by the two great impediments to the transfer of model checking. These were: a required methodology change for model checking and required infrastructure for defining properties to be checked. The required methodology change was accomplished through a process of small steps, each of which demonstrated positive value. This is why it took so long (and it still continues). The required infrastructure for defining properties was established through standardization of property specification languages. The gating issues for these technologies remains speed and capacity. Speed is continuously improving as technology advances. Capacity is improving as well, but is limited by the intrinsic infeasibility of the technologies. To circumvent the capacity limitation, the only known general strategy is abstraction-based divide-and-conquer. This is where the cutting edge research is focused.

References

[BCC+99]   Biere, A., Cimatti, A., Clarke, E.M., Fujita, M., Zhu, Y.: Symbolic model checking using SAT procedures instead of BDDs. In: Proc. 36th Design Automation Conference, pp. 317–320. IEEE Computer Society Press, Los Alamitos (1999)

[BG92]   Berry, G., Gonthier, G.: The Esterel Synchronous Programming Language: Design, Semantics, Implementation. Science of Computer Programming, vol. 19, pp. 87–152 (1992)

[BL84]   Bledsoe, W.W., Loveland, D.W. (eds.): Automated Theorem Proving: After 25 Years, Contemporary Math. 29, pp. 119–132. Amer. Math. Soc. (1984); Especially the paper Proof-Checking, Theorem-Proving and Program Verification by R. S. Boyer and J. S. Moore

[BR02]   Ball, T., Rajamani, S.K.: The SLAM Project: Debugging System Software via Static Analysis. In: Symposium on Principles of Programming Languages (POPL), pp. 1–3. ACM (January 2002)

[Büc62]   Büchi, J.R.: On a Decision Method in Restricted Second-Order Arithmetic. In: Methodology and Philosophy of Science, Proc., 1960 Stanford Intern. Congr., pp. 1–11. Stanford Univ. Press, Stanford (1962)

[CBRZ01]   Clarke, E.M., Biere, A., Raimi, R., Zhu, Y.: Bounded model checking using satisfiability solving. In: Formal Methods in System Design, vol. 19, Kluwer Academic Publishers (July 2001)

[CE82]   Clarke, E.M., Emerson, E.A.: Design and Synthesis of Synchronization Skeletons for Branching Time Temporal Logic. In: Logic of Programs 1981. LNCS, vol. 131, pp. 52–71 (1982)

[CGJ+00]   Clarke, E.M., Grumberg, O., Jha, S., Lu, Y., Veith, H.: Counterexample-guided abstraction refinement. In: Computer Aided Verification, pp. 154–169 (2000)

[CKL04]   Clarke, E., Kroening, D., Lerda, F.: A Tool for Checking ANSI-C Programs. In: Jensen, K., Podelski, A. (eds.) TACAS 2004. LNCS, vol. 2988, pp. 168–176. Springer, Heidelberg (2004)

[Coe95]   Coe, T.: Inside the Pentium FDIV Bug. Dr. Dobbs Journal 20, 129–135 (1995)

[DDHY92] Dill, D.L., Drexler, A.J., Hu, A.J., Yang, C.H.: Protocol Verification as a Hardware Design Aid. In: IEEE International Conference on Computer Design: VLSI in Computers and Processors, pp. 522–525. IEEE Computer Society (1992)

[GMW79]   Gordon, M., Milner, R., Wadsworth, C.P.: Edinburgh LCF: A Mechanised Logic of Computation. LNCS, vol. 78 (1979)

[HHK96]   Hardin, R.H., Har'El, Z., Kurshan, R.P.: COSPAN. In: Alur, R., Henzinger, T.A. (eds.) CAV 1996. LNCS, vol. 1102, pp. 423–427. Springer, Heidelberg (1996)

[JM05]   Jhala, R., McMillan, K.L.: Interpolant-based transition relation approximation. In: Etessami, K., Rajamani, S.K. (eds.) CAV 2005. LNCS, vol. 3576, pp. 39–51. Springer, Heidelberg (2005)

[KH90]   Kurshan, R.P., Har'El, Z.: Software for analytical development of communication protocols. AT&T Tech. J. 69(1), 45–59 (1990)

[Kur94]   Kurshan, R.P.: Computer-Aided Verification of Coordinating Processes: The Automata-Theoretic Approach. Princeton University Press (1994)

[Kur00]   Kurshan, R.P.: Program Verification. Notices of the AMS 47(5), 534–545 (2000)

[MA03]   McMillan, K.L., Amla, N.: Automatic Abstraction without Counterexamples. In: Garavel, H., Hatcliff, J. (eds.) ETAPS 2003 and TACAS 2003. LNCS, vol. 2619, pp. 2–17. Springer, Heidelberg (2003)

[McM93]   McMillan, K.L.: Symbolic Model Checking. Kluwer Academic Publishers (1993)

[McM03]   Kenneth, L., McMillan, K.L.: Interpolation and sat-based model checking. In: Hunt Jr., W.A., Somenzi, F. (eds.) CAV 2003. LNCS, vol. 2725, pp. 1–13. Springer, Heidelberg (2003)

[Pnu77]   Pnueli, A.: The Temporal Logic of Programs. In: Proc. of the Eighteenth Symposium on Foundations of Computer Science (FOCS), Providence, RI, pp. 46–57 (1977)

[QS82]   Queille, J.P., Sifakis, J.: Programming 1982. LNCS, vol. 137, pp. 337–351 (1982)

[Rob65]   Robinson, J.A.: Machine-Oriented Logic Based on the Resolution Principle. Journal of the Association for Computing Machinery 12, 23–41 (1965)

[RS59]   Rabin, M.O., Scott, D.: Finite Automata and Their Decisions Problems. IBM J. Res. and Dev. 3, 114–125 (1959)

[RW82]   Rudin, H., West, C.: A validation technique for tightly coupled protocols. Transactions on Computers (April 1982)

[Tur36]   Turing, A.: On Computable Numbers, With an Application to the Entscheidungsproblem. In: Proceedings of the London Mathematical Society, vol. 42 (1936)

[VW86]   Vardi, M.Y., Wolper, P.: An Automata-Theoretic Approach to Automatic Program Verification. In: Proc (1st) IEEE Symposium on Logic in Computer Science (LICS), Boston, pp. 322–331 (1986)

[Wes78]   West, C.H.: Generalized technique for communication protocol validation. IBM Journal of Res. and Devel. 22, 393–404 (1978)

[WR13]   Alfred North Whitehead and Bertrand Russell. Principia Mathematica, pp. 1910–1913. Cambridge University Press (1913)

New Challenges in Model Checking

Gerard J. Holzmann, Rajeev Joshi, and Alex Groce

NASA/JPL Laboratory for Reliable Software, Pasadena, CA 91109, USA
{Gerard.Holzmann,Rajeev.Joshi,Alex.Groce}@jpl.nasa.gov

Abstract. In the last 25 years, the notion of performing software verification with logic model checking techniques has evolved from intellectual curiosity to accepted technology with significant potential for broad practical application. In this paper we look back at the main steps in this evolution and illustrate how the challenges have changed over the years, as we sharpened our theories and tools. Next we discuss a typical challenge in software verification that we face today – and that perhaps we can look back on in another 25 years as having inspired the next logical step towards a broader integration of model checking into the software development process.

Keywords: Logic model checking, software verification, software reliability, software structure, grand challenge project, flash file system challenge.

1 Introduction

The idea to build a practically useful tool to check the correctness of program code quite possibly already occurred to the first people who attempted to write code. Not by coincidence, many of those people were mathematicians. Goldstein and Von Neumann took a first step in 1947 when they introduced the notion of an assertion in program design [7] (see also [5]):

> For this reason we will denote each area in which the validity of such limitations is being asserted, by a special box, which we call an 'assertion box.'

A series of foundational papers on program analysis and program verification techniques appeared in the sixties and seventies, including seminal work by Robert Floyd, Tony Hoare, and Edsger Dijkstra, that we will not attempt to summarize here. More closely related to the topic of this paper and the theme of this symposium is work that started in the late seventies on model based verification techniques. Among the earliest models used for this purpose were Petri nets and finite automata, initially paired with manual analysis procedures (e.g., [3]). Carl Sunshine described a basic reachability analysis method for automata models in 1975 [20], a variant of which was applied in a verification tool built by West and Zafiropulo at IBM [24]. The latter tool attracted attention by uncovering relatively simple defects in trusted international standards for data communication. A favored example of an automaton model from this period was also the simple alternating bit protocol [2]. It is in retrospect

O. Grumberg and H. Veith (Eds.): 25MC Festschrift, LNCS 5000, pp. 65–76, 2008.
© Springer-Verlag Berlin Heidelberg 2008

remarkable that some of the early verification tools could not yet handle the complexity of this very basic protocol.

Work on what later became the SPIN model checker started in 1980 at Bell Laboratories. This first tool, named *pan*, was also based on an optimized reachability analysis procedure, though initially supported by an algebraic specification formalism [8]. Like the IBM tool, this tool attracted attention within AT&T by successfully uncovering defects in models of trusted telephony software. Pan was restricted to the verification of safety properties, and was therefore not a true *logic* model checking system as intended in [4]. The restriction to safety properties did however allow us to verify models with up to millions of reachable states, although the latter could take a good week of computation on the fastest available hardware at that time. We did not contemplate an extension of the verification system to properties specified in linear temporal logic, and more broadly the set of omega-regular properties, until the late eighties, when available compute power had increased, and our verification techniques had sharpened.

Looking back, we can recognize some patterns in what we considered to be the main obstacles to a broader application of model checking techniques to problems in *software* verification. As obstacles were overcome, new challenges were identified and targeted. The following list sketches some of the deciding issues that influenced the evolution of the SPIN model checker.

1. *Specification formalisms*: The initial challenge, in a period that we can indicate very approximately as 1975-1985, was to find a usable formalism for constructing **models** with verifiable properties. The focus in this period was on the identification of specification formalisms that could facilitate analysis. Ultimately, automata-based models were found to provide the most solid foundation, and much work has since been focused on them. *Trace*, the successor to *pan* and the next step in the evolution of SPIN, dropped *pan*'s process algebra specification formalism in favor of automata models in 1983, leading the way for SPIN to easily conform to the automata-theoretic foundation from [22].

2. *Efficient Algorithms*: The next challenge, between approximately 1985 and 1995, was on developing new data structures and **algorithms** that could improve the range and efficiency of model checking systems. This development produced BDD-based and symbolic verification methods, as well as the partial order reduction methods that are at the core of model checking systems today. Partial order reduction was integrated into SPIN in the early nineties [9].

3. *Model Extraction from Code*: The third challenge, between 1995 and 2005, was to find ways to apply model checking techniques more directly to implementation level code, using software abstraction and **model extraction** techniques. This work led to the extension of the SPIN model checker with support for embedded software in abstract models. This change enabled the application of SPIN to the verification of unmodified, implementation level software for call processing in a commercial voice and data switch, and as such perhaps the first application of formal software verification at this scale

[10]. Similarly, this third challenge led to the successes at Microsoft in the formal verification of device driver code [19], and the work at Stanford on the CMC model checker [17].

4. *Today's Challenge*: This brings us to the next, and current, challenge for work that may well turn out to define the primary emphasis for our work in logic model checking for the period 2005 to 2015. This fourth challenge is to find effective ways to **structure software** such that formal verification techniques, and especially logic model checking techniques, become simpler to use and more effective in identifying potential violations of correctness properties in executable code.

We will devote the remainder of this paper to a description of this new challenge.

2 The New Challenge

The "Grand Challenge in Verification" recently posed by Sir Tony Hoare [23], prompted us to propose a mini-version, which is to design and implement a verifiable file system for non-volatile memory [14]. This mini-challenge was of course not chosen arbitrarily. Space exploration missions need a reliable capability to record data that is either received from earth (e.g., commands and parameters), or to be returned to earth (e.g., telemetry and images). Often a spacecraft is temporarily pointed away from earth to capture an image or take a measurement. The data can only be returned later, sometimes much later, when communication with the Deep Space Network on earth is restored.

The MER Rovers that currently explore the surface of Mars, for instance, use flash memory cards to store critical data. The reliability of hardware components can often be increased by adding nominally redundant backups. The flash memory cards used on spacecraft are special radiation-hardened designs that can be duplicated for redundancy if needed. For software, though, increasing reliability is not nearly as simple to achieve, and a number of mission anomalies related to data storage on flash memory cards can be traced back to software flaws. Curiously, the software used for the management of flash memory cards in missions to date has consisted of off-the-shelf code that was designed and built primarily for use in cameras and home computers, but not for reliable operation in space, resisting hardware failures, power-loss, and sudden reboots. What makes failures in this software so difficult to accept is that a file system is easily one of the best understood modules on a spacecraft in terms of its required functionality. It should be possible to design an ultra-reliable version of this type of software. These observations provided the motivation behind our mini-version of the grand challenge. The real challenge, though, is somewhat broader:

> *Is there a way to structure software in such a way that the application*
> *of logic model checking techniques becomes a trivial exercise?*

It is of course all too easy to pose a challenge problem and wait for others to solve it. We have therefore decided take our own challenge and to pursue a full design, a full verification, *and* a complete implementation of a flight-qualified file system module that can withstand the rigors of space. We have also committed to building the module to standards that satisfy all existing flight software development requirements at

JPL. This decision rules out a number of choices for the design and development that otherwise might have been possible. It means, for instance, that the target programming language is most conveniently C (the language most commonly used at JPL for implementing mission critical software), the target operating system VxWorks® (a real-time operating system), and the process followed must comply with all reporting and book-keeping requirements for software development at our host institution. Naturally, our desire is to not just comply with the existing process, but to show how it can be exceeded. Our goal is further to chart a course for reliable software development that can later plausibly be followed by non-experts in formal software verification.

At the time of writing, we have completed a first implementation of the file system software that we will use as a reference for our formal verification attempts. The prototype is written to a high standard of reliability, compliant with all JPL coding requirements, as well as conforming to a small set of fairly strict additional coding rules, described in [15]. These additional rules are in part meant to simplify, if not enable, formal verification with logic model checking techniques.

3 Our Plan

We started on our mini challenge in the middle of 2005, initially pursuing three tracks in parallel.

1. The first track is to build a simulation environment for a file system that can reproduce all relevant behavior of the target hardware. A software simulation of the environment will simplify the use of model-driven verification techniques, as outlined in [12]. We have meanwhile completed several versions of this hardware simulation layer, supporting different levels of abstraction. The most accurate simulation module supports a bit-level accurate representation of a typical flash memory card.

2. The second track is to develop a formalization of all relevant requirements, including standard POSIX requirements for the user interface to the file system [18]. As always with requirements specifications, identifying and capturing a representative set of requirements is a non-trivial task. The primary requirements for file systems, for instance, are functional and not temporal in nature, and there are few if any adequate formalisms available for expressing such requirements. We currently plan to capture most requirements of this type as system invariants, and as pre- and post-conditions on basic file system operations.

3. The third track includes the detailed design of the file system itself. This is in principle a white-board design, aspects of which are currently being verified with the SPIN model checker [13] and with the ACL2 theorem-prover [1].

3.1 Constraints

To give a flavor for the design requirements, note that flash-memory is typically logically organized into separately mountable file system partitions (sometimes called volumes), but physically they are organized in pages, blocks, and banks. On a typical NAND flash memory card there may be 2 banks, 1024 blocks per bank, and 32 pages per block, each page able to record 4096 bytes of information.

Pages on NAND-flash devices must always be written in their entirety, in one operation. The information can be read back in portions, but only sequentially and not randomly. A page can be read any number of times without degrading the information that is stored in it, but it should be written only once. After a page has been written, it should be erased before it is reused for new write operations. A page, of course, holds no useful information until it is written. The reason for the single-write requirement is that a page erase operation on flash memory sets all bits on the page to one, and subsequent write operations can only set bits to zero. Once a bit is zero, it can only be reset to one in an erase operation.

To make things more interesting still, pages on a flash memory card can only be erased in multiples of blocks (i.e., 32 pages at a time). This means that there are in principle only three types of operations that can be performed on a flash disk: *read a page*, *write a page*, and *erase a block* of pages. A block, finally, can only be erased a limited number of times, e.g., 100,000 times, and the reliability of the pages in a block degrades with the number of erasures that have taken place. Since we don't want some blocks to wear out long before others, blocks have to be erased and reused in such a way that the wear on all blocks is roughly the same. This process is called *wear-leveling*. Page read- and write-operations, and block erase operations can fail, sometimes intermittently, sometimes permanently. On such a failure, a block may have to be marked as *bad*, to indicate that no further write or erase operations should be attempted on that block. When a block goes bad, the pages in that block can no longer be written or erased, although any correctly written page in the block may still be read.

A first observation about the target design for our file system is that no information can be stored in a fixed location on disk, not even information that is unlikely to change. The wear-leveling requirement means that all stored data may have to move from time to time, so that all blocks can be erased and reused roughly equally. Since stored data is the only information that will survive a reboot, it must also be possible to reconstruct all relevant information about the file system from scratch, without knowing in advance where it is stored on disk. Another requirement, orthogonal to the wear-leveling requirement, is that the consistency of the file system must be maintained at all times, even in the presence of arbitrary reboots or a sudden loss of power. That means that all operations on the file system must be interruptible. No data should be lost or corrupted when the system is interrupted at a random point in its execution. A user of the file system must be able to assume that changes in the stored data are atomic, even if they take multiple page writes to complete. A strong design requirement is that, with very few exceptions, file system operations must either succeed completely or fail completely, never leaving visible evidence of intermediate states when interrupted.

In the target environment, the file system should also be able to deal with random data errors caused by radiation, which can be particularly severe during solar flares. To give one small example of the problems that this can pose: a so-called Single Event Upset (SEU) in the address register of a flash memory device during a *read_page* operation could alter the page address and result in the wrong page being read, without an error condition being flagged (i.e., the data read from the page can pass a checksum test successfully). The same type of error during a *write_page* operation could result in a page different than the one intended being written, again without detectable error unless special precautions are taken in the design that is adopted.

3.2 Verification Challenges

A key challenge in this project is to provide the ability to prove the integrity of the file system under all types of hardware error, and power-loss scenarios. A model of the flash hardware can capture the relevant assumptions about the lower interface to the hardware, and a model of nominal user behavior can capture our assumptions about the upper interface. This leads to a *sandwich* model of the file system: enclosed between two SPIN models that define the environment in which it is meant to operate and against which it must be verified, as illustrated in Figure 1.

The user behavior, though conceptually simple, can add a surprising amount of complexity. Note that for even very small systems, there are a very large number of possible ways to define directory hierarchies, file contents, and file and directory names. Rename operations can move files arbitrarily between different locations in the directory hierarchy, and seek operations can change where new contents are written to or read from in a file. Files may be truncated, moved, removed, recreated, etc. This means that it is not simple to define a single user model and hope to perform an exhaustive verification against that model. To alleviate some of these problems, different levels of abstraction and different subsets of possible user behaviors can be defined to perform a series of targeted verification runs against a relevant subset of the correctness properties.

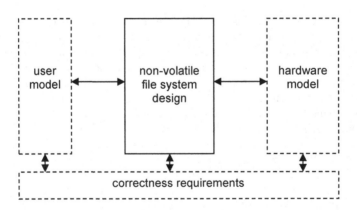

Fig. 1. Sandwich Model for File System Verification

A simple model of user behavior could, for instance, specify the manipulation of a single file by a user, performing random reads and writes to that file, resetting the file pointer to the start of the file at arbitrary points, while the hardware model fails read and write operations arbitrarily. We have been able to demonstrate that such a model can indeed be verified exhaustively, when applied to the prototype software implementation, using model driven verification techniques and fairly straightforward conservative abstractions of the file system state.

A simple version of an abstract model for the flash hardware is shown in Figure 2. This model captures only basic behavior of the hardware, allowing page reads and writes, with the possibility of failure and the sudden appearance of bad blocks, and

```
active proctype flash_disk()
{    byte b, p;
     bool v;

     do
     :: flash?readpage(b,p,_) ->
            assert(b < NBL);
            assert(p < PPB);
            if      /* non-deterministic choice */
            :: blocks[b].meta[p] != free ->
                    user!success
            :: blocks[b].meta[p] != verified ->
                    user!error
            fi

     :: flash?writepage(b,p,v) ->
            assert(b < NBL);
            assert(p < PPB);
            assert(blocks[b].meta[p] == free);
            if
            :: blocks[b].bad -> user!error
            :: else ->
                    if
                    :: blocks[b].meta[p] = v;
                            user!success
                    :: blocks[b].bad = true ->
                            user!error
            fi      fi

     :: flash?eraseblock(b,_,_) ->
            assert(b < NBL);
            if
            :: blocks[b].bad -> user!error
            :: else ->
                    if
                    :: blocks[b].bad = true ->
                            user!error
                    :: erase_pages(b) ->
                            user!success
            fi      fi
     od
}
```

Fig. 2. Simplified Model of the Flash Hardware

allowing for a distinction between meta-data (directory information) and regular file data. Meta-data is typically stored with a verified write cycle, which is slower than regular write operations, but lowers the probability of subsequent page read errors. In a verified write operation the information is read back and compared with the original data to make sure it can be retrieved correctly.

A sample correctness property for the file system is that no page is written more than once before it is erased. This property could be expressed in LTL as follows:

$$[] (pw -> X (!pw \ U \ be))$$

where pw indicates the occurrence of write operation on an arbitrary given page, and be indicates a block erase operation on the block that contains the given page.

A more complete model of the flash hardware will also record page header information; so that one can track which pages are current and which are obsolete and erasable, in the verification of the properties of the file system software. With that model we should also be able to prove that a block with only obsolete pages and no free pages will eventually be erased for reuse, for instance expressed as:

$$[] (ob -> <> be)$$

where ob is true when some given block contains only obsolete pages, and be is true when that block is erased.

4   On Code Structure

One focus of our project is to study if the adoption of specific code and data structures can enable stronger types of verification, and make it easier to apply existing software verification methods. Clearly, code can be written in such a way that most properties of interest become unprovable. It is unfortunately easier to demonstrate this point than it is to show that the opposite is also possible. To achieve the opposite, to write code in such a way that it *can* be verified, takes more planning, but the additional level of effort required may still be relatively small. We adopted strong coding rules for our project, that include a restricted use of pointers, statically verifiable bounds on all loops, absence of dynamic memory allocation, and even the absence of direct and indirect recursion [15].

A loop to traverse a linked list, for instance, can be bounded as follows:

```
SET_BOUND(MAX);
for (ptr = start; ptr != null; ptr = ptr->nxt)
{      ...
       CHECK_BOUND();
}
```

Where SET_BOUND and CHECK_BOUND are macros. The first macro call will initialize a predefined loop variable to the boundary value that should never be exceeded. The second macro call decrements the variable value and asserts that the result remains positive. The protection here is against infinite loops, so the precise bound is often not that important, as long as it is a finite number. (Nested loops should be rare in high integrity code, and are handled separately since they will require us to track more than one loop bound.)

Assertions are also handled differently. The standard assertion definition from the C `assert.h` library is not really adequate for our purposes. An abort on assertion failure is rarely the right response in embedded systems, and in most, if not all, cases processing should also *not* continue normally when an assertion fails. Instead, some type of corrective or recovery action should be initiated to handle the unexpected situation. We therefore define an assertion as a Boolean pseudo-function that normally returns *true*, but will optionally print a diagnostic message when it fails and then return *false*, so that the caller of the assertion can take the required corrective action. With some C preprocessor magic, this can be written as follows:

```
#define ASSERT(e)  ((e) ? (1) : \
                    output("%s:%d assert(%s) failed\n",
                    __FILE__, __LINE__, #e), 0)
```

The macro definition makes use of the predefined preprocessor names __FILE__ and __LINE__ to print the location of the assertion in the source files, and of the C preprocessor operator # to reproduce the text of the failing assertion. Assertions, then are *always* used as expressions in a conditional and *never* as standalone statements.

The use of an assertion to defend against a null-pointer dereference could for instance be written as follows:

```
if (!ASSERT(ptr != NULL))
{    return ERROR;
}
```

This forces the programmer to think about the corrective action that would be needed in case the assertion fails.

For embedded code, where there is typically no mechanism for printing output, the assertion can be redefined *after* testing with the variant:

```
#define ASSERT(e)  (e)
```

which maintains the protection and the original functionality of the assertion (so that all test results remain valid), but removes the diagnostic output on failure.

The rules we adopted allow us to derive bounds on memory and stack use, and to prove the finiteness of all file system operations. Without recursion, the function call graph is acyclic and can be analyzed with traditional logic model checking techniques. We use, for instance, the *uno* static analyzer [11,21] to generate the function call graph for the software, and convert it with a small awk-script into a SPIN model, that is automatically annotated with relevant operations (e.g., semaphore operations). Then we use the SPIN model checker to prove additional properties of the code such as proper locking orders, bounds on stack use, and absence of direct or indirect recursion.

Importantly, the data structures for the prototype file system are organized in such a way that it becomes easy to set up a connection with the model checker for model-driven verification runs. Just two data structures (a mount table and a partition structure) hold all state information that must be tracked in the model checking process, and the required tracking statements are trivially defined – possibly even mechanically derivable from the source code. It is also relatively straightforward, thanks to these structuring conventions, to set up abstraction functions for the model checker over the relevant state data, that will allow us to exploit, for instance, symmetry abstractions. We further make sure that the level of atomicity in the source code, enforced through VxWorks semaphores, matches the level of granularity that the model driven verification method handles best (i.e., function level atomicity).

5 Testing?

To perform an initial check of the working of our prototype implementation, we have relied on a number of methods that include strong static source code analysis, and randomized differential testing [16]. These more conventional testing methods serve not only for us as designers to gain confidence in our initial prototype, they also help to win the trust of colleagues who may need to be convinced of the added value of a more formal verification effort of the same code. We have not attempted to generate implementation level code from high level design models (e.g., Spin models), although we may revisit that decision later once the full design and its verification challenges are thoroughly understood.

A few more words on the random differential testing method we used may be of interest. For these tests, one or more reference systems are needed to serve as a judge of the validity of operations that are performed on the system under test. Fortunately, for a standard file system, reference implementations are readily available. As part of our tests, we ran randomly generated usage scenarios on the flash file system, comparing against reference file systems on Solaris, Linux, and Cygwin. Perhaps not surprisingly, we found defects not only in our own prototype software but also in some of the widely-used reference implementations. The Linux implementation proved to be the most reliable, and was used for the majority of our tests. A test fails in this setup when the file system created by the module under test differs from that created on the reference system when given the same sequence of POSIX operations. Each such test failure is inspected manually and in cases of doubt the official POSIX requirements are consulted to determine which implementation is at fault: the prototype file system or the reference system. The test harness used in these tests randomly injects simulated hardware faults, such as bad blocks and sudden reboots. Because these faults cannot easily be reproduced on the reference system, our integrity requirement was that the module under test either completes an operation fully, matching the result of the completed operation on the reference system, or fails the operation completely, matching the state of the reference system before the operation is executed, but never creating an intermediate or a corrupted state. Long error scenarios found through this method are minimized with a method based on Zeller's delta-debugging system [6] and all error scenarios found are preserved in a regression test suite.

The differential test method is easily automated. The random tests run in principle non-stop in the background on our machines. Even at that pace, there is of course no hope that these tests can be exhaustive, yet our experience so far is that new defects in the code are found quickly.

There is an opportunity to replace at least part of the differential test system with a stronger Spin driven verification system, using models along the lines of what is shown in Figure 2, where we replace the random choices from the tester with non-deterministic choices that are controlled by the model checker. Our real challenge here is to make the model driven software verification methods work as easily, and be as effective as the original differential test method.

A switch to the model driven verification method will allow us to formulate and verify more complicated correctness properties in linear temporal logic, to perform the verifications more systematically, and has the potential for a significantly greater accuracy in catching requirements violations.

6 Summary

In this paper we have posed a challenge that illustrates where we believe the new frontier in the application of logic model checking techniques rests today. To realize the full potential of logic model checking techniques for software verification, we will need to find ways to structure code in such a way that verification becomes easier. We believe that the main potential in this area is in the application of model-driven verification techniques. To give substance to these ideas, we have described a specific challenge problem that we, and we hope many others, will try to solve fully in the coming years. The domain in which we have phrased this problem is that of space exploration, but it could be any other application domain where the correctness of software is critically important. Like many organizations, JPL and NASA already have strict requirements for the development of mission-critical software components. Still, anomalies that can be traced to software defects do occur, and have on occasion led to mission failures. Stronger types of software verification are therefore essential to reach higher levels of software reliability.

JPL today lists among its strategic goals in software development the adoption of formal methods for software design, an increased use of model-driven software verification techniques, and routine application of logic model checking techniques to mission software by the year 2013. The work we have sketched is an attempt to realize at least some of these goals.

Acknowledgements. We are grateful to Len Day for building the bit-level accurate software simulator for flash hardware, and to Cheng Hu for his initial formalization of the POSIX requirements for our file system.

The research described in this paper was carried out at the Jet Propulsion Laboratory, California Institute of Technology, under a contract with the National Aeronautics and Space Administration.

References

[1] Kaufmann, M., Manolios, P., Strother Moore, J.: Computer-Aided Reasoning: An Approach. Kluwer Academic Publishers (July 2000),
   http://www.cs.utexas.edu/users/moore/publications/acl2-books/car/index.html
[2] Bartlett, K.A., Scantlebury, R.A., Wilkinson, P.T.: A note on reliable full-duplex transmission over half-duplex lines. Comm. ACM 12(5), 260–265

[3] Bochmann, G.V.: Finite state description of communication protocols, Publ. 236, Dept. d'Informatique, University of Montreal (July 1976)

[4] Clarke, E.M., Emerson, E.A., Sistla, A.P.: Automatic verification of finite-state concurrent systems using temporal logic specifications. ACM Trans. On Programming Languages and Systems 8(2), 244–263 (1986)

[5] Clarke, L.A., Rosenblum, D.S.: A historical perspective on runtime assertion checking in software development. ACM SIGSOFT Software Engineering Notes 31(3), 25–37 (2006)

[6] http://www.st.cs.uni-sb.de/dd/ on delta debugging techniques

[7] Goldstein, H.H., Von Neumann, J.: Planning and coding problems for an electronic computing instrument. Part II, vol. 1, Princeton (April 1947)

[8] Holzmann, G.J.: PAN: a protocol specification analyzer, Tech Report TM81-11271-5, AT&T Bell Laboratories (March 1981)

[9] Holzmann, G.J., Peled, D.: An improvement in formal verification. In: Proc. 7th Int. Conf. on Formal Description Techniques (FORTE) 1994, pp. 197–211. Chapman and Hall (1994)

[10] Holzmann, G.J., Smith, M.H.: Automating software feature verification. Bell Labs Technical Journal 5(2), 72–87 (2000)

[11] Holzmann, G.J.: Static source code checking for user-defined properties. In: Proc. 6th World Conference on Integrated Design & Process Technology (IDPT), Pasadena CA, USA (June 2002)

[12] Holzmann, G.J., Joshi, R.: Model-Driven Software Verification. In: Graf, S., Mounier, L. (eds.) SPIN 2004. LNCS, vol. 2989, pp. 77–92. Springer, Heidelberg (2004)

[13] Holzmann, G.J.: The SPIN Model Checker: Primer and Reference Manual. Addison-Wesley (2003)

[14] Holzmann, G.J., Joshi, R.: A mini grand challenge: build a verifiable file-system (position paper), Grand Challenge in Verified Software – Theories, Tools, Experiments, Zurich, Switzerland (October 2005)

[15] Holzmann, G.J.: The Power of Ten: rules for developing safety critical code. IEEE Computer (June 2006)

[16] McKeeman, W.M.: Differential testing for software. Digital Technical Journal 10(1), 100–107 (1998)

[17] Musuvathi, M., Park, D.Y.W., Chou, A., Engler, D.R., Dill, D.L.: CMC: A pragmatic approach to model checking real code. In: Proc. Fifth Symposium on Operating Systems Design and Implementation, OSDI (December 2002)

[18] http://www.opengroup.org/

[19] Rajamani, S.K., Ball, T.: Automatically Validating Temporal Safety Properties of Interfaces. In: Dwyer, M.B. (ed.) SPIN 2001. LNCS, vol. 2057. Springer, Heidelberg (2001)

[20] Sunshine, C.A.: Interprocess Communication Protocols for Computer Networks, Ph.D. Thesis, Dept. of Computer Science, Stanford Univ., Stanford, CA (1975)

[21] http://spinroot.com/uno/

[22] Vardi, M., Wolper, P.: An authomata-theoretic approacj to automatic program verification. In: Proc. 1st Annual Symposium on Logic in Computer Science, LICS, pp. 332–344 (1986)

[23] Grand Challenge in Verified Software – Theories, Tools, Experiments (VSTTE), Zurich, Switzerland (October 2005), http://vstte.ethz.ch/

[24] West, C.H., Zafiropulo, P.: Automated validation of a communications protocol: the CCITT X. 21 recommendation, IBM J. Res. Develop. 22(1), 60–71 (1978)

A Retrospective on Murφ

David L. Dill

Stanford University
dill@stanford.edu

Abstract. Murφ is a formal verification system for finite-state concurrent systems developed as a research project at Stanford University. It has been widely used for many protocols especially for multiprocessor cache coherence protocols and cryptographic protocols. This paper reviews the history of Murφ, some of results that of the project, and lessons learned.

1 Introduction

Murφ (pronounced "Murphy") is a formal verification system for finite-state concurrent systems. It was developed by my group in the Stanford University Computer Systems Laboratory during the 1990's. It has been a fairly successful project, resulting in a widely-used tool and in a number of published research results that have influenced other systems. Based on my discussions with members of design teams, it seems that Murφ has been used at some point in the development of the cache coherence protocols for almost every major commercial shared memory multiprocessor system. Murφ has also been used for a variety of other problems, including verification of cryptographic protocols [1,2].

I learned much from the Murφ project about formal verification, the design of practical tools in an academic setting, and research strategy. This paper is a first-person recollection of how the Murφ project unfolded. It is intended to provide an overview of some of the issues and technical advances in explicit state model checking, a realistic portrayal of how a research project actually happened (information that does not appear in the technical papers about Murφ), and as a source of some hard-earned knowledge about building a formal verification tool in an academic environment.

2 Early Years

2.1 The Motivation for the Project

The Murφ project came out of a desire to show that formal verification tools could have practical value. When I arrived at Stanford, in 1987, several faculty and many students in my building were involved in the DASH project [3], a large effort to design and build a shared-memory multiprocessor. The heart of the DASH system was a cache coherence protocol to maintain consistency between multiple distributed cached copies of data from memory. Not surprisingly, when I polled these colleagues about important problems in the hardware verification area, they frequently mentioned the challenge of assuring the correctness of cache coherence protocols.

O. Grumberg and H. Veith (Eds.): 25MC Festschrift, LNCS 5000, pp. 77–88, 2008.
© Springer-Verlag Berlin Heidelberg 2008

At about the same time, my research group was exploring the use of Boolean decision diagrams (BDDs) for symbolic model checking of large state spaces [4]. A BDD is a data structure that compactly represents Boolean functions that arise in practice [5]. The essence of BDD-based model checking is to compute the reachable state space using only operations on BDDs, so that explicit lists or tables of states never have to be saved. BDD verification connected with cache coherence when I saw a talk by Ken McMillan, then a PhD student in Computer Science at Carnegie Mellon University, on verification of the Gigamax cache coherence protocol using BDDs [6].

A group of three PhD students, Andreas J. Drexler and Alan J. Hu and C. Han Yang and I decided to try the same techniques on a different cache coherence protocol. Ken had used the "m4" macro processing language to improvise a description language that could be translated into BDDs. We attempted a similar approach, but, after a few weeks, the students expressed the unanimous view that the method was far too labor-intensive, and that we could accelerate the project by first building a translator for a more user-friendly description language. That language eventually became Murφ.

2.2   The Murφ Description Language Design

The basic concepts of the Murφ description language sprang from the UNITY modeling language of Misra and Chandy [7], which I had learned about a few years earlier, and found to be simple and appealing. In the UNITY model, a concurrent system is represented as a set of global variables and guarded commands. Each guarded command consists of predicate on the state variables, called a *guard*, and a set of assignments that update those variables to change the state. The "control structure" of a UNITY program consists of a single infinite loop, which repeatedly executes two steps: (1) evaluate all the guards, given the current values of the global variables and (2) arbitrarily choose one of the commands whose guard is true and execute it, updating the variables.

A UNITY model defines an implicit state graph, where each state is an assignment of values to the global variables. The initial values of the variables are specified as part of the model. The commands define the next-state relationship: if a command has a guard that is true in state s, and state t is obtained by executing the assignments of that command, then there is an edge from s to t in the global state graph.

Modeling concurrency in UNITY is trivial. UNITY has no notion of a process or thread, but a process can be represented as a set of variables and commands. The joint behavior of several processes is simply the union of the variables and commands for each process. This approach provides an asynchronous, interleaving model of concurrency, where all synchronization and communication is through global variables. Non-deterministic choices by a scheduler are subsumed by the nondeterministic choice of which guarded command to execute on each iteration of UNITY's loop.

While preserving the basic concepts of UNITY, we quickly found that it was very helpful to have more conventional programming language constructs for the basic data types of the language (records, arrays, integer subranges, enumerated types, etc.) and for the predicates and statements appearing in the commands. We even included "while" loops in the commands, in spite of some initial concerns about potential problems from non-terminating commands (in retrospect, these concerns were completely unimportant – infinite loops in commands are are rare, and easily detected and fixed). Pointers and heap-allocated memory were not included because of a desire to discourage the writing of descriptions requiring very large state representations. It is not clear to me that this was a good decision, since it resulted in significant inconvenience when modeling some software applications.

Murφ could check several kinds of properties. It could detect deadlocks, which were defined as a state with no successors other than (possibly) itself. Murφ descriptions are supposed to be deadlock-free. The user could also specify *invariants,* which are predicates on the state variables (in the Murφ language) that are supposed to hold in all global states. We soon discovered that assertions and error statements embedded in commands also very useful, because it is often easier to specify an error condition in the context of the logic of a rule than to separate it from the rule. For example, users frequently handle a range of possibilities with a "case" statement or nested conditionals, and want to add "otherwise, it is an error" for all the cases that are not supposed to occur. Whenever a new state is constructed, these properties are all checked and an error message and error trace are produced if one is violated.

The Murφ model could be translated to logic by writing each command as a logical relation, and then representing the next-state relation as a disjunction of predicates, one for each Murφ command. This translation seemed attractive for BDD-based verification, because BDD-based evaluation of reachability has an outermost existentially quantified variable which can be distributed over the disjunction of predicates, minimizing the size of intermediate BDDs generated during the computation (this trick is very important to BDD computations; it is called "early quantification").

The three students began implementing the system. My recollection is that Andreas worked on the description language translation, Alan worked on the BDD verifier, and Han worked on examples. Unfortunately, we soon ran into a barrier: There were efficiency problems with the BDD verifier. As a interim measure to allow Han to work on examples before the BDD verifier was functioning we decided to implement a simple explicit-state on-the-fly verifier for Murφ, with the intention of throwing it away in a few months.

Explicit on-the-fly verification is a simple depth-first or breadth-first search of the state graph for a state that violates a property. An on-the-fly algorithm checks each state as it is created, so that an error can be reported before the entire set of reachable states is explored. Such methods had already been used for protocol verification for over a decade. The search algorithm uses two large data structures: a queue of states whose successor states need to be searched (the *queue*) and a hash table of states that do not need to be visited again (the *state table*).

2.3 Murφ's First Major Application

Shortly after we had our first working prototype of Murφ, I connected with Andreas Nowatzyk, who was designing an experimental shared-memory multiprocessor at Sun Microsystems called S3.mp [8]. I knew Andreas from the PhD program at Carnegie Mellon University, where he had shared an office with Michael Browne, another student of Ed Clarke's who was working on model checking. Andreas became familiar with model checking through his officemate, and later worked with Ken McMillan, who found a bug in an early version of the cache coherence protocol that Andreas was designing. We decided to apply Murφ to this problem. I, personally, did much of the work on this, and soon became the main user of Murφ. I generated a long list of requests for improvement in the language and the system to make it more usable. Murφ improved rapidly, and we found several bugs and other issues in the protocol. Later, Han Yang applied Murφ to many problems related to S3.mp.

When working on the S3.mp protocol, we learned some things about how to use Murφ. For example, we discovered the importance of *downscaling*. It was impossible to represent the protocol at the scale it was implemented, with potentially hundreds of processors and millions of cache lines. Instead, bugs could be often found with scaled-down models having, for example, three processors and one "cache line" with only one bit of data. Using such a model, the verifier could exercise many subtle scenarios and find bugs quickly in such a model that would be very difficult to find with system-level simulation. Also, when a problem with a scaled-down model was discovered, it was much easier to understand the problem than it would have been using a larger-scale model [9]. Indeed, it was a good idea to try the smallest possible model that made any sense at all, find and fix any bugs, and then scale the model up slightly and repeat the process. Changing scales was also useful when Murφ ran up against capacity limits, by allowing the user to increase the scale of one dimension (*e.g.*,the number of cache lines) while decreasing the scale of another dimension (*e.g.*, the number of processors).

It became obvious that Murφ needed to support verification of the same model at different scales with minimal changes to the description. We found that easy rescalability could be achieved with three simple features: (1) named constants, (2) arrays, and (3) parameterized sets of commands. For example, a generic model could be written for n processors. Each processor could have an associated numerical index in the range $1 \ldots n$, the global state variables for processor i could be stored in one or more arrays at index i, and the guarded commands for the processor could be nested inside a *ruleset*, a new Murφ construct that defines a symbolic parameter to represent a process index. Each command inside a ruleset was actually a *family* of commands, one for each possible value of the ruleset parameter. Each command could use the process index to access the appropriate array element, and as a storeable value for the name of the process (for example, the process index might be stored in a variable representing the owner of a cache line). With such a representation, the number of processors verified could be changed simply by re-defining the symbolic constant n.

After these improvements, we found that useful results could be obtained with our "interim" explicit-state implementation, and that we could compensate for some of the obvious efficiency problems with the verifier by judicious use of abstractions, as well as generally minimizing the number of state variables.

2.4 BDD Research

Meanwhile, Alan Hu was still struggling with the BDD-based verifier for Murφ. He defined a somewhat simpler input language (eventually called "EVER"), so that he could find out if BDDs could be made to work efficiently for the problems of interest before investing the effort to handle the entire Murφ description language. It seemed that our distributed cache implementations led to BDD blowup regardless of what we did. It eventually dawned on us that there was an inherent problem: Many of the transactions in the cache model involved sending a message from processor A to processor B and storing the message. In the midst of such a transaction, processor A would be in a state waiting for a response to the message it sent, processor B would be in a state waiting for a message, and the message itself would have "from" address of A and a "to" address of B. All of these relationships would be implicit in a BDD representing the reachable states of the system.

BDD variables must be placed in a single total order. As a rule, BDDs explode in size when highly correlated variables are widely separated in this total order. But there seemed to be no way to avoid separating closely correlated variables in the system we were modeling, because there could be many transactions in process at the same time, and transactions could involve any pair of processors. So, a variable order that put the variables for processor A and B near each other would separate variables for A and C, A and D, etc., which also correlated. So the BDDs would always blow up.

We came up with a two ideas for reducing this problem. The first was to note that, in many cases, when there were several related variables, some of them were actually redundant – their values could be inferred from the values of other variables. For example, the state of a process that has just sent a message might be a determinable from the contents of the message. One idea was to declare variables that are *functionally dependent* on other variables, and treat them as abbreviations rather than as separate variables [10]. This reduces some of the redundancy that causing BDD blowup. Since the declarations of functional dependencies could be wrong, the verification algorithm verifies that there really is a functional dependency before exploiting it.

Another, more general, idea was to maintain a list of separate BDDs for sets of related variables, such as those in an individual processor or in the network, the conjunction of which represented the reachable state space. Most BDDs would capture the relationships between a small set of related variables, such as the variables describing the state of a processor. Since these BDDs had a small number of variables, the related variables could be close together. Other BDDs could focus on different properties involve different sets of variables (the sets of variables did not have to be disjoint). There would be a BDD at the end of the list that included all the variables, but the relations captured in the earlier, smaller BDDs in the list would be factored out of the large one, to keep it small. So, in the best case, we would have several small BDDs instead of one huge BDD [11,12].

Both of these ideas worked moderately well on artificial examples, but we still could not handle the S3.mp cache coherence protocol, and we eventually concluded that there were several different causes of blowup, each of which was going to require a complicated solution – if all were even solvable. We were never able to verify distributed cache coherence algorithms with BDDs. To my knowledge, no one else has been able to use BDDs successfully for this problem, even now.

3   Optimizations

3.1   State Reduction

Subsequently, another student, C. Norris Ip, joined the project. Norris and I noticed that, in many of the examples, Murφ was searching many redundant states because of symmetry in the system description. For example, some of our cache coherence examples would have three different kinds of symmetry. Processors, cache lines, and memory locations could all be interchanged in a state without changing the future behavior of the system in any important way. More precisely, once a state had been visited and its descendents searched without finding a bug, it was pointless to search a state that was identical except for a permutation of the processors [13,14].

We also noticed that symmetries in our descriptions corresponded to the use of numerical indices, which were represented as subrange types in Murφ. Equivalent states corresponded to different permutations of the elements of these subranges. If Murφ could standardize each state to find an equivalent representative state before looking it up in the state table, the search algorithm would only search the descendents of the representative state instead of all the states equivalent to it. It turned out that standardizing states was a difficult problem (at least as hard as graph isomorphism), but it was possible to find reasonably accurate and fast heuristics.

However, if symmetry reduction were applied inappropriately, identifying states that were not equivalent, Murφ could miss errors. The solution was to invent a new, more abstract type for subranges (which we called a "scalarset") values of which could only be assigned to variables, used as array indices, or used as ruleset parameters. Under these restrictions, it could be guaranteed that permuting the elements of a scalarset (which were represented as small integers) would preserve state equivalence. So, symmetry could be "declared" by change subrange declarations to scalarsets, and the Murφ compiler would detect any symmetry-breaking operations that might lead to missed error states.

We made an important discovery when looking at graphs of the numbers of states searched as a function of scalarset sizes. For some scalarsets, the number of states stopped increasing even as the size of the scalarset was increased. We realized that Murφ could automatically verify an infinite family of systems, completely automatically, under certain circumstances! For example, if the scalarset type s was only stored in three places in a state, the representative state would map the original values to 0, 1, and 2 – even if s had a hundred possible values. We called scalarsets that were used in this limited way "data scalarsets," and the phenomenon where the state graph stops growing "data saturation."

Scalar sets only capture *full symmetry*, in which the members of the set can be permuted arbitrarily. Other researchers have explored other types of symmetry that can occur in systems, [15,16,17,18] but full symmetry is easy to express, occurs frequently in practice, and saves more states than other types of symmetry, so we made a choice, in the engineering of Murφ and in our research strategy, not to pursue the topic more deeply.

3.2   Reducing the Primary Memory Bottleneck

One of the major problems with explicit on-the-fly verification, as described above, is poor locality of reference in the state table. The queue needs to store entire states, because all of the information in each state may be necessary to compute the successor states, so it uses a lot of memory. But the queue has good locality of reference – states that are in use tend to be located in memory near other states that are in use – so most of the states can be migrated to the disk without major losses in efficiency when they verifier is not using them. However, the state table, being a large hash table, has no locality of reference. Once the size of the state table approaches the size of available primary memory, parts of it are paged out to the disk, resulting in slowdowns of many orders of magnitude. Thus, available primary memory effectively limits the number of states than can be searched.

Ulrich Stern, then a visiting student from Germany, joined our group and began investigating whether we could reduce memory usage by using probabilistic techniques such as the bit-state hashing method pioneered by Holzmann [19,20] or the hash compaction method that had recently been published by Wolper and Leroy [21,22]. These techniques save memory, but at the expense of some probability that states (and, possibly, errors) will be missed. Bit-state hashing does not provide any guarantees about that probability, but Wolper and Leroy could provide an upper bound on the probability of missing an error, if the verifier completed without finding any errors.

Instead of storing full states in the state table, the Wolper/Leroy scheme stored numerical signatures, computed using a hash function. The signatures were much smaller than the states. In this method, states could be missed when they have the same signature. If the signature of state s_1 is stored in the table, and s_2 with the same signature is looked up, the verifier will find the signature of s_2 in the state table and mistakenly conclude that the descendents of s_2 have already been searched, and never visit them. If all of the error states are descendents of s_2, this can result in missed errors.

Wolper and Leroy could bound the probability of missed errors after the completion of the search by counting the number of states actually visited and computing the probability that two of them had the same signature. This number could be made reasonably small if there were sufficiently many bits in the signatures. In theory, the user could raise that small probability to the nth power by verifying n times with different hash functions.

Uli's first improvement to this scheme was to improve the probability bound by noticing that a state could only be missed if it had the same signature as another state *and* hashed to the same location in the hash table – so the log of the number of buckets in the hash table could be used in place of bits in the signatures.

A more significant improvement came from using breadth-first search. A particular error state, e, can be missed only if some state on a path from the start state to e is missed due to a signature collision. Hence, the probability of missing e can be minimized by minimizing the lengths of the paths searched by the verifier – which is what breadth-first search does. If search completes with no errors, the probability that this answer is incorrect is no greater than the probability that state e was missed. That probability can be computed, after verification, from the maximum number of breadth-first search levels and the number of states in the hash table. Empirically, many of the state graphs of our applications had small number of levels, so this improvement resulted in another 50% reduction in the number of bits required per state, while preserving the same small probability of missed errors.

Uli also discovered a way to make effective use of secondary storage for the state table. This idea was inspired by an earlier algorithm by A.W. Roscoe [23]. Uli discovered a simpler and more efficient scheme, which again relied on breadth-first search. Only the current level of breadth-first search states are kept in primary memory. Redundant states within the same level are detected using a hash table in primary memory. After all the states in a level have been generated, the stored states on the disk are scanned linearly, and states are deleted from the newly-computed breadth-first layer when those states are read off the disk. In practice, this algorithm allowed orders of magnitude more states to be searched, with a small percentage increase in computational overhead.

Parallel Murφ

Hash compaction and the improved use of disk storage converted the storage bottleneck to a CPU-time bottleneck, in many cases. Fortunately, Uli also devised a search algorithm that made effective use of parallel computing to reduce the CPU bottleneck.

The basic algorithm is simple. The state table is partitioned among many processors, and each processor "owns" the states that hash to its part of the state table, so, essentially, the states are allocated randomly to processors. Newly created states are sent to the processors that own them. Those processors check whether the states they were sent are already in the state table. If not, the processor computes the successors of the state and sends those to their owners. Uli also devised an efficient (and correct) distributed termination detection algorithm that worked well in practice.

Parallel Murφ is surprisingly effective at balancing the load. It exhibited linear speedup and high efficiency even with relatively large numbers of processors (e.g., a speedup of a factor of 44 to 53 when running on a 63-processor system).

Conflict with Liveness Checking

The original plan for Murφ was to implement checking for liveness properties as well as simple safety properties and deadlock checking. Seungjoon Park, another Stanford PhD student, implemented checking for properties a simple subset of linear temporal logic (LTL) formulas that captured some of the most common liveness and fairness properties, using a modified depth-first search algorithm. However, it seemed that every major efficiency improvement conflicted with these algorithms. Symmetry reduction of a state graph, as described above, does not preserve liveness properties, and it is not simple to modify the symmetry reduction or liveness checking algorithms to make them compatible (Later, Gyuris, Sistla and Emerson implemented clever liveness checking algorithms that exploit symmetry reduction [18,24]).

The state table and disk optimizations relied heavily on breadth-first search. But on-the-fly verification of liveness properties seem generally rely on depth-first search algorithms. Unfortunately, an efficient on-the-fly breadth-first search algorithm for liveness properties still does not exist.

Given a choice between verifying safety properties and liveness properties, safety properties are probably more important in practice. However, it would be better not to have to choose, because liveness properties are also extremely important. I have had several students in class projects develop protocols that they verify successfully in Murφ only because the protocols livelock before they can reach an error state.

4 Lessons Learned

Our team learned many lessons about verification, research strategy, and tool design from the Murφ project. Unfortunately, I have validated many of these lessons by ignoring them in other projects, and suffering the consequences. Findings such as these are rarely written in technical papers. I am writing them here in the hope that they may be of value to others.

Bug Hunting is More Rewarding than Proving Correctness. I had already learned this in my graduate work, but our work on Murφ strongly reinforced the lesson. Finding bugs in a system is usually much easier than proving correctness, and the impact is usually greater. Designers of systems implicitly believe that the systems are correct, so they are impressed, if not pleased, when a bug is found. Additionally, some people don't believe proofs of correctness, but a bug is explainable and demonstrable. This is the justification for using Murφ and similar tools on partial, abstracted, scaled-down models of systems.

Start Using the Tool to Solve Real Problems as Early as Possible, and Make Whatever Changes are Necessary to Maximize the Tool's Usefulness. In the the best case, the user is an implementer of the system (or, even better, the manager of the project, as I was in the early days). The tool should be put to use as early as possible, so that improvements in the tool can be driven by the demands of the problem. Every PhD student who maintained (and rewrote) Murφ was also worked on challenging verification problems using Murφ.

This heuristic is helpful to ensure that a tool is useful for at least one thing. That may not seem to be an ambitious goal, but it is frighteningly easy to make tool that is useful for *no* applications, because of faulty intuition about the answers to crucial questions, such as "What are the critical language features?" and "Where are the performance bottlenecks?" However, using the tool on a real problem very rapidly reveals these misconceptions. Useful additional features and optimizations will become apparent with use; more importantly, many complex and difficult features will never be implemented because they are never really needed.

To keep the tool in use, it is necessary to respond to demands quickly. This pressure leads to creative enhancements to the tool that solve the user's problems with minimal redesign and implementation – and these solutions often turn out to be better for the system and user than a feature requiring more elaborate implementation. (However, over time, a certain number of sub-optimal but expedient decisions accumulate, and the tool needs to be redesigned and reimplemented more-or-less from scratch. Murφ has been completely re-written at least four times.)

Almost every decision in the design of the Murφ language and verifier was profoundly affected by this application-oriented philosophy. We abandoned BDDs because we found they did not work for the application, and the explicit state verifier evolved from incremental improvements from an algorithm that we initially thought would be impractical. The invention of scalarsets came from examination of the symmetries in the application, and from the pervasive use of small integer subranges to represent sets that turned out to be symmetric.

Make it Easy for People to Audition the Tool. Potential users are impatient, and they have to encounter many broken and/or useless tools on the Internet. It is time-consuming and frustrating to sort through all the advertised systems that are available for a particular process to find out which ones actually work. My unscientific estimate is that the potential user community for a tool declines exponentially with the number of minutes it takes to see whether a tool works.

The tool should be easy to download and run. I'm amazed at the number of tools that require a user to download five different programs and libraries from different sources before anything will compile. Of course, some of those programs are broken, or conflict with other software on the user's system, etc. It is best to make pre-compiled binaries available, and statically link them (when possible) so that library version problems don't arise, and otherwise do whatever can be done to make sure the tool works "out of the box." When a tool doesn't work, sometimes highly motivated or obsessive users will fix it, if they have access to the source code – so it is good to distribute source code.

Murφ did well in some regards and not so well in others. We *did* distribute binaries for linux and some other Unix operating systems. We did not support Windows – although, at that time, most interested users were probably running on Unix systems. The biggest problem with Murφ was that the compiler translated the Murφ description to a C++ program that then had to be compiled and executed to search the state space (this idea was borrowed from SPIN [25]). The problem with this approach is that C++ semantics would shift from version to version of the compiler. In particular, semantic analysis often became more stringent with new releases, so that generated C++ code would suddenly produce errors or warnings because a user tried to compile with a newer version of g++. A more pragmatic solution would have been to compile to a least-common-denominator dialect of C, but a series of implementers of Murφ found it much easier to generate C++ – so that's what they did.

Minimize Intellectual Property Issues. We initially considered whether we should protect the potential commercial value of Murφ by restricting the license for noncommercial use. After conversations with potential users at some very large corporations, it eventually became clear that we, as well as potential users, would have to spend far too much time talking to lawyers before someone at these companies could use our tool. Even the Gnu Public License (GPL) created complications. We thought explicitly about our strategy, and concluded that the impact of our research would be maximized if we made the license terms as liberal as possible. We then adopted something very similar to the MIT and Berkeley licenses, which allow users great freedom in using, modifying, and incorporating code into other systems. I'm not sure Murφ would have been at all successful had we done otherwise.

Acknowledgments

Murφ was the work of many students, and occasional post-docs and staff, at Stanford. The roles of Andreas Drexler, Alan J. Hu, and C. Han Yang, Norris Ip, Seungjoon Park, and Ulrich Stern are partially described above. Andreas, Norris, and Uli each almost completely rewrote the system. Unfortunately, space does not permit discussion of many of the contributions of each, including large examples verified, variations of Murφ developed, and papers written.

In addition, Ralph Melton (an undergraduate at that time) maintained and almost completely rewrote the system, and Denis Leroy (a Master's student at the time) maintained and improved it. There have been so many helpful collaborators that I'm bound to forget some, but some of them were Satyaki Das, Steven German, Ganesh Gopalakrishnan, Richard Ho, Paul Loewenstein, John L. Mitchell, Andreas Nowatzyk, John Rushby, Jens Skakkebaek, and Vitaly Shmatikov.

The Murφ project was supported financially by a series of sponsors, including the National Science Foundation MIP-8858807, the Defense Advanced Research Projects Agency (through contact number N00039-91-C-0138, and, later, NASA grant NAG-2-891).), the Semiconductor Research Foundation (contract 95-DJ-389), financial gifts from the Powell Foundation, Mitsubishi Electronics Research Laboratories, the Stanford Center for Integrated Systems, equipment gifts from Sun Microsystems, Hewlett-Packard, IBM, and Intel.

The Murφ project resulted in a tool that has no doubt made widely-used systems notably more reliable. It also trained some of the most talented computer technologists in the country, who are now key contributors at companies and universities. I believe that the support of the above sponsors has yielded benefits to the U.S. and the world that are many times greater than the investment. I would like not only to thank the sponsoring organizations, but the individuals within them who were responsible for deciding to fund our project in the hope that we would produce something of value.

Of course, any statements, findings, conclusions, or recommendations above are my own, and do not necessarily reflect the views of any of the project funders.

References

1. Mitchell, J.C., Mitchell, M., Stern, U.: Automated analysis of cryptographic protocols using murφ. In: IEEE Symposium on Security and Privacy, pp. 141–153 (1997)
2. Mitchell, J.C.: Finite-state analysis of security protocols. In: Computer Aided Verification. LNCS, pp. 71–76 (1998)
3. Lenoski, D., Laudon, J., Gharachorloo, K., Weber, W.D., Gupta, A., Hennessy, J., Horowitz, M., Lam, M.: The Stanford DASH multiprocessor. Computer 25(3) (1992)
4. Burch, J., Clarke, E., McMillan, K., Dill, D., Hwang, L.: Symbolic model checking: 10^{20} states and beyond. In: 5th IEEE Symposium on Logic in Computer Science (1990)
5. Bryant, R.E.: Graph-based algorithms for Boolean function manipulation. IEEE Transactions on Computers C-35(8) (1986)
6. McMillan, K.L., Schwalbe, J.: Formal verification of the gigamax cache-consistency protocol. In: Proceedings of the International Symposium on Shared Memory Multiprocessing, Information Processing Society of Japan, pp. 242–251 (1991)
7. Chandy, K.M., Misra, J.: Parallel Program Design — a Foundation. Addison-Wesley (1988)
8. Nowatzyk, A., Aybay, G., Browne, M., Kelly, E., Parkin, M., Radke, W., Vishin, S.: The s3.mp scalable shared memory multiprocessor. In: International Conference on Parallel Processing (1995)
9. Dill, D.L., Drexler, A.J., Hu, A.J., Yang, C.H.: Protocol verification as a hardware design aid. In: IEEE International Conference on Computer Design: VLSI in Computers and Processors, pp. 522–525 (1992)

10. Hu, A.J., Dill, D.L.: Reducing BDD size by exploiting functional dependencies. In: 30th Design Automation Conference, pp. 266–271 (1993)
11. Hu, A.J., Dill, D.L.: Efficient verification with BDDs using implicitly conjoined invariants. In: 5th International Conference on Computer-Aided Verification (1993)
12. Hu, A.J., York, G., Dill, D.L.: New techniques for efficient verification with implicitly conjoined bdds. In: 31th Design Automation Conference, pp. 276–282 (1994)
13. Ip, C.N., Dill, D.L.: Better verification through symmetry. In: 11th International Symposium on Computer Hardware Description Languages and Their Applications, pp. 87–100 (1993)
14. Ip, C.N., Dill, D.L.: Better verification through symmetry. Formal Methods in System Design 9(1/2), 41–75 (1996)
15. Clarke, E., Enders, R., Filkorn, T., Jha, S.: Exploiting symmetry in temporal logic model checking. Formal Methods in System Design 9(1/2), 77–104 (1996)
16. Emerson, E.A., Sistla, A.P.: Symmetry and model checking. Formal Methods in System Design 9(1/2), 105–131 (1996)
17. Emerson, E., Sistla, A.: Utilizing symmetry when model checking under fairness assumptions: An automata-theoretic approach. In: 7th International Conference on Computer-Aided Verification (1995)
18. Gyuris, V., Sistla, A.P.: On-the-fly model checking under fairness that exploits symmetry. Formal Methods in System Design 15(3), 217–238 (1999)
19. Holzmann, G.J.: On limits and possibilities of automated protocol analysis. In: Protocol Specification, Testing, and Verification. 7th International Conference, pp. 339–344 (1987)
20. Holzmann, G.J.: Design and Validation of Computer Protocols. Prentice-Hall, Englewood Cliffs (1991)
21. Wolper, P., Leroy, D.: Reliable hashing without collision detection. In: Computer Aided Verification. 5th International Conference, pp. 59–70 (1993)
22. Wolper, P., Leroy, D.: Reliable hashing without collision detection (unpublished revised version of [21])
23. Roscoe, A.: Model-checking CSP. Prentice-Hall (1994)
24. Sistla, A.P., Gyuris, V., Emerson, E.A.: Smc: a symmetry-based model checker for verification of safety and liveness properties. ACM Transactions Software Engineering Methodolgy 9(2), 133–166 (2000)
25. Holzmann, G.: Design and validation of computer protocols. Prentice-Hall (1991)

Model Checking: From Tools to Theory*

Rajeev Alur

University of Pennsylvania

Abstract. Model checking is often cited as a success story for transitioning and engineering ideas rooted in logics and automata to practice. In this paper, we discuss how the efforts aimed at improving the scope and effectiveness of model checking tools have revived the study of logics and automata leading to unexpected theoretical advances whose impact is not limited to model checking. In particular, we describe how our efforts to add context-free specifications to software model checking led us to the model of *nested words* as a representation of data with both a linear ordering and a hierarchically nested matching of items. Such dual structure occurs in diverse corners of computer science ranging from executions of structured programs where there is a well-nested matching of entries to and exits from functions and procedures, to XML documents with the hierarchical structure specified by start-tags matched with end-tags. Finite-state acceptors of nested words define the class of regular languages of nested words that has all the appealing theoretical properties that the class of regular word languages enjoys. We review the emerging theory of nested words, its extension to nested trees, and its potential applications.

1 Introduction

The abstract for the talk titled "The Birth of Model Checking" by Ed Clarke at the *25 Years of Model Checking* symposium begins as follows

> The most important problem in model checking is the *State Explosion Problem*. In particular, it is far more important than the logic or specification formalism that is used – CTL, LTL, CTL*, Büchi automata, or the μ-calculus.

Indeed, without the spectacular progress on combating the state explosion problem, it is not clear if model checking would have had any impact on industrial practice at all. However, we would like to argue that theory, in particular, specification languages based on temporal logics, automata, and fixpoint logics, have contributed significantly to the success of model checking. First, theory of regular languages of finite and infinite words and trees, gives a clear understanding of which properties are algorithmically checkable. Second, modern

---

* This research was partially supported by NSF grants CPA 0541149, CNS 0524059, and CCR 0410662.

O. Grumberg and H. Veith (Eds.): 25MC Festschrift, LNCS 5000, pp. 89–106, 2008.

industrial-strength specification languages such as PSL are rooted in the theory of temporal logics [PSL05]. Such standardized specification languages have an important role beyond model checking, namely, in testing as well as simulation. Third, since fixpoint logic has a strong computational flavor, logics have suggested ways of implementing symbolic model checkers. Finally, the vigorous debate on relative merits of different specification languages has contributed to the intellectual health and growth of the field. It is also worth noting that one key manner in which model checking differs from program analysis is the use of specification languages: model checking typically has focussed on efficiently checking generic classes of properties such as safety and liveness, while program analysis has emphasized specific analysis questions such as pointer analysis and buffer overflows.

The foundational work on monadic second order logics and ω-automata over words and trees dates back to research in 1960s. Particularly noteworthy results include

1. Büchi's Theorem: A language of infinite words is definable using monadic second order logic of linear order (S1S) iff it is accepted by a (finite) Büchi automaton [Büc62].
2. Kamp's Theorem: A property of infinite words is expressible in first-order theory of linear order iff it is expressible in linear temporal logic LTL [Kam68].
3. Rabin's Theorem: The monadic second order theory of binary trees (S2S) is decidable [Rab69].

The automata-theoretic approach to verification, advocated by Vardi and others, connects model checking tools to the above results and their subsequent refinements, and has been celebrated with numerous awards including the 2006 ACM Kannellakis Theory in Practice Award [WVS83, VW94, KVW00, Tho90, Hol97, Kur94]. We wish to argue that, as the success of model checking tools brought intense focus on expressiveness and decidability boundary, and this led to fundamental advances in theory. Since automata and logics have applications to other areas of computing, such as databases, document processing, and planning, model checking continues to contribute to these areas. We list two such developments for illustrative purposes.

Tree automata, μ-calculus, and parity games: The use of branching-time logics such as CTL [CE81] and μ-calculus [Koz83] in symbolic model checking tools such as SMV [McM93] led researchers revisit the theory of infinite trees. While classical theory of trees considers binary trees and their regular properties, programs are best modeled by trees that are unordered and unranked, and we want to focus on properties that do not distinguish among bisimilar systems (the notion of bisimilarity was introduced in theory of concurrency [Mil89]). The resulting body of research led to new notions of automata such as *alternating tree automata* [EJ91, JW96, MS85, CDG+02]. We now know that, for a set L of infinite, unordered, unranked trees, the following are equivalent: (1) L is bisimulation-closed and definable using monadic second order logic, (2) L is definable in μ-calculus, and (3) L is accepted by an alternating parity tree automaton. This work also connects to deciding two-player games with parity winning condition, and provides the basis for *synthesis* of correct controllers with respect to LTL specifications and modular verification of open systems [Tho02, KVW01, AHK02].

Timed automata: Traditional automata do not admit an explicit modeling of time, and consequently, in order to extend model checking techniques to timed circuits, *timed automata* [AD94] were introduced as a formal notation to model the behavior of real-time systems. Timed automata accept *timed languages* consisting of sequences of events tagged with their occurrence times. Many analysis problems for timed automata are solvable, and this has led to tools such as Uppaal for verifying finite-state real-time systems [LPY97, DOTY96]. Theory of regular timed languages has also been developed with an accompanying study of real-time temporal logics [ACD93, AH94, AH93, HRS98]. Timed automata are now used as a formal model of real-time computation in contexts beyond model checking (see, for instance, textbooks on Signals and systems [LV02] and control theory [CL99]). The main technique for analysis of timed automata relies on constructing a finite quotient of the infinite space of real-valued state vectors [AD94], and this has led to many abstraction techniques for dynamical and hybrid systems [AHLP00, PS02].

In the rest of this paper, we focus in detail on our current line of research. We describe how our efforts to understand limits of algorithmically checkable properties of pushdown models led us to the model of nested words as a representation of data with both a linear ordering and a hierarchically nested matching of items. Such dual structure occurs in diverse corners of computer science ranging from executions of structured programs where there is a well-nested matching of entries to and exits from functions and procedures, to XML documents with the well-nested structure given by start-tags matched with end-tags. We review the emerging theory of nested words and its potential applications [AM04, AEM04, AKMV05, ACM06a, ACM06b, AM06, KMV06a, Alu07, AAB+07].

2 History of Verification of Pushdown Systems

Pushdown automata naturally model the control flow of sequential computation in typical programming languages with nested, and potentially recursive, invocations of program modules such as procedures and method calls. Consequently, a variety of program analysis, compiler optimization, and model checking questions can be formulated as decision problems for pushdown automata.

When viewed as a generator of words, a pushdown model specifies a context-free language of words. Decidability of regular requirements of pushdown models, then, follows from classical results on pushdown automata: the product of a pushdown automaton and a finite-state automaton gives a pushdown automaton, and the emptiness of the language of a pushdown automaton can be checked in polynomial-time (see any standard textbook on automata theory, such as, [HU79]). The decision procedure for emptiness of pushdown automata, in fact, forms the basis for many inter-procedural dataflow analysis problems [SP81, RHS95] (see [Rep98] for a survey).

In the context of model checking, a pushdown automaton can be interpreted as a generator of a context-free language of infinite words. Model checking of LTL requirements against pushdown models is known to be decidable [BS92, BEM97] (see, also, [ABE+05] for refined complexity bounds). Checking μ-calculus requirements of pushdown models, and similarly, solving games over pushdown graphs with winning condition specified in LTL, are also known to be decidable [Wal01]. The emergence of software model checking, as implemented in tools such as SLAM and BLAST, brought pushdown verification to forefront [BR01, HJM+02]. In these tools, a C program is mapped to a pushdown model (more specifically, to Boolean programs that allow stack-based control flow, but with only Boolean data variables) using predicate abstraction, and then symbolic model checking is used to analyze the resulting model.

The typical program analysis tools over control-flow graphs and BDD-based model checking tools such as Bebop, are based on the so-called summary computation for pushdown models [BR00, Rep98]. Intuitively, the analysis algorithm computes, for each procedure or a component, summaries of the form (x, y), meaning that if the component is invoked with input x, it may return with output y. The number of such summaries is finite, and can be computed by an inductive fixpoint computation. An alternative view is based on the so-called *regular model checking* [BEM97]. In a pushdown model, the state is completely described by the control state and a finite word over the alphabet of stack symbols describing the contents of the stack. It turns out that the set of reachable states of a model is regular and can be represented by a finite-state automaton. Model checking can be viewed as computation of the edges of this automaton, and the model checker Moped is based on this approach [EHRS00]. Finally, there exist interesting decidability results for logics interpreted over pushdown graphs, typically using interpretation over trees [Cau03, KPV02].

While many analysis problems can be captured as regular requirements, and hence, specifiable in LTL or μ-calculus, many others require inspection of the stack or matching of calls and returns, and are context-free. Even though the general problem of checking context-free properties of pushdown automata is undecidable, algorithmic solutions have been proposed for checking many different kinds of non-regular properties. For example, access control requirements such as "a module A should be invoked only if the module B belongs to the call-stack," and bounds on stack size such as "the number of interrupt-handlers in the call-stack should never exceed 5," require inspection of the stack, and decision procedures for certain classes of stack properties already exist [JMT99, CW02, EKS03, CMM+04]. Our own efforts to add expressiveness to LTL, while maintaining decidability of model checking with respect to pushdown models, led to the definition of temporal logic CARET that allows matching of calls and returns. CARET can express the classical correctness requirements of program modules with pre and post conditions, such as "if p holds when a module is invoked, the module must return, and q holds upon return" [AEM04].

This suggests that the answer to the question "which class of properties are algorithmically checkable against pushdown models?" should be more general than "regular." The key feature of checkable requirements, such as stack inspection and matching calls and returns, is that the stacks in the model and the property are correlated: while the stacks are not identical, the two synchronize on when to push and when to pop, and are always of the same depth. We first formalized this intuition by defining *visibly pushdown automata* (VPA). Such an automaton operates over words over an alphabet that is partitioned into three disjoint sets of calls, returns, and internal symbols. While reading a *call* symbol, the automaton must push, while reading a *return* symbol, it must pop (if the stack is non-empty), and while reading an *internal* symbol, it can only update its control state. A language over a partitioned alphabet is a *visibly pushdown language* if there is such an automaton that accepts it. This class has desirable closure properties, tractable decision problems, multiple equivalent characterizations, and adequate for formulating program analysis questions.

We now believe that a better way of exposing the matching call-return structure of the input word is by explicitly adding nesting edges [AM06]. Nested words integrate trees and words as the underlying signature has both a linear order and a hierarchical nesting relation. Finite-state acceptors of nested words define the class of regular languages of nested words that has all the appealing theoretical properties that the class of classical regular word languages enjoys. As we will describe, this allows us to view programs as finite-state generators of regular languages of nested words, as opposed to (infinite-state) pushdown generators of (restricted classes of) context-free languages of words, thereby allowing model checking of stronger requirements.

3   Nested Words

A nested word consists of a sequence of linearly ordered positions, augmented with nesting edges connecting calls to returns (or open-tags to close-tags). The edges create a properly nested hierarchical structure, while allowing some of the edges to be pending. We will present definitions for finite nested words, but the theory extends to infinite words.

We use edges starting at $-\infty$ and edges ending at $+\infty$ to model "pending" edges. A *nesting relation* $\leadsto$ of length ℓ is a subset of $\{-\infty, 1, 2, \ldots \ell\} \times \{1, 2, \ldots \ell, +\infty\}$ such that if $i \leadsto j$ then $i < j$; if $i \leadsto j$ and $i \leadsto j'$ and $i \neq -\infty$ then $j = j'$, if $i \leadsto j$ and $i' \leadsto j$ and $j \neq +\infty$ then $i = i'$, and if $i \leadsto j$ and $i' \leadsto j'$ then it is not the case that $i < i' \leq j < j'$. The definition ensures that nesting edges go only forward, do not cross, and every position is involved in at most one nesting edge. Source positions for nesting edges are *call* positions, target positions for nesting edges are *return* positions, and a position that is neither a call or a return is called *internal*. A *nested word* n over an alphabet Σ is a pair $(a_1 \ldots a_\ell, \leadsto)$, such that a_i, for each $1 \leq i \leq \ell$, is a symbol in Σ, and $\leadsto$ is a nesting relation of length ℓ.

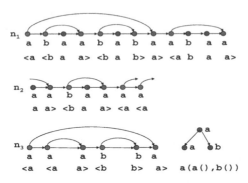

Fig. 1. Sample nested words

This nesting structure can be uniquely represented by a sequence specifying the types of positions (calls, returns, and internals). In particular, we assume that $\langle$ and $\rangle$ are special symbols that do not appear in the alphabet Σ. Then, define the *tagged alphabet* $\hat{\Sigma}$ to be the set that contains the symbols $\langle a$, a, and $a \rangle$ for each $a \in \Sigma$. Given a nested word over Σ, we can map it to a word over $\hat{\Sigma}$: at every call position labeled a, output $\langle a$; at every return position labeled a, output $a \rangle$; and at every internal position labeled a, output a. This correspondence between nested words and words over tagged symbols is a bijection. Figure 1 shows some nested words over the alphabet $\{a, b\}$ along with their linear encodings.

Finite-state acceptors over nested words can process both linear and hierarchical structure. A *nested word automaton* (NWA) A over an alphabet Σ consists of a finite set Q of states, an initial state $q_0 \in Q$, a set of final states $F \subseteq Q$, a call-transition function $\delta_c : Q \times \Sigma \mapsto Q \times Q$, an internal-transition function $\delta_i : Q \times \Sigma \mapsto Q$, and a return-transition function $\delta_r : Q \times Q \times \Sigma \mapsto Q$. The automaton A starts in the initial state, and reads the nested word from left to right. The state is propagated along the linear edges as in case of a standard word automaton. However, at a call, the nested word automaton can propagate a state along the outgoing nesting edge also. At a return, the new state is determined based on the states propagated along the linear as well as the nesting incoming edges. Formally, a *run* r of the automaton A over a nested word $n = (a_1 \ldots a_\ell, \leadsto)$ is a linear sequence $q_0, \ldots, q_\ell$ of states and a nesting sequence q_{ij}, for $i \leadsto j$, of states such that for each position $1 \leq i \leq \ell$, if i is a call with $i \leadsto j$, then $\delta_c(q_{i-1}, a_i) = (q_i, q_{ij})$; if i is an internal, then $\delta_i(q_{i-1}, a_i) = q_i$; and if i is a return such that $j \leadsto i$, then $\delta_r(q_{i-1}, q_{ji}, a_i) = q_i$, where if $j = -\infty$ then $q_{ji} = q_0$. For a given nested word n, the automaton has precisely one run over n. The automaton A accepts the nested word n if in this run, $q_\ell \in F$. The language $L(A)$ of a nested-word automaton A is the set of nested words it accepts. The resulting class of *regular* languages of nested words seems to have all the appealing theoretical properties that the classes of classical regular word and tree languages enjoy.

It is easy to see that if L is a regular language of nested words, then the corresponding language of words over tagged symbols is a context-free language.

This is because a nested word automaton can be interpreted as a pushdown automaton over words: call transitions can be simulated by pushing the state along nesting edge, and return transitions can access this state by popping the stack. Languages of words with well-bracketed structure have been studied as Dyck languages and *parenthesis* languages, and shown to have some special properties compared to context-free languages (for example, decidable equivalence problem) [McN67, Knu67]. The new insight is that the matching among left and right parenthesis can be considered to be an explicit component of the input structure, and this leads to a robust notion of regular languages using finite-state acceptors.

There is an emerging and growing body of literature studying nested word automata, and we review some of the results below.

Closure: The class of regular languages of nested words is (effectively) closed under union, intersection, complementation, concatenation, and Kleene-∗. If L is a regular language of nested words then all the following languages are regular: the set of all prefixes of all the words in L; the set of all suffixes of all the words in L; the set of reversals of all the words in L. Regular languages are closed under tree-like operations that use hierarchical structure.

Determinization: A *nondeterministic* NWA A has finite set Q of states, a set of initial states $Q_0 \subseteq Q$, a set $F \subseteq Q$ of final states, a call-transition relation $\delta_c \subseteq Q \times \Sigma \times Q \times Q$, an internal-transition relation $\delta_i \subseteq Q \times \Sigma \times Q$, and a return-transition relation $\delta_r \subseteq Q \times Q \times \Sigma \times Q$. The automaton now has a choice at every step, and accepts a word if one of the possible runs accepts. Nondeterministic nested word automata are no more expressive than the deterministic ones: given a nondeterministic automaton A with s states, one can effectively construct a deterministic NWA B with 2^{s^2} states such that $L(B) = L(A)$. The construction is a generalization of the classical subset construction for determinizing word automata, and a state of B is set of pairs of states of A.

Logic based characterization: The classical correspondence between monadic second order logic and finite recognizability for words and trees continues to hold for nested words. The *monadic second-order logic of nested words* (MSO) is given by the syntax:

$$\phi := Q_a(x) \mid x \leq y \mid x \rightsquigarrow y \mid \phi \vee \phi \mid \neg \phi \mid \exists x.\phi \mid \exists X.\phi,$$

where $a \in \Sigma$, x, y are first-order variables, and X is a second order variable. The semantics is defined over nested words in a natural way. A language L of nested words over Σ is regular iff there is an MSO sentence ϕ over Σ such that L is the set of all nested words that satisfy ϕ.

The correspondence between linear temporal logic and first-order logic continues to hold too. The logic *Nested Word Temporal Logic* (NWTL) has atomic propositions, logical connectives, the linear *next* and *previous* operators, the hierarchical next and previous operators (e.g., "hierarchical-next φ" holds at a call position iff φ holds at the matching return), and *until* and *since* operators that are interpreted over the "summary" paths. The summary path between two positions i and j is the shortest path in the graph of the nested word: if the summary path from i to j reaches a call position k such that $i \leq k \rightsquigarrow k' \leq j$, then it will follow the nesting edge from k to k'. A language L of nested words is definable in first-order logic of nested words (that is, the logic above without the second-order variables X) iff it is expressible in the temporal logic NWTL [AAB$^+$07].

Decision problems: Given a nested word automaton A and a nested word n, the membership problem (is n in $L(A)$?) can be solved in linear time. The space required is proportional to the depth of n since one needs to remember the labeling of pending nesting edges at every position. If A is nondeterministic, membership problem can be solved in time $O(|A|^3 \ell)$ using dynamic programming similar to the one used for membership for pushdown word automata.

The emptiness problem for nested word automata(is $L(A)$ empty?) can be solved in cubic time using techniques similar to the ones used for pushdown word automata or tree automata.

Problems such as language inclusion and language equivalence are decidable. These problems can be solved using constructions for complementation and language intersection, and emptiness test. If one of the automata is nondeterministic, then this would require determinization, and both language inclusion and equivalence are EXPTIME-complete for nondeterministic NWAs.

4   Revised Formulation of Software Model Checking

Traditionally, execution of a program is modeled as a word over an alphabet Σ, where the choice of Σ depends on the desired level of detail. As an example, suppose we are interested in tracking read/write accesses to a program variable x. Then, we can choose the following set of symbols: rd to denote a read access to x, wr to denote a write access to x, en to denote beginning of a new scope (such as a call to a function or a procedure), and ex to denote the ending of the current scope, and sk to denote all other actions of the program. A program P generates, then, a set $L(P)$ of words over this alphabet. The specification S is given as a set of "desirable" words, and verification corresponds to checking whether the inclusion $L(P) \subseteq S$ holds. Since typical programming languages are Turing complete, the verification problem is undecidable. The first step in algorithmic program verification is to approximate a program using *data abstraction*, where the data in a program is abstracted using a finite set of boolean variables that stand for predicates on the data-space [SH97,BMMR01,HJM$^+$02]. The resulting model P' hence has finite data and stack-based control flow (see Boolean programs [BR00] and recursive state machines [ABE$^+$05] as concrete instances of pushdown models of programs). The language $L(P')$ is a context-free language of words. If the specification S is a regular language, then the verification question $L(P') \subseteq S$ can be solved. Consider the requirement that every write access is followed by a read access. This can be expressed by the LTL formula $\Box(wr \rightarrow \Diamond rd)$, and is indeed a regular property. However, if we want to express the requirement that "if a procedure writes to x, it must read x," we must capture the scope of each procedure by matching of en and ex symbols, and the requirement is not a regular language, and thus, not expressible in the specification languages supported by existing software model checkers such as SLAM [BR00] and BLAST [HJM+02]. The specification is a context-free language, but this is not useful for algorithmic verification since context-free languages are not closed under intersection, and decision problems such as language inclusion and emptiness of intersection of two languages are undecidable for context-free languages.

In the revised formulation, an execution is modeled as a nested word. In addition to the linear sequence of symbols given by the program execution, from each entry symbol en, there is a nesting edge to the matching exit symbol ex. Following the nesting edge corresponds to skipping the called procedure, and a path that uses only nesting and internal edges gives the part of the execution that is local to a procedure. We can interpret the abstracted program P' as a nested word automaton, and associate with it a regular language $L'(P')$ of nested words. It is worth noting that, in general, pushdown models can be interpreted as nested word automata as syntactically the two definitions are same (in NWAs, stack alphabet coincides with the set of states, acceptance is by final state, call transitions are same as push transitions, and return transitions are same as pop transitions). The difference is only in the semantics: pushdown automata define word languages while NWAs define nested word languages.

The specification, now, is given as a language S' over nested words, and verification reduces to the language-inclusion problem for nested words: $L'(P') \subseteq S'$. The question is solvable as long as S' is a regular language of nested words. Clearly, every regular language of words is also a regular language of nested words. The requirement that "if a procedure writes to x, it must read x" also becomes regular now, and there is a natural two-state deterministic nested-word automaton that specifies it. The initial state is q_0, and has no pending obligations, and is the only final state. The state q_1 denotes that along the local path of the current scope, a write-access has been encountered, with no following read access. The transitions are: for $j = 0, 1$, $\delta_i(q_j, rd) = q_0$; $\delta_i(q_j, wr) = q_1$; $\delta_i(q_j, sk) = q_j$; $\delta_c(q_j, en) = (q_0, q_j)$; and $\delta_r(q_0, q_j, ex) = q_j$. The automaton reinitializes the state to q_0 upon entry, while processing internal read/write symbols, it updates the state as in a finite-state word automaton, and at a return, if the current state is q_0 (meaning the called context satisfies the desired requirement), it restores the state of the calling context.

Further, we can design temporal logics for programs that exploit the nested structure. An example of such a temporal logic is CARET [AEM04], which extends linear temporal logic by *local* modalities such as $\bigcirc^a \phi$, which holds at a call if the return-successor of the call satisfies ϕ. The formula $\square(wr \rightarrow \lozenge^a rd)$ captures the specification "if a procedure writes to x, it must read x." CARET can state many interesting properties of programs, including stack-inspection properties, pre-post conditions of programs, local flows in programs, etc. Analogous to the theorem that a linear temporal formula can be compiled into an automaton that accepts its models [VW94], any CARET formula can be compiled into a nested word automaton that accepts its models. Decidability of inclusion then yields a decidable model-checking problem for program models against CaRet [AM04, AEM04].

Software model checking tools such as SLAM and BLAST support an assertion language for writing monitors checking for violations of safety properties. The monitor M is observing the executions of P, and reaches an error state if an undesirable execution is detected. The verification question is to check if the monitor can reach an error state. Given a C program P and a monitor M written in the query language, the model checker first constructs an annotated C program P' such that the verification problem reduces to analysis of P'. While current assertion languages for monitors support automata over words, now we can strengthen them to allow automata over nested words. The transformation of P to the annotated program P', to account for M, can be done with equal ease even for this more expressive language. The resulting program P' can be subjected to different analysis techniques such as testing, runtime monitoring, static analysis, and model checking. Thus, the nested-word formulation can be useful for any analysis technique. Even though we have emphasized pushdown models in the theory of nested words, the proposed reformulation is useful even if programs are not recursive as long as they are structured with stack-based control flow.

5   Fixpoints for Local and Global Program Flows

In the branching-time approach to program verification, a program P is modeled by an unranked unordered infinite tree T_P such that nodes in T_P are labeled with program states, and paths in T_P correspond to executions of P. The branching-time specification specifies the set S of desirable trees, and model checking corresponds to the membership test $T_P \in S$. The μ-calculus [Koz83] is a modal logic with fixpoints, and is an extensively studied branching-time specification formalism with applications to program analysis, computer-aided verification, and database query languages [Eme90, Sti91]. From a theoretical perspective, its status as the *canonical* temporal logic for regular requirements is due to the fact that its expressiveness exceeds all commonly used temporal logics such as LTL, CTL, and CTL*, and equals *alternating parity tree automata* or the bisimulation-closed fragment of monadic second-order theory over trees [EJ91, JW96]. From a practical standpoint, iterative computation of fixpoints naturally suggests symbolic evaluation, and symbolic model checkers such as SMV check CTL properties of finite-state models by compiling them into μ-calculus formulas [BCD+92, McM93].

There are at least three reasons that motivated us to extend the theory of nested words to the branching-time case. First, while algorithmic verification of μ-calculus properties of pushdown models is possible [Wal01, BS99], classical μ-calculus cannot express pushdown specifications that require inspection of the stack or matching of calls and returns. This raises the question about the right theoretical extension of μ-calculus that can capture CaRet and nested word automata. Second, in the program analysis literature, it has been argued that data flow analysis, such as the computation of live variables and very busy expressions, can be viewed as evaluating μ-calculus formulas over abstractions of programs [Ste91, Sch98]. This correspondence does not hold when we need to account for *local* data flow paths. For instance, for an expression e that involves a variable local to a procedure P, the set of control points within P at which e is very busy (that is, e is guaranteed to be used before any of its variables get modified), cannot be specified using a μ-calculus formula even though interprocedural dataflow analysis can compute this information. Can we extend μ-calculus so that it can capture interprocedural dataflow analysis? Finally, the standard reachability property "some p-state is reachable" is expressed by the μ-calculus formula $\varphi = \mu X.(p \vee \bigcirc X)$. The meaning of φ is the smallest set X such that if a state satisfies p or has a successor in X then it is in X. While this formula captures reachability over all models, over finite-state models, the specification also encodes the symbolic algorithm for computing the set of states satisfying φ by successive approximations of the fixpoint: let X_0 to be the set of states satisfying p, and at each step i, compute X_{i+1} from X_i by adding states that can reach X_i in one step (termination is obtained when $X_i = X_{i+1}$). Over pushdown models, such a computation may not terminate. The correct way to compute reachability, as implemented in dataflow analysis or tools such as SLAM, is based on "summarization" of paths. The summarization algorithm can be viewed as a fixpoint computation over pairs of states of the form (x, y) meaning that state y is reachable if the current procedure is called with input state x. This raises the question if there is a different way of expressing reachability over pushdown models.

A *nested tree* is a labeled tree T augmented with a nesting relation $\rightsquigarrow$ over the vertices of T such that every path through the tree is a nested word (see [ACM06a] for precise definition). In context of program verification, the tree T_P corresponding to a program P, will be unranked, unordered, and infinite, and the nesting relation is obtained by adding edges from call nodes to matching returns. Note that a call node can have multiple matching returns (and, no matching returns along some paths corresponding to executions in which the called procedure does not return). It turns out there is an appealing fixpoint calculus NT_μ over nested trees that has the following properties:

1. The model-checking problem for NT_μ is effectively solvable against pushdown models with no more effort than that required for weaker logics such as CTL (EXPTIME-complete).

2. Evaluating NT_μ formulas over pushdown models captures the standard summary-based analysis algorithms, and thus, expressing a property in NT_μ amounts to describing symbolic computation for evaluation.

3. The logic NT_μ encompasses all properties expressed by nested word automata as well as by the classical μ-calculus. This makes NT_μ the most expressive known program logic for which algorithmic software model checking is feasible. In fact, the decidability of most known program logics (μ-calculus, temporal logics LTL and CTL, CARET, etc.) can be understood by their

interpretation in the monadic second-order logic over trees. This is not true for the logic NT_μ, making it a new powerful tractable program logic.

4. The logic NT_μ can capture local as well as global program flows, and thus, interprocedural dataflow analysis problems can be stated in NT_μ.

5. Expressiveness of NT_μ coincides with *alternating parity automata* over nested trees (APNTA). An APNTA is a finite-state tree automaton such that (a) its transition relation is alternating, so along an edge it can send multiple copies, (b) its acceptance condition is defined using parity condition over the infinite run, and (c) like a nested word automaton, at a call node, the automaton sends states to the immediate tree successor as well as to the return successors along nesting edges, and at a return node, the state can depend on the state at the immediate tree parent as well as the state along the nesting edge from the matching call parent.

6. While the correspondence between alternating tree automata and fixpoint calculus holds as in the classical tree case, the correspondence between monadic second order logic and fixpoint calculus fails: the monadic second order logic over nested trees and NT_μ seem to have incomparable expressiveness (though this is not proved formally yet). Both logics have undecidable satisfiability problem [ACM06b].

We intuitively describe the logic NT_μ below. The variables of the calculus evaluate not over sets of vertices, but rather over sets of subtrees that capture *summaries* of computations in the "current" program block. The fixpoint operators in the logic then compute fixpoints of summaries. For a given vertex s of a nested tree, consider the subtree rooted at s such that the leaves correspond to the matching returns as specified by the nesting relation (while modeling program, such a subtree captures all the computations till the procedure that s belongs to returns). In order to be able to relate paths in this subtree to the trees rooted at the leaves, we allow marking of the leaves: a 1-ary summary is specified by the root s and a subset U of the leaves of the subtree rooted at s. Each formula of the logic is evaluated over such a summary. The central construct of the logic corresponds to concatenation of call trees: the formula $\langle call \rangle \varphi \{\psi\}$ holds at a summary $\langle s, U \rangle$ if the vertex s has a call-edge to a vertex t, and there exists a summary $\langle t, V \rangle$ satisfying φ and for each leaf v that belongs to V, the subtree $\langle v, U \rangle$ satisfies ψ.

This logic is best explained using the specification of local reachability: let us identify the set of all summaries $\langle s, U \rangle$ such that there is a *local* path from s to some node in U (i.e. all calls from the initial procedure must have returned before reaching U). In our logic, this is written as the formula $\varphi = \mu X. \langle ret \rangle R_1 \vee \langle loc \rangle X \vee \langle call \rangle X \{X\}$. The above means that X is the smallest set of summaries of the form $\langle s, U \rangle$ such that (1) there is a return-edge from s to some node in U, (2) there is an internal edge from s to t and there is a summary $\langle t, U \rangle$ in X, or (3) there is a call-edge from s to t and a summary $\langle t, V \rangle$ in X such that from each $v \in V$, $\langle v, U \rangle$ is a summary in X. Notice that the above formula identifies the summaries in the natural way it will be *computed* on a pushdown system:

compute the local summaries of each procedure, and update the reachability relation using the call-to-return summaries found in the procedures called.

Using the above formula, we can state local reachability of a state satisfying p as: $\mu Y.(p \vee \langle loc \rangle Y \vee \langle call \rangle \varphi\{Y\})$ which intuitively states that Y is the set of summaries (s, U) where there is a local path from s to U that goes through a state satisfying p. The initial summary (involving the initial state of the program) satisfies the formula only if a p-labeled state is reachable in the top-most context, which cannot be stated in the standard μ-calculus. This example also illustrates how local flows in the context of dataflow analysis can be captured using our logic.

6   Modeling and Processing Linear-Hierarchical Data

While nested words were motivated by program verification, they can potentially be used to model data with the dual–linear and hierarchical, structure. Such dual structure exists naturally in many contexts including XML documents, annotated linguistic data, and primary/secondary bonds in genomic sequences. Also, in some applications, even though the only logical structure on data is hierarchical, linear sequencing is added either for storage or for stream processing. Data with linear-hierarchical structure is traditionally modeled using binary (or more generally, ordered) trees and queried using tree automata (see [Nev02, Lib05, Sch04] for recent surveys on applications of tree automata and tree logics to document processing).

Even though tree models and tree automata are extensively studied with a well-developed theory with appealing properties (see [CDG$^+$02]), they seem ill suited to capture and query the linear structure. First, tree-based approach implicitly assumes that the input linear document can be parsed into a tree, and thus, one cannot represent and process data that may not parse correctly. Word operations such as prefixes, suffixes, and concatenation, while natural for document processing, do not have analogous tree operations. Second, tree automata do not generalize word automata. Finite-state word automata can be exponentially more succinct than tree automata. For example, the query that patterns $p_1, \ldots p_n$ appear in the document in that order (that is, the regular expression $\Sigma^* p_1 \Sigma^* \ldots p_n \Sigma^*$) compiles into a deterministic word automaton with $n + 1$ states, but standard deterministic bottom-up tree automaton for this query must be of size exponential in n. This deficiency shows up more dramatically if we consider pushdown acceptors: a query such as "the document contains an equal number of occurrences of patterns p and q" is a context-free word language but is not a context-free tree language.

In a nutshell, binary/ordered trees encode both linear and hierarchical structure, but not on an equal footing. Recently we have argued that the model of nested words is a better integration of the two orderings, and can either simplify or improve existing ways of document processing [KMV06b, Alu07]. We have already seen that words are nested words where all positions are internals. Ordered trees can be interpreted as nested words using the following traversal:

to process an a-labeled node, first print an a-labeled call, process all children in order, and print an a-labeled return. Binary trees, ranked trees, unranked trees, forests, and documents that do not parse correctly, all can be represented with equal ease. Figure 1 shows the ordered tree corresponding to the third nested word, the first two do not correspond to trees.

Since XML documents already contain tags that specify the position type, they can be interpreted as tagged encoding of nested words without any pre-processing. As we have seen already, the class of regular languages of nested words seems to have all the appealing theoretical properties that the classes of classical regular word and tree languages enjoy, and decision problems such as membership, emptiness, language inclusion, and language equivalence are all decidable, typically with the same complexity as the corresponding problem for tree automata.

In order to study the relationship of nested word automata to various kinds of word and tree automata, let us consider restricted classes of nested word automata and the impact of these restrictions on expressiveness and succinctness [Alu07]. *Flat* automata do not propagate information along the nesting edges at calls, and correspond exactly to classical word automata accepting the weaker class of regular word languages. *Bottom-up* automata, on the other hand, do not propagate information along the linear edges at calls. Over the subclass of nested words corresponding to ordered trees, these automata correspond exactly to bottom-up tree automata for binary trees and stepwise bottom-up tree automata [BKMW01] for unranked trees. However, there is an exponential price in terms of succinctness due to this restriction. The class of *joinless* automata avoids a nontrivial join of information along the linear and nesting edges at returns, and this concept is a generalization of the classical top-down tree automata. While deterministic joinless automata are strictly less expressive, nondeterministic ones can accept all regular languages of nested words. The succinctness gap between nested word automata and traditional tree automata holds even if we restrict attention to paths (that is, unary trees): nested word automata are exponentially more succinct than both bottom-up and top-down automata. We have also studied *pushdown nested word automata* by adding a stack to the finite-state control of nondeterministic joinless automata. Both pushdown word automata and pushdown tree automata are special cases, but pushdown nested word automata are strictly more expressive than both. In terms of complexity of analysis problems, they are similar to pushdown tree automata: membership is NP-complete and emptiness is EXPTIME-complete.

These results suggest that nested words and nested word automata may be a more suitable way to model and process linear-hierarchical data. We need to explore if compiling existing XML query languages into nested word automata reduces query processing time in practice.

Acknowledgements. I would also like to thank Marcelo Arenas, Pablo Barcelo, Swarat Chaudhuri, Kousha Etessami, Neil Immerman, Leonid Libkin, P. Madhusudan, Benjamin Pierce, and Mahesh Viswanathan, for past and ongoing research collaboration on nested words.

References

[AAB+07]   Alur, R., Arenas, M., Barcelo, P., Etessami, K., Immerman, N., Libkin, L.:
            First-order and temporal logics for nested words (unpublished manuscript,
            2007)

[ABE+05]   Alur, R., Benedikt, M., Etessami, K., Godefroid, P., Reps, T., Yannakakis,
            M.: Analysis of recursive state machines. ACM Transactions on Program-
            ming Languages and Systems 27(4), 786–818 (2005)

[ACD93]   Alur, R., Courcoubetis, C., Dill, D.L.: Model-checking in dense real-time.
            Information and Computation 104(1), 2–34 (1993)

[ACM06a]   Alur, R., Chaudhuri, S., Madhusudan, P.: A fixpoint calculus for local and
            global program flows. In: Proceedings of the 33rd Annual ACM Symposium
            on Principles of Programming Languages, pp. 153–165 (2006)

[ACM06b]   Alur, R., Madhusudan, P., Chaudhuri, S.: Languages of Nested Trees. In:
            Ball, T., Jones, R.B. (eds.) CAV 2006. LNCS, vol. 4144, pp. 329–342.
            Springer, Heidelberg (2006)

[AD94]   Alur, R., Dill, D.L.: A theory of timed automata. Theoretical Computer
            Science 126, 183–235 (1994)

[AEM04]   Alur, R., Etessami, K., Madhusudan, P.: A Temporal Logic of Nested
            Calls and Returns. In: Jensen, K., Podelski, A. (eds.) TACAS 2004. LNCS,
            vol. 2988, pp. 467–481. Springer, Heidelberg (2004)

[AH93]   Alur, R., Henzinger, T.A.: Real-time logics: complexity and expressiveness.
            Information and Computation 104(1), 35–77 (1993)

[AH94]   Alur, R., Henzinger, T.A.: A really temporal logic. Journal of the
            ACM 41(1), 181–204 (1994)

[AHK02]   Alur, R., Henzinger, T.A., Kupferman, O.: Alternating-time temporal
            logic. Journal of the ACM 49(5), 1–42 (2002)

[AHLP00]   Alur, R., Henzinger, T.A., Lafferriere, G., Pappas, G.: Discrete abstrac-
            tions of hybrid systems. Proceedings of the IEEE 88(7), 971–984 (2000)

[AKMV05]   Alur, R., Madhusudan, P., Viswanathan, M., Kumar, V.: Congruences for
            Visibly Pushdown Languages. In: Caires, L., Italiano, G.F., Monteiro, L.,
            Palamidessi, C., Yung, M. (eds.) ICALP 2005. LNCS, vol. 3580, pp. 1102–
            1114. Springer, Heidelberg (2005)

[Alu07]   Alur, R.: Marrying words and trees (unpublished manuscript, 2007)

[AM04]   Alur, R., Madhusudan, P.: Visibly pushdown languages. In: Proceedings of
            the 36th ACM Symposium on Theory of Computing, pp. 202–211 (2004)

[AM06]   Alur, R., Madhusudan, P.: Adding Nesting Structure to Words. In: H.
            Ibarra, O., Dang, Z. (eds.) DLT 2006. LNCS, vol. 4036, pp. 1–13. Springer,
            Heidelberg (2006)

[BCD+92]   Burch, J.R., Clarke, E.M., Dill, D.L., Hwang, L.J., McMillan, K.L.: Sym-
            bolic model checking: 10^{20} states and beyond. Information and Computa-
            tion 98(2), 142–170 (1992)

[BEM97]   Boujjani, A., Esparza, J., Maler, O.: Reachability analysis of pushdown au-
            tomata: Applications to model checking. In: Mazurkiewicz, A., Winkowski,
            J. (eds.) CONCUR 1997. LNCS, vol. 1243, pp. 135–150. Springer, Heidel-
            berg (1997)

[BKMW01]   Brüggemann-Klein, A., Murata, M., Wood, D.: Regular tree and regu-
            lar hedge languages over unranked alphabets: Version 1. Technical Report
            HKUST-TCSC-2001-0, The Hongkong University of Science and Technol-
            ogy (2001)

[BMMR01] Ball, T., Majumdar, R., Millstein, T.D., Rajamani, S.K.: Automatic predi-
          cate abstraction of C programs. In: SIGPLAN Conference on Programming
          Language Design and Implementation, pp. 203–213 (2001)
[BR00]   Ball, T., Rajamani, S.: Bebop: A symbolic model checker for boolean pro-
          grams. In: Havelund, K., Penix, J., Visser, W. (eds.) SPIN 2000. LNCS,
          vol. 1885, pp. 113–130. Springer, Heidelberg (2000)
[BR01]   Ball, T., Rajamani, S.: The SLAM toolkit. In: Computer Aided Verifica-
          tion, 13th International Conference (2001)
[BS92]   Burkart, O., Steffen, B.: Model checking for context-free processes. In:
          Cleaveland, W.R. (ed.) CONCUR 1992. LNCS, vol. 630, pp. 123–137.
          Springer, Heidelberg (1992)
[BS99]   Burkart, O., Steffen, B.: Model checking the full modal mu-calculus for
          infinite sequential processes. Theoretical Computer Science 221, 251–270
          (1999)
[Büc62]   Büchi, J.R.: On a decision method in restricted second-order arithmetic.
          In: Proceedings of the International Congress on Logic, Methodology, and
          Philosophy of Science 1960, pp. 1–12. Stanford University Press (1962)
[Cau03]   Caucal, D.: On infinite transition graphs having a decidable monadic the-
          ory. Theoretical Computer Science 290(1), 79–115 (2003)
[CDG+02] Comon, H., Dauchet, M., Gilleron, R., Lugiez, D., Tison, S., Tom-
          masi, M.: Tree automata techniques and applications. Draft (2002),
          http://www.grappa.univ-lille3.fr/tata/
[CE81]   Clarke, E.M., Emerson, E.A.: Design and synthesis of synchronization
          skeletons using branching time temporal logic. In: Kozen, D. (ed.) Logic
          of Programs 1981. LNCS, vol. 131, pp. 52–71. Springer, Heidelberg (1982)
[CL99]   Cassandras, C.G., Lafortune, S.: Introduction to discrete event systems.
          Kluwer Academic Publishers, Dordrecht (1999)
[CMM+04] Chatterjee, K., Ma, D., Majumdar, R., Zhao, T., Henzinger, T.A., Pals-
          berg, J.: Stack size analysis for interrupt driven programs. Information and
          Computation 194(2), 144–174 (2004)
[CW02]   Chen, H., Wagner, D.: Mops: an infrastructure for examining security prop-
          erties of software. In: Proceedings of ACM Conference on Computer and
          Communications Security, pp. 235–244 (2002)
[DOTY96] Daws, C., Olivero, A., Tripakis, S., Yovine, S.: The tool KRONOS. In:
          Alur, R., Sontag, E.D., Henzinger, T.A. (eds.) HS 1995. LNCS, vol. 1066,
          pp. 208–219. Springer, Heidelberg (1996)
[EHRS00] Esparza, J., Hansel, D., Rossmanith, P., Schwoon, S.: Efficient algorithms
          for model checking pushdown systems. In: Emerson, E.A., Sistla, A.P.
          (eds.) CAV 2000. LNCS, vol. 1855, pp. 232–247. Springer, Heidelberg
          (2000)
[EJ91]   Emerson, E.A., Jutla, C.S.: Tree automata, mu-calculus, and determinacy.
          In: Proceedings of the 32nd IEEE Symposium on Foundations of Computer
          Science, pp. 368–377 (1991)
[EKS03]   Esparza, J., Kucera, A., Schwoon, S.S.: Model-checking LTL with regular
          valuations for pushdown systems. Information and Computation 186(2),
          355–376 (2003)
[Eme90]   Emerson, E.A.: Temporal and modal logic. In: van Leeuwen, J. (ed.) Hand-
          book of Theoretical Computer Science, vol. B, pp. 995–1072. Elsevier Sci-
          ence Publishers, Amsterdam (1990)

[HJM+02]   Henzinger, T.A., Jhala, R., Majumdar, R., Necula, G.C., Sutre, G., Weimer, W.: Temporal-Safety Proofs for Systems Code. In: Brinksma, E., Larsen, K.G. (eds.) CAV 2002. LNCS, vol. 2404, pp. 526–538. Springer, Heidelberg (2002)

[Hol97]   Holzmann, G.J.: The model checker SPIN. IEEE Transactions on Software Engineering 23(5), 279–295 (1997)

[HRS98]   Henzinger, T.A., Raskin, J.-F., Schobbens, P.: The Regular Real-Time Languages. In: Larsen, K.G., Skyum, S., Winskel, G. (eds.) ICALP 1998. LNCS, vol. 1443, pp. 580–593. Springer, Heidelberg (1998)

[HU79]   Hopcroft, J.E., Ullman, J.D.: Introduction to Automata Theory, Languages, and Computation. Addison-Wesley (1979)

[JMT99]   Jensen, T., Le Metayer, D., Thorn, T.: Verification of control flow based security properties. In: Proceedings of the IEEE Symposium on Security and Privacy, pp. 89–103 (1999)

[JW96]   Janin, D., Walukiewicz, I.: On the expressive completeness of the propositional mu- calculus with respect to monadic second order logic. In: Sassone, V., Montanari, U. (eds.) CONCUR 1996. LNCS, vol. 1119, pp. 263–277. Springer, Heidelberg (1996)

[Kam68]   Kamp, J.: Tense Logic and the Theory of Linear Order. PhD thesis, University of California, Los Angeles (1968)

[KMV06a]   Kumar, V., Madhusudan, P., Viswanathan, M.: Minimization, Learning, and Conformance Testing of Boolean Programs. In: Baier, C., Hermanns, H. (eds.) CONCUR 2006. LNCS, vol. 4137, pp. 203–217. Springer, Heidelberg (2006)

[KMV06b]   Kumar, V., Madhusudan, P., Viswanathan, M.: Visibly pushdown languages for XML. Technical Report UIUCDCS-R-2006-2704, UIUC (2006)

[Knu67]   Knuth, D.E.: A characterization of parenthesis languages. Information and Control 11(3), 269–289 (1967)

[Koz83]   Kozen, D.: Results on the propositional mu-calculus. Theoretical Computer Science 27, 333–354 (1983)

[KPV02]   Kupferman, O., Piterman, N., Vardi, M.Y.: Model Checking Linear Properties of Prefix-Recognizable Systems. In: Brinksma, E., Larsen, K.G. (eds.) CAV 2002. LNCS, vol. 2404, pp. 371–385. Springer, Heidelberg (2002)

[Kur94]   Kurshan, R.P.: Computer-aided Verification of Coordinating Processes: the automata-theoretic approach. Princeton University Press (1994)

[KVW00]   Kupferman, O., Vardi, M.Y., Wolper, P.: An automata-theoretic approach to branching-time model checking. Journal of the ACM 47(2), 312–360 (2000)

[KVW01]   Kupferman, O., Vardi, M.Y., Wolper, P.: Module checking. Information and Computation 164(2), 322–344 (2001)

[Lib05]   Libkin, L.: Logics for Unranked Trees: An Overview. In: Caires, L., Italiano, G.F., Monteiro, L., Palamidessi, C., Yung, M. (eds.) ICALP 2005. LNCS, vol. 3580, pp. 35–50. Springer, Heidelberg (2005)

[LPY97]   Larsen, K., Pettersson, P., Yi, W.: UPPAAL in a nutshell. Springer International Journal of Software Tools for Technology Transfer 1 (1997)

[LV02]   Lee, E.A., Varaiya, P.: Structure and interpretation of signals and systems. Addison-Wesley (2002)

[McM93]   McMillan, K.L.: Symbolic model checking: an approach to the state explosion problem. Kluwer Academic Publishers (1993)

[McN67]   McNaughton, R.: Parenthesis grammars. Journal of the ACM 14(3), 490–500 (1967)

[Mil89]   Milner, R.: Communication and Concurrency. Prentice-Hall (1989)

[MS85]   Muller, D.E., Schupp, P.E.: The theory of ends, pushdown automata, and second-order logic. Theoretical Computer Science 37, 51–75 (1985)

[Nev02]   Neven, F.: Automata, Logic, and XML. In: Bradfield, J.C. (ed.) CSL 2002 and EACSL 2002. LNCS, vol. 2471, pp. 2–26. Springer, Heidelberg (2002)

[PS02]   Pappas, G.J., Simic, S.: Consistent abstractions of affine control systems. IEEE Transactions on Automatic Control 47(5), 745–756 (2002)

[PSL05]   IEEE 1850 standard for property specification language (PSL) (2005)

[Rab69]   Rabin, M.O.: Decidability of second order theories and automata on infinite trees. Transactions of the AMS 141, 1–35 (1969)

[Rep98]   Reps, T.: Program analysis via graph reachability. Information and Software Technology 40(11-12), 701–726 (1998)

[RHS95]   Reps, T., Horwitz, S., Sagiv, S.: Precise interprocedural dataflow analysis via graph reachability. In: Proceedings of the ACM Symposium on Principles of Programming Languages, pp. 49–61 (1995)

[Sch98]   Schmidt, D.A.: Data flow analysis is model checking of abstract interpretations. In: Proceedings of the 25th Annual ACM Symposium on Principles of Programming Languages, pp. 68–78 (1998)

[Sch04]   Schwentick, T.: Automata for XML – a survey. Technical report, University of Dortmund (2004)

[SH97]   Graf, S., Saidi, H.: Construction of abstract state graphs with PVS. In: Grumberg, O. (ed.) CAV 1997. LNCS, vol. 1254, pp. 72–83. Springer, Heidelberg (1997)

[SP81]   Sharir, M., Pnueli, A.: Two approaches to inter-procedural data-flow analysis. In: Program flow analysis: Theory and applications. Prentice-Hall, Englewood Cliffs (1981)

[Ste91]   Steffen, B.: Data flow analysis as model checking. In: Ito, T., Meyer, A.R. (eds.) TACS 1991. LNCS, vol. 526, pp. 346–365. Springer, Heidelberg (1991)

[Sti91]   Stirling, C.S.: Modal and temporal logic. In: Handbook of Logic in Computer Science, pp. 477–563. Oxford University Press (1991)

[Tho90]   Thomas, W.: Automata on infinite objects. In: van Leeuwen, J. (ed.) Handbook of Theoretical Computer Science, vol. B, pp. 133–191. Elsevier Science Publishers (1990)

[Tho02]   Thomas, W.: Infinite Games and Verification. In: Brinksma, E., Larsen, K.G. (eds.) CAV 2002. LNCS, vol. 2404, pp. 58–64. Springer, Heidelberg (2002)

[VW94]   Vardi, M.Y., Wolper, P.: Reasoning about infinite computations. Information and Computation 115(1), 1–37 (1994)

[Wal01]   Walukiewicz, I.: Pushdown processes: Games and model-checking. Information and Computation 164(2), 234–263 (2001)

[WVS83]   Wolper, P., Vardi, M.Y., Sistla, A.P.: Reasoning about infinite computation paths. In: Proceedings of the 24th IEEE Symposium on Foundations of Computer Science, pp. 185–194 (1983)

Value Iteration*

Krishnendu Chatterjee[1] and Thomas A. Henzinger[1,2]

[1] University of California, Berkeley
[2] EPFL, Switzerland

Abstract. We survey value iteration algorithms on graphs. Such algorithms can be used for determining the existence of certain paths (*model checking*), the existence of certain strategies (*game solving*), and the probabilities of certain events (*performance analysis*). We classify the algorithms according to the value domain (boolean, probabilistic, or quantitative); according to the graph structure (nondeterministic, probabilistic, or multi-player); according to the desired property of paths (Borel level 1, 2, or 3); and according to the alternation depth and convergence rate of fixpoint computations.

1 Introduction

Symbolic model checking is an instance of value iteration on graphs. In value iteration, each vertex of a graph is assigned a value, and the values are iteratively improved until a fixpoint is reached. The improvement function is local, meaning that the new, improved value at a vertex depends on the old values at neighboring vertices. For symbolic model checking, the value domain is a boolean algebra of atomic propositions. Termination is guaranteed if the number of vertices is finite.

We take a systematic look at value iteration along four dimensions. First, we consider three different *value domains*. In the boolean domain, a value represents the truth or falsehood of atomic propositions. In the probabilistic domain, a value represents a probability. In the quantitative domain, a value is a real number (possibly greater than 1) which represents a reward, i.e., some quantitative information associated with a vertex. In the two nonboolean cases, the termination of value iteration is not guaranteed even for finite sets of vertices. However, an acceleration towards the fixpoint may be possible to ensure finite convergence. If even this proves difficult, then we investigate whether by value iteration the fixpoint can be approximated within any given error bound.

Second, as carrier of values, we consider three different kinds of *graph structures*, and their combinations. Simple graphs are nondeterministic generators of paths. Game graphs generate paths according to the competitive decisions made by two players. Probabilistic graphs represent stochastic processes that generate paths. Over simple graphs, value iteration can be used to determine the existence of certain paths, e.g., paths that satisfy a specification; over game graphs, it can be

---

* This research was supported in part by the Swiss National Science Foundation and by the NSF grants CCR-0225610 and CCR-0234690.

O. Grumberg and H. Veith (Eds.): 25MC Festschrift, LNCS 5000, pp. 107–138, 2008.

used to determine the existence of certain strategies, e.g., strategies that achieve an objective; and over probabilistic graphs, it can be used to determine the probability of certain events, where an event is a measurable set of paths.

Third, we consider increasingly complex specifications, objectives, and events; for uniformity, we refer to all of these as *objectives*. Objectives can be classified according to their Borel complexity. The values of Borel level-1 objectives are determined by finite paths. For example, reachability and safety specifications are Borel level-1, and so are the objectives to maximize or minimize a one-time reward. The Borel level-2 objectives are the simplest objectives whose values depend on infinite paths. For example, deterministic Büchi and coBüchi specifications are Borel level-2, and so are the objectives to maximize or minimize an infinitely recurring reward (i.e., limsup and liminf objectives). More general kinds of objectives include ω-regular specifications (Borel level-$2\frac{1}{2}$), and objectives to maximize or minimize the average of infinitely many rewards (Borel level-3).

Fourth, we consider three increasingly complex *value iteration* (or *fixpoint computation*) *schemes*. Alternation-free value iteration computes an increasing or decreasing sequence of values at each vertex. Value iteration of alternation depth-1 computes an increasing sequence of decreasing value sequences (or vice versa). General value iteration arbitrarily alternates the successive approximation of least and greatest fixpoints. Alternation-free value iteration can be used to compute the values of Borel level-1 objectives (e.g., symbolic CTL model checking; solving reachability and safety games). Value iteration of alternation depth-1 can be used to compute the values of Borel level-2 objectives (e.g., symbolic CTL model checking on structures with weak-fairness constraints; solving Büchi and coBüchi games). General value iteration can be used to compute the values of ω-regular objectives (e.g., symbolic CTL model checking on structures with strong fairness constraints; LTL model checking; solving parity games). However, by adjusting the value domain, even the values of complex Borel objectives (e.g., parity games and limit-average games) can be computed by an alternation-free value iteration. In this paper we only survey and generalize some known results; there remains much room for a detailed investigation of the connections and trade-offs between the complexity of the value domain, the Borel level of the objective, and the alternation depth of the fixpoint computation.

Section 2 defines the graph structures we consider. Sections 3 and 4 present alternation-free value iteration for Borel level-1 objectives, and alternation depth-1 value iteration for Borel level-2 objectives. Section 5 provides some remarks on more general objectives. Section 6 concludes with thoughts on related topics, such as strategy iteration (as opposed to value iteration) and discounting.

2   Graph Models of Systems

The states and transitions of a system can be viewed as vertices and edges of a graph. Often the states carry values, such as truth values for observable propositions, or quantitative values that represent resource data (e.g., buffer size, power consumption). This leads us to the model of valued graphs.

2.1 Valued Graphs

A *valued graph* (S, E, D) consists of the following components.

1. A finite set S of *states*.

2. A binary *transition relation* $E \subseteq S \times S$. For a state $s \in S$, we write $E(s) = \{s' \in S \mid (s, s') \in E\}$ for the set of *successors*. We require that every state has at least one successor; that is, $E(s) \neq \emptyset$ for all $s \in S$.

3. A complete lattice D of *values*. In the cases that we consider in this paper, the value set D is a subset of the real numbers, and the lattice order is the usual ordering $\leq$ on the reals. We will encounter the following three cases.

   Boolean. The value set D is the set $\mathbb{B} = \{0, 1\}$ of booleans. The least upper bound is disjunction; the greatest lower bound, conjunction.

   Probabilistic. The value set D is the closed interval $[0, 1]$ of reals between 0 and 1. The least upper bound is max (for infinite sets, sup); the greatest lower bound, min (for infinite sets, inf).

   Quantitative. The value set D is the set $\mathbb{R}_{\geq 0}^{\infty} = \mathbb{R}_{\geq 0} \cup \{\infty\}$ of nonnegative reals together with the top element ∞. Upper and lower bounds are as in the probabilistic case.

Throughout the paper, we use $\boldsymbol{n} = |S|$ for the number of states, and $\boldsymbol{m} = |E|$ for the number of transitions. Note that $\boldsymbol{m} \geq \boldsymbol{n}$, because every state has a successor.

Valuations. A *valuation* is a function $v \colon S \to D$ that maps every state to a value. In the boolean case, where $D = \mathbb{B}$, a valuation corresponds to a set $v \subseteq S$ of states; in this case, for a valuation v and a state s, we use the two expressions "$v(s) = 1$" and "$s \in v$" interchangeably. We write V for the set of valuations. The ordering on values is lifted to valuations in a pointwise fashion: for two valuations $v_1, v_2 \in V$, we write $v_1 \leq v_2$ iff $v_1(s) \leq v_2(s)$ for all states $s \in S$. The valuations with ordering $\leq$ form a complete lattice. In this lattice, a *chain* is an infinite sequence $C = \langle v_0, v_1, v_2, \ldots \rangle$ of valuations such that either $v_0 \leq v_1 \leq v_2 \leq \cdots$, or $v_0 \geq v_1 \geq v_2 \geq \cdots$. In the former case, the chain is *increasing*, and $\lim C = \text{lub } C$ denotes its least upper bound; in the latter case, the chain is *decreasing*, and $\lim C = \text{glb } C$ denotes its greatest lower bound.

Objectives. A *path* is an infinite sequence $\langle s_0, s_1, s_2, \ldots \rangle$ of states such that $(s_i, s_{i+1}) \in E$ for all $i \geq 0$. We write Ω the set of paths, and Ω_s for the set of paths that start from a given state $s \in S$. An *objective* is a Borel function $W \colon \Omega \to D$ that maps every path to a value.[1] In the boolean case, an objective corresponds to a Borel set $W \subseteq \Omega$ of paths; in this case, for an objective W and a path ω, we use the two expressions "$W(\omega) = 1$" and "$\omega \in W$" interchangeably.

---

[1] We require objectives to be Borel (with respect to the Cantor topology on paths and the order topology on values) for measurability.

2.2 Generalized Graphs

We define several extensions of valued graphs: deterministic games; probabilistic graphs; probabilistic games; and concurrent games.

Deterministic games. A *deterministic game* consists of (1) a valued graph (S, E, D) and (2) a partition (S_1, S_2) of the set S of states into two subsets, S_1 and S_2. We refer to the states in S_1 as *player-1 states*; and to the states in S_2, as *player-2 states*. At player-1 states, player 1 chooses a successor; at player-2 states, player 2 chooses a successor.

Probabilistic graphs. A *probabilistic graph* consists of (1) a valued graph (S, E, D); (2) a partition (S_1, S_*) of the set S of states into the two subsets S_1 (player-1 states) and S_* (*probabilistic states*); and (3) a probabilistic transition function $\delta\colon S_* \to \mathrm{Dist}(S)$ that maps every probabilistic state to a probability distribution of successors.[2] We require that for all states $s \in S_*$ and $s' \in S$, we have $(s, s') \in E$ iff $\delta(s)(s') > 0$. At a probabilistic state s, a successor $s' \in E(s)$ is chosen with probability $\delta(s)(s')$. The probabilistic graphs are commonly known as *Markov decision processes*.

Probabilistic games. A *probabilistic game* consists of (1) a valued graph (S, E, D); (2) a partition (S_1, S_2, S_*) of the set S of states into three subsets (player-1, player-2, and probabilistic states); and (3) a probabilistic transition function $\delta\colon S_* \to \mathrm{Dist}(S)$. As for probabilistic graphs, we require that for all states $s \in S_*$ and $s' \in S$, we have $(s, s') \in E$ iff $\delta(s)(s') > 0$. Note that the deterministic games ($S_* = \emptyset$), the probabilistic graphs ($S_2 = \emptyset$), and the valued graphs (both $S_2 = \emptyset$ and $S_* = \emptyset$) are special cases of probabilistic games.

Concurrent games. The most general class of graph models we consider are the concurrent games. A *concurrent game* consists of (1) a valued graph (S, E, D); (2) two finite sets A_1 and A_2 of *player-1* and *player-2 moves*; and (3) a probabilistic transition function $\delta\colon S \times A_1 \times A_2 \to \mathrm{Dist}(S)$. We require that for all states $s, s' \in S$, we have $(s, s') \in E$ iff $\delta(s, a_1, a_2)(s') > 0$ for some moves $a_1 \in A_1$ and $a_2 \in A_2$. Given a state $s \in S$ and two moves $a_1 \in A_1$ and $a_2 \in A_2$, let $E(s, a_1, a_2) = \{s' \in S \mid \delta(s, a_1, a_2)(s') > 0\}$. At a state s, both players choose moves simultaneously and independently; if player 1 chooses move $a_1 \in A_1$, and player 2 chooses $a_2 \in A_2$, then a successor $s' \in E(s, a_1, a_2)$ is chosen with probability $\delta(s, a_1, a_2)(s')$. The probabilistic games are equivalent to the special case of concurrent games where for all states $s \in S$ and all moves $a_1 \in A_1$ and $a_2 \in A_2$, either $\delta(s, a_1, a_2) = \delta(s, a_1, a_2')$ for all player-2 moves $a_2' \in A_2$, or $\delta(s, a_1, a_2) = \delta(s, a_1', a_2)$ for all player-1 moves $a_1' \in A_1$; that is, in each state only one of the two players can influence the choice of successor. This is why, in contrast to the more general concurrent games, the probabilistic games are also known as *turn-based games*.

---

[2] For a finite set X, we write $\mathrm{Dist}(X)$ for the set of probability distributions on X.

3 Level-1 Objectives and Alternation-Free Value Iteration

The simplest kind of objectives are boolean reachability and safety objectives. In the quantitative case, these Borel level-1 objectives generalize to maximizing and minimizing objectives.

3.1 Maximizing and Minimizing Objectives

Consider a valued graph (S, E, D). A *reward function* $p: S \to D$ is a valuation; the value $p(s)$ at a state s is interpreted as a reward that is collected when s is visited. We assume that $p(s) > 0$ for some state $s \in S$. Given a reward function p, the *maximizing objective* $\mathsf{Max}(p): \Omega \to D$ is the function that maps every path to the maximal reward appearing along the path. Formally, for all paths $\omega = \langle s_0, s_1, s_2, \ldots \rangle$,

$$\mathsf{Max}(p)(\omega) \;=\; \max\{p(s_i) \mid i \geq 0\}.$$

In the boolean case, where $D = \mathbb{B}$, maximizing objectives are reachability objectives; they require a path to visit a *target* set p: we have $\omega \in \mathsf{Max}(p)$ iff $s_i \in p$ for some $i \geq 0$. The *minimizing objective* $\mathsf{Min}(p): \Omega \to D$ is defined dually, by

$$\mathsf{Min}(p)(\omega) = \min\{p(s_i) \mid i \geq 0\}.$$

Boolean minimizing objectives are safety objectives; they require a path to stay in a *safe* set p: we have $\omega \in \mathsf{Min}(p)$ iff $s_i \in p$ for all $i \geq 0$. While the boolean $\mathsf{Max}(p)$ objective corresponds to the formula $\Diamond p$ of linear temporal logic (a logic that is interpreted over paths), the boolean $\mathsf{Min}(p)$ objective corresponds to the formula $\Box p$. Both maximizing and minimizing objectives lie on level 1 of the Borel hierarchy.

3.2 Value Improvement

We refer to alternation-free value iteration as *value improvement*. The value improvement algorithm operates on a valued graph $G = (S, E, D)$ using two functions: an improvement function and a limit function.

Improvement functions. An *improvement function* $\mathsf{Imp}: V \to V$ is a function on valuations which satisfies the following requirements.

Monotone. For all valuations $v_1, v_2 \in V$, if $v_1 \leq v_2$, then $\mathsf{Imp}(v_1) \leq \mathsf{Imp}(v_2)$.

Continuous. For every chain $C = \langle v_0, v_1, v_2, \ldots \rangle$ of valuations, the monotonicity of Imp ensures that $\mathsf{Imp}(C) = \langle \mathsf{Imp}(v_0), \mathsf{Imp}(v_1), \mathsf{Imp}(v_2), \ldots \rangle$ is a chain. We require that $\mathsf{Imp}(\lim C) = \lim \mathsf{Imp}(C)$.

Directed. Either $v \leq \mathsf{Imp}(v)$ for all valuations $v \in V$; or $v \geq \mathsf{Imp}(v)$ for all valuations $v \in V$. In the former case, the function Imp is *extensive*; in the latter case, *reductive*.

Algorithm 1. ValueImprovement

Input: valued graph G, improvement function Imp, limit function Lim,
precision $\alpha \in \mathbb{R}_{\geq 0}$, and initial valuation $v^0 \in V$.
Output: valuation $v^* \in V$.

$i := 0$;
do {
$\quad v^{i+1} := \mathsf{Imp}(v^i)$;
$\quad i := i + 1$;
$\quad$ } **until** $\mathrm{diff}(v^{i-1}, v^i) \leq \alpha$;
return $v^* := \mathsf{Lim}(v^i, \alpha)$.

The improvement functions we consider satisfy also the property of *locality*, which is defined as follows: for all states $s \in S$ and all valuations $v_1, v_2 \in V$, if $v_1(s') = v_2(s')$ for all successors $s' \in E(s)$, then $\mathsf{Imp}(v_1)(s) = \mathsf{Imp}(v_2)(s)$. Locality states that the value of the improvement function at a state s only depends on the values of the states that are successors of s. Locality restricts the power of improvement functions.

Limit functions. We define a distance between valuations: for two valuations $v_1, v_2 \in V$, let $\mathrm{diff}(v_1, v_2) = \max\{|v_1(s) - v_2(s)| \mid s \in S\}$. A *limit function* Lim: $V \times \mathbb{R}_{\geq 0} \to V$ maps each valuation $v \in V$ and real $\alpha \geq 0$ to a valuation $\mathsf{Lim}(v, \alpha)$ such that $\mathrm{diff}(\mathsf{Lim}(v, \alpha), v) \leq \alpha$; that is, at each state, the input and output values of Lim do not differ by more than α. In particular, if $\alpha = 0$, then $\mathsf{Lim}(v, \alpha) = v$.

The value improvement algorithm. The value improvement algorithm (Algorithm 1) takes as input a valued graph, an improvement function Imp, a limit function Lim, a precision $\alpha \in \mathbb{R}_{\geq 0}$, and an initial valuation $v^0 \in V$. Starting from the initial valuation, the algorithm iteratively "improves" the valuation by applying the directed improvement function Imp: it computes a prefix of the *improvement chain* $C(v^0, \mathsf{Imp}) = \langle v^0, v^1, v^2, \ldots \rangle$, where $v^{i+1} = \mathsf{Imp}(v^i)$ for all $i \geq 0$. For boolean values, the improvement chain converges in a finite number of steps —that is, $v^{i+1} = v^i$ for some $i \geq 0$— and (provided the precision α is less than 1) the algorithm returns $\mathsf{Lim}(v^{i+1}, \alpha) = v^i$, which is the limit of the improvement chain. However, for probabilistic and quantitative values, finite convergence is not guaranteed. This is where the precision and the limit function come into play. If $\mathrm{diff}(v^i, v^{i+1}) \leq \alpha$ for some $i \geq 0$, then the algorithm applies the limit function and returns the valuation $\mathsf{Lim}(v^{i+1}, \alpha)$. Thus, for precisions $\alpha > 0$, the algorithm may terminate even if the improvement chain does not converge in a finite number of steps.

Fixpoint characterization. Since $(V, \leq)$ is a complete lattice, and Imp is a monotone and continuous function, the limit $v^\infty = \lim C(v^0, \mathsf{Imp})$ of the improvement chain is a fixpoint of the improvement function, i.e., $\mathsf{Imp}(v^\infty) = v^\infty$. We refer to v^∞ as the *improvement fixpoint*. By Kleene's fixpoint theorem, if

Imp is extensive, then v^∞ is the least fixpoint of Imp above v^0; that is,

$$v^\infty = \text{glb}\{v \in V \mid v \geq v^0 \text{ and } \text{Imp}(v) = v\} = (\mu X \geq v^0) \text{ Imp}(X),$$

where the notation of the right-most expression is borrowed from the μ-calculus [10]. Symmetrically, if Imp is reductive, then v^∞ is the greatest fixpoint of Imp below v^0; that is,

$$v^\infty = \text{lub}\{v \in V \mid v \leq v^0 \text{ and } \text{Imp}(v) = v\} = (\nu X \leq v^0) \text{ Imp}(X).$$

Rate of convergence. In the limit, the improvement chain always converges to the improvement fixpoint. From an algorithmic perspective, the rate of convergence is important. Given a valued graph G, an improvement function Imp, a limit function Lim, and a complexity class $\mathbb{C}$, we are interested in the following three questions.

Finitely reachable fixpoint. Does Algorithm 1 terminate for all initial valuations v^0 and precision $\alpha = 0$? Finite reachability asks if the improvement fixpoint is reached in finitely many iterations of the improvement function: for all $v^0 \in V$, does there exist an $i \geq 0$ such that $\text{Imp}(v^i) = v^i$? If the answer is Yes, then $v^* = v^\infty$; that is, the algorithm returns the improvement fixpoint. We furthermore wish to know if the required number i of iterations, given as a function of the valued graph G and the initial valuation v^0, lies in the complexity class $\mathbb{C}$.

Finitely computable fixpoint. Does there exist a precision $\alpha > 0$ such that for all initial valuations v^0, Algorithm 1 terminates and returns the improvement fixpoint $v^* = v^\infty$? Finite computability asks if the improvement fixpoint can be computed using the limit function after finitely many iterations of the improvement function: is there an $\alpha > 0$ such that for all $v^0 \in V$, we have (1) for all $i \geq 0$, if $\text{diff}(v^i, v^{i+1}) \leq \alpha$, then $\text{Lim}(v^{i+1}, \alpha) = v^\infty$; and (2) there exists an $i \geq 0$ such that $\text{diff}(v^i, v^{i+1}) \leq \alpha$. If the answer is Yes, then when given a suitable $\alpha > 0$ as input, the algorithm returns the improvement fixpoint. More precisely we wish to know if there exists such a suitable α such that required number i of iterations, given as a function of the valued graph G and the initial valuation v^0, lies in the complexity class $\mathbb{C}$.

Finitely approximable fixpoint. For every real $\varepsilon > 0$ and initial valuation $v^0 \in V$, there exists an $i \geq 0$ such that $\text{diff}(v^i, v^\infty) \leq \varepsilon$. We wish to know if the required number i of iterations, given as a function of the valued graph G and the initial valuation v^0, lies in the complexity class $\mathbb{C}$. In other words, finite approximability asks if the improvement fixpoint can be approximated within error ε using only the resources (time or space) provided by the complexity class $\mathbb{C}$. If the answer is Yes, then Algorithm 1 can be run with precision $\alpha = 0$ and stopped after i iterations with output v^i, which is guaranteed to deviate from the improvement fixpoint v^∞ by at most ε.

Whenever the finite reachability of an improvement fixpoint is not ensured, we investigate its finite computability, i.e., the existence of a suitable limit function.

In cases where finite computability cannot be guaranteed for any α, we study finite approximability. We will also address the finer algorithmic question whether a value improvement scheme can be implemented (possibly with auxiliary data structures) so that its running time matches the best known upper bound for computing (or ε-approximating) the improvement fixpoint.

3.3   Graphs

Graph values of objectives. On a valued graph $G = (S, E, D)$, every objective W defines a valuation $\sup W \colon S \to D$, namely,

$$\sup W(s) \;=\; \sup\{W(\omega) \mid \omega \in \Omega_s\}$$

for all states $s \in S$. We refer to $\sup W$ as the *graph valuation* of the objective W. The graph value of a maximizing objective $\mathsf{Max}(p)$ at a state s is the maximal reward that appears along any path from s. In the boolean case, for a state $s \in S$, we have $s \in \sup \mathsf{Max}(p)$ iff some path from s leads to a state in p; and $s \in \sup \mathsf{Min}(p)$ iff some path from s contains only states in p. In other words, the graph valuation of the boolean $\mathsf{Max}(p)$ objective corresponds to the formula $\exists \Diamond p$ of branching temporal logic (a logic that is interpreted over states); and the graph valuation of the boolean $\mathsf{Min}(p)$ objective corresponds to the formula $\exists \Box p$. The dual, universal interpretation of objectives can be defined by $\inf W(s) = \inf\{W(\omega) \mid \omega \in \Omega_s\}$; however, we will not further pursue this case, which is symmetric.

Maximizing and minimizing problems on graphs. Given a valued graph G and a reward function p, we wish to compute the graph valuations of the objectives $\mathsf{Max}(p)$ and $\mathsf{Min}(p)$ over G. In the boolean case, this corresponds to the model-checking problem for the branching temporal logic CTL [10].

Graph predecessor operator. The *graph predecessor operator* $\mathsf{maxPre} \colon V \to V$ is the function on valuations defined by

$$\mathsf{maxPre}(v)(s) \;=\; \max\{v(s') \mid s' \in E(s)\}$$

for all valuations $v \in V$ and all states $s \in S$; that is, the value of $\mathsf{maxPre}(v)$ at a state s is the maximal value of v at the states that are successors of s. In the boolean case, we have $s \in \mathsf{maxPre}(v)$ iff there exists a successor $s' \in E(s)$ such that $s' \in v$. The function maxPre is monotone, continuous, and local.

Graph valuations as improvement fixpoints. The graph valuations of maximizing and minimizing objectives can be computed as finitely reachable improvement fixpoints. Consider a reward function p, and the corresponding objectives $\mathsf{Max}(p)$ and $\mathsf{Min}(p)$. We define two improvement functions:

$$\mathsf{maxImp}(v)(s) \;=\; \max\{v(s), \mathsf{maxPre}(v)(s)\};$$
$$\mathsf{minImp}(v)(s) \;=\; \min\{v(s), \mathsf{maxPre}(v)(s)\};$$

for all valuations $v \in V$ and all states $s \in S$. Note that maxImp is extensive, and minImp reductive. In the boolean case, $\mathsf{maxImp}(v) = v \cup \mathsf{maxPre}(v)$

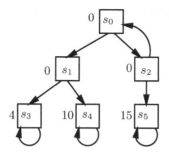

Fig. 1. Graph with maximizing objective

and $\mathsf{minImp}(v) = v \cap \mathsf{maxPre}(v)$. The improvement fixpoint $\lim C(p, \mathsf{maxImp})$ for the initial valuation p and the improvement function maxImp is the graph valuation $\sup \mathsf{Max}(p)$ of the maximizing objective. Similarly, the improvement fixpoint $\lim C(p, \mathsf{minImp})$ is the graph valuation $\sup \mathsf{Min}(p)$ of the minimizing objective. Both fixpoints are finitely reachable, and the number of improvement steps is bounded by the number of states. Hence the value improvement algorithm (Algorithm 1) with initial valuation $v^0 = p$, improvement function maxImp (resp. minImp), and precision $\alpha = 0$, returns the valuation $v^* = v^i = \sup \mathsf{Max}(p)$ (resp. $v^* = v^i = \sup \mathsf{Min}(p)$) after at most $i = n$ iterations (regardless of the limit function, because $\alpha = 0$).

Example 1 (Graph with maximizing objective). Consider the valued graph shown in Figure 1. The reward function p is given by the state labels. We consider the objective $\mathsf{Max}(p)$ for player 1. The value improvement algorithm proceeds by computing value vectors, which consist of one value for each state. We denote by v^i the value vector at iteration i. The j-th component of v^i indicates the value for state s_{j-1} at iteration i. The initial value vector is given by p, that is, $v^0 = \langle 0, 0, 0, 4, 10, 15 \rangle$. Applying the improvement function maxImp to v^0, we obtain $v^1 = \langle 0, 10, 15, 4, 10, 15 \rangle$. This vector contains, for each state, the maximal reward that can be obtained in a single transition. Applying maxImp to v^1, we obtain $v^2 = \langle 15, 10, 15, 4, 10, 15 \rangle$, which indicates for each state the maximal reward that can be obtained in two transitions. Since $\mathsf{maxImp}(v^2) = v^2$, this is the improvement fixpoint; that is, the vector v^2 contains for each state the maximal reachable reward. □

Optimality. Every improvement step (i.e., each application of the function maxImp or minImp) can be computed in $O(m)$ time. Hence a direct implementation of Algorithm 1 has the time complexity $O(mn)$. However, in the boolean case, the value improvement scheme can be implemented to run in $O(m)$ time. This is because each transition, once considered in the computation of some valuation v^i, is never revisited in subsequent iterations. Thus, in the boolean case, value improvement yields an optimal, linear-time algorithm for solving the maximizing and minimizing problems on graphs. In the quantitative case, the two problems can be solved in $O(m + n \log n)$ time by first sorting the rewards of all states, and then computing the states from which a reward can be reached, in descending (or ascending) order of rewards. We know of no implementation of value improvement which matches this time complexity.

3.4 Deterministic Games

Deterministic strategies. Central to games is the notion of strategies. For games played on graphs, a strategy is a recipe that instructs a player which successor state to choose. Let $G = ((S, S_1, S_2), E, D)$ be a deterministic game. For player $k \in \{1, 2\}$, given a finite prefix of a path which represents the history of the game played so far, and which ends in a player-k state, a deterministic strategy for player k specifies how to extend the path by a transition. Formally, a *deterministic player-k strategy* is a function $\sigma\colon S^* \cdot S_k \to S$ such that $\sigma(w \cdot s) \in E(s)$ for all $w \in S^*$ and all $s \in S_k$. We write Σ^D and Π^D for the sets of deterministic player-1 and player-2 strategies, respectively. Given two deterministic strategies $\sigma \in \Sigma^D$ and $\pi \in \Pi^D$, and a state $s \in S$, we write $\omega_s^{\sigma,\pi}$ for the path $\langle s_0, s_1, s_2, \ldots \rangle \in \Omega$ such that (1) $s_0 = s$ and (2) for all $i \geq 0$, we have $\sigma(\langle s_0, s_1, \ldots, s_i \rangle) = s_{i+1}$ if $s_i \in S_1$, and $\pi(\langle s_0, s_1, \ldots, s_i \rangle) = s_{i+1}$ if $s_i \in S_2$; that is, if the game is started in state s and the two players play according to the strategies σ and π, then the result is the path $\omega_s^{\sigma,\pi}$.

Game values of objectives. On a deterministic game G, every objective W defines a valuation $\mathsf{supinf}\, W\colon S \to D$, namely,

$$\mathsf{supinf}\, W(s) \;=\; \sup_{\sigma \in \Sigma^D} \inf_{\pi \in \Pi^D} W(\omega_s^{\sigma,\pi}).$$

We refer to $\mathsf{supinf}\, W$ as the *deterministic game valuation* of the objective W. The game value of a maximizing objective $\mathsf{Max}(p)$ at a state s is the maximal reward that player 1 can ensure to appear along a path from s, against any strategy for player 2. In the boolean case, for a state $s \in S$, we have $s \in \mathsf{supinf}\,\mathsf{Max}(p)$ iff there exists a player-1 strategy σ such that for every player-2 strategy π, the path from s given σ and π leads to a state in p. Similarly, if $D = \mathbb{B}$, then $s \in \mathsf{supinf}\,\mathsf{Min}(p)$ iff there exists a player-1 strategy σ such that for every player-2 strategy π, the path from s given σ and π contains only states in p. Thus, the game valuation of the boolean $\mathsf{Max}(p)$ objective corresponds to the formula $\langle\langle 1 \rangle\rangle \Diamond p$ of the alternating temporal logic ATL [1]; and the game valuation of the boolean $\mathsf{Min}(p)$ objective corresponds to the ATL formula $\langle\langle 1 \rangle\rangle \Box p$.

Maximizing and minimizing problems on deterministic games. Given a deterministic game G and a reward function p, we wish to compute the deterministic game valuations of the objectives $\mathsf{Max}(p)$ and $\mathsf{Min}(p)$. In the boolean case, this corresponds to the model-checking problem for ATL.

Game predecessor operator. The *deterministic game predecessor operator* $\mathsf{maxminPre}\colon V \to V$ is the function on valuations defined by

$$\mathsf{maxminPre}(v)(s) \;=\; \begin{cases} \max\{v(s') \mid s' \in E(s)\} & \text{if } s \in S_1; \\ \min\{v(s') \mid s' \in E(s)\} & \text{if } s \in S_2; \end{cases}$$

that is, the value of maxminPre(v) at a player-1 state s is the maximal value of v at the successors of s, and at a player-2 state s it is the minimal value of v at the successors of s. In the boolean case, we have $s \in$ maxminPre(v) iff (1) if $s \in S_1$, then there exists a successor $s' \in E(s)$ such that $s' \in v$; and (2) if $s \in S_2$, then $s' \in v$ for all successors $s' \in E(s)$. The function maxminPre is monotone, continuous, and local.

Deterministic game valuations as improvement fixpoints. As in the case of graphs, the deterministic game valuations of maximizing and minimizing objectives can be computed as finitely reachable improvement fixpoints. Consider a reward function p, and the corresponding objectives Max(p) and Min(p). We redefine the two improvement functions:

$$maxImp(v)(s) = \max\{v(s), maxminPre(v)(s)\};$$
$$minImp(v)(s) = \min\{v(s), maxminPre(v)(s)\}.$$

Note that maxImp is still extensive, and minImp reductive. The improvement fixpoint $\lim C(p, maxImp)$ for the initial valuation p and the improvement function maxImp is the deterministic game valuation supinf Max(p) of the maximizing objective. Similarly, the improvement fixpoint $\lim C(p, minImp)$ is the deterministic game valuation supinf Min(p) of the minimizing objective. Both fixpoints are finitely reachable, and as in the case of graphs, the number of improvement steps is bounded by the number of states. Hence the value improvement algorithm (Algorithm 1) with initial valuation $v^0 = p$, improvement function maxImp (resp. minImp), and precision $\alpha = 0$, returns the valuation $v^* = v^i =$ supinf Max(p) (resp. $v^* = v^i =$ supinf Min(p)) after at most $i = n$ iterations.

Example 2 (Deterministic game with maximizing objective). Consider the deterministic game shown in Figure 2. The $\square$ states are player 1 states, and the $\diamond$ state is a player 2 state (we will follow this graphical convention in all figures of this paper). We consider the objective Max(p) for player 1. From the initial valuation $v^0 = \langle 0, 0, 0, 4, 10, 15 \rangle$ given by the reward function p (indicated by the state labels), we obtain $v^1 = \langle 0, 10, 0, 4, 10, 15 \rangle$. Note that state s_2 chooses the successor with the minimum value, i.e., the value of s_0. Applying maxImp again, we obtain $v^2 = \langle 10, 10, 0, 4, 10, 15 \rangle$, and then $v^3 = \langle 10, 10, 10, 4, 10, 15 \rangle$. This is the improvement fixpoint, which represents the value of the deterministic maximizing game at each state.   □

Optimality. The situation is similar to the case of graphs. Each application of maxImp or minImp can be computed in $O(m)$ time, yielding the time complexity $O(mn)$ for Algorithm 1. In the boolean case, the value improvement scheme can be implemented to run in $O(m)$ time, which is optimal. Consider the case of a reachability (i.e., boolean maximizing) objective. We maintain a counter for each state s, which is initialized to 0 and incremented whenever a transition from s to some valuation v^i is visited. If $s \in S_1$, then s is included in v^{i+1} as soon as the counter becomes positive (i.e., some successor of s lies in v^i); if $s \in S_2$, then s is included in v^{i+1} when the counter reaches the outdegree of s (i.e., all successors

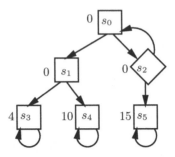

Fig. 2. Deterministic game with maximizing objective

of s lie in v^i). In this way, each transition is visited only once. In the quantitative case, the maximizing and minimizing problems on deterministic games can be solved in $O(m + n \log n)$ time [2], but we know of no implementation of value improvement which matches this bound.

3.5 Probabilistic Graphs

Probabilistic strategies. A probabilistic strategy extends a finite path by a probability distribution of successors. Although probabilistic graphs do not contain player-2 states, we define probabilistic strategies right away for the more general case of probabilistic games. Let $((S, S_1, S_2, S_*), (E, \delta), D)$ be a probabilistic game, and let $k \in \{1, 2\}$. A *probabilistic player-k strategy* is a function $\sigma \colon S^* \cdot S_k \to \mathrm{Dist}(S)$ such that for all $w \in S^*$ and all $s, s' \in S_k$, if $\sigma(w \cdot s)(s') > 0$, then $s' \in E(s)$. We write Σ^P and Π^P for the sets of probabilistic player-1 and player-2 strategies, respectively. Given two probabilistic strategies $\sigma \in \Sigma^P$ and $\pi \in \Pi^P$, and a state $s \in S$, we write $\mathrm{Pr}_s^{\sigma,\pi}$ for the probability measure on the set Ω of paths which is defined inductively as follows: for all $w \in S^*$ and all $t, t' \in S$, (1) $\mathrm{Pr}_s^{\sigma,\pi}(t \cdot S^\omega)$ is 1 if $t = s$, and it is 0 otherwise; and (2) if $\mathrm{Pr}_s^{\sigma,\pi}(w \cdot t \cdot S^\omega) = x$, then $\mathrm{Pr}_s^{\sigma,\pi}(w \cdot t \cdot t' \cdot S^\omega)$ is $x \cdot \sigma(w \cdot t)(t')$ if $t \in S_1$, it is $x \cdot \pi(w \cdot t)(t')$ if $t \in S_2$, and it is $x \cdot \delta(t)(t')$ if $t \in S_*$. From this definition of $\mathrm{Pr}_s^{\sigma,\pi}$ for all basic open sets of paths, we obtain probabilities for all Borel sets. For an objective $W \subseteq \Omega$, we write $\mathrm{E}_s^{\sigma,\pi}[W]$ for the expected value of W under the probability measure $\mathrm{Pr}_s^{\sigma,\pi}$.

Example 3 (Probabilistic graph). Consider the probabilistic graph shown in Figure 3, with the single probabilistic state s_2 (probabilistic states are indicated by circles). The probabilities of the transitions from s_2 to s_0 and to s_5 are both $\frac{1}{2}$. We consider the following three deterministic strategies σ_1, σ_2, and σ_3 for player 1: strategy σ_1 chooses at state s_0 the successor s_1, and at s_1 the successor s_3; strategy σ_2 chooses at state s_0 the successor s_1, and at s_1 the successor s_4; and strategy σ_3 chooses at state s_0 the successor s_2. Given strategy σ_1 and start state s_0, the outcome is the path $\omega_{s_0}^{\sigma_1} = s_0 \cdot s_1 \cdot s_3^\omega$; given σ_2 and s_0, the outcome is the path $\omega_{s_0}^{\sigma_2} = s_0 \cdot s_1 \cdot s_4^\omega$. Given strategy σ_3 and start state s_0, the outcome is a set of possible paths, namely, $((s_0 \cdot s_2)^* \cdot s_5^\omega) \cup (s_0 \cdot s_2)^\omega$. Observe that the probability

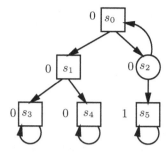

Fig. 3. Probabilistic graph with reachability objective

of visiting s_2 for n times and never visiting s_5 is $(\frac{1}{2})^n$, which goes to 0 as n goes to ∞. Therefore $\Pr_{s_0}^{\sigma_3}((s_0 \cdot s_2)^* \cdot s_5^\omega) = 1$, and $\Pr_{s_0}^{\sigma_3}((s_0 \cdot s_2)^\omega) = 0$.   □

Probabilistic graph values of objectives. On a probabilistic graph $G = ((S, S_1, S_*), (E, \delta), D)$, an objective W defines the valuation $\sup W \colon S \to D$ given by

$$\sup W(s) \;=\; \sup\{E_s^\sigma[W] \mid \sigma \in \Sigma^P\}.$$

We refer to $\sup W$ as the *probabilistic graph valuation* of the objective W. The probabilistic graph value of a maximizing objective $\mathsf{Max}(p)$ at a state s is the maximal expectation of the function $\mathsf{Max}(p)$ that player 1 can ensure from s. Note that if W is a boolean objective (that is, $W \colon \Omega \to \mathbb{B}$), in general the valuation $\sup W$ has probabilistic values (that is, $\sup W \colon S \to [0,1]$). If W is a quantitative objective (that is, $W \colon \Omega \to \mathbb{R}_{\geq 0}^\infty$), then $\sup W$ is a quantitative valuation.

Maximizing and minimizing problems on probabilistic graphs. Given a probabilistic graph G and a reward function p, we wish to compute the probabilistic graph valuations of the objectives $\mathsf{Max}(p)$ and $\mathsf{Min}(p)$.

Probabilistic graph predecessor operator. The *probabilistic graph predecessor operator* $\mathsf{maxPre}^P \colon V \to V$ is the function on valuations defined by

$$\mathsf{maxPre}^P(v)(s) \;=\; \begin{cases} \max\{v(s') \mid s' \in E(s)\} & \text{if } s \in S_1; \\ \sum_{s' \in E(s)} v(s') \cdot \delta(s)(s') & \text{if } s \in S_*; \end{cases}$$

that is, the value of $\mathsf{maxPre}^P(v)$ at a player-1 state s is the maximal value of v at the successors of s, and at a probabilistic state s it is the average value of v at the successors of s. Note that if v is a boolean valuation (that is, $v \colon S \to \mathbb{B}$), in general the predecessor valuation $\mathsf{maxPre}^P(v)$ has probabilistic values (that is, $\mathsf{maxPre}^P(v) \colon S \to [0,1]$). If v is a quantitative valuation, then so is $\mathsf{maxPre}^P(v)$. In all cases, the function maxPre^P is monotone, continuous, and local.

Probabilistic graph valuations as improvement fixpoints. The probabilistic graph valuations of maximizing and minimizing objectives can be expressed as improvement fixpoints, but these fixpoints are not finitely reachable. Consider a reward function p, and the corresponding objectives $\mathsf{Max}(p)$ and $\mathsf{Min}(p)$. We redefine the two improvement functions:

$$\mathsf{maxImp}(v)(s) = \max\{v(s), \mathsf{maxPre}^P(v)(s)\};$$
$$\mathsf{minImp}(v)(s) = \min\{v(s), \mathsf{maxPre}^P(v)(s)\}.$$

Note that maxImp is still extensive, and minImp reductive. The improvement fixpoint $\lim C(p, \mathsf{maxImp})$ for the initial valuation $v^0 = p$ and the improvement function maxImp is the probabilistic graph valuation $\sup \mathsf{Max}(p)$ of the maximizing objective [16]. Similarly, the improvement fixpoint $\lim C(p, \mathsf{minImp})$ is the probabilistic graph valuation $\sup \mathsf{Min}(p)$ of the minimizing objective. Example 4 (below) shows that the two fixpoints are not finitely reachable.

Precision of values. We assume that all transition probabilities and rewards are given as rational numbers. From results of [12,35] it follows that all values of the probabilistic graph valuations $\sup \mathsf{Max}(p)$ and $\sup \mathsf{Min}(p)$ are again rationals, and that the denominators can be bounded. Let $\delta_u = \max\{d \mid \delta(s)(s') = \frac{n}{d}$ for $s \in S_*$ and $s' \in E(s)\}$ be the largest denominator of all transition probabilities. Let $p_u = \mathrm{lcm}\{d \mid p(s) = \frac{n}{d}$ for $s \in S\}$ be the least common multiple of all reward denominators. Let $p_{\max} = \max\{n \mid p(s) = \frac{n}{d}$ for $s \in S\}$ be the largest numerator of all rewards; note that $p_{\max} > 0$ because at least one reward is positive. Then, for all states $s \in S$, both $\sup \mathsf{Max}(p)(s)$ and $\sup \mathsf{Min}(p)(s)$ have the form $\frac{n}{d}$ for a nonnegative integer n and a positive integer $d \leq \gamma$, where

$$\gamma = \delta_u^{4m} \cdot p_u \cdot p_{\max}.$$

This *boundedness* property of probabilistic graph values for maximizing and minimizing objectives is the key for proving the finite computability of the two improvement fixpoints $\sup \mathsf{Max}(p) = \lim C(p, \mathsf{maxImp})$ and $\sup \mathsf{Min}(p) = \lim C(p, \mathsf{minImp})$. The value improvement algorithm (Algorithm 1) with initial valuation $v^0 = p$, improvement function maxImp (resp. minImp), and precision $\alpha = \frac{1}{2\gamma}$, computes a valuation v^i such that $\mathrm{diff}(v^i, v^{i+1}) \leq \alpha$ within a number $i \in O(\gamma^2)$ of iterations. In particular, the number of iterations depends exponentially on the number of states and on the size of rewards. The limit function Lim to obtain v^* from v^i is defined as follows: for each state $s \in S$, round the value $v^i(s)$ to the nearest multiple of $\frac{1}{\gamma}$. Then v^* is the desired improvement fixpoint; that is, $v^* = \sup \mathsf{Max}(p)$ (resp. $v^* = \sup \mathsf{Min}(p)$).

Example 4 (Probabilistic graph with reachability objective). Recall the probabilistic graph from Figure 3, and consider the boolean maximizing objective to reach state s_5 (the reward at s_5 is 1, and the rewards at all other states are 0). We focus on the value improvements at the two states s_0 and s_2. Initially, both values are 0. After $2i$ improvement steps, both values are $\frac{2^i - 1}{2^i}$. To see this, observe that in the $(2i + 1)$-st iteration, the value at s_2 becomes

$$\frac{1}{2} \cdot \left(\frac{2^i - 1}{2^i} + 1\right) = \frac{2^{i+1} - 1}{2^{i+1}};$$

and in the $(2i + 2)$-nd iteration, the value at s_0 becomes $\frac{2^{i+1}-1}{2^{i+1}}$. Hence both values approach 1. Indeed, as we argued in Example 3, the player-1 strategy σ_3 ensures that the target state s_5 is reached with probability 1. Moreover, by the boundedness property of probabilistic graph values, once the values at s_0 and s_1 exceed $1 - \frac{1}{2^{37}}$, we can conclude that both values are 1.   □

Optimality. The maximizing and minimizing problems on probabilistic graphs can be solved in polynomial time using linear programming [18]. The linear-programming approach works equally for boolean and quantitative objectives. However, no better bound than an exponential bound in the number of states is known for the value improvement algorithm on probabilistic graphs, even in the special case of boolean reachability objectives.

3.6 Probabilistic Games

Probabilistic game values of objectives. On a probabilistic game $G = ((S, S_1, S_2, S_*), (E, \delta), D)$, an objective W defines the valuation $\text{supinf } W \colon S \to D$ given by

$$\text{supinf } W(s) = \sup_{\sigma \in \Sigma^P} \inf_{\pi \in \Pi^P} \text{E}_s^{\sigma, \pi}[W].$$

We refer to $\text{supinf } W$ as the *probabilistic game valuation* of the objective W. The probabilistic game value of a maximizing objective $\text{Max}(p)$ at a state s is the maximal expectation of the function $\text{Max}(p)$ that player 1 can ensure from s against any strategy for player 2. The maximizing and minimizing problems on probabilistic games ask, given a probabilistic game G and a reward function p, to compute the probabilistic game valuations $\text{supinf } \text{Max}(p)$ and $\text{supinf } \text{Min}(p)$.

Probabilistic game predecessor operator. The *probabilistic game predecessor operator* $\text{maxminPre}^P \colon V \to V$ is the function on valuations defined by

$$\text{maxminPre}^P(v)(s) = \begin{cases} \max\{v(s') \mid s' \in E(s)\} & \text{if } s \in S_1; \\ \min\{v(s') \mid s' \in E(s)\} & \text{if } s \in S_2; \\ \sum_{s' \in E(s)} v(s') \cdot \delta(s)(s') & \text{if } s \in S_*. \end{cases}$$

The function maxminPre^P is monotone, continuous, and local.

Probabilistic game valuations as improvement fixpoints. Consider a reward function p, and the corresponding objectives $\text{Max}(p)$ and $\text{Min}(p)$. We redefine the two improvement functions:

$$\text{maxImp}(v)(s) = \max\{v(s), \text{maxminPre}^P(v)(s)\};$$
$$\text{minImp}(v)(s) = \min\{v(s), \text{maxminPre}^P(v)(s)\}.$$

Note that maxImp is still extensive, and minImp reductive. The improvement fixpoint $\lim C(p, \text{maxImp})$ for the initial valuation $v^0 = p$ and the improvement function maxImp is the probabilistic game valuation $\text{supinf } \text{Max}(p)$ of the maximizing objective [16], and the improvement fixpoint $\lim C(p, \text{minImp})$ is the probabilistic game valuation supinf Min(p) of the minimizing objective. Since the probabilistic games generalize the probabilistic graphs, the two fixpoints are not finitely reachable. However, as in the case of probabilistic graphs, we have finite computability. If all transition properties and rewards are rational, then we can show the following boundedness property: for all states $s \in S$, both sup Max(p)(s) and sup Min(p)(s) have the form $\frac{n}{d}$ for a nonnegative integer n and a positive integer $d \leq \gamma$, where the bound γ is defined as for probabilistic graphs [12,35]. Furthermore, the value improvement algorithm (Algorithm 1) with initial valuation $v^0 = p$, improvement function maxImp (resp. minImp), and precision $\alpha = \frac{1}{2\gamma}$, computes a valuation v^i such that diff(v^i, v^{i+1}) $\leq \alpha$ within a number $i \in O(\gamma^2)$ of iterations. Thus the limit function Lim can be defined as for probabilistic graphs, and guarantees that Algorithm 1 returns supinf Max(p) (resp. supinf Min(p)).

Optimality. The maximizing and minimizing problems on probabilistic games lie in NP ∩ coNP. This was shown for boolean reachability objectives in [11], and the argument can be generalized to quantitative objectives. No polynomial-time algorithms are known for solving the maximizing and minimizing problems on probabilistic games, even in the special case of boolean reachability objectives. In particular, the linear-programming approach for probabilistic graphs does not generalize to probabilistic games.

3.7   Concurrent Games

Concurrent strategies. Concurrent strategies are probabilistic. However, in concurrent games, the players choose distributions of moves, not of successor states. Let $G = (S, A_1, A_2, (E, \delta), D)$ be a concurrent game. For $k \in \{1, 2\}$, a *concurrent player-k strategy* is a function $\sigma : S^+ \to \text{Dist}(A_k)$. We write Σ and Π for the sets of concurrent player-1 and player-2 strategies, respectively. Given two concurrent strategies $\sigma \in \Sigma$ and $\pi \in \Pi$, and a state $s \in S$, we write $\Pr_s^{\sigma,\pi}$ for the probability measure on the set Ω of paths which is defined as follows: for all $w \in S^*$ and all $t, t' \in S$, (1) $\Pr_s^{\sigma,\pi}(t \cdot S^\omega)$ is 1 if $t = s$, and it is 0 otherwise; and (2) if $\Pr_s^{\sigma,\pi}(w \cdot t \cdot S^\omega) = x$, then $\Pr_s^{\sigma,\pi}(w \cdot t \cdot t' \cdot S^\omega) = x \cdot \sum_{a_1 \in A_1} \sum_{a_2 \in A_2} \sigma(w \cdot t)(a_1) \cdot \pi(w \cdot t)(a_2) \cdot \delta(t, a_1, a_2)(t')$. This definition of $\Pr_s^{\sigma,\pi}$ for the basic open sets of paths suffices to obtain probabilities for all Borel sets.

Concurrent game values of objectives. On a concurrent game G, an objective W defines the valuation supinf $W : S \to D$ given by

$$\text{supinf } W(s) \;=\; \sup_{\sigma \in \Sigma} \inf_{\pi \in \Pi} \text{E}_s^{\sigma,\pi}[W].$$

We refer to supinf W as the *concurrent game valuation* of the objective W. The maximizing and minimizing problems on concurrent games ask, given a concurrent game G and a reward function p, to compute the concurrent game valuations supinf Max(p) and supinf Min(p).

Concurrent game predecessor operator. The *concurrent game predecessor operator* supinfPre: $V \to V$ is the function on valuations defined by

$$\text{supinfPre}(v)(s) =$$
$$\sup_{\tau_1 \in \text{Dist}(A_1)} \inf_{\tau_2 \in \text{Dist}(A_2)} \sum_{s' \in S} \sum_{a_1 \in A_1} \sum_{a_2 \in A_2} v(s') \cdot \tau_1(s)(a_1) \cdot \tau_2(s)(a_2) \cdot \delta(s, a_1, a_2)(s');$$

that is, the value of supinfPre(v) at a state s is the maximal value of v which player 1 can ensure at a successor of v, against all probabilistic choices of moves for player 2. In other words, the predecessor operator supinfPre solves a matrix game whose payoff function is specified by the valuation v. The function supinfPre is monotone, continuous and local.

Concurrent game valuations as improvement fixpoints. The concurrent game valuations of maximizing and minimizing objectives can be expressed as improvement fixpoints, but these fixpoints are not known to be finitely computable. Consider a reward function p, and the corresponding objectives $\text{Max}(p)$ and $\text{Min}(p)$. We redefine the two improvement functions:

$$\text{maxImp}(v)(s) = \max\{v(s), \text{supinfPre}(v)(s)\};$$
$$\text{minImp}(v)(s) = \min\{v(s), \text{supinfPre}(v)(s)\}.$$

Note that maxImp is still extensive, and minImp reductive. The improvement fixpoint $\lim C(p, \text{maxImp})$ for the initial valuation $v^0 = p$ and the improvement function maxImp is the concurrent game valuation supinf $\text{Max}(p)$ of the maximizing objective, and the improvement fixpoint $\lim C(p, \text{minImp})$ is the concurrent game valuation supinf $\text{Min}(p)$ of the minimizing objective. This was shown for boolean objectives in [16], and the argument can be generalized to quantitative objectives. It is an open problem if the two improvement fixpoints are finitely computable. Indeed, even if all transition probabilities are rational, in general the values of boolean reachability objectives are irrational (but algebraic) [16]. This is in stark contrast to turn-based probabilistic games. For concurrent games, it is not even known if the improvement fixpoints are finitely approximable. More precisely, we do not know a time-bounded complexity class $\mathbb{C}$ such that for every real $\varepsilon > 0$ and every initial valuation v^0, there exists a function $f \in \mathbb{C}$ such that $\text{diff}(v^i, v^\infty) \leq \varepsilon$ for $v^\infty = \lim C(p, \text{maxImp})$ and $i = f(G, v^0, \varepsilon)$.

Optimality. The best known complexity bound for the maximizing and minimizing problems on concurrent games is EXPTIME. Specifically, since all improvement functions we consider can be defined in the theory of the reals with addition and multiplication, we can also express improvement fixpoints in this theory, which can be decided in EXPTIME. For boolean objectives a better bound is known: given a rational r in binary and an integer $d > 0$ in unary, there exists an NP Turing machine that is guaranteed to answer Yes if the concurrent game value of a boolean maximizing (or minimizing) objective at a state is greater than $r + \frac{1}{d}$, and No if it is less than $r - \frac{1}{d}$. This was shown (but misstated) in [4]. However, the argument does not generalize to quantitative objectives.

Table 1. Value improvement for maximizing and minimizing objectives. Recall that γ is such that $16^n \in O(\gamma)$.

n states	Objective Max(p)	Objective Min(p)
Valued graphs	$\mathsf{Imp}(v) = \max\{v, \mathsf{maxPre}(v)\}$ iteration converges in n steps	$\mathsf{Imp}(v) = \min\{v, \mathsf{maxPre}(v)\}$ iteration converges in n steps
Deterministic games	$\mathsf{Imp}(v) = \max\{v, \mathsf{maxminPre}(v)\}$ iteration converges in n steps	$\mathsf{Imp}(v) = \min\{v, \mathsf{maxminPre}(v)\}$ iteration converges in n steps
Probabilistic graphs	$\mathsf{Imp}(v) = \max\{v, \mathsf{maxPre}^P(v)\}$ iteration converges in $O(\gamma^2)$ steps	$\mathsf{Imp} = \min\{v, \mathsf{maxPre}^P(v)\}$ iteration converges in $O(\gamma^2)$ steps
Probabilistic games	$\mathsf{Imp}(v) = \max\{v, \mathsf{maxminPre}^P(v)\}$ iteration converges in $O(\gamma^2)$ steps	$\mathsf{Imp}(v) = \min\{v, \mathsf{maxminPre}^P(v)\}$ iteration converges in $O(\gamma^2)$ steps
Concurrent games	$\mathsf{Imp}(v) = \max\{v, \mathsf{supinfPre}(v)\}$ iteration converges in the limit (no known bound)	$\mathsf{Imp}(v) = \min\{v, \mathsf{supinfPre}(v)\}$ iteration converges in the limit (no known bound)

Summary. We summarize the situation for maximizing and minimizing objectives in Table 1.

4   Level-2 Objectives and Depth-1 Value Iteration

Maximizing and minimizing objectives are obtained within a finite number of transitions. The simplest kind of infinite objectives are boolean Büchi and coBüchi objectives. In the quantitative case, these Borel level-2 objectives generalize to limsup and liminf objectives.

4.1   Limsup and liminf Objectives

Consider a valued graph (S, E, D) and a reward function $p: S \to D$. The *limsup objective* $\mathsf{LimSup}(p)$: $\Omega \to D$ is the function that maps every path to the maximal reward appearing infinitely often along the path. Formally, for all paths $\omega = \langle s_0, s_1, s_2, \ldots \rangle$,

$$\mathsf{LimSup}(p)(\omega) = \lim_{n \to \infty} \max\{p(s_i) \mid i \geq n\}.$$

Observe that $C = \langle p_0, p_1, p_2, \ldots \rangle$, where $p_n = \max\{p(s_i) \mid i \geq n\}$ for all $n \geq 0$, is a decreasing sequence (chain) of values, and its limit is the greatest lower bound of C. In the boolean case, limsup objectives are Büchi objectives; they require a path to visit a *recurrent* set p infinitely often: we have $\omega \in \mathsf{LimSup}(p)$ iff $s_i \in p$ for infinitely many $i \geq 0$. The *liminf objective* $\mathsf{LimInf}(p)$: $\Omega \to D$ is defined dually, by

$$\mathsf{LimInf}(p)(\omega) = \lim_{n \to \infty} \min\{p(s_i) \mid i \geq n\};$$

that is, $\mathsf{LimInf}(p)$ is a least upper bound. Boolean LimInf objectives are coBüchi objectives; they require a path to eventually stay in a *persistent* set p: we have

Algorithm 2. NestedValueImprovement

Input: valued graph G, binary improvement function $\mathsf{Imp2}$, limit function Lim,
precision $\alpha \in \mathbb{R}_{\geq 0}$, and two initial valuations $v^0, u^0 \in V$.
Output: valuation $v^* \in V$.

$i := 0;$
do {
    $v^{i+1} := \mathrm{innerLoop}(v^i, u^0);$
    $i := i + 1;$
    } **until** $\mathrm{diff}(v^{i-1}, v^i) \leq \alpha;$
return $v^* := \mathsf{Lim}(v^i, \alpha).$

procedure $\mathrm{innerLoop}(v^i, u_i^0)$:
    $j := 0;$
    do {
        $u_i^{j+1} := \mathsf{Imp2}(v^i, u_i^j);$
        $j := j + 1;$
        } **until** $\mathrm{diff}(u_i^{j-1}, u_i^j) \leq \alpha;$
    return $u_i^* := \mathsf{Lim}(u_i^j, \alpha).$

$\omega \in \mathsf{LimInf}(p)$ iff $s_i \in p$ for all but finitely many $i \geq 0$. While the boolean $\mathsf{LimSup}(p)$ objective corresponds to the formula $\square \lozenge p$ of linear temporal logic, the boolean $\mathsf{LimInf}(p)$ objective corresponds to the formula $\lozenge \square p$. Both limsup and liminf objectives lie on level 2 of the Borel hierarchy.

Limsup and liminf problems. Given a valued graph G (resp. a deterministic game; a probabilistic graph; a probabilistic game; or a concurrent game), and a reward function p, we wish to compute the valuations $\sup \mathsf{LimSup}(p)$ and $\sup \mathsf{LimInf}(p)$ over G. Note that the graph valuation of the boolean $\mathsf{LimSup}(p)$ objective corresponds to the formula $\exists \square \lozenge p$ of branching temporal logic; and the graph valuation of the boolean $\mathsf{LimInf}(p)$ objective corresponds to the formula $\exists \lozenge \square p$. Hence in the boolean case, the limsup and liminf problems on graphs (resp. games) arise in model checking CTL (resp. ATL) over structures with weak-fairness (Büchi) constraints [10]. Also the model-checking problem for the linear temporal logic LTL can be reduced to the boolean limsup problem on graphs (or probabilistic graphs), by converting the negation of a given LTL formula into a nondeterministic Büchi automaton of exponential size [13,10].

4.2 Nested Value Improvement

We refer to value iteration schemes of alternation depth-1 as *nested value improvement*. The nested value improvement algorithm operates on a valued graph $G = (S, E, D)$ using a binary improvement function $\mathsf{Imp2}$ and a limit function Lim. A binary improvement function maps a pair of valuations to a new valuation.

Binary improvement functions. The valuation pairs $V \times V$ form a complete lattice —the product lattice— with the following ordering: for two valuation pairs $(v_1, u_1), (v_2, u_2) \in V \times V$, let $(v_1, u_1) \leq (v_2, u_2)$ iff both $v_1 \leq v_2$ and $u_1 \leq u_2$. Thus all infinite increasing and decreasing sequences (chains) of valuation pairs have limits. Every chain $C = \langle (v_0, u_0), (v_1, u_1), (v_2, u_2), \ldots \rangle$ of valuation pairs consists of two chains $C_1 = \langle v_0, v_1, v_2, \ldots \rangle$ and $C_2 = \langle u_0, u_1, u_2, \ldots \rangle$ of valuations; note that $\lim C = (\lim C_1, \lim C_2)$. A *binary improvement function* $\mathsf{Imp2} : V \times V \to V$ is a function on valuation pairs which satisfies the following requirements.

Monotone. For all valuation pairs $(v_1, u_1), (v_2, u_2) \in V \times V$, if $(v_1, u_1) \leq (v_2, u_2)$, then $\mathsf{Imp2}(v_1, u_1) \leq \mathsf{Imp2}(v_2, u_2)$.

Continuous. For every chain $C = \langle (v_0, u_0), (v_1, u_1), (v_2, u_2), \ldots \rangle$ of valuation pairs, the sequence $\mathsf{Imp2}(C) = \langle \mathsf{Imp2}(v_0, u_0), \mathsf{Imp2}(v_1, u_1), \mathsf{Imp2}(v_2, u_2), \ldots \rangle$ is a chain of valuations because of the monotonicity of $\mathsf{Imp2}$. We require that $\mathsf{Imp2}(\lim C) = \lim \mathsf{Imp2}(C)$.

Directed. Either $v \leq \mathsf{Imp2}(v, u) \leq u$ for all valuations $v, u \in V$ with $v \leq u$; or $v \geq \mathsf{Imp2}(v, u) \geq u$ for all valuations $v, u \in V$ with $v \geq u$.

The binary improvement functions we consider also satisfy the following *locality* property: for all states $s \in S$ and all valuation pairs $(v_1, u_1), (v_2, u_2) \in V \times V$, if $v_1(s') = v_2(s')$ and $u_1(s') = u_2(s')$ for all successors $s' \in E(s)$, then $\mathsf{Imp2}(v_1, u_1)(s) = \mathsf{Imp2}(v_2, u_2)(s)$.

The nested value improvement algorithm. The nested value improvement algorithm (Algorithm 2) takes as input a valued graph, a binary improvement function $\mathsf{Imp2}$, a limit function Lim, a precision $\alpha \in \mathbb{R}_{\geq 0}$, an *outer* initial valuation $v^0 \in V$, and an *inner* initial valuation $u^0 \in V$. The algorithm returns a valuation $v^* \in V$ that lies between v^0 and u^0 with respect to the lattice ordering of valuations. It suffices to choose the initial valuations v^0 and u^0 such that the desired result v^* lies between v^0 and u^0. Thus, it is possible to choose either v^0 to be the bottom element of the lattice, and u^0 the top, or vice versa. Alternatively, in our uses of the algorithm, we can always choose one of them to be $\min p$ and the other one $\max p$, where $(\min p)(s) = \min\{p(t) \mid t \in S\}$ and $(\max p)(s) = \max\{p(t) \mid t \in S\}$ for all states $s \in S$. This is because the values of the rewards that appear infinitely often along a path, or that appear all but finitely often along a path, lie between $\min p$ and $\max p$. However, the result v^* of the algorithm depends on the ordering of the two initial valuations; that is, it is important whether the outer initial valuation is less than the inner initial valuation (case $v^0 \leq u^0$), or greater (case $v^0 \geq u^0$).

Starting from the outer initial valuation v^0, the algorithm iteratively improves the valuation in order to compute the limit v^∞ of an *outer improvement chain* $C_1(v^0, u^0, \mathsf{Imp2}) = \langle v^0, v^1, v^2, \ldots \rangle$ of valuations. Each outer improvement step is itself the result of computing the limit of an inner improvement chain: we have $v^{i+1} = u_i^\infty = \lim C_2^i(v^i, u^0, \mathsf{Imp2})$ for all $i \geq 0$. For each $i \geq 0$, the i-th *inner improvement chain* $C_2^i(v^i, u^0, \mathsf{Imp2}) = \langle u_i^0, u_i^1, u_i^2, \ldots \rangle$ of valuations results from iteratively applying the directed improvement function Imp2 to the inner initial valuation u^0: we have $u_i^0 = u^0$, and $u_i^{j+1} = \text{Imp2}(v^i, u_i^j)$ for all $j \geq 0$. In other words,

$$v^\infty = \lim_{i \to \infty} u_i^\infty = \lim_{i \to \infty} \lim_{j \to \infty} u_i^j.$$

In case $v^0 \leq u^0$, since Imp2 is directed, for all $i \geq 0$, the inner improvement chain $C_2^i(v^i, u^0, \text{Imp2})$ is decreasing. Since Imp2 is directed, we also have $v^i \leq u_i^j$ for all $i, j \geq 0$. Hence $v^i \leq u_i^\infty = v^{i+1}$, and thus the outer improvement chain $C_1(v^0, u^0, \text{Imp2})$ is increasing. On the other hand, in case $v^0 \geq u^0$, all inner improvement chains $C_2^i(v^i, u^0, \text{Imp2})$ are increasing, and the outer improvement chain $C_1(v^0, u^0, \text{Imp2})$ is decreasing. Observe that, as Imp2 is monotone, also $u_i^j \leq u_{i+1}^j$ for all $i, j \geq 0$ if $v^0 \leq u^0$, and $u_i^j \geq u_{i+1}^j$ for all $i, j \geq 0$ if $v^0 \geq u^0$.

If successful, the algorithm returns the limit v^∞ of the outer improvement chain. As in the alternation-free case, success means either that all limits u_i^∞, for $i \geq 0$, and v^∞ are finitely reachable, or that they are finitely computable using the precision α and the limit function Lim for acceleration. If finite computability fails, then we ask the question of finite approximability of the outer limit v^∞.

Fixpoint characterization. We consider first the case $v^0 \leq u^0$. For all $i \geq 0$, the limit u_i^∞ of the i-th inner improvement chain $C_2^i(v^i, u^0, \text{Imp2})$ is the greatest fixpoint below u^0 of the monotone and continuous function $\text{Imp2}(v^i, \cdot) \colon V \to V$. The limit v^∞ of the outer improvement chain $C_1(v^0, u^0, \text{Imp2})$ is the least fixpoint above v^0 of the function $f \colon V \to V$, which is defined by $f(v) = \text{lub}\{u \in V \mid u \leq u^0 \text{ and } \text{Imp2}(v, u) = u\}$ for all valuations $v \in V$. Note that f is again monotone and continuous. Thus, in this case, the outer limit v^∞ is the least fixpoint of a function whose values are greatest fixpoints. In μ-calculus notation,

$$v^\infty = (\mu X \geq v^0)(\nu Y \leq u^0)\, \text{Imp2}(X, Y).$$

The case $v^0 \geq u^0$ is symmetric. In this case, the outer limit v^∞ is the greatest fixpoint of a function whose values are least fixpoints, namely,

$$v^\infty = (\nu X \leq v^0)(\mu Y \geq u^0)\, \text{Imp2}(X, Y).$$

We henceforth refer to v^∞ as *outer improvement fixpoint*, and to u_i^∞ as i-th *inner improvement fixpoint*, for $i \geq 0$.

Parametric improvement functions. We define binary improvement functions with a parameter Pre that, for different classes of graph models, will be instantiated by different predecessor operators. Consider a reward function p, and the corresponding objectives $\text{LimSup}(p)$ and $\text{LimInf}(p)$. Given a function $\text{Pre} \colon V \to V$, we define the two parametric functions $\text{limsupImp}[\text{Pre}] \colon V \times V \to V$ and $\text{liminfImp}[\text{Pre}] \colon V \times V \to V$ by

$$\text{limsupImp}[\text{Pre}](v, u) = \min\{\max\{p, u, \text{Pre}(u)\}, v, \max\{u, \text{Pre}(v)\}\};$$
$$\text{liminfImp}[\text{Pre}](v, u) = \max\{\min\{p, u, \text{Pre}(u)\}, v, \min\{u, \text{Pre}(v)\}\};$$

for all valuations $v, u \in V$ (the functions max and min are lifted from values to valuations in a pointwise fashion). Observe that if $v \geq u$, then $v \geq$

limsupImp[Pre]$(v, u) \geq u$; and if $v \leq u$, then $v \leq$ liminfImp[Pre]$(v, u) \leq u$. Thus both limsupImp[Pre] and liminfImp[Pre] are directed. For different graph models, we will instantiate the parameter Pre by one of the predecessor operators maxPre, maxminPre, maxPre^P, maxminPre^P, or supinfPre from Section 3. It should be remarked that in the cases we consider, we can simplify the definitions of the binary improvement functions as follows:

$$\text{limsupImp[Pre]}(v, u) = \min\{\max\{p, u, \text{Pre}(u)\}, v, \text{Pre}(v)\};$$
$$\text{liminfImp[Pre]}(v, u) = \max\{\min\{p, u, \text{Pre}(u)\}, v, \text{Pre}(v)\};$$

for all valuations $v, u \in V$. To see why the simplification works, let $u^{j+1} =$ limsupImp[Pre](v, u^j) (according to the original, unsimplified definition) for all $j \geq 0$. For all valuations $v \geq u^0$, if Pre$(v) \geq u^0$, then for all $j \geq 0$, both $v \geq u^j$ and Pre$(v) \geq u^j$, and therefore $u^{j+1} = \min\{\max\{p, u^j, \text{Pre}(u^j)\}, v, \text{Pre}(v)\}$. If $u^0 = \min p$, and Pre is one of maxPre, maxminPre, maxPre^P, maxminPre^P, or supinfPre, then for all valuations $v \geq u^0$, we have Pre$(v) \geq u^0$, and thus the above simplification works. The case $u^0 = \max p$ and liminfImp[Pre] is symmetric.

4.3   Graphs

Finitely reachable nested fixpoints. The graph valuations of limsup and liminf objectives can be computed by nested value improvement. On a valued graph $G = (S, E, D)$, the outer improvement fixpoint $\lim C_1(v^0, u^0, \text{Imp2})$, for the outer initial valuation $v^0 = \max p$, the inner initial valuation $u^0 = \min p$, and the improvement function Imp2 = limsupImp[maxPre], is the graph valuation sup LimSup(p) of the limsup objective. Similarly, the outer improvement fixpoint $\lim C_1(\min p, \max p, \text{liminfImp[maxPre]})$ is the graph valuation sup LimInf(p) of the liminf objective. Each inner improvement fixpoint is finitely reachable within at most n steps, and the outer improvement fixpoints are finitely reachable within at most n computations of inner improvement fixpoints. Hence the total number of applications of the improvement function Imp2 in Algorithm 2 is bounded by n^2 when computing sup LimSup(p) or sup LimInf(p) on graphs.

Optimality. Every improvement step (i.e., each application of the function limsupImp or liminfImp) can be computed in $O(m)$ time. Hence a direct implementation of Algorithm 2 has the time complexity $O(mn^2)$. In the boolean case, the nested value improvement scheme can be sped up to run in $O(mn)$ time by computing inner improvement fixpoints using techniques similar to the $O(m)$ implementations of Max and Min objectives. Yet, unlike in the case of maximizing and minimizing objectives, the nested value improvement scheme is not known to have an optimal implementation even in the boolean case. This is because the graph valuations of Büchi and coBüchi objectives (i.e., boolean limsup and liminf objectives) can be computed in $O(m)$ time by finding the maximal strongly connected components of a graph. In the quantitative case, the limsup and liminf problems on graphs can be solved in $O(m + n \log n)$ time by sorting the rewards of all states, computing maximal strongly connected components, and applying the algorithms for Max (resp. Min) objectives in descending (resp. ascending) order of rewards. We know of no implementation of the nested value improvement scheme which matches this complexity.

4.4 Deterministic Games

Finitely reachable nested fixpoints. The deterministic game valuations of limsup and liminf objectives can again be computed by nested value improvement, using a different predecessor operator. On a deterministic game $G = ((S, S_1, S_2), E, D)$, the outer improvement fixpoint $\lim C_1(\max p, \min p, \mathsf{limsupImp}[\mathsf{maxminPre}])$ is the deterministic game valuation $\mathsf{supinf}\,\mathsf{LimSup}(p)$ of the limsup objective, and $\lim C_1(\min p, \max p, \mathsf{liminfImp}[\mathsf{maxminPre}])$ is the deterministic game valuation $\mathsf{supinf}\,\mathsf{LimInf}(p)$ of the liminf objective. Each inner improvement fixpoint is finitely reachable within at most n steps, and the outer improvement fixpoints are finitely reachable within at most n computations of inner improvement fixpoints. Hence, as in the case of graphs, the total number of applications of the improvement function $\mathsf{Imp2}$ in Algorithm 2 is bounded by n^2 when computing $\mathsf{supinf}\,\mathsf{LimSup}(p)$ or $\mathsf{supinf}\,\mathsf{LimInf}(p)$ on deterministic games.

Example 5 (Deterministic game with limsup objective). Consider the deterministic game shown in Figure 4, where the reward function p is indicated by state labels. We consider the objective $\mathsf{LimSup}(p)$ for player 1 (the $\square$ player). We specify valuations as value vectors as before; the outer initial valuation is $v^0 = \langle 15, 15, 15, 15, 15 \rangle$, and the inner initial valuation is $u^0 = \langle 5, 5, 5, 5, 5 \rangle$. We compute the first inner improvement fixpoint: $u_0^0 = \langle 5, 5, 5, 5, 5 \rangle$, and since

$$u_0^{j+1} = \min\{\max\{p, u_0^j, \mathsf{maxminPre}(u_0^j)\}, v^0, \mathsf{maxminPre}(v^0)\}$$

for all $j \geq 0$, where $v^0 = \mathsf{maxminPre}(v^0) = \langle 15, 15, 15, 15, 15 \rangle$, we obtain $u_0^1 = \langle 5, 5, 15, 10, 5 \rangle$. Note that u_0^1 coincides with the reward function p. Next we obtain $u_0^2 = \langle 10, 5, 15, 10, 10 \rangle$, because $\max\{p, u_0^1, \mathsf{maxminPre}(u_0^1)\} = \langle 10, 5, 15, 10, 10 \rangle$. Finally $u_0^3 = u_0^4 = \langle 10, 10, 15, 10, 10 \rangle$, which is the first inner improvement fixpoint v^1. The second inner improvement chain starts with $u_1^0 = \langle 5, 5, 5, 5, 5 \rangle$ using

$$u_1^{j+1} = \min\{\max\{p, u_1^j, \mathsf{maxminPre}(u_1^j)\}, v^1, \mathsf{maxminPre}(v^1)\},$$

where $v^1 = \langle 10, 10, 15, 10, 10 \rangle$ and $\mathsf{maxminPre}(v^1) = \langle 10, 10, 10, 10, 10 \rangle$. Since $\max\{p, u_1^0, \mathsf{maxminPre}(u_1^0)\} = \langle 5, 5, 15, 10, 5 \rangle$, we obtain $u_1^2 = \langle 10, 5, 10, 10, 10 \rangle$. Then $u_1^3 = u_1^4 = \langle 10, 10, 10, 10, 10 \rangle$, which is the second inner improvement fixpoint v^2. This is also the desired outer improvement fixpoint; that is, $v^\infty = v^2 = v^3 = \langle 10, 10, 10, 10, 10 \rangle$. The player-1 strategy that chooses at state s_0 the successor s_3 ensures that against all strategies of player 2, the reward 10 will be visited infinitely often. Dually, the player-2 strategy that chooses at s_1 the successor s_0 ensures that against all strategies of player 1, the reward 15 will be visited at most once. Hence $\langle 10, 10, 10, 10, 10 \rangle$ is the deterministic game valuation of the player-1 objective $\mathsf{LimSup}(p)$: from any start state, player 1 can

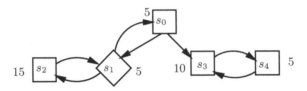

Fig. 4. Deterministic game with limsup objective

ensure that reward 10 will be visited infinitely often, but she cannot do so for reward 15.   □

Optimality. The situation is similar to the case of graphs. The direct implementation of nested value improvement yields a $O(mn^2)$ time complexity. In the boolean case, the scheme can be sped up to run in $O(mn)$ time by using $O(m)$ implementations for Max and Min objectives to compute inner improvement fixpoints. However, unlike in the case of graphs, $O(mn)$ is the best known time bound for solving deterministic games with Büchi or coBüchi objectives; that is, nested value improvement for deterministic games with boolean objectives is optimal. In the quantitative case, the limsup and liminf problems on deterministic games can be solved in $O((m + \log n) \cdot n)$ time [2], but we know of no implementation of nested value improvement which matches this complexity.

4.5   Probabilistic Graphs

Finitely computable nested fixpoints. The probabilistic graph valuations of limsup and liminf objectives can be expressed as nested improvement fixpoints; while these fixpoints are not finitely reachable, they are finitely computable. On a probabilistic graph $G = ((S, S_1, S_*), (E, \delta), D)$, the outer improvement fixpoint $\lim C_1(\max p, \min p, \mathsf{limsupImp}[\mathsf{maxPre}^P])$ is the probabilistic graph valuation $\sup \mathsf{LimSup}(p)$ of the limsup objective, and $\lim C_1(\min p, \max p, \mathsf{liminfImp}[\mathsf{maxPre}^P])$ is the probabilistic graph valuation $\sup \mathsf{LimInf}(p)$ of the liminf objective. Neither the inner nor the outer improvement fixpoints are finitely reachable. However, the boundedness property of probabilistic graph values for maximizing and minimizing objectives carries over to limsup and liminf objectives. This is the key for proving the finite computability: the nested value improvement algorithm (Algorithm 2) with precision $\alpha = \frac{1}{2\gamma}$, where γ is defined as in Section 3, achieves the following: (1) in the outer loop, Algorithm 2 computes a valuation v^i such that $\mathrm{diff}(v^i, v^{i+1}) \leq \alpha$ within a number $i \in O(\gamma^2)$ of iterations; and (2) in the inner loop, for each $i \geq 0$, Algorithm 2 computes a valuation u_i^j such that $\mathrm{diff}(u_i^j, u_i^{j+1}) \leq \alpha$ within a number $j \in O(\gamma^2)$ of iterations. Thus the limit function Lim to obtain v^* from v^i, and each u_i^* from u_i^j, can be defined as follows: for every state $s \in S$, round the value $v^i(s)$ (resp. $u_i^j(s)$) to the nearest multiple of $\frac{1}{\gamma}$. Then for each $i \geq 0$, the accelerated valuation u_i^* is the i-th inner improvement fixpoint u_i^∞, and v^* is the outer improvement fixpoint v^∞.

Optimality. While no better bound than an exponential bound in the number of states is known for the nested value improvement scheme, the probabilistic graph valuations of limsup and liminf objectives can be computed in polynomial time. In the boolean case, for Büchi and coBüchi objectives, the polynomial-time computation proceeds as follows: first compute the *value-1* set $T \subseteq S$ of the given Büchi or coBüchi objective (i.e., the set of states s such that the probabilistic graph valuation at s is 1), and then compute the probabilistic graph valuation of the reachability objective with target set T; the latter values can be computed by linear programming (see Section 3 on maximizing and minimizing objectives). A polynomial-time algorithm for computing the value-1 set T for Büchi and coBüchi objectives is presented in [14,8]. In the quantitative case, the probabilistic graph valuations of limsup and liminf objectives can be obtained by first computing the value-1 sets for Büchi (resp. coBüchi) objectives in descending (resp. ascending) order of the rewards, and then using the linear-programming approach to compute the probabilistic graph valuations for maximizing (resp. minimizing) objectives. As pointed out in Section 3, these techniques based on linear programming do not generalize to probabilistic games, even in the special case of boolean objectives.

4.6   Probabilistic Games

Finitely computable nested fixpoints. The probabilistic game valuations of limsup and liminf objectives can again be expressed as nested improvement fixpoints: on a probabilistic game $G = ((S, S_1, S_2, S_*), (E, \delta), D)$, the outer improvement fixpoint $\lim C_1(\max p, \min p, \mathsf{limsupImp}[\mathsf{maxminPre}^P])$ is the probabilistic game valuation $\mathsf{supinf} \, \mathsf{LimSup}(p)$ of the limsup objective, and $\lim C_1(\min p, \max p, \mathsf{liminfImp}[\mathsf{maxminPre}^P])$ is the probabilistic game valuation $\mathsf{supinf} \, \mathsf{LimInf}(p)$ of the liminf objective. The boundedness property and finite-computability results for limsup and liminf objectives on probabilistic graphs carry over to probabilistic games; see Table 2.

Optimality. Unlike in the case of probabilistic graphs, no polynomial-time algorithms are known for solving the limsup and liminf problems on probabilistic games, not even in the special case of boolean (Büchi and coBüchi) objectives. The problems of computing probabilistic game valuations for general (quantitative) limsup and liminf objectives can be shown to lie in NP $\cap$ coNP.

4.7   Concurrent Games

Nested improvement fixpoints. The concurrent game valuations of Büchi and coBüchi objectives can be expressed as nested improvement fixpoints, but these fixpoints are not known to be finitely computable. On a concurrent game $G = (S, A_1, A_2, (E, \delta), D)$, the outer improvement fixpoint $\lim C_1(\max p, \min p, \mathsf{limsupImp}[\mathsf{supinfPre}])$ is the concurrent game valuation $\mathsf{supinf} \, \square\lozenge p$ of the boolean limsup (Büchi) objective, and $\lim C_1(\min p, \max p, \mathsf{liminfImp}[\mathsf{supinfPre}])$ is the concurrent game valuation

Table 2. Nested value improvement for limsup and liminf objectives. Recall that γ is such that $16^n \in O(\gamma)$.

n states	Objective $\mathsf{LimSup}(p)$	Objective $\mathsf{LimInf}(p)$
Valued graphs	$\mathsf{Imp2}(v, u) =$ $\mathsf{limsupImp}[\mathsf{maxPre}](v, u)$ iteration converges in n^2 steps	$\mathsf{Imp2}(v, u) =$ $\mathsf{liminfImp}[\mathsf{maxPre}](v, u)$ iteration converges in n^2 steps
Deterministic games	$\mathsf{Imp2}(v, u) =$ $\mathsf{limsupImp}[\mathsf{maxminPre}](v, u)$ iteration converges in n^2 steps	$\mathsf{Imp2}(v, u) =$ $\mathsf{liminfImp}[\mathsf{maxminPre}](v, u)$ iteration converges in n^2 steps
Probabilistic graphs	$\mathsf{Imp2}(v, u) =$ $\mathsf{limsupImp}[\mathsf{maxPre}^P](v, u)$ iteration converges in $O(\gamma^4)$ steps	$\mathsf{Imp2}(v, u) =$ $\mathsf{liminfImp}[\mathsf{maxPre}^P](v, u)$ iteration converges in $O(\gamma^4)$ steps
Probabilistic games	$\mathsf{Imp2}(v, u) =$ $\mathsf{limsupImp}[\mathsf{maxminPre}^P](v, u)$ iteration converges in $O(\gamma^4)$ steps	$\mathsf{Imp2}(v, u) =$ $\mathsf{liminfImp}[\mathsf{maxminPre}^P](v, u)$ iteration converges in $O(\gamma^4)$ steps
Concurrent games (boolean p)	$\mathsf{Imp2}(v, u) =$ $\mathsf{limsupImp}[\mathsf{supinfPre}](v, u)$ iteration converges in the limit (no known bound)	$\mathsf{Imp2}(v, u) =$ $\mathsf{liminfImp}[\mathsf{supinfPre}](v, u)$ iteration converges in the limit (no known bound)

supinf $\Diamond\Box p$ of the boolean liminf (coBüchi) objective [16]. Neither the inner nor outer improvement fixpoints are known to be finitely computable. As in the case of reachability and safety objectives, it is not even known if any improvement fixpoints are finitely approximable. The quantitative case has not been studied in the literature: we conjecture that the above characterizations of the concurrent game valuations for Büchi and coBüchi objectives generalize to quantitative limsup and liminf objectives.

Optimality. The complexity results for concurrent games with reachability and safety objectives (see Section 3) generalize to Büchi and coBüchi objectives.

Summary. We summarize the situation for limsup and liminf objectives in Table 2.

5   Level-3 Objectives

We briefly discuss the most important objectives above Borel level 2: parity objectives and limit-average objectives. The parity objectives are a canonical form to express all ω-regular objectives, and the limit-average (often called *mean-payoff*) objectives are studied widely in game theory. For parity objectives, the value lattice is a finite linear order (or alternatively, a finite product of two-valued boolean lattices); for limit-average objectives, the value lattice is quantitative.

Parity objectives. Let $D = \{0, 1, \ldots, d-1\}$ or $D = \{1, 2, \ldots, d\}$; the d integers in D are called *priorities*. Consider a valued graph (S, E, D) and a reward function $p\colon S \to D$. The *parity objective* $\mathsf{Parity}(p)\colon \Omega \to \mathbb{B}$ is the function that maps a path to 1 if the maximal priority that appears along the path infinitely often is even. Formally,

$$\mathsf{Parity}(p) \;=\; \{\omega \in \Omega \mid \mathsf{LimSup}(p)(\omega) \text{ is even}\}.$$

Büchi and coBüchi objectives are special cases of parity objectives with two priorities: for Büchi objectives, let $D = \{1,2\}$, and $p(s) = 2$ iff s is in the recurrent set; for coBüchi objectives, let $D = \{0,1\}$, and $p(s) = 0$ iff s is in the persistent set.

Limit-average objectives. Let $D = \mathbb{R}_{\geq 0}^{\infty}$. Consider a valued graph (S, E, D) and a reward function $p \colon S \to D$. The *limit-average objective* $\mathsf{LimAvg}(p) \colon \Omega \to D$ is the function that maps every path to the long-run average of the rewards that appear along the path. Formally, for all paths $\omega = \langle s_0, s_1, s_2, \ldots \rangle$,

$$\mathsf{LimAvg}(p)(\omega) \;=\; \lim_{n \to \infty} \inf \{ \frac{1}{k} \cdot \sum_{i=0}^{k-1} p(s_i) \mid k \geq n \}.$$

Borel complexity. The parity objectives lie in the intersection of the third levels of the Borel hierarchy, in $\Sigma_3 \cap \Pi_3$; they are hard for the second levels, i.e., both Σ_2-hard and Π_2-hard [31]. The limit-average objectives are Π_3-complete: for every real $\beta \geq 0$, the set of paths $\omega \in \Omega$ with $\mathsf{LimAvg}(p)(\omega) \geq \beta$ is definable in Π_3 by

$$(\forall m \geq 1)(\exists n \geq 0)(\forall k \geq n)(\frac{1}{k} \cdot \sum_{i=0}^{k-1} p(s_i) \geq \beta - \frac{1}{m});$$

and the set of paths $\omega \in \Omega$ with $\mathsf{LimAvg}(p)(\omega) \leq \beta$ is definable in Π_2 by

$$(\forall n \geq 0)(\exists k \geq n)(\frac{1}{k} \cdot \sum_{i=0}^{k-1} p(s_i) \leq \beta).$$

The Π_3-hardness of limit-average objectives is proved in [3].

Parity and limit-average problems. Given a valued graph G (resp. a deterministic game; a probabilistic graph; a probabilistic game; or a concurrent game), and a reward function p, we wish to compute the graph valuations $\sup \mathsf{Parity}(p)$ and $\sup \mathsf{LimAvg}(p)$ (resp. the game valuations $\mathsf{supinf}\,\mathsf{Parity}(p)$ and $\mathsf{supinf}\,\mathsf{LimAvg}(p)$) over G. The parity problem on graphs (resp. games) arises in model checking CTL (resp. ATL) over structures with strong-fairness (Streett) constraints, which can be converted to parity constraints. Also the synthesis problem for LTL can be reduced to a parity problem on games, by converting a given LTL formula into a deterministic parity automaton of double-exponential size [29].

5.1   Parity Objectives

Value iteration solutions for parity (and limit-average) objectives were proposed first for deterministic games; so we start with this case.

Deterministic games. The parity problem on deterministic games is equivalent to μ-calculus model checking [17]: given a value set with d priorities, the deterministic game valuation sup Parity(p) can be computed by evaluating a μ-calculus expression over the deterministic game predecessor operator maxminPre. The μ-calculus expression has alternation depth $d - 1$, that is, it contains $d - 1$ alternations of the least-fixpoint operator μ and the greatest-fixpoint operator ν (the μ-calculus formulas for Büchi and coBüchi objectives from Section 4, which have alternation depth 1, are obtained as special cases for $d = 2$). The μ-calculus expression defines a value iteration scheme that computes d nested fixpoints. All fixpoints are finitely reachable, and thus the value iteration algorithm runs in $O(mn^{d-1})$ time.

For the value iteration scheme obtained from the μ-calculus expression of [17], the values are boolean. In [21], a different value lattice is considered, namely, tuples of nonnegative integers with lexicographic ordering. A valuation assigns to each state a so-called *rank* (or *small-progress measure*), which is a d-tuple such that every even coordinate is 0, and every odd coordinate is an integer between 0 and n. For such "rich" valuations, an alternation-free value iteration scheme (similar to Algorithm 1) can be used to solve parity games. The value improvement fixpoint is finitely reachable and can be computed in $O(mn^{\lfloor d/2 \rfloor})$ time [21]. It is an interesting question when and how in general the complexity of a value iteration scheme can be traded off against the complexity of a modified value domain. If $d \leq \sqrt{n}$, then [21] is the best known algorithm. In [22], a subexponential-time algorithm for solving deterministic parity games is given; the running time of that algorithm is $n^{O(\sqrt{n})}$, which improves on [21] when $d \notin O(\sqrt{n})$. No polynomial-time algorithm is known for the parity problem on deterministic games, which lies in NP ∩ coNP [17].

Graphs. The parity problem on graphs can be solved in $O(m \log d)$ time [24]. Value iteration is not optimal, because the value iteration solutions that have been devised for deterministic games require exponentially many iterations even when applied to the special case of graphs. A reduction from parity objectives to limit-average objectives [20], followed by value iteration for graphs with limit-average objectives [27] (see below), yields an $O(mn^2)$ value iteration solution for the parity problem on graphs, which is still not optimal.

Probabilistic graphs. The parity problem on probabilistic graphs can be solved in polynomial time by first computing the value-1 set T of the given parity objective, and then computing (by linear programming; see Section 3) the probabilistic graph valuation of the reachability objective with target set T [14,8]. The known value iteration solutions require exponentially many iterations.

Probabilistic games. The parity problem on probabilistic games lies in NP ∩ coNP [8]. A value iteration scheme can obtained from the μ-calculus expression for deterministic games, essentially by replacing the deterministic game predecessor operator maxminPre with the probabilistic game predecessor operator maxminPre^P [16]. The nested fixpoints are not finitely reachable, but finitely computable, as in the case of Büchi and coBüchi objectives (see Section 4). This leads to a $O(\gamma^{2d})$ value iteration solution for the parity problem on probabilistic games (recall that γ is such that $16^n \in O(\gamma)$).

Concurrent games. The value characterization of [17] for deterministic games can be extended to concurrent games [16]: given a value set with d priorities, the concurrent game valuation supinf Parity(p) can be defined by a μ-calculus expression of alternation depth $d - 1$. The fixpoint expression is very similar to the expression of [17], except that it uses the concurrent game predecessor operator supinfPre instead of the deterministic game predecessor operator maxminPre. However, as explained in Section 3, no bounds are known for the finite approximability of fixpoints even in the very special case of reachability objectives. The known complexity bounds for the parity problem on concurrent games are the same as for the reachability problem on concurrent games [4] (see Section 3). All fixpoints can be defined in the theory of the reals with addition and multiplication [16]; however, for parity objectives the reduction to the theory of reals yields a decision procedure in 3EXPTIME [16].

5.2   Limit-Average Objectives

Deterministic games. A value improvement solution for the limit-average problem on deterministic games is given in [35]. For measuring complexity, we consider all values to be rational numbers (rather than reals). Given a reward function $p : S \to \mathbb{Q}_{\geq 0}$, let $p = \sum_{s \in S} |p(s)|$, where $|p(s)|$ denotes the space required to express the rational $p(s)$ in binary. We run Algorithm 1 with the initial valuation $v^0 = p$ and the improvement function

$$\mathsf{Imp}(v)(s) \;=\; \begin{cases} p(s) + \max\{v(s') \mid s' \in E(s)\} & \text{if } s \in S_1; \\ p(s) + \min\{v(s') \mid s' \in E(s)\} & \text{if } s \in S_2; \end{cases}$$

for all valuations $v \in V$. The value improvement fixpoint is not finitely reachable, but finitely computable. The improvement function is applied $k = mn^3 \cdot 2^p$ times. If $v^{i+1} = \mathsf{Imp}(v^i)$ for all $i \geq 0$, then for every state $s \in S$, the value sup LimAvg$(p)(s)$ is very close to $v^k(s)/k$. Thus the deterministic game valuation sup LimAvg(p) can be constructed from the valuation v^k by applying a suitable limit function [35]. The running time of the value improvement algorithm is pseudo-polynomial. No polynomial-time algorithm is known for the limit-average problem on deterministic games, which lies in NP $\cap$ coNP [35].

Graphs. The limit-average problem on graphs can be solved in $O(mn)$ time, by computing the maximum-mean cycle of a directed graph [23]. The best known value iteration solution requires $O(mn^2)$ time [27].

Probabilistic graphs. The limit-average problem on probabilistic graphs can be solved in polynomial time by linear programming [18]. Again value iteration, which requires exponentially many iterations [26,32], is not optimal.

Probabilistic games. The limit-average problem on probabilistic games lies in NP $\cap$ coNP [25]. No polynomial-time algorithm is known. We conjecture that the value improvement solution of [35], with a suitable modification of the improvement function to account for probabilistic states, can be used to solve the limit-average problem on probabilistic games, and requires exponentially many iterations.

Concurrent games. A value improvement algorithm to compute the values of limit-average objectives for concurrent games is, to our knowledge, not known. The limit-average problem on concurrent games can be solved in EXPTIME [9]. The best known lower bound is PTIME-hardness (by reduction from alternating reachability), which applies already to deterministic games.

5.3   Relation between Parity and Limit-Average Objectives

The parity and limit-average problems are related. The parity problem on deterministic games can be polynomial-time reduced to the limit-average problem on deterministic games [20]. The reduction has recently been extended to the case of probabilistic games [6]. The polynomial-time reducibility of concurrent games with parity objectives to concurrent games with limit-average objectives remains an open problem. Since parity objectives lie in $\Sigma_3 \cap \Pi_3$, while limit-average objectives are Π_3-complete, no Wadge reduction [34], and thus no polynomial-time reduction, exists from the limit-average problem to the parity problem on a given class of graphs (e.g., on deterministic games). However, a polynomial-time reduction from deterministic games with limit-average objectives to probabilistic games with reachability objectives is available [35].

6   Concluding Remarks

We briefly mention two topics related to value iteration, which we have not discussed in this paper.

Strategy improvement. An alternative approach to compute the values of games is to iterate over strategies rather than over valuations. Given an objective, a player-1 strategy σ defines a valuation v_σ on graphs and probabilistic graphs, namely, the values that player 1 achieves by following the strategy σ. On deterministic games, probabilistic games, and concurrent games, let v_σ be the optimal valuation obtainable by player 2 if player 1 follows the strategy σ. A strategy improvement algorithm iterates over strategies: given a player-1 strategy σ, the algorithm computes v_σ and then locally improves the strategy σ to achieve a better valuation for player 1. This process is repeated until no improvement is possible. In other words, the strategy improvement approach iterates over local optimizations of strategies instead of over local optimizations of values. For deterministic games with parity objectives, although the best known bound for strategy improvement is exponential, the algorithm works well in practice, and it is an open problem to find a family of examples for which strategy improvement requires a super-polynomial number of iterations [33]. Strategy improvement algorithms are also known for probabilistic games with reachability objectives [12], for probabilistic games with parity objectives [7], and for concurrent games with reachability objectives [5].

Discounted games. An improvement function Imp is *contractive* if there exists a real $0 \leq \beta < 1$ such that for all valuations v_1 and v_2, we have $\text{diff}(\text{Imp}(v_1), \text{Imp}(v_2)) \leq \beta \cdot \text{diff}(v_1, v_2)$. For contractive improvement functions, the value improvement algorithm (Algorithm 1) converges to a fixpoint because of Banach's fixpoint theorem. While the improvement functions we discussed in this paper are not necessarily contractive, in the setting of games with discounted reward objectives [30], improvement functions are contractive. The analysis of discounted games is therefore simpler [15]: (1) a contractive improvement function ensures that there is an unique fixpoint, and hence the nested analysis of least and greatest fixpoints can be avoided; and (2) a contractive improvement function ensures the geometric convergence of valuations, guaranteeing finite approximability even for concurrent games. Moreover, the values of undiscounted games with parity and limit-average objectives can be obtained as appropriate limits of the values of certain discounted reward objectives, as the discount factor goes to 1. This was shown for concurrent games with parity objectives in [15,19], and for concurrent games with limit-average objectives in [28]. Probabilistic graphs with discounted reward objectives can be solved in polynomial time [18], but no polynomial-time algorithm is known for deterministic games with discounted reward objectives. The problem of computing the values of discounted reward objectives for probabilistic games can be shown to lie in NP ∩ coNP.

Acknowledgment. We thank Laurent Doyen for helpful comments on a draft.

References

1. Alur, R., Henzinger, T.A., Kupferman, O.: Alternating-time temporal logic. Journal of the ACM 49, 672–713 (2002)
2. Chakrabarti, A., de Alfaro, L., Henzinger, T.A., Stoelinga, M.: Resource Interfaces. In: Alur, R., Lee, I. (eds.) EMSOFT 2003. LNCS, vol. 2855, pp. 117–133. Springer, Heidelberg (2003)
3. Chatterjee, K.: Concurrent games with tail objectives. Technical Report EECS-2005-1385, UC Berkeley (2005)
4. Chatterjee, K., de Alfaro, L., Henzinger, T.A.: The complexity of quantitative concurrent parity games. In: SODA 2006, pp. 678–687. ACM-SIAM (2006)
5. Chatterjee, K., de Alfaro, L., Henzinger, T.A.: Strategy improvement for concurrent reachability games. In: QEST 2006, pp. 291–300. IEEE (2006)
6. Chatterjee, K., Henzinger, T.A.: Reduction of stochastic parity to stochastic mean-payoff games. Technical Report EECS-2006-140, UC Berkeley (2006)
7. Henzinger, T.A., Chatterjee, K.: Strategy Improvement and Randomized Subexponential Algorithms for Stochastic Parity Games. In: Durand, B., Thomas, W. (eds.) STACS 2006. LNCS, vol. 3884, pp. 512–523. Springer, Heidelberg (2006)
8. Chatterjee, K., Jurdziński, M., Henzinger, T.A.: Quantitative stochastic parity games. In: SODA 2004, pp. 121–130. ACM-SIAM (2004)
9. Chatterjee, K., Majumdar, R., Henzinger, T.A.: Stochastic limit-average games are in EXPTIME. Technical Report EECS-2006-143, UC Berkeley (2006)
10. Clarke, E.M., Grumberg, O., Peled, D.: Model Checking. MIT Press (1999)
11. Condon, A.: The complexity of stochastic games. Information and Computation 96, 203–224 (1992)

12. Condon, A.: On algorithms for simple stochastic games. In: Advances in Computational Complexity Theory. DIMACS Series in Discrete Mathematics and Theoretical Computer Science, vol. 13, pp. 51–73. AMS (1993)
13. Courcoubetis, C., Yannakakis, M.: The complexity of probabilistic verification. Journal of the ACM 42, 857–907 (1995)
14. de Alfaro, L.: Formal Verification of Probabilistic Systems. PhD thesis, Stanford University (1997)
15. de Alfaro, L., Henzinger, T.A., Majumdar, R.: Discounting the future in systems theory. In: Baeten, J.C.M., Lenstra, J.K., Parrow, J., Woeginger, G.J. (eds.) ICALP 2003. LNCS, vol. 2719, pp. 1022–1037. Springer, Heidelberg (2003)
16. de Alfaro, L., Majumdar, R.: Quantitative solution of ω-regular games. Journal of Computer and System Sciences 68, 374–397 (2004)
17. Emerson, E.A., Jutla, C.: Tree automata, μ-calculus, and determinacy. In: FOCS 1991, pp. 368–377. IEEE (1991)
18. Filar, J., Vrieze, K.: Competitive Markov Decision Processes. Springer (1997)
19. Gimbert, H., Zielonka, W.: Discounting infinite games, but how and why? ENTCS 119, 3–9 (2005)
20. Jurdziński, M.: Deciding the winner in parity games is in UP ∩ coUP. Information Processing Letters 68, 119–124 (1998)
21. Jurdziński, M.: Small Progress Measures for Solving Parity Games. In: Reichel, H., Tison, S. (eds.) STACS 2000. LNCS, vol. 1770, pp. 290–301. Springer, Heidelberg (2000)
22. Jurdziński, M., Paterson, M., Zwick, U.: A deterministic subexponential algorithm for solving parity games. In: SODA 2006, pp. 117–123. ACM-SIAM (2006)
23. Karp, R.M.: A characterization of the minimum cycle mean in a digraph. Discrete Mathematics 23, 309–311 (1978)
24. Vardi, M.Y., Kupferman, O., King, V.: On the Complexity of Parity Word Automata. In: Honsell, F., Miculan, M. (eds.) ETAPS 2001 and FOSSACS 2001. LNCS, vol. 2030, pp. 276–286. Springer, Heidelberg (2001)
25. Liggett, T.A., Lippman, S.A.: Stochastic games with perfect information and time average payoff. SIAM Review 11, 604–607 (1969)
26. Littman, M.L.: Algorithms for Sequential Decision Making. PhD thesis, Brown University (1996)
27. Madani, O.: Polynomial value iteration algorithms for deterministic MDPs. In: UAI 2002, pp. 311–318. Morgan Kaufmann (2002)
28. Mertens, J.F., Neyman, A.: Stochastic games. International Journal of Game Theory 10, 53–66 (1981)
29. Safra, S.: On the complexity of ω-automata. In: FOCS 1988, pp. 319–327. IEEE (1988)
30. Shapley, L.S.: Stochastic games. Proceedings of the National Academy of Sciences 39, 1095–1100 (1953)
31. Thomas, W.: Languages, automata, and logic. In: Rozenberg, G., Salomaa, A. (eds.) Handbook of Formal Languages, vol. 3, pp. 389–455. Springer (1997)
32. Tseng, P.: Solving H-horizon stationary Markov decision problems in time proportional to log(H). Operations Research Letters 9, 287–297 (1990)
33. Vöge, J., Jurdziński, M.: A discrete strategy improvement algorithm for solving parity games. In: Emerson, E.A., Sistla, A.P. (eds.) CAV 2000. LNCS, vol. 1855, pp. 202–215. Springer, Heidelberg (2000)
34. Wadge, W.W.: Reducibility and Determinateness of Baire Spaces. PhD thesis, UC Berkeley (1984)
35. Zwick, U., Paterson, M.: The complexity of mean-payoff games on graphs. Theoretical Computer Science 158, 343–359 (1996)

Fifteen Years of Formal Property Verification in Intel

Limor Fix

Intel Research Pittsburgh
Limor.fix@intel.com

Abstract. Model checking technologies have been applied to hardware verification in the last 15 years. Pioneering work has been conducted in Intel since 1990 using model checking technologies to build industrial hardware verification systems. This paper reviews the evolution and the success of these systems in Intel and in particular it summarizes the many challenges and learning that have resulted from changing how hardware validation is performed in Intel to include formal property verification. The paper ends with a discussion on how the learning from hardware verification can be used to accelerate the industrial deployment of model-checking technologies for software verification.

Keywords: Model checking, formal specification, formal property verification.

1 Hardware Verification in Intel

1.1 The First Generation

Since 1995 Intel engineers have been using formal verification tools to verify properties of hardware designs. The first generation of Intel formal property verification tools [1, 2, 3, 4, 5, 6], called *Prover*, included an enhanced version of SMV, the BDD-based model checker developed by Ken McMillan [17], and a specification language, called FSL, that was a hardware linear temporal language inspired by LTL, the linear temporal logic proposed by Pnueli [18]. The compiler for FSL translated the linear logic into automata using algorithms similar to [19]. FSL was used both to specify *formal properties* to be verified by the model checker and to specify *checkers* to be checked dynamically during simulation of the hardware designs.

Two lead CPU design teams used Prover from 1995 till 1999. Both teams reported successful usage of the new verification technology and in particular *high quality bugs* have been discovered. These bugs were classified as bugs that either would have been found by other validation tools much later in the design cycle or bugs that might otherwise would have escaped all the validation tools and reach the silicon. Very important leanings were generated by the two design teams about how, where, when and by whom hardware formal verification tools should be used and moreover the remaining technology challenges were identified.

How - Automated abstraction [1, 4] and *modular verification [20]* using *assume-guarantee paradigm* were used to overcome the limited capacity of the tools. Properties were developed to capture the intended behavior of the inputs and the

O. Grumberg and H. Veith (Eds.): 25MC Festschrift, LNCS 5000, pp. 139–144, 2008.

outputs of each module. Properties on the outputs of a module were verified using the assumptions on the inputs of the module. Properties on the output signals of the module served also as assumptions on the inputs of the neighboring module.

Where - Only selected areas of the CPU were formally verified. These were areas of high risk in which new complex functionality was added or areas in which the properties to be proven were obvious. For example, the arithmetic units of the CPU had both characteristic.

When - The decision on when to use the formal tools was not easy. On the one hand, using the tools very early in the design cycle even before the entire design was coded, that is before the RTL simulation can start, was very successful. Bugs were revealed early and did not even reach the early simulation models. On the other hand, since at that time the RTL was unstable, changes to the RTL required recoding of the properties and assumptions again and again. The team ended up using the tools relatively late in the design cycle and indicated that support for early verification would be very beneficial.

By Whom - Traditionally, limited validation was done by the RTL designers and most of the in depth verification was carried out by the validation engineers. We encouraged both groups, the designers and the validators to use Prover. In terms of number of users, we had better success with the validation groups. More resources were devoted in the validation teams to use the new formal property verification system. The small number of designers that used the tools indicated bigger success in finding more bugs with less efforts. The designers had an easier task because they were very familiar with the design and developing appropriate assumptions and properties was much easier for them.

Among the main challenges that have been identified, it became clear that it was very difficult to develop good specifications. It was hard for designers to develop high level properties that do not mimic the details of the implementation, it was hard to train the designers to use a linear temporal language, it was impossible to know if enough properties were developed to express the entire desired behavior of the design, and it was hard to maintain the properties since the design was changing and as a result the properties had to be changed accordingly.

Other challenges were also identified. One obvious challenge was the limited capacity of the model checker. As mentioned before, modularization and abstraction techniques were developed. The design was divided into smaller components and assumptions were placed on the inputs of the blocks. The introduction of assumptions created additional challenges: it was hard to know which assumptions were needed, it was hard to identify circular reasoning, and it was hard to make sure all assumptions were verified. As for abstraction, semi-manual abstraction techniques were developed, however, it was impossible to deploy them because whenever the design changed the abstract model had to be re-built. We ended up focusing on automated abstraction only [1, 4].

The most important learning from the first deployment of formal property verification tools in two real complex design projects was the need to either identify which previously existing validation activity can be omitted and replaced by the formal verification effort. Or, alternatively, the need to smoothly integrate the formal verification activity into the rest of the design and validation efforts while minimizing any additional manual effort by either the designers or the validators.

1.2 The Second Generation

In the following years, Intel formal verification system developed very fast, moving from a single BDD-based model checking engine to multiple engines. A SAT-based model checker [21, 7] and a symbolic simulation engine [22, 8] were added. Formal specification coverage tools were introduced to be able to measure the quality and the completeness of the set of properties that have been developed [10, 11, 12, 14]. These tools indicated which parts of the implementation were not specified by the properties, which properties were vacuously true with respect to the given design and how one set of properties covers another set of properties. A database of properties and assumptions was developed to help detect circular reasoning and track the status of all properties.

With high effort, a new generation of the specification language, called ForSpec [9, 10], was developed. This language had two versions, a standalone version in which the properties are developed in a separate file detached from the RTL design and an embedded version in which properties were developed as assertions embedded inside the RTL model, that is, as part of the Verilog code. In 2003, Intel donated ForSpec to Accelera, part of the effort to make ForSpec an IEEE standard for formal verification language [23]. The resulting IEEE 1850 Standard, has adopted major parts of ForSpec standalone version. The IEEE standard for SystemVerilog has adopted major parts of ForSpec embedded version for the SystemVerilog assertions, also called SVA.

The barrier to moving from a limited deployment to wide spread deployment of formal property verification in Intel was crossed mainly due to two developments: the first was the introduction of ForSpec assertions inside the Verilog code, thus allowing the designers to easily code and maintain the properties (assertions). The second was the integration of the formal verification activity with other validation efforts. In particular, the RTL designer had two reasons to annotate his/her code with assertions. The assertions were always checked during simulation and in addition the assertions served as assumptions and properties for formal verification. In case an assertion was too complex to be verified formally it was still very useful as a checker in simulation.

In the last two years we have extended the use of formal verification technology to other parts of the design. A very successful system has been developed for the verification of microcode [15].

2 Industrial Deployment of Model Checking for SW Verification

A large body of very successful research already exists in the area of formal software verification. The goal of using these techniques widely by software developers, has not been achieved yet. As our experience in hardware verification taught us the following questions need to be answered: how, where, when and by whom. Below I present my beliefs that are based only on my hardware experience.

2.1 How

Embedded assertions have been proven very successful in hardware verification, thus, I believe assertions embedded in programs is a very most promising approach. For assertions to be successful, they need to be dense enough, that is, enough assertions need to be manually inserted by the programmer or generated automatically by the compilers. A very successful method to increase the number of assertions is to develop a library of parameterized assertions that express common requirements for software correctness.

Once assertions are embedded in the program they need to be utilized for several purposes, for example, for compiler optimization, for debugging using gdb-like debuggers and for formal verification. Databases of assertions need to be generated automatically from the program code for managing the status of the assertions.

2.2 Where

While parallel programming and distributed algorithms were very active research fields 20 years ago but had limited deployment, these days parallel programming becomes a necessity. Due to the power wall in silicon technology all state of the art computing devices have multiple processing units and the transition to chip multiprocessors is happening very fast. New programming paradigms are being developed to combat the difficulties of parallel programming, e.g., transaction memory programming. This transition and the need for new programming paradigms and languages create opportunities for formal verification of software. The new developed parallel programming paradigm should include embedded assertions as integral part its design.

An additional area in which formal verification of software should apply to is security. The problems of viruses, spyware, and worms are growing fast and have very high costs. Extra efforts to reduce vulnerability of software are likely to be invested to prevent these costs.

2.3 When

As with hardware, the best person to develop the assertions is the developer (programmer) himself. Assertions development should become an integral part of writing software and assertions should be embedded in the code while the code is generated and they should be as dense as possible. The compilers should also generate embedded assertions in addition to the ones inserted by the programmer.

2.4 By Whom

In large software companies, just as in hardware companies, large validation groups are focused on raising the quality of the code by intensive debugging. I believe most assertions need to be developed by the programmers themselves and should be always turned on. The validation teams may add more assertions later and most importantly they need to work with the assertion database to complete the verification of all assertions.

Acknowledgments. The success of formal verification in Intel was the result of a great collaboration between industry and academia. Intel formal verification systems have been developed with intensive collaboration with researchers around the world.

In particular, my team has worked with Moshe Vardi, Amir Pnueli, Orna Grumberg, Zohar Manna, Ed Clarke, Randy Bryant, David Dill, Sharad Malik, Assaf Schuster, P.P. Chakrabarti, P. Dasgupta, Scott Hazelhurst, Enrico Giuchilia. It also required great openness and willingness to take risk from the managers of the design teams and the managers of Intel internal CAD group.

References

1. Kamhi, G., Weissberg, O., Fix, L., Binyamini, Z., Shtadler, Z.: Automatic data-path extraction for efficient usage of HDD. In: Grumberg, O. (ed.) CAV 1997. LNCS, vol. 1254, pp. 95–106. Springer, Heidelberg (1997)
2. Kamhi, G., Fix, L.: Adaptive variable reordering for symbolic model checking. In: IEEE/ACM International Conference on Computer Aided Design (ICCAD) (1998)
3. Kamhi, G., Fix, L., Binyamini, Z.: Symbolic Model Checking Visualization. In: Gopalakrishnan, G.C., Windley, P. (eds.) FMCAD 1998. LNCS, vol. 1522, pp. 290–302. Springer, Heidelberg (1998)
4. Mador-Haim, S., Fix, L.: Inputs elimination and data abstraction in model checking. In: Gopalakrishnan, G.C., Windley, P. (eds.) FMCAD 1998. LNCS, vol. 1522. Springer, Heidelberg (1998)
5. Fraer, R., Kamhi, G., Fix, L., Vardi, M.: Evaluating Semi-Exhaustive Verification Techniques for Bug Hunting. In: SMC, 1999 (CAV 1999 workshop) (1999)
6. Fraer, R., Kamhi, G., Ziv, B., Vardi, M.Y., Fix, L.: Prioritized Traversal: Efficient Reachability Analysis for Verification and Falsification. In: CAV (2000)
7. Vardi, M.Y., Giunchiglia, E., Tacchella, A., Kamhi, G., Fix, L., Fraer, R., Copty, F.: Benefits of Bounded Model Checking at an Industrial Setting. In: Berry, G., Comon, H., Finkel, A. (eds.) CAV 2001. LNCS, vol. 2102. Springer, Heidelberg (2001)
8. Hazelhurst, S., Wiessberg, O., Kamhi, G., Fix, L.: A hybrid verification approach: getting deep into the design. In: DAC 2002 (2002)
9. Armoni, R., Fix, L., Flaisher, A., Gerth, R., Ginsburg, B., Kanza, T., Landver, A., Mador-Haim, S., Singerman, E., Tiemeyer, A., Vardi, M., Zbar, Y.: The ForSpec temporal Logic: A new Temporal Property Specification Language. In: Katoen, J.-P., Stevens, P. (eds.) ETAPS 2002 and TACAS 2002. LNCS, vol. 2280, pp. 296–311. Springer, Heidelberg (2002)
10. Vardi, M.Y., Grumberg, O., Armoni, R., Piterman, N., Fix, L., Flaisher, A., Tiemeyer, A.: Enhanced Vacuity Detection in Linear Temporal Logic. In: Hunt Jr., W.A., Somenzi, F. (eds.) CAV 2003. LNCS, vol. 2725, pp. 368–380. Springer, Heidelberg (2003)
11. Basu, P., Das, S., Dasgupta, P., Chakrabarti, P.P., Mohan, C.R., Fix, L.: Formal Verification Coverage: are the RTL-properties covering the design's architectural intent. In: DATE 2004, pp. 668–669 (2004)
12. Basu, P., Das, S., Dasgupta, P., Chakrabarti, P.P., Mohan, C.R., Fix, L.: Formal Verification Coverage: Computing the coverage gap between temporal specifications. In: ICCAD 2004 (2004)
13. Armoni, R., Fix, L., Fraer, R., Huddleston, S., Piterman, N., Vardi, M.: SAT-based induction for temporal safety properties. In: BMC workshop at CAV 2004 (2004)
14. Basu, P., Das, S., Dasgupta, P., Chakrabarti, P.P., Mohan, C.R., Fix, L.: Formal methods for analyzing the completeness of assertions suite against a high level fault model. In: VLSI Design 2005 conference at Kokata (to be published)

15. Arons, T., Elster, E., Fix, L., Mador-Haim, S., Mishaeli, M., Shalev, J., Singerman, E., Tiemeyer, A., Vardi, M., Zuck, L.: Formal Verification of Backward compatibility of Microcode. In: 17th International Conference on Computer Aided Verification, Edinburgh (July 2005)
16. Fix, L., Grumberg, O., Heyman, T., Schuster, A.: Verifying very large industrial circuits using 100 processes and beyond. In: Third International Symposium on Automated Technology for Verification and Analysis (October 2005) Best paper award
17. McMillan, K.L.: Symbolic Model Checking: an approach to the state explosion problem, PhD Thesis. CMU CS-929131 (1992)
18. Pnueli, A.: The temporal logic of programs. In: Proc. 18th IEEE Symposium on Foundation of Computer Science (1977)
19. Clarke, E., Grumberg, O., Hamaguchi, H.: Another Look at LTL Model Checking. Formal Methods in System Design 10(1) (February 1997); In: Dill, D.L. (ed.) CAV 1994. LNCS, vol. 818. Springer, Heidelberg (1994)
20. Pnueli, A.: In Transition from Global to Modular Temporal Reasoning about Programs. In: Apt, K.R. (ed.) Logics and Models of Concurrent Systems. sub-series F: Computer and System Science, pp. 123–144. Springer (1985)
21. Clarke, E., Biere, A., Cimatti, A., Zhu, Y.: Symbolic Model Checking without BDDs. In: Cleaveland, W.R. (ed.) ETAPS 1999 and TACAS 1999. LNCS, vol. 1579. Springer, Heidelberg (1999)
22. Bryant, R.E., Seger, C.-J.: Formal verification of digital circuits using symbolic ternary system models. In: Clarke, E.M., Kurshan, R.P. (eds.) CAV 1990. LNCS, vol. 531. Springer (1990)
23. Vardi, M.: From Church and Prior to PSL: Standing on The Shoulders of Giants. This volume

A View from the Engine Room: Computational Support for Symbolic Model Checking*

Randal E. Bryant

School of Computer Science
Carnegie Mellon University
Pittsburgh, PA 15213, USA
Randy.Bryant@cs.cmu.edu

1 Introduction

Symbolic model checking owes much of its success to powerful methods for reasoning about Boolean functions. The first symbolic model checkers used Ordered Binary Decision Diagrams (OBDDs) [1] to represent system transition relations and sets of system states [9]. All of the steps required for checking a model can be expressed as a series of operations on these representations, without ever enumerating individual states or transitions. More recently, bounded [3] and unbounded [10,11] model checkers have been devised that use Boolean satisfiability (SAT) solvers as their core computational engines. Methods having a SAT solver work on a detailed system model and OBDDs operate on an abstracted model have shown that the combination of these two reasoning techniques can be more powerful than either operating on its own [4]. Boolean methods have enabled model checkers to scale to handle some of the complex verification problems arising from real-world hardware and software designs.

Given the importance of Boolean reasoning in symbolic checking, we take this opportunity to examine the capabilities of SAT solvers and BDD packages. We use several simple experimental evaluations to illustrate some strengths and weaknesses of current approaches, and suggest directions for future research.

2 Experiments in (Un)SAT

Verification problems typically use SAT solver to find an error in the design, and hence the task is to prove that a formula is unsatisfiable. Currently, the Davis-Putnam-Logemann-Loveland (DPLL) method [5] for solving SAT problems by backtracking search is heavily favored among complete SAT algorithms. Recent progress in these solvers has led to remarkable gains in speed and capacity [13], especially in proving that a formula is unsatisfiable. By contrast, using OBDDs seems like an inefficient approach to solving SAT problems, since it will generate a representation of all possible solutions, rather than a single solution. There are some common, and seemingly simple problems, for which DPLL performs poorly. We illustrate this and compare the performance of OBDDs for two sets of benchmarks.

---

* This research was supported by the Semiconductor Research Corporation, Contract RID 1355.001

O. Grumberg and H. Veith (Eds.): 25MC Festschrift, LNCS 5000, pp. 145–149, 2008.

Size	Exhaustive	LIMMAT	ZCHAFF	SIEGE	MINISAT	CUDD
8	< 0.1	< 0.1	< 0.1	< 0.1	< 0.1	< 0.1
16	< 0.1	< 0.1	< 0.1	< 0.1	< 0.1	< 0.1
24	3.6	10.0	0.6	0.5	0.3	< 0.1
32	TIME	TIME	13.0	3.8	3.7	< 0.1
40	TIME	TIME	TIME	72.0	162.2	< 0.1
48	TIME	TIME	TIME	TIME	TIME	< 0.1

Fig. 1. SAT Solver Performance on Parity Tree Benchmarks. Each number is the median time for comparing 16 different random trees to a linear chain. The timeout limit was set to 900 seconds.

Our first set of benchmarks compares functions for computing the parity of a set of n Boolean values using a tree of exclusive-or operators. Each instance of the problem compares a randomly generated tree to a linear chain. We generated 16 different trees for six different values of n, ranging from 8 to 48. The results, run on an 3.2 GHz Intel Pentium 4 Xeon, are shown in Figure 1. Since SAT solvers times can vary greatly depending on minor differences in the problem encoding, we report the median time for the 16 cases for each value of n. We set a timeout limit of 900 seconds for each instance.

These parity tree problems are known to be difficult cases for DPLL, or in fact any method based on resolution principle. Zhang and Malik submitted one such problem for $n = 36$ as a benchmark for the SAT solver competition held in conjunction with the SAT 2002 [14]. None of the solvers at the time could solve the problem within the 40-minute time limit on an Intel Pentium III.

We tested six different solution methods:

Exhaustive. Enumerate all 2^n possible solutions and test each one.

LIMMAT. The LIMMAT solver by Armin Biere from 2002. This solver uses the innovations introduced by the GRASP [8] and CHAFF solvers [13], but without the level of tuning found in more recent solvers.

ZCHAFF. The ZCHAFF 2004 solver, carrying on the work by Malik and his students [13].

SIEGE. The SIEGE version 4 solver, winner of the 2003 SAT competition.

MINISAT. The MINISAT version 1.14 solver, winner of the 2005 SAT competition.

CUDD. An OBDD-based implementation using the CUDD library from the University of Colorado.

As can be seen from the results of Figure 1, exhaustive evaluation can readily handle problems up to $n = 24$, but it becomes impractical very quickly due to the exponential scaling. The LIMMAT solver actually performs slightly worse than exhaustive evaluation. The other DPLL solvers (ZCHAFF, SIEGE, and MINISAT) can handle all 16 instances for $n = 32$. Only MINISAT can handle all 16 instances for $n = 40$, and even it can solve only 4 of the 16 instances for $n = 48$. These experiments illustrate that DPLL solvers have progressed considerably since the 2002 SAT competition, but they all experience exponential growth for this class of problems.

By contrast, OBDDs can solve parity tree problems with hardly any effort, never requiring more than 0.1 seconds for any of the instances. Parity functions have OBDD representations of linear complexity [1], and hence the tree comparison problem can be solved in worst-case $O(n^2)$ time using OBDDs. It would be feasible to solve instances of this problem for $n = 1000$ or more.

As a second class of benchmarks, we consider ones that model the bit-level behavior of arithmetic operations. Consider the problem of proving that integer addition and multiplication are associative. That is, we wish to show that the following two C functions always return the value 1:

```c
int assocA(int x, int y, int z)
{
   return (x+y)+z == x+(y+z);
}

int assocM(int x, int y, int z)
{
   return (x*y)*z == x*(y*z);
}
```

We created a set of benchmark problems from these C functions, where we varied the number of bits n in the argument words x, y, and z, up to a maximum of $n = 32$. Since there are three arguments, the number of possible argument combinations is 8^n.

Problem	Exhaustive	CUDD	MINISAT
Addition	12	> 32	> 32
Multiplication	12	8	5

Fig. 2. Performance in Solving Associativity Problems Numbers indicate the maximum word size that can be solved in under 900 seconds of CPU time

Figure 2 shows the performance for this benchmark by exhaustive evaluation, OBDDs using the CUDD package, and MINISAT (the best DPLL-based approach tested). In each case, we show the maximum number of argument bits n for which the problem can be solved within a 900 second time limit. Exhaustive evaluation works up to $n = 12$, but then becomes impractical, with each additional bit requiring eight times more evaluations. Both DPLL and OBDDs can show that addition is associative up to the maximum value tested. For multiplication, we see that OBDDs outperform DPLL, but neither does as well as brute-force, exhaustive evaluation. For OBDDs, we know that the Boolean functions for integer multiplication require OBDDs of exponential size [2], and hence OBDD-based methods for this problem incur exponential space and time. Evidently, DPLL-based methods also suffer from exponential time performance.

3   Observations

Our first set of benchmarks illustrates one of the challenges of the Boolean satisfiability problem. While DPLL works well on many problems, it has severe weaknesses, some of which can be filled by more "niche" approaches, such as OBDDs. Some attempts have been made to develop SAT solvers that use different combinations of DPLL and OBDDs, e.g., [7], but none of these has demonstrated consistent improvements over DPLL. In particular, it seems like the main advantage of current DPLL/OBDD hybrids is that they can solve problems that are tractable using either DPLL or OBDDs. We have not seen meaningful examples of them solving problems that cannot be solved by one of the two approaches operating in isolation.

An additional concern of ours is that the recent success of DPLL methods is having the effect that the research field is narrowly focusing on this approach to SAT solving. Researchers have found they can do better in SAT competitions by fine tuning DPLL solvers rather than trying fundamentally different approaches. While this tuning has led to remarkable improvements, it is not healthy for the field to narrow the "gene pool" of SAT techniques. Rather, we should be encouraging researchers to explore new approaches, even if they only outperform DPLL on small classes of problems, as long as these classes have practical applications. Steps in this direction include recent work by Jain, et al [6].

Our arithmetic problems illustrate that, while both DPLL and OBDDs are adequate for addition and related functions, neither performs well for operations related to integer multiplication. Indeed, companies that market circuit equivalence checkers have had to devise *ad hoc* workarounds for checking circuits containing multipliers. We believe that the research community should invest more effort in tackling problems that are well beyond the capability of existing SAT solvers. Examples of challenging problems arise in the fields of cryptanalysis [12] and combinatorial optimization.

4   Conclusion

2006 marks the twenty-fifth anniversary of model checking, but also the twentieth anniversary of powerful tools for Boolean reasoning, first with OBDDs and more recently with DPLL-based SAT solvers. The field has advanced considerably due to both clever ideas and careful engineering. Model checking and many other application areas have directly benefited from these tools. It is important that the research community keeps pushing ahead with new approaches and new improvements in Boolean reasoning. There remain many important problems that are beyond the reach of today's methods.

References

1. Bryant, R.E.: Graph-based algorithms for Boolean function manipulation. IEEE Transactions on Computers C-35(8), 677–691 (1986)
2. Bryant, R.E.: On the complexity of VLSI implementations and graph representations of Boolean functions with application to integer multiplication. IEEE Transactions on Computers 40(2), 205–213 (1991)
3. Clarke, E.M., Biere, A., Raimi, R., Zhu, Y.: Bounded model checking using satisfiability solving. Formal Methods in System Design 19(1), 7–34 (2001)
4. Clarke, E.M., Grumberg, O., Jha, S., Lu, Y., Veith, H.: Counterexample-guided abstraction refinement for symbolic model checking. JACM 50(5), 752–794 (2003)

5. Davis, M., Logemann, G., Loveland, D.: A machine program for theorem proving. Communcations of the ACM 5(7), 394–397 (1962)
6. Jain, H., Bartzis, C., Clarke, E.M.: Satisfiability Checking of Non-clausal Formulas Using General Matings. In: Biere, A., Gomes, C.P. (eds.) SAT 2006. LNCS, vol. 4121, pp. 75–89. Springer, Heidelberg (2006)
7. Jin, H., Somenzi, F.: CirCUs: A Hybrid Satisfiability Solver. In: Hoos, H.H., Mitchell, D.G. (eds.) SAT 2004. LNCS, vol. 3542, pp. 211–223. Springer, Heidelberg (2005)
8. Marques-Silva, J.P., Sakallah, K.A.: GRASP: A search algorithm for propositional satisfiability. IEEE Transactions on Computers 48(5), 506–521 (1999)
9. McMillan, K.: Symbolic Model Checking. Kluwer Academic Publishers (1992)
10. McMillan, K.L.: Applying SAT Methods in Unbounded Symbolic Model Checking. In: Brinksma, E., Larsen, K.G. (eds.) CAV 2002. LNCS, vol. 2404. Springer, Heidelberg (2002)
11. McMillan, K.L.: Interpolation and SAT-Based Model Checking. In: Hunt Jr., W.A., Somenzi, F. (eds.) CAV 2003. LNCS, vol. 2725, pp. 1–13. Springer, Heidelberg (2003)
12. Mironov, I., Zhang, L.: Applications of SAT Solvers to Cryptanalysis of Hash Functions. In: Biere, A., Gomes, C.P. (eds.) SAT 2006. LNCS, vol. 4121, pp. 102–115. Springer, Heidelberg (2006)
13. Moskewicz, M., Madigan, C., Zhao, Y., Zhang, L., Malik, S.: Chaff: Engineering an efficient SAT solver. In: 38th Design Automation Conference (DAC 2001), pp. 530–535 (2001)
14. Simon, L., Le Berre, D., Hirsch, E.A.: The SAT 2002 competition. Annals of Mathematics and Artificial Intelligence 43(1–4) (2005)

From Church and Prior to PSL

Moshe Y. Vardi*

Rice University, Department of Computer Science, Rice University,
Houston, TX 77251-1892, U.S.A.
vardi@cs.rice.edu
http://www.cs.rice.edu/~vardi

Abstract. One of the surprising developments in the area of program verification is how ideas introduced originally by logicians in the 1950s ended up yielding by 2003 an industrial-standard property-specification language called PSL. This development was enabled by the equally unlikely transformation of the mathematical machinery of automata on infinite words, introduced in the early 1960s for second-order arithmetics, into effective algorithms for model-checking tools. This paper attempts to trace the tangled threads of this development.

1 Thread I: Classical Logic of Time

1.1 Reasoning about Sequential Circuits

The field of hardware verification seems to have been started in a little known 1957 paper by Alonzo Church, 1903–1995, in which he described the use of logic to specify *sequential circuits* [24]. A sequential circuit is a switching circuit whose output depends not only upon its input, but also on what its input has been in the past. A sequential circuit is a particular type of finite-state machine, which became a subject of study in mathematical logic and computer science in the 1950s.

Formally, a sequential circuit $C = (I, O, R, f, g, \mathbf{r}_0)$ consists of a finite set I of Boolean input signals, a finite set O of Boolean output signals, a finite set R of Boolean sequential elements, a transition function $f : 2^I \times 2^R \to 2^R$, an output function $g : 2^R \to 2^O$, and an initial state $\mathbf{r}_0 \in 2^R$. (We refer to elements of $I \cup O \cup R$ as *circuit elements*, and assume that I, O, and R are disjoint.) Intuitively, a state of the circuit is a Boolean assignment to the sequential elements. The initial state is $\mathbf{r}_0$. In a state $\mathbf{r} \in 2^R$, the Boolean assignment to the output signals is $g(\mathbf{r})$. When the circuit is in state $\mathbf{r} \in 2^R$ and it reads an input assignment $\mathbf{i} \in 2^I$, it changes its state to $f(\mathbf{i}, \mathbf{r})$.

A *trace* over a set V of Boolean variables is an infinite word over the alphabet 2^V, i.e., an element of $(2^V)^\omega$. A trace of the sequential circuit C is a trace over $I \cup O \cup R$ that satisfies some conditions. Specifically, a sequence $\tau = (\mathbf{i}_0, \mathbf{r}_0, \mathbf{o}_0), (\mathbf{i}_1, \mathbf{r}_1, \mathbf{o}_1), \ldots,$ where $\mathbf{i}_j \in 2^I$, $\mathbf{o}_j \in 2^O$, and $\mathbf{r}_j \in 2^R$, is a trace of C if $\mathbf{r}_{j+1} = f(\mathbf{i}_j, \mathbf{r}_j)$ and $\mathbf{o}_j = g(\mathbf{r}_j)$, for $j \geq 0$. Thus, in modern terminology, Church was following the *linear-time* approach [81] (see discussion in Section 2.1). The set of traces of C is denoted by $\mathrm{traces}(C)$.

---

* Supported in part by NSF grants CCR-9988322, CCR-0124077, CCR-0311326, and ANI-0216467, by BSF grant 9800096, and by a gift from the Intel Corporation. The "Y" in the author's middle name stands for "Ya'akov".

Church observed that we can associate with an infinite word $w = a_0, a_1, \ldots$ over an alphabet 2^V, a relational structure $M_w = (I\!N, \leq, V)$, with the naturals $I\!N$ as the domain, ordered by $\leq$, and extended by the set V of unary predicates, where $j \in p$, for $p \in V$, precisely when p holds (i.e., is assigned 1) in a_i.[1] We refer to such structures as *word structures*. When we refer to the *vocabulary* of such a structure, we refer explicitly only to V, taking $\leq$ for granted.

We can now specify traces using first-order logic (FO) sentences constructed from atomic formulas of the form $x = y$, $x \leq y$, and $p(x)$ for $p \in V = I \cup R \cup O$.[2] For example, the FO sentence

$$(\forall x)(\exists y)(x < y \land p(y))$$

says that p holds infinitely often in the trace. In a follow-up paper in 1963 [25], Church considered also specifying traces using *monadic second-order logic* (MSO), where in addition to first-order quantifiers, which range over the elements of $I\!N$, we allow also monadic second-order quantifiers, ranging over subsets of $I\!N$, and atomic formulas of the form $Q(x)$, where Q is a monadic predicate variable. (This logic is also called *S1S*, the "second-order theory of one successor function".) For example, the MSO sentence,

$$(\exists P)(\forall x)(\forall y)((((P(x) \land y = x + 1) \rightarrow (\neg P(y)))\land$$
$$(((\neg P(x)) \land y = x + 1) \rightarrow P(y)))\land$$
$$(x = 0 \rightarrow P(x)) \land (P(x) \rightarrow q(x))),$$

where $x = 0$ is an abbreviation for $(\neg(\exists z)(z < x))$ and $y = x + 1$ is an abbreviation for $(y > x \land \neg(\exists z)(x < z \land z < y))$, says that q holds at every even point on the trace. MSO was introduced in [15, 17, 43, 120].) In effect, Church was proposing to use classical logic (FO or MSO) as a logic of time, by focusing on word structures. The set of models of an FO or MSO sentence φ is denoted by $\mathrm{models}(\varphi)$.

Church posed two problems related to sequential circuits [24]:

- The DECISION problem: Given circuit C and a sentence φ, does φ hold in all traces of C? That is, does $\mathrm{traces}(C) \subseteq \mathrm{models}(\varphi)$ hold?
- The SYNTHESIS problem: Given sets I and O of input and output signals, and a sentence φ over the vocabulary $I \cup O$, construct, if possible, a sequential circuit C with input signals I and output signals O such that φ holds in all traces of C. That is, construct C such that $\mathrm{traces}(C) \subseteq \mathrm{models}(\varphi)$ holds.

In modern terminology, Church's DECISION problem is precisely the MODEL-CHECKING problem in the linear-time approach (see Section 2.2). This problem did not receive much attention after [24,25], until the introduction of model checking in the early 1980s. In contrast, the SYNTHESIS problem has remained a subject of ongoing research; see [18,75,77,105,119]. One reason that the DECISION problem did not remain a subject of study, is the easy observation in [25] that the DECISION problem can be reduced to the VALIDITY problem in the underlying logic (FO or MSO). Given a sequential circuit C, we can easily generate an FO sentence α_C that holds in precisely all structures associated with traces of C. Intuitively, the sentence α_C simply has to encode the transition

---

[1] We overload notation here and treat p as both a Boolean variable and a predicate.

[2] We overload notation here and treat p as both a circuit element and a predicate symbol.

and output functions of C, which are Boolean functions. Then φ holds in all traces of C precisely when $\alpha_C \rightarrow \varphi$ holds in all word structures (of the appropriate vocabulary). Thus, to solve the DECISION problem we need to solve the VALIDITY problem over word structures. As we see next, this problem was solved in 1962.

1.2   Reasoning about Words

Church's DECISION problem was essentially solved in 1962 by Julius Richard Büchi, 1924–1984, who showed that the VALIDITY problem over word structures is decidable [16]. Actually, Büchi showed the decidability of the dual problem, which is the SATISFIABILITY problem for MSO over word structures. Büchi's approach consisted of extending the *automata-theoretic approach*, which was introduced a few years earlier [15, 43, 120] for finite word structures, to (infinite) word structures. To that end, Büchi extended automata theory to automata on infinite words.

A *nondeterministic Büchi automaton on words* (NBW) $A = (\Sigma, S, S_0, \rho, F)$ consists of a finite input alphabet Σ, a finite state set S, an initial state set $S_0 \subseteq S$, a transition relation $\rho \subseteq S \times \Sigma \times S$, and an accepting state set $F \subseteq S$. An NBW runs over an infinite input word $w = a_0, a_1, \ldots \in \Sigma^\omega$. A *run* of A on w is an infinite sequence $r = s_0, s_1, \ldots$ of states in S such that $s_0 \in S_0$, and $(s_i, a_i, s_{i+1}) \in \rho$, for $i \geq 0$. The run r is *accepting* if F is visited by r infinitely often; that is, $s_i \in F$ for infinitely many i's. The word w is *accepted* by A if A has an accepting run on w. The *language* of A, denoted $L(A)$, is the set of words accepted by A.

Example 1. We describe graphically an NBW that accepts all words over the alphabet $\{0, 1\}$ that contain infinitely many occurrences of 1. The arrow on the left designates the initial state, and the circle on the right designates an accepting state.

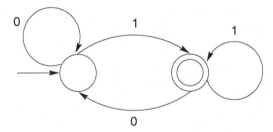

The class of languages accepted by NBWs forms the class of ω-*regular* languages, which are defined in terms of regular expressions augmented with the ω-power operator (e^ω denotes an infinitary iteration of e) [16].

The paradigmatic idea of the automata-theoretic approach is that we can compile high-level logical specifications into an equivalent low-level finite-state formalism.

Theorem 1.   [16] *Given an MSO sentence φ over a vocabulary V, one can construct an NBW A_φ with alphabet 2^V such that a word w in $(2^V)^\omega$ is accepted by A_φ iff φ holds in the associated word structure M_w.*

The theorem says that models(φ) $= L(A_\varphi)$. Thus, the class of languages defined by MSO sentences is precisely the class of ω-regular languages. This result was inspired by an analogous earlier theorem for MSO over finite words [15, 43, 120], which showed that MSO over finite words defines precisely the class of regular languages.

To decide whether sentence φ is satisfiable, that is, whether models(φ) $\neq \emptyset$, we need to check that $L(A_\varphi) \neq \emptyset$. This turns out to be an easy problem. Let $A = (\Sigma, S, S_0, \rho, F)$ be an NBW. Construct a directed graph $G_A = (S, E_A)$, with S as the set of nodes, and $E_A = \{(s, t) : (s, a, t) \in \rho \text{ for some } a \in \Sigma\}$. The following lemma is implicit in [16] and more explicit in [121].

Lemma 1. $L(A) \neq \emptyset$ iff there are states $s_0 \in S^0$ and $t \in F$ such that in G_A there is a path from s_0 to t and a path from t to itself.

We thus obtain an algorithm for the SATISFIABILITY problem of MSO over word structures: given an MSO sentence φ, construct the NBW A_φ and check whether $L(A) \neq \emptyset$. Since the DECISION problem can be reduced to the SATISFIABILITY problem, this also solves the DECISION problem.

Neither Büchi nor Church analyzed the complexity of the DECISION problem. This had to wait until 1974. Define the function $exp(k, n)$ inductively as follows: $exp(0, n) = n$ and $exp(k + 1, n) = 2^{exp(k,n)}$. We say that a problem is *nonelementary* if it can not be solved by an algorithm whose running time is bounded by $exp(k, n)$ for some fixed $k \geq 0$; that is, the running time cannot be bounded by a tower of exponentials of a fixed height. It is not too difficult to observe that the construction of the automaton A_φ in [16] is nonelementary. It was shown in [87, 113] that the SATISFIABILITY problem for MSO is nonelementary. In fact, the problem is already nonelementary for FO over finite words [113].

2 Thread II: Temporal Logic

2.1 From Aristotle to Kamp

The history of time in logic goes back to ancient times.[3] Aristotle pondered how to interpret sentences such as "Tomorrow there will be a sea fight," or "Tomorrow there will not be a sea fight." Medieval philosophers also pondered the issue of time.[4] By the Renaissance period, philosophical interest in the logic of time seems to have waned. There were some stirrings of interest in the 19th century, by Boole and Peirce. Peirce wrote:

---

[3] For a detailed history of temporal logic from ancient times to the modern period, see [91].

[4] For example, William of Ockham, 1288–1348, wrote (rather obscurely for the modern reader): "Wherefore the difference between present tense propositions and past and future tense propositions is that the predicate in a present tense proposition stands in the same way as the subject, unless something added to it stops this; but in a past tense and a future tense proposition it varies, for the predicate does not merely stand for those things concerning which it is truly predicated in the past and future tense propositions, because in order for such a proposition to be true, it is not sufficient that that thing of which the predicate is truly predicated (whether by a verb in the present tense or in the future tense) is that which the subject denotes, although it is required that the very same predicate is truly predicated of that which the subject denotes, by means of what is asserted by such a proposition."

"Time has usually been considered by logicians to be what is called 'extra-logical' matter. I have never shared this opinion. But I have thought that logic had not yet reached the state of development at which the introduction of temporal modifications of its forms would not result in great confusion; and I am much of that way of thinking yet."

There were also some stirrings of interest in the first half of the 20th century, but the birth of modern temporal logic is unquestionably credited to Arthur Norman Prior, 1914-1969. Prior was a philosopher, who was interested in theological and ethical issues. His own religious path was somewhat convoluted; he was born a Methodist, converted to Presbytarianism, became an atheist, and ended up an agnostic. In 1949, he published a book titled "Logic and The Basis of Ethics". He was particularly interested in the conflict between the assumption of *free will* ("the future is to some extent, even if it is only a very small extent, something we can make for ourselves"), *foredestination* ("of what will be, it has now been the case that it will be"), and *foreknowledge* ("there is a deity who infallibly knows the entire future"). He was also interested in modal logic [102]. This confluence of interests led Prior to the development of *temporal logic*. [5] His wife, Mary Prior, recalled after his death:

"I remember his waking me one night [in 1953], coming and sitting on my bed, ..., and saying he thought one could make a formalised tense logic."

Prior lectured on his new work when he was the John Locke Lecturer at the University of Oxford in 1955-6, and published his book "Time and Modality" in 1957 [100].[6] In this book, he presented a temporal logic that is propositional logic extended with two temporal connectives, F and P, corresponding to "sometime in the future" and "sometime in the past". A crucial feature of this logic is that it has an implicit notion of "now", which is treated as an *indexical*, that is, it depends on the context of utterance for its meaning. Both future and past are defined with respect to this implicit "now".

It is interesting to note that the *linear* vs. *branching* time dichotomy, which has been a subject of some controversy in the computer science literature since 1980 (see [126]), has been present from the very beginning of temporal-logic development. In Prior's early work on temporal logic, he assumed that time was linear. In 1958, he received a letter from Saul Kripke,[7] who wrote

"In an indetermined system, we perhaps should not regard time as a linear series, as you have done. Given the present moment, there are several possibilities for what the next moment may be like – and for each possible next moment, there are several possibilities for the moment after that. Thus the situation takes the form, not of a linear sequence, but of a 'tree'."

---

[5] An earlier term was *tense logic*; the term *temporal logic* was introduced in [90]. The technical distinction between the two terms seems fuzzy.

[6] Due to the arcane infix notation of the time, the book may not be too accessible to modern readers, who may have difficulties parsing formulas such as $CKMpMqAMKpMqMKqMp$.

[7] Kripke was a high-school student, not quite 18, in Omaha, Nebraska. Kripke's interest in modal logic was inspired by a paper by Prior on this subject [103]. Prior turned out to be the referee of Kripke's first paper [74].

Prior immediately saw the merit of Kripke's suggestion: "the determinist sees time as a line, and the indeterminist sees times as a system of forking paths." He went on to develop two theories of branching time, which he called "Ockhamist" and "Peircean". (Prior did not use path quantifiers; those were introduced later, in the 1980s. See Section 3.2.)

While the introduction of branching time seems quite reasonable in the context of trying to formalize free will, it is far from being simple philosophically. Prior argued that the nature of the course of time is branching, while the nature of a course of events is linear [101]. In contrast, it was argued in [90] that the nature of time is linear, but the nature of the course of events is branching: "We have 'branching *in* time,' not 'branching *of* time'."[8]

During the 1960s, the development of temporal logic continued through both the linear-time approach and the branching-time approach. There was little connection, however, between research on temporal logic and research on classical logics, as described in Section 1. That changed in 1968, when Johan Anthony Willem (Hans) Kamp tied together the two threads in his doctoral dissertation.

Theorem 2. [70] *Linear temporal logic with past and binary temporal connectives ("strict until" and "strict since") has precisely the expressive power of FO over the ordered naturals (with monadic vocabularies).*

It should be noted that Kamp's Theorem is actually more general and asserts expressive equivalence of FO and temporal logic over all "Dedekind-closed orders". The introduction of binary temporal connectives by Kamp was necessary for reaching the expressive power of FO; *unary* linear temporal logic, which has only unary temporal connectives, is weaker than FO [51]. The theorem refers to FO formulas with one free variable, which are satisfied at an element of a structure, analogously to temporal logic formulas, which are satisfied at a point of time.

It should be noted that one direction of Kamp's Theorem, the translation from temporal logic to FO, is quite straightforward; the hard direction is the translation from FO to temporal logic. Both directions are algorithmically effective; translating from temporal logic to FO involves a linear blowup, but translation in the other direction involves a nonelementary blowup.

If we focus on FO sentences rather than FO formulas, then they define sets of traces (a sentence φ defines models(φ)). A characterization of of the expressiveness of FO sentences over the naturals, in terms of their ability to define sets of traces, was obtained in 1979.

Theorem 3. [118] *FO sentences over naturals have the expressive power of $*$-free ω-regular expressions.*

Recall that MSO defines the class of ω-regular languages. It was already shown in [44] that FO over the naturals is weaker expressively than MSO over the naturals. Theorem 3 was inspired by an analogous theorem in [86] for finite words.

---

[8] One is reminded of St. Augustin, who said in his *Confessions*: "What, then, is time? If no one asks me, I know; but if I wish to explain it to some who should ask me, I do not know."

2.2 The Temporal Logic of Programs

There were some early observations that temporal logic can be applied to programs. Prior stated: "There are practical gains to be had from this study too, for example, in the representation of time-delay in computer circuits" [101]. Also, a discussion of the application of temporal logic to processes, which are defined as "programmed sequences of states, deterministic or stochastic" appeared in [90].

The "big bang" for the application of temporal logic to program correctness occurred with Amir Pnueli's 1977 paper [93]. In this paper, Pnueli, inspired by [90], advocated using future linear temporal logic (LTL) as a logic for the specification of non-terminating programs.

LTL is a temporal logic with two temporal connectives, "next" and "until".[9] In LTL, formulas are constructed from a set $Prop$ of atomic propositions using the usual Boolean connectives as well as the unary temporal connective X ("next"), and the binary temporal connective U ("until"). Additional unary temporal connectives F ("eventually"), and G ("always") can be defined in terms of U. Note that all temporal connectives refer to the future here, in contrast to Kamp's "strict since" operator, which refers to the past. Thus, LTL is a *future temporal logic*. For extensions with past temporal connectives, see [83, 84, 123].

LTL is interpreted over traces over the set $Prop$ of atomic propositions. For a trace τ and a point $i \in I\!N$, the notation $\tau, i \models \varphi$ indicates that the formula φ holds at the point i of the trace τ. Thus, the point i is the implicit "now" with respect to which the formula is interpreted. We have that

- $\tau, i \models p$ if p holds at $\tau(i)$,
- $\tau, i \models X\varphi$ if $\tau, i+1 \models \varphi$, and
- $\tau, i \models \varphi U \psi$ if for some $j \geq i$, we have $\tau, j \models \psi$ and for all k, $i \leq k < j$, we have $\tau, k \models \varphi$.

The temporal connectives F and G can be defined in terms of the temporal connective U; $F\varphi$ is defined as $\mathbf{true}\ U\varphi$, and $G\varphi$ is defined as $\neg F \neg \varphi$. We say that τ *satisfies* a formula φ, denoted $\tau \models \varphi$, iff $\tau, 0 \models \varphi$. We denote by models(φ) the set of traces satisfying φ.

As an example, the LTL formula $G(request \rightarrow F\ grant)$, which refers to the atomic propositions *request* and *grant*, is true in a trace precisely when every state in the trace in which *request* holds is followed by some state in the (non-strict) future in which *grant* holds. Also, the LTL formula $G(request \rightarrow (request\ U\ grant))$ is true in a trace precisely if, whenever *request* holds in a state of the trace, it holds until a state in which *grant* holds is reached.

The focus on satisfaction at 0, called *initial semantics*, is motivated by the desire to specify computations at their starting point. It enables an alternative version of Kamp's Theorem, which does not require past temporal connectives, but focuses on initial semantics.

---

[9] Unlike Kamp's "strict until" ("p strict until q" requires q to hold in the strict future), Pnueli's "until" is not strict ("p until q" can be satisfied by q holding now), which is why the "next" connective is required.

Theorem 4. [56] *LTL has precisely the expressive power of FO over the ordered naturals (with monadic vocabularies) with respect to initial semantics.*

As we saw earlier, FO has the expressive power of star-free ω-regular expressions over the naturals. Thus, LTL has the expressive power of star-free ω-regular expressions (see [95]), and is strictly weaker than MSO. An interesting outcome of the above theorem is that it lead to the following assertion regarding LTL [88]: "The corollary due to Meyer – I have to get in my controversial remark – is that that [Theorem 4] makes it theoretically uninteresting." Developments since 1980 have proven this assertion to be overly pessimistic on the merits of LTL.

Pnueli also discussed the analog of Church's DECISION problem: given a finite-state program P and an LTL formula φ, decide if φ holds in all traces of P. Just like Church, Pnueli observed that this problem can be solved by reduction to MSO. Rather than focus on sequential circuits, Pnueli focused on programs, modeled as (labeled) *transition systems* [71]. A transition system $M = (W, W_0, R, V)$ consists of a set W of states that the system can be in, a set $W_0 \subseteq W$ of initial states, a transition relation $R \subseteq W^2$ that indicates the allowable state transitions of the system, and an assignment $V : W \to 2^{Prop}$ of truth values to the atomic propositions in each state of the system. (A transition system is essentially a Kripke structure [10].) A *path* in M that *starts at u* is a possible infinite behavior of the system starting at u, i.e., it is an infinite sequence $u_0, u_1 \ldots$ of states in W such that $u_0 = u$, and $(u_i, u_{i+1}) \in R$ for all $i \geq 0$. The sequence $V(u_0), V(u_1) \ldots$ is a *trace* of M that *starts at u*. It is the sequence of truth assignments visited by the path. The *language* of M, denoted $L(M)$, consists of all traces of M that start at a state in W_0. Note that $L(M)$ is a language of infinite words over the alphabet 2^{Prop}. The language $L(M)$ can be viewed as an abstract description of the system M, describing all possible traces. We say that M *satisfies* an LTL formula φ if all traces in $L(M)$ satisfy φ, that is, if $L(M) \subseteq \text{models}(\varphi)$. When W is finite, we have a finite-state system, and can apply algorithmic techniques.

What about the complexity of LTL reasoning? Recall from Section 1 that satisfiability of FO over trace structures is nonelementary. In contrast, it was shown in [60, 61, 108, 109, 110, 132, 133] that LTL SATISFIABILITY is elementary; in fact, it is PSPACE-complete. It was also shown that the DECISION problem for LTL with respect to finite transition systems is PSPACE-complete [108, 109, 110]. The basic technique for proving these elementary upper bounds is the *tableau* technique, which was adapted from *dynamic logics* [98] (see Section 3.1). Thus, even though FO and LTL are expressively equivalent, they have dramatically different computational properties, as LTL reasoning is in PSPACE, while FO reasoning is nonelementary.

The second "big bang" in the application of temporal logic to program correctness was the introduction of *model checking* by Edmund Melson Clarke and Ernest Allen Emerson [28] and by Jean-Pierre Queille and Joseph Sifakis [104]. The two papers used two different branching-time logics. Clarke and Emerson used CTL (inspired by the branching-time logic UB of [9]), which extends LTL with existential and universal path quantifiers E and A. Queille and Sifakis used a logic introduced by Leslie Lamport [81], which extends propositional logic with the temporal connectives POT (which corresponds to the CTL operator EF) and $INEV$ (which corresponds to the CTL operator AF). The focus in both papers was on model checking, which is essentially what Church called the DECISION problem: does a given finite-state program, viewed as a finite transition system, satisfy its given temporal specification. In particular, Clarke and Emerson showed that model checking transition systems of size m with respect to formulas of size n can be done in time polynomial in m and n. This was refined later to $O(mn)$ (even in the presence of *fairness* constraints, which restrict attention to certain infinite paths in the underlying transition system) [29,30]. We drop the term "DECISION problem" from now on, and replace it with the term "MODEL-CHECKING problem".[10]

It should be noted that the linear complexity of model checking refers to the size of the transition system, rather than the size of the program that gave rise to that system. For sequential circuits, transition-system size is essentially exponential in the size of the description of the circuit (say, in some Hardware Description Language). This is referred to as the "state-explosion problem" [31]. In spite of the state-explosion problem, in the first few years after the publication of the first model-checking papers in 1981-2, Clarke and his students demonstrated that model checking is a highly successful technique for automated program verification [13,33]. By the late 1980s, automated verification had become a recognized research area. Also by the late 1980s, *symbolic* model checking was developed [19,20], and the SMV tool, developed at CMU by Kenneth Laughlin McMillan [85], was starting to have an industrial impact. See [27] for more details.

The detailed complexity analysis in [29] inspired a similar detailed analysis of linear time model checking. It was shown in [82] that model checking transition systems of size m with respect to LTL formulas of size n can be done in time $m2^{O(n)}$. (This again was shown using a tableau-based technique.) While the bound here is exponential in n, the argument was that n is typically rather small, and therefore an exponential bound is acceptable.

2.3 Back to Automata

Since LTL can be translated to FO, and FO can be translated to NBW, it is clear that LTL can be translated to NBW. Going through FO, however, would incur, in general, a nonelementary blowup. In 1983, Pierre Wolper, Aravinda Prasad Sistla, and I showed that this nonelementary blowup can be avoided.

Theorem 5. [130, 134] *Given an LTL formula φ of size n, one can construct an NBW A_φ of size $2^{O(n)}$ such that a trace σ satisfies φ if and only if σ is accepted by A_φ.*

It now follows that we can obtain a PSPACE algorithm for LTL SATISFIABILITY: given an LTL formula φ, we construct A_φ and check that $A_\varphi \neq \emptyset$ using the graph-theoretic approach described earlier. We can avoid using exponential space, by constructing the automaton *on the fly* [130, 134].

What about model checking? We know that a transition system M satisfies an LTL formula φ if $L(M) \subseteq \text{models}(\varphi)$. It was then observed in [129] that the following are equivalent:

---

[10] The model-checking problem is analogous to database query evaluation, where we check the truth of a logical formula, representing a query, with respect to a database, viewed as a finite relational structure. Interestingly, the study of the complexity of database query evaluation started about the same time as that of model checking [122].

- M satisfies φ
- $L(M) \subseteq \text{models}(\varphi)$
- $L(M) \subseteq L(A_\varphi)$
- $L(M) \cap ((2^{Prop})^\omega - L(A_\varphi)) = \emptyset$
- $L(M) \cap L(A_{\neg\varphi}) = \emptyset$
- $L(M \times A_{\neg\varphi}) = \emptyset$

Thus, rather than complementing A_φ using an exponential complementation construction [16, 76, 112], we complement the LTL property using logical negation. It is easy to see that we can now get the same bound as in [82]: model checking programs of size m with respect to LTL formulas of size n can be done in time $m2^{O(n)}$. Thus, the optimal bounds for LTL satisfiability and model checking can be obtained without resorting to ad-hoc tableau-based techniques; the key is the exponential translation of LTL to NBW.

One may wonder whether this theory is practical. Reduction to practice took over a decade of further research, which saw the development of

- an optimized search algorithm for explicit-state model checking [36, 37],
- a symbolic, BDD-based[11] algorithm for NBW nonemptiness [19, 20, 49],
- symbolic algorithms for LTL to NBW translation [19, 20, 32], and
- an optimized explicit algorithm for LTL to NBW translation [58].

By 1995, there were two model-checking tools that implemented LTL model checking via the automata-theoretic approach: Spin [68] is an explicit-state LTL model checker, and Cadence's SMV is a symbolic LTL model checker.[12] See [127] for a description of algorithmic developments since the mid 1990s. Additional tools today are *VIS* [12], *NuSMV* [26], and *SPOT* [38].

It should be noted that Robert Kurshan developed the automata-theoretic approach independently, also going back to the 1980s [1, 2, 78]. In his approach (as also in [106, 134]), one uses automata to represent both the system and its specification [79].[13] The first implementation of COSPAN, a model-checking tool that is based on this approach [62], also goes back to the 1980s; see [80].

2.4   Enhancing Expressiveness

Can the development of LTL model checking [82, 129] be viewed as a satisfactory solution to Church's DECISION problem? Almost, but not quite, since, as we observed earlier, LTL is not as expressive as MSO, which means that LTL is expressively weaker than NBW. Why do we need the expressive power of NBWs? First, note that once we add fairness to transitions systems (sse [29, 30]), they can be viewed as variants of NBWs. Second, there are good reasons to expect the specification language to be as expressive as the underlying model of programs [94]. Thus, achieving the expressive

---

[11] To be precise, one should use the acronym ROBDD, for Reduced Ordered Binary Decision Diagrams [14].

[12] Cadence's SMV is also a CTL model checker. See www.cadence.com/webforms/cbl_software/index.aspx.

[13] The connection to automata is somewhat difficult to discern in the early papers [1, 2].

power of NBWs, which we refer to as ω-*regularity*, is a desirable goal. This motivated efforts since the early 1980s to extend LTL.

The first attempt along this line was made by Wolper [132, 133], who defined ETL (for *Extended Temporal Logic*), which is LTL extended with grammar operators. He showed that ETL is more expressive than LTL, while its SATISFIABILITY problem can still be solved in exponential time (and even PSPACE [108, 109, 110]). Then, Sistla, Wolper and I showed how to extend LTL with automata connectives, reaching ω-regularity, without losing the PSPACE upper bound for the SATISFIABILITY problem [130, 134]. Actually, three syntactical variations, denoted ETL_f, ETL_l, and ETL_r were shown to be expressively equivalent and have these properties [130, 134].

Two other ways to achieve ω-regularity were discovered in the 1980s. The first is to enhance LTL with monadic second-order quantifiers as in MSO, which yields a logic, QPTL, with a nonelementary SATISFIABILITY problem [111, 112]. The second is to enhance LTL with least and greatest fixpoints [6, 124], which yields a logic, μLTL, that achieves ω-regularity, and has a PSPACE upper bound on its SATISFIABILITY and MODEL-CHECKING problems [124]. For example, the (not too readable) formula

$$(\nu P)(\mu Q)(P \wedge X(p \vee Q)),$$

where ν and μ denote greatest and least fixpoint operators, respectively, is equivalent to the LTL formula GFp, which says that p holds infinitely often.

3   Thread III: Dynamic and Branching-Time Logics

3.1   Dynamic Logics

In 1976, a year before Pnueli proposed using LTL to specify programs, Vaughan Ronald Pratt proposed using *dynamic logic*, an extension of modal logic, to specify programs [96].[14] In modal logic $\Box\varphi$ means that φ holds in all worlds that are possible with respect to the current world [10]. Thus, $\Box\varphi$ can be taken to mean that φ holds after an execution of a program step, taking the transition relation of the program to be the possibility relation of a Kripke structure. Pratt proposed the addition of dynamic modalities $[e]\varphi$, where e is a program, which asserts that φ holds in all states reachable by an execution of the program e. Dynamic logic can then be viewed as an extension of Hoare logic, since $\psi \to [e]\varphi$ corresponds to the Hoare triple $\{\psi\}e\{\varphi\}$ (see [3]). See [64] for an extensive coverage of dynamic logic.

In 1977, a propositional version of Pratt's dynamic logic, called PDL, was proposed, in which programs are regular expressions over atomic programs [52, 53]. It was shown there that the SATISFIABILITY problem for PDL is in NEXPTIME and EXPTIME-hard. Pratt then proved an EXPTIME upper bound, adapting tableau techniques from modal logic [97, 98]. (We saw earlier that Wolper then adapted these techniques to linear-time logic.)

Pratt's dynamic logic was designed for terminating programs, while Pnueli was interested in nonterminating programs. This motivated various extensions of dynamic

---

[14] See discussion of precursor and related developments, such as [21, 34, 50, 107], in [64].

logic to nonterminating programs [67, 115, 114, 116]. Nevertheless, these logics are much less natural for the specification of ongoing behavior than temporal logic. They inspired, however, the introduction of the (*modal*) μ-*calculus* by Dexter Kozen [72,73]. The μ-calculus is an extension of modal logic with least and greatest fixpoints. It subsumes expressively essentially all dynamic and temporal logics [11]. Kozen's paper was inspired by previous papers that showed the usefulness of fixpoints in characterizing correctness properties of programs [45, 92] (see also [99]). In turn, the μ-calculus inspired the introduction of μLTL, mentioned earlier. The μ-calculus also played an important role in the development of symbolic model checking [19, 20, 49].

3.2   Branching-Time Logics

Dynamic logic provided a branching-time approach to reasoning about programs, in contrast to Pnueli's linear-time approach. Lamport was the first to study the dichotomy between linear and branching time in the context of program correctness [81]. This was followed by the introduction of the branching-time logic UB, which extends unary LTL (LTL without the temporal connective "until") with the existential and universal path quantifiers, E and A [9]. Path quantifiers enable us to quantify over different future behavior of the system. By adapting Pratt's tableau-based method for PDL to UB, it was shown that its SATISFIABILITY problem is in EXPTIME [9]. Clarke and Emerson then added the temporal connective "until" to UB and obtained CTL [28]. (They did not focus on the SATISFIABILITY problem for CTL, but, as we saw earlier, on its MODEL-CHECKING problem; the SATISFIABILITY problem was shown later to be solvable in EXPTIME [47].) Finally, it was shown that LTL and CTL have incomparable expressive power, leading to the introduction of the branching-time logic CTL*, which unifies LTL and CTL [46,48].

The key feature of branching-time logics in the 1980s was the introduction of explicit path quantifiers in [9]. This was an idea that was not discovered by Prior and his followers in the 1960s and 1970s. Most likely, Prior would have found CTL* satisfactory for his philosophical applications and would have seen no need to introduce the "Ockhamist" and "Peircean" approaches.

3.3   Combining Dynamic and Temporal Logics

By the early 1980s it became clear that temporal logics and dynamic logics provide two distinct perspectives for specifying programs: the first is *state* based, while the second is *action* based. Various efforts have been made to combine the two approaches. These include the introduction of *Process Logic* [63] (branching time), *Yet Another Process Logic* [128] (branching time), *Regular Process Logic* [66] (linear time), *Dynamic LTL* [59] (linear time), and *RCTL* [8] (branching time), which ultimately evolved into *Sugar* [7]. RCTL/Sugar is unique among these logics in that it did not attempt to borrow the action-based part of dynamic logic. It is a state-based branching-time logic with no notion of actions. Rather, what it borrowed from dynamic logic was the use of regular-expression-based dynamic modalities. Unlike dynamic logic, which uses regular expressions over program statements, RCTL/Sugar uses regular expressions over state predicates, analogously to the automata of ETL [130, 134], which run over sequences of formulas.

4   Thread IV: From LTL to ForSpec and PSL

In the late 1990s and early 2000s, model checking was having an increasing industrial impact. That led to the development of two industrial temporal logics based on LTL: *ForSpec*, developed by Intel, and *PSL*, developed by an industrial standards committee.

4.1   From LTL to ForSpec

Intel's involvement with model checking started in 1990, when Kurshan, spending a sabbatical year in Israel, conducted a successful feasibility study at the Intel Design Center (IDC) in Haifa, using COSPAN, which at that point was a prototype tool; see [80]. In 1992, IDC started a pilot project using SMV. By 1995, model checking was used by several design projects at Intel, using an internally developed model checker based on SMV. Intel users have found CTL to be lacking in expressive power and the Design Technology group at Intel developed its own specification language, FSL. The FSL language was a linear-time logic, and it was model checked using the automata-theoretic approach, but its design was rather ad-hoc, and its expressive power was unclear; see [54].

In 1997, Intel's Design Technology group at IDC embarked on the development of a second-generation model-checking technology. The goal was to develop a model-checking engine from scratch, as well as a new specification language. A BDD-based model checker was released in 1999 [55], and a SAT-based model checker was released in 2000 [35].

I got involved in the design of the second-generation specification language in 1997. That language, ForSpec, was released in 2000 [5]. The first issue to be decided was whether the language should be linear or branching. This led to an in-depth examination of this issue [126], and the decision was to pursue a linear-time language. An obvious candidate was LTL; we saw that by the mid 1990s there were both explicit-state and symbolic model checkers for LTL, so there was no question of feasibility. I had numerous conversations with Limor Fix, Michael Hadash, Yonit Kesten, and Moshe Sananes on this issue. The conclusion was that LTL is not expressive enough for industrial usage. In particular, many properties that are expressible in FSL are not expressible in LTL. Thus, it turned out that the theoretical considerations regarding the expressiveness of LTL, i.e., its lack of ω-regularity, had practical significance. I offered two extensions of LTL; as we saw earlier both ETL and μLTL achieve ω-regularity and have the same complexity as LTL. Neither of these proposals was accepted, due to the perceived difficulty of usage of such logics by Intel validation engineers, who typically have only basic familiarity with automata theory and logic.

These conversations continued in 1998, now with Avner Landver. Avner also argued that Intel validation engineers would not be receptive to the automata-based formalism of ETL. Being familiar with RCTL/Sugar and its dynamic modalities [7,8], he asked me about regular expressions, and my answer was that regular expressions are equivalent to automata [69], so the automata of ETL$_f$, which extends LTL with automata on *finite* words, can be replaced by regular expressions over state predicates. This lead to the development of *RELTL*, which is LTL augmented by the dynamic regular modalities of dynamic logic (interpreted linearly, as in ETL). Instead of the dynamic-logic notation $[e]\varphi$, ForSpec uses the more readable (to engineers) (e triggers φ), where e is a regular expression over state predicates (e.g., $(p \lor q)^*$, $(p \land q)$), and φ is a formula. Semantically, $\tau, i \models (e$ triggers $\varphi)$ if, for all $j \geq i$, if $\tau[i, j]$ (that is, the finite word $\tau(i), \ldots, \tau(j)$) "matches" e (in the intuitive formal sense), then $\tau, j \models \varphi$; see [22]. Using the ω-regularity of ETL_f, it is now easy to show that RELTL also achieves ω-regularity [5].

While the addition of dynamic modalities to LTL is sufficient to achieve ω-regularity, we decided to also offer direct support to two specification modes often used by verification engineers at Intel: *clocks* and *resets*. Both clocks and resets are features that are needed to address the fact that modern semiconductor designs consist of interacting parallel modules. While clocks and resets have a simple underlying intuition, defining their semantics formally is quite nontrivial. ForSpec is essentially RELTL, augmented with features corresponding to clocks and resets, as we now explain.

Today's semiconductor designs are still dominated by synchronous circuits. In synchronous circuits, clock signals synchronize the sequential logic, providing the designer with a simple operational model. While the asynchronous approach holds the promise of greater speed (see [23]), designing asynchronous circuits is significantly harder than designing synchronous circuits. Current design methodology attempts to strike a compromise between the two approaches by using multiple clocks. This results in architectures that are globally asynchronous but locally synchronous. The temporal-logic literature mostly ignores the issue of explicitly supporting clocks. ForSpec supports multiple clocks via the notion of *current clock*. Specifically, ForSpec has a construct change_on $c \, \varphi$, which states that the temporal formula φ is to be evaluated with respect to the clock c; that is, the formula φ is to be evaluated in the trace defined by the high phases of the clock c. The key feature of clocks in ForSpec is that each subformula may advance according to a different clock [5].

Another feature of modern designs' consisting of interacting parallel modules is the fact that a process running on one module can be reset by a signal coming from another module. As noted in [117], reset control has long been a critical aspect of embedded control design. ForSpec directly supports reset signals. The formula accept_on $a \, \varphi$ states that the property φ should be checked only until the arrival of the reset signal a, at which point the check is considered to have *succeeded*. In contrast, reject_on $r \, \varphi$ states that the property φ should be checked only until the arrival of the reset signal r, at which point the check is considered to have *failed*. The key feature of resets in ForSpec is that each subformula may be reset (positively or negatively) by a different reset signal; for a longer discussion see [5].

ForSpec is an industrial property-specification language that supports hardware-oriented constructs as well as uniform semantics for formal and dynamic validation, while at the same time it has a well understood expressiveness (ω-regularity) and computational complexity (SATISFIABILITY and MODEL-CHECKING problems have the same complexity for ForSpec as for LTL) [5]. The design effort strove to find an acceptable compromise, with trade-offs clarified by theory, between conflicting demands, such as expressiveness, usability, and implementability. Clocks and resets, both important to hardware designers, have a clear intuitive semantics, but formalizing this semantics is nontrivial. The rigorous semantics, however, not only enabled mechanical verification of various theorems about the language, but also served as a reference document for the implementors. The implementation of model checking for ForSpec followed the automata-theoretic approach, using *alternating* automata as advocated in [125] (see [57]).

4.2   From ForSpec to PSL

In 2000, the Electronic Design Automation Association instituted a standardization body called *Accellera*.[15] Accellera's mission is to drive worldwide development and use of standards required by systems, semiconductor and design tools companies. Accellera decided that the development of a standard specification language is a requirement for formal verification to become an industrial reality (see [80]). Since the focus was on specifying properties of designs rather than designs themselves, the chosen term was "property specification language" (PSL). The PSL standard committee solicited industrial contributions and received four language contributions: *CBV*, from Motorola, ForSpec, from Intel, *Temporal e*, from Verisity [89], and Sugar, from IBM.

The committee's discussions were quite fierce.[16] Ultimately, it became clear that while technical considerations play an important role, industrial committees' decisions are ultimately made for business considerations. In that contention, IBM had the upper hand, and Accellera chose Sugar as the base language for PSL in 2003. At the same time, the technical merits of ForSpec were accepted and PSL adopted all the main features of ForSpec. In essence, PSL (the current version 1.1) is LTL, extended with dynamic modalities (referred to as the *regular layer*), clocks, and resets (called *aborts*). PSL did inherit the syntax of Sugar, and does include a branching-time extension as an acknowledgment to Sugar.[17]

There was some evolution of PSL with respect to ForSpec. After some debate on the proper way to define resets [4], ForSpec's approach was essentially accepted after some reformulation [41]. ForSpec's fundamental approach to clocks, which is semantic, was accepted, but modified in some important details [42]. In addition to the dynamic modalities, borrowed from dynamic logic, PSL also has weak dynamic modalities [40], which are reminiscent of "looping" modalities in dynamic logic [67, 65]. Today PSL 1.1 is an IEEE Standard 1850–2005, and continues to be refined by the IEEE P1850 PSL Working Group.[18]

Practical use of ForSpec and PSL has shown that the regular layer (that is, the dynamic modalities), is highly popular with verification engineers. Another standardized property specification language, called *SVA* (for SystemVerilog Assertions), is based, in essence, on that regular layer [131].

---

[15] See http://www.accellera.org/.

[16] See http://www.eda-stds.org/vfv/.

[17] See [39] and language reference manual at
    http://www.eda.org/vfv/docs/PSL-v1.1.pdf and

[18] See http://www.eda.org/ieee-1850/.

5   Contemplation

The evolution of ideas, from Church and Prior to PSL, seems to be an amazing development. It reminds me of the medieval period, when building a cathedral spanned more than a mason's lifetime. Many masons spend their whole lives working on a cathedral, never seeing it to completion. We are fortunate to see the completion of this particular "cathedral". Just like the medieval masons, our contributions are often smaller than we'd like to consider them, but even small contributions can have a major impact. Unlike the medieval cathedrals, the scientific cathedral has no architect; the construction is driven by a complex process, whose outcome is unpredictable. Much that has been discovered is forgotten and has to be rediscovered. It is hard to fathom what our particular "cathedral" will look like in 50 years.

Acknowledgments. I am grateful to E. Clarke, A. Emerson, R. Goldblatt, A. Pnueli, P. Sistla, P. Wolper for helping me trace the many threads of this story, to D. Fisman, C. Eisner, J. Halpern, D. Harel and T. Wilke for their many useful comments on earlier drafts of this paper, and to S. Nain, K. Rozier, and D. Tabakov for proofreading earlier drafts. I'd also like to thank K. Rozier for her help with graphics.

References

1. Aggarwal, S., Kurshan, R.P.: Automated implementation from formal specification. In: Proc. 4th Int'l Workshop on Protocol Specification, Testing and Verification, pp. 127–136. North-Holland (1984)
2. Aggarwal, S., Kurshan, R.P., Sharma, D.: A language for the specification and analysis of protocols. In: Proc. 3rd Int'l Workshop on Protocol Specification, Testing, and Verification, pp. 35–50. North-Holland (1983)
3. Apt, K., Olderog, E.R.: Verification of Sequential and Concurrent Programs. Springer (2006)
4. Armoni, R., Bustan, D., Kupferman, O., Vardi, M.Y.: Resets vs. aborts in linear temporal logic. In: Garavel, H., Hatcliff, J. (eds.) ETAPS 2003 and TACAS 2003. LNCS, vol. 2619, pp. 65–80. Springer, Heidelberg (2003)
5. Armoni, R., Fix, L., Flaisher, A., Gerth, R., Ginsburg, B., Kanza, T., Landver, A., Mador-Haim, S., Singerman, E., Tiemeyer, A., Vardi, M.Y., Zbar, Y.: The ForSpec temporal logic: A new temporal property-specification logic. In: Katoen, J.-P., Stevens, P. (eds.) ETAPS 2002 and TACAS 2002. LNCS, vol. 2280, pp. 211–296. Springer, Heidelberg (2002)
6. Banieqbal, B., Barringer, H.: Temporal logic with fixed points. In: Banieqbal, B., Barringer, H., Pnueli, A. (eds.) Temporal Logic in Specification. LNCS, vol. 398, pp. 62–74. Springer, Heidelberg (1989)
7. Beer, I., Ben-David, S., Eisner, C., Fisman, D., Gringauze, A., Rodeh, Y.: The temporal logic Sugar. In: Berry, G., Comon, H., Finkel, A. (eds.) CAV 2001. LNCS, vol. 2102, pp. 363–367. Springer, Heidelberg (2001)
8. Beer, I., Ben-David, S., Landver, A.: On-the-fly model checking of RCTL formulas. In: Y. Vardi, M. (ed.) CAV 1998. LNCS, vol. 1427, pp. 184–194. Springer, Heidelberg (1998)
9. Ben-Ari, M., Manna, Z., Pnueli, A.: The logic of nexttime. In: Proc. 8th ACM Symp. on Principles of Programming Languages, pp. 164–176 (1981)
10. Blackburn, P., de Rijke, M., Venema, Y.: Modal Logic. Cambridge University Press (2002)

11. Bradfield, J., Stirling, C.: PDL and modal μ-calculus. In: Blackburn, P., van Benthem, J., Wolter, F. (eds.) Handbook of Modal Logic, Elsevier (2006)
12. Brayton, R.K., Hachtel, G.D., Sangiovanni-Vincentelli, A., Somenzi, F., Aziz, A., Cheng, S.-T., Edwards, S., Khatri, S., Kukimoto, T., Pardo, A., Qadeer, S., Ranjan, R.K., Sarwary, S., Shiple, T.R., Swamy, G., Villa, T.: VIS: a system for verification and synthesis. In: Alur, R., Henzinger, T.A. (eds.) CAV 1996. LNCS, vol. 1102, pp. 428–432. Springer, Heidelberg (1996)
13. Browne, M.C., Clarke, E.M., Dill, D.L., Mishra, B.: Automatic verification of sequential circuits using temporal logic. IEEE Transactions on Computing C-35, 1035–1044 (1986)
14. Bryant, R.E.: Graph-based algorithms for Boolean-function manipulation. IEEE Transactions on Computing C-35(8), 677–691 (1986)
15. Büchi, J.R.: Weak second-order arithmetic and finite automata. Zeit. Math. Logik und Grundl. Math. 6, 66–92 (1960)
16. Büchi, J.R.: On a decision method in restricted second order arithmetic. In: Proc. Int. Congress on Logic, Method, and Philosophy of Science. 1960, pp. 1–12. Stanford University Press (1962)
17. Büchi, J.R., Elgot, C.C., Wright, J.B.: The non-existence of certain algorithms for finite automata theory (abstract). Notices Amer. Math. Soc. 5, 98 (1958)
18. Büchi, J.R., Landweber, L.H.: Solving sequential conditions by finite-state strategies. Trans. AMS 138, 295–311 (1969)
19. Burch, J.R., Clarke, E.M., McMillan, K.L., Dill, D.L., Hwang, L.J.: Symbolic model checking: 10^{20} states and beyond. In: Proc. 5th IEEE Symp. on Logic in Computer Science, pp. 428–439 (1990)
20. Burch, J.R., Clarke, E.M., McMillan, K.L., Dill, D.L., Hwang, L.J.: Symbolic model checking: 10^{20} states and beyond. Information and Computation 98(2), 142–170 (1992)
21. Burstall, R.M.: Program proving as hand simulation with a little induction. In: Information Processing 1974, Stockholm, Sweden, pp. 308–312. International Federation for Information Processing, North-Holland (1974)
22. Bustan, D., Flaisher, A., Grumberg, O., Kupferman, O., Vardi, M.Y.: Regular vacuity. In: Borrione, D., Paul, W. (eds.) CHARME 2005. LNCS, vol. 3725, pp. 191–206. Springer, Heidelberg (2005)
23. Nowick, S.M., van Berkel, C.H., Josephs, M.B.: Applications of asynchronous circuits. Proceedings of the IEEE 87(2), 223–233 (1999)
24. Church, A.: Applicaton of recursive arithmetics to the problem of circuit synthesis. In: Summaries of Talks Presented at The Summer Institute for Symbolic Logic. Communications Research Division, Institute for Defense Analysis, pp. 3–50 (1957)
25. Church, A.: Logic, arithmetics, and automata. In: Proc. Int. Congress of Mathematicians, 1962, Institut Mittag-Leffler, pp. 23–35 (1963)
26. Cimatti, A., Clarke, E.M., Giunchiglia, E., Giunchiglia, F., Pistore, M., Roveri, M., Sebastiani, R., Tacchella, A.: Nusmv 2: An opensource tool for symbolic model checking. In: Brinksma, E., Larsen, K.G. (eds.) CAV 2002. LNCS, vol. 2404, pp. 359–364. Springer, Heidelberg (2002)
27. Clarke, E.M.: The birth of model checking. In: Grumberg, O., Veith, H. (eds.) 25 Years of Model Checking. LNCS, vol. 5000, pp. 1–26. Springer, Heidelberg (2008, this volume)
28. Clarke, E.M., Emerson, E.A.: Design and synthesis of synchronization skeletons using branching time temporal logic. In: Kozen, D. (ed.) Logic of Programs. LNCS, vol. 131, pp. 52–71. Springer, Heidelberg (1981)
29. Clarke, E.M., Emerson, E.A., Sistla, A.P.: Automatic verification of finite state concurrent systems using temporal logic specifications: A practical approach. In: Proc. 10th ACM Symp. on Principles of Programming Languages, pp. 117–126 (1983)

30. Clarke, E.M., Emerson, E.A., Sistla, A.P.: Automatic verification of finite-state concurrent systems using temporal logic specifications. ACM Transactions on Programming Languagues and Systems 8(2), 244–263 (1986)
31. Clarke, E.M., Grumberg, O.: Avoiding the state explosion problem in temporal logic model-checking algorithms. In: Proc. 16th ACM Symp. on Principles of Distributed Computing, pp. 294–303 (1987)
32. Clarke, E.M., Grumberg, O., Hamaguchi, K.: Another look at LTL model checking. In: Dill, D.L. (ed.) CAV 1994. LNCS, vol. 818, pp. 415–427. Springer, Heidelberg (1994)
33. Clarke, E.M., Mishra, B.: Hierarchical verification of asynchronous circuits using temporal logic. Theoretical Computer Science 38, 269–291 (1985)
34. Constable, R.L.: On the theory of programming logics. In: Proc. 9th ACM Symp. on Theory of Computing, pp. 269–285 (1977)
35. Copty, F., Fix, L., Fraer, R., Giunchiglia, E., Kamhi, G., Tacchella, A., Vardi, M.Y.: Benefits of bounded model checking at an industrial setting. In: Berry, G., Comon, H., Finkel, A. (eds.) CAV 2001. LNCS, vol. 2102, pp. 436–453. Springer, Heidelberg (2001)
36. Courcoubetis, C., Vardi, M.Y., Wolper, P., Yannakakis, M.: Memory efficient algorithms for the verification of temporal properties. In: Clarke, E., Kurshan, R.P. (eds.) CAV 1990. LNCS, vol. 531, pp. 233–242. Springer, Heidelberg (1991)
37. Courcoubetis, C., Vardi, M.Y., Wolper, P., Yannakakis, M.: Memory efficient algorithms for the verification of temporal properties. Formal Methods in System Design 1, 275–288 (1992)
38. Duret-Lutz, A., Poitrenaud, D.: SPOT: An extensible model checking library using transition-based generalized büchi automata. In: Proc. 12th Int'l Workshop on Modeling, Analysis, and Simulation of Computer and Telecommunication Systems, pp. 76–83. IEEE Computer Society (2004)
39. Eisner, C., Fisman, D.: A Practical Introduction to PSL. Springer (2006)
40. Eisner, C., Fisman, D., Havlicek, J.: A topological characterization of weakness. In: Proc. 24th ACM Symp. on Principles of Distributed Computing, pp. 1–8 (2005)
41. Eisner, C., Fisman, D., Havlicek, J., Lustig, Y., McIsaac, A., Van Campenhout, D.: Reasoning with temporal logic on truncated paths. In: Hunt Jr., W.A., Somenzi, F. (eds.) CAV 2003. LNCS, vol. 2725, pp. 27–39. Springer, Heidelberg (2003)
42. Eisner, C., Fisman, D., Havlicek, J., McIsaac, A., Van Campenhout, D.: The definition of a temporal clock operator. In: Baeten, J.C.M., Lenstra, J.K., Parrow, J., Woeginger, G.J. (eds.) ICALP 2003. LNCS, vol. 2719, pp. 857–870. Springer, Heidelberg (2003)
43. Elgot, C.: Decision problems of finite-automata design and related arithmetics. Trans. Amer. Math. Soc. 98, 21–51 (1961)
44. Elgot, C.C., Wright, J.: Quantifier elimination in a problem of logical design. Michigan Math. J. 6, 65–69 (1959)
45. Emerson, E.A., Clarke, E.M.: Characterizing correctness properties of parallel programs using fixpoints. In: Proc. 7th Int. Colloq. on Automata, Languages, and Programming, pp. 169–181 (1980)
46. Emerson, E.A., Halpern, J.Y.: "Sometimes" and "not never" revisited: On branching versus linear time. In: Proc. 10th ACM Symp. on Principles of Programming Languages, pp. 127–140 (1983)
47. Emerson, E.A., Halpern, J.Y.: Decision procedures and expressiveness in the temporal logic of branching time. Journal of Computer and Systems Science 30, 1–24 (1985)
48. Emerson, E.A., Halpern, J.Y.: Sometimes and not never revisited: On branching versus linear time. Journal of the ACM 33(1), 151–178 (1986)
49. Emerson, E.A., Lei, C.-L.: Efficient model checking in fragments of the propositional μ-calculus. In: Proc. 1st IEEE Symp. on Logic in Computer Science, pp. 267–278 (1986)

50. Engeler, E.: Algorithmic properties of structures. Math. Syst. Theory 1, 183–195 (1967)
51. Etessami, K., Vardi, M.Y., Wilke, T.: First-order logic with two variables and unary temporal logic. Inf. Comput. 179(2), 279–295 (2002)
52. Fischer, M.J., Ladner, R.E.: Propositional modal logic of programs (extended abstract). In: Proc. 9th ACM Symp. on Theory of Computing, pp. 286–294 (1977)
53. Fischer, M.J., Ladner, R.E.: Propositional dynamic logic of regular programs. Journal of Computer and Systems Science 18, 194–211 (1979)
54. Fix, L.: Fifteen years of formal property verification at intel. This Volume (2007)
55. Fix, L., Kamhi, G.: Adaptive variable reordering for symbolic model checking. In: Proc. ACM/IEEE Int'l Conf. on Computer Aided Design, pp. 359–365 (1998)
56. Gabbay, D., Pnueli, A., Shelah, S., Stavi, J.: On the temporal analysis of fairness. In: Proc. 7th ACM Symp. on Principles of Programming Languages, pp. 163–173 (1980)
57. Gastin, P., Oddoux, D.: Fast LTL to Büchi automata translation. In: Berry, G., Comon, H., Finkel, A. (eds.) CAV 2001. LNCS, vol. 2102, pp. 53–65. Springer, Heidelberg (2001)
58. Gerth, R., Peled, D., Vardi, M.Y., Wolper, P.: Simple on-the-fly automatic verification of linear temporal logic. In: Dembiski, P., Sredniawa, M. (eds.) Protocol Specification, Testing, and Verification, pp. 3–18. Chapman & Hall (1995)
59. Hafer, T., Thomas, W.: Computation tree logic CTL* and path quantifiers in the monadic theory of the binary tree. In: Ottmann, T. (ed.) Automata, Languages and Programming. LNCS, vol. 267, pp. 269–279. Springer, Heidelberg (1987)
60. Halpern, J.Y., Reif, J.H.: The propositional dynamic logic of deterministic, well-structured programs (extended abstract). In: Proc. 22nd IEEE Symp. on Foundations of Computer Science, pp. 322–334 (1981)
61. Halpern, J.Y., Reif, J.H.: The propositional dynamic logic of deterministic, well-structured programs. Theor. Comput. Sci. 27, 127–165 (1983)
62. Hardin, R.H., Har'el, Z., Kurshan, R.P.: COSPAN. In: Alur, R., Henzinger, T.A. (eds.) CAV 1996. LNCS, vol. 1102, pp. 423–427. Springer, Heidelberg (1996)
63. Harel, D., Kozen, D., Parikh, R.: Process logic: Expressiveness, decidability, completeness. J. Comput. Syst. Sci. 25(2), 144–170 (1982)
64. Harel, D., Kozen, D., Tiuryn, J.: Dynamic Logic. MIT Press (2000)
65. Harel, D., Peleg, D.: More on looping vs. repeating in dynamic logic. Inf. Process. Lett. 20(2), 87–90 (1985)
66. Harel, D., Peleg, D.: Process logic with regular formulas. Theoreti. Comp. Sci. 38(2–3), 307–322 (1985)
67. Harel, D., Sherman, R.: Looping vs. repeating in dynamic logic. Inf. Comput. 55(1–3), 175–192 (1982)
68. Holzmann, G.J.: The model checker SPIN. IEEE Transactions on Software Engineering 23(5), 279–295 (1997)
69. Hopcroft, J.E., Ullman, J.D.: Introduction to Automata Theory, Languages, and Computation. Addison-Wesley (1979)
70. Kamp, J.A.W.: Tense Logic and the Theory of Order. PhD thesis, UCLA (1968)
71. Keller, R.M.: Formal verification of parallel programs. Communications of the ACM 19, 371–384 (1976)
72. Kozen, D.: Results on the propositional μ-calculus. In: Nielsen, M., Schmidt, E.M. (eds.) ICALP 1982. LNCS, vol. 140, pp. 348–359. Springer, Heidelberg (1982)
73. Kozen, D.: Results on the propositional μ-calculus. Theoretical Computer Science 27, 333–354 (1983)
74. Kripke, S.: A completeness theorem in modal logic. Journal of Symbolic Logic 24, 1–14 (1959)
75. Kupferman, O., Piterman, N., Vardi, M.Y.: Safraless compositional synthesis. In: Ball, T., Jones, R.B. (eds.) CAV 2006. LNCS, vol. 4144, pp. 31–44. Springer, Heidelberg (2006)

76. Kupferman, O., Vardi, M.Y.: Weak alternating automata are not that weak. ACM Transactions on Computational Logic 2(2), 408–429 (2001)
77. Kupferman, O., Vardi, M.Y.: Safraless decision procedures. In: Proc. 46th IEEE Symp. on Foundations of Computer Science, pp. 531–540 (2005)
78. Kurshan, R.P.: Analysis of discrete event coordination. In: de Bakker, J.W., de Roever, W.-P., Rozenberg, G. (eds.) REX 1989. LNCS, vol. 430, pp. 414–453. Springer, Heidelberg (1990)
79. Kurshan, R.P.: Computer Aided Verification of Coordinating Processes. Princeton Univ. Press (1994)
80. Kurshan, R.P.: Verification technology transfer. In: Grumberg, O., Veith, H. (eds.) 25 Years of Model Checking. LNCS, vol. 5000, pp. 46–64. Springer, Heidelberg (2008, this volume)
81. Lamport, L.: "Sometimes" is sometimes "not never" - on the temporal logic of programs. In: Proc. 7th ACM Symp. on Principles of Programming Languages, pp. 174–185 (1980)
82. Lichtenstein, O., Pnueli, A.: Checking that finite state concurrent programs satisfy their linear specification. In: Proc. 12th ACM Symp. on Principles of Programming Languages, pp. 97–107 (1985)
83. Lichtenstein, O., Pnueli, A., Zuck, L.: The glory of the past. In: Parikh, R. (ed.) Logic of Programs 1985. LNCS, vol. 193, pp. 196–218. Springer, Heidelberg (1985)
84. Markey, N.: Temporal logic with past is exponentially more succinct. EATCS Bulletin 79, 122–128 (2003)
85. McMillan, K.L.: Symbolic Model Checking. Kluwer Academic Publishers (1993)
86. McNaughton, R., Papert, S.: Counter-Free Automata. MIT Pres (1971)
87. Meyer, A.R.: Weak monadic second order theory of successor is not elementary recursive. In: Proc. Logic Colloquium. Lecture Notes in Mathematics, vol. 453, pp. 132–154. Springer (1975)
88. Meyer, A.R.: Ten thousand and one logics of programming. Technical report, MIT, MIT-LCS-TM-150 (1980)
89. Morley, M.J.: Semantics of temporal e. In: Melham, T.F., Moller, F.G. (eds.) Banff 1999 Higher Order Workshop (Formal Methods in Computation), University of Glasgow, Department of Computing Science Technical Report (1999)
90. Urquhart, A., Rescher, N.: Temporal Logic. Springer (1971)
91. Øhrstrøm, P., Hasle, P.F.V.: Temporal Logic: from Ancient Times to Artificial Intelligence. Studies in Linguistics and Philosophy, vol. 57. Kluwer (1995)
92. Park, D.: Finiteness is μ-ineffable. Theoretical Computer Science 3, 173–181 (1976)
93. Pnueli, A.: The temporal logic of programs. In: Proc. 18th IEEE Symp. on Foundations of Computer Science, pp. 46–57 (1977)
94. Pnueli, A.: Linear and branching structures in the semantics and logics of reactive systems. In: Brauer, W. (ed.) ICALP 1985. LNCS, vol. 194, pp. 15–32. Springer, Heidelberg (1985)
95. Pnueli, A., Zuck, L.: In and out of temporal logic. In: Proc. 8th IEEE Symp. on Logic in Computer Science, pp. 124–135 (1993)
96. Pratt, V.R.: Semantical considerations on Floyd-Hoare logic. In: Proc. 17th IEEE Symp. on Foundations of Computer Science, pp. 109–121 (1976)
97. Pratt, V.R.: A practical decision method for propositional dynamic logic: Preliminary report. In: Proc. 10th Annual ACM Symposium on Theory of Computing, pp. 326–337 (1978)
98. Pratt, V.R.: A near-optimal method for reasoning about action. Journal of Computer and Systems Science 20(2), 231–254 (1980)
99. Pratt, V.R.: A decidable μ-calculus: preliminary report. In: Proc. 22nd IEEE Symp. on Foundations of Computer Science, pp. 421–427 (1981)
100. Prior, A.: Time and Modality. Oxford University Press (1957)
101. Prior, A.: Past, Present, and Future. Clarendon Press (1967)

102. Prior, A.N.: Modality de dicto and modality de re. Theoria 18, 174–180 (1952)
103. Prior, A.N.: Modality and quantification in s5. J. Symbolic Logic 21, 60–62 (1956)
104. Queille, J.P., Sifakis, J.: Specification and verification of concurrent systems in Cesar. In: Dezani-Ciancaglini, M., Montanari, U. (eds.) Programming 1982. LNCS, vol. 137, pp. 337–351. Springer, Heidelberg (1982)
105. Rabin, M.O.: Automata on infinite objects and Church's problem. Amer. Mathematical Society (1972)
106. Sabnani, K., Wolper, P., Lapone, A.: An algorithmic technique for protocol verification. In: Proc. Globecom 1985 (1985)
107. Salwicki, A.: Algorithmic logic: a tool for investigations of programs. In: Butts, R.E., Hintikka, J. (eds.) Logic Foundations of Mathematics and Computability Theory, pp. 281–295. Reidel (1977)
108. Sistla, A.P.: Theoretical issues in the design of distributed and concurrent systems. PhD thesis, Harvard University (1983)
109. Sistla, A.P., Clarke, E.M.: The complexity of propositional linear temporal logics. In: Proc. 14th Annual ACM Symposium on Theory of Computing, pp. 159–168 (1982)
110. Sistla, A.P., Clarke, E.M.: The complexity of propositional linear temporal logic. Journal of the ACM 32, 733–749 (1985)
111. Sistla, A.P., Vardi, M.Y., Wolper, P.: The complementation problem for Büchi automata with applications to temporal logic. In: Brauer, W. (ed.) ICALP 1985. LNCS, vol. 194, pp. 465–474. Springer, Heidelberg (1985)
112. Sistla, A.P., Vardi, M.Y., Wolper, P.: The complementation problem for Büchi automata with applications to temporal logic. Theoretical Computer Science 49, 217–237 (1987)
113. Stockmeyer, L.J.: The complexity of decision procedures in Automata Theory and Logic. PhD thesis, MIT, Project MAC Technical Report TR-133 (1974)
114. Street, R.S.: Propositional dynamic logic of looping and converse. In: Proc. 13th ACM Symp. on Theory of Computing, pp. 375–383 (1981)
115. Streett, R.S.: A propositional dynamic logic for reasoning about program divergence. PhD thesis, M.Sc. Thesis, MIT (1980)
116. Streett, R.S.: Propositional dynamic logic of looping and converse. Information and Control 54, 121–141 (1982)
117. A comparison of reset control methods: Application note 11, Summit Microelectronics, Inc. (1999),
    http://www.summitmicro.com/tech_support/notes/note11.htm
118. Thomas, W.: Star-free regular sets of ω-sequences. Information and Control 42(2), 148–156 (1979)
119. Thomas, W.: On the synthesis of strategies in infinite games. In: Mayr, E.W., Puech, C. (eds.) STACS 1995. LNCS, vol. 900, pp. 1–13. Springer, Heidelberg (1995)
120. Trakhtenbrot, B.: The synthesis of logical nets whose operators are described in terms of one-place predicate calculus. Doklady Akad. Nauk SSSR 118(4), 646–649 (1958)
121. Trakhtenbrot, B.A., Barzdin, Y.M.: Finite Automata. North Holland (1973)
122. Vardi, M.Y.: The complexity of relational query languages. In: Proc. 14th ACM Symp. on Theory of Computing, pp. 137–146 (1982)
123. Vardi, M.Y.: A temporal fixpoint calculus. In: Proc. 15th ACM Symp. on Principles of Programming Languages, pp. 250–259 (1988)
124. Vardi, M.Y.: Unified verification theory. In: Banieqbal, B., Pnueli, A., Barringer, H. (eds.) Temporal Logic in Specification. LNCS, vol. 398, pp. 202–212. Springer, Heidelberg (1989)
125. Vardi, M.Y.: Nontraditional applications of automata theory. In: Hagiya, M., Mitchell, J.C. (eds.) TACS 1994. LNCS, vol. 789, pp. 575–597. Springer, Heidelberg (1994)
126. Vardi, M.Y.: Branching vs. linear time: Final showdown. In: Margaria, T., Yi, W. (eds.) ETAPS 2001 and TACAS 2001. LNCS, vol. 2031, pp. 1–22. Springer, Heidelberg (2001)

127. Vardi, M.Y.: Automata-theoretic model checking revisited. In: Cook, B., Podelski, A. (eds.) VMCAI 2007. LNCS, vol. 4349, pp. 137–150. Springer, Heidelberg (2007)
128. Vardi, M.Y., Wolper, P.: Yet another process logic. In: Clarke, E., Kozen, D. (eds.) Logic of Programs 1983. LNCS, vol. 164, pp. 501–512. Springer, Heidelberg (1984)
129. Vardi, M.Y., Wolper, P.: An automata-theoretic approach to automatic program verification. In: Proc. 1st IEEE Symp. on Logic in Computer Science, pp. 332–344 (1986)
130. Vardi, M.Y., Wolper, P.: Reasoning about infinite computations. Information and Computation 115(1), 1–37 (1994)
131. Vijayaraghavan, S., Ramanathan, M.: A Practical Guide for SystemVerilog Assertions. Springer (2005)
132. Wolper, P.: Temporal logic can be more expressive. In: Proc. 22nd IEEE Symp. on Foundations of Computer Science, pp. 340–348 (1981)
133. Wolper, P.: Temporal logic can be more expressive. Information and Control 56(1–2), 72–99 (1983)
134. Wolper, P., Vardi, M.Y., Sistla, A.P.: Reasoning about infinite computation paths. In: Proc. 24th IEEE Symp. on Foundations of Computer Science, pp. 185–194 (1983)

On the Merits of Temporal Testers*

A. Pnueli and A. Zaks

New York University, New York,
{amir,zaks}@cs.nyu.edu

Abstract. The paper discusses the merits of *temporal testers*, which can serve
as a compositional basis for automata construction corresponding to temporal
formulas in the context of LTL, PSL, and MITL logics. Temporal testers can be
viewed as (non-deterministic) transducers that, at any point, output a boolean
value which is 1 iff the corresponding temporal formula holds starting at the
current position.

The main advantage of testers, compared to acceptors (such as Büchi automata) is their compositionality. Namely, a tester for a compound formula can
be constructed out of the testers for its sub-formulas. Besides providing the construction of testers for formulas specified in LTL, PSL, and MITL, the paper also
presents a general overview of the tester methodology, and highlights some of the
unique features and applications of transducers including compositional deductive verification of LTL properties.

1 Introduction

Automata theory plays a central role in formal methods. For example, the classical
way of model checking an LTL property φ over a finite-state system S, represented by
the automaton M_s, is based on the construction of an ω-automaton $\mathcal{A}_{\neg\varphi}$ that accepts
all sequences that violate the property φ. Having both the system and its specification
represented by automata, we may form the product automaton $M_s \times \mathcal{A}_{\neg\varphi}$ and check
that it accepts the empty language, implying that there exists no computation of S which
refutes φ [24]. For the working of this algorithm, it is sufficient that the automaton
is a proper recognizer for the language $\mathcal{L}(\neg\varphi)$ specified by the formula $\neg\varphi$. It is no
surprise that acceptors such as ω-automata is a formalism widely used by researchers
and engineers alike.

However, with the advancements in the field of the formal verification, several draw-
backs of acceptors became noticeable. First of all, modern model checkers may expect
the automaton to be symbolic (BDD-based). Therefore, if one is to use the standard
tableau-based construction, some encoding may be necessary. In addition, new temporal languages such as PSL [1] have been developed to address the need for formalizing
more elaborate and intricate specifications. In particular, PSL has several features to
support bottom-up construction of complex properties, where lower level properties are
composed to construct more complex properties. Acceptors do not fit into this paradigm
very well since they do not compose. That is, having constructed automata $\mathcal{A}_\varphi$ and $\mathcal{A}_\psi$

---

* This research was supported in part by the European community project Prosyd, ONR grant
N00014-99-1-0131, and SRC grant 2004-TJ-1256.

O. Grumberg and H. Veith (Eds.): 25MC Festschrift, LNCS 5000, pp. 172–195, 2008.

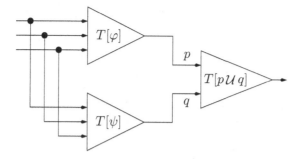

Fig. 1. Composition of transducers to form $T[\varphi\,\mathcal{U}\,\psi]$

for LTL formulas φ and ψ, there is no simple recipe for constructing the automaton for a compound formula that combines φ and ψ, such as $\varphi\,\mathcal{U}\,\psi$.

One remedy to this problem is to enhance ω-automata with universal non-determinism (i.e., alternating ω-automata) [6]. In this approach, there are no special requirements on the sub-automata, and any two acceptors can be composed using alternation. An orthogonal solution to the problem is to impose the responsibility of being composable on the sub-automata themselves. In particular, we suggest that an automaton not only tells whether the entire (infinite) input sequence is in the language, but does so for every suffix of the input word. We call such an automaton a *temporal tester*, which has been introduced first in [13]. More formally, a tester for a formula φ can be viewed as a *transducer* that keeps observing a state sequence σ and, at every position $j \geq 0$, outputs a boolean value which equals 1 iff $(\sigma, j) \models \varphi$.

While acceptors, such as the Büchi automata $\mathcal{A}_\varphi$, do not easily compose, temporal testers do. In Fig. 1, we show how transducers for the formulas φ, ψ, and $p\,\mathcal{U}\,q$ can be composed into a transducer for the formula $\varphi\,\mathcal{U}\,\psi$.

Below is a summary of several important features of temporal testers that make them very useful:

- The construction is compositional. Therefore, it is sufficient to specify testers for the basic temporal formulas. In case of LTL, we only need to consider the formulas $X! p^1$ and $p\,\mathcal{U}\,q$, where p and q are assertions (state formulas). Testers for more complex formulas can be derived by composition as in Fig. 1.
- The testers for the basic formulas are naturally symbolic. Thus, a general tester, which is a synchronous parallel composition (automata product) of symbolic modules can also be easily represented symbolically. As was shown in [21], the basic processes of model checking and run-time monitoring can be performed directly on the symbolic representation of the testers. There is no need for partial determinization to handle alternation nor conversion from explicit state representation.
- Extensions of an existing logic can be handled by constructing testers only for the newly introduced basic operators. This feature has been utilized to a great advantage when a compositional approach to the construction of transducers

---

[1] Inspired by the PSL notation, we write $X! p$ for "next p".

corresponding to LTL formulas [13] has been extended to handle the logics PSL [21] and MITL [16] which are extensions of LTL.

- In spite of the fact that transducers are more functionally complex than acceptors, the complexity of constructing a transducer (temporal tester) for an arbitrary LTL, PSL, or MITL formula is not worse than that of the lower-functionality acceptor. In its symbolic representation, the size of a tester is linear in the size of the formula. This implies that the worst-case state complexity is exponential for LTL and PSL formulas, which is an established lower bound.

Note that we can always regard a temporal tester as an acceptor. Therefore, it is interesting to compare automata construction using temporal testers to other techniques such as tableau construction for LTL [15] and alternating-automata based construction for PSL [8]. First, we note that the complexity of all of these techniques as well as that of the testers approach equally match the established lower bound. Of course, there is plenty of room for practical considerations and local improvements. Surprisingly, for LTL, a tableau-based approach [15] yields an automaton identical to the one induced by the transducer constructed according to [13]. Similarly, for PSL, the tester construction of [21] induces an acceptor almost identical to the one obtained in [8]. Actually, the two automata become exactly alike after several optimizations are applied to an alternating automata based approach, most of the optimizations become much more obvious once we realize how to build a proper transducer for these operators.

Nevertheless, the testers approach offers a conceptually new methodology, and while similarities are not accidental and rather striking, the differences are equally remarkable. Let us again compare temporal testers to tableau construction and alternation techniques, but now with an emphasis on the process itself rather than on the final result. The main building blocks of tableau construction are the expansion formulas, like $b_1 \mathcal{U} b_2 \iff b_2 \vee (b_1 \wedge X![b_1 \mathcal{U} b_2])$. Such expansion formulas, which exist for all the temporal operators, relate the value of an expression involving the operator at the current position to the values of its arguments in the current and next position and to the value of the expression in the next position. For past operators, the expansion formula relates the value of the expression and its arguments in the current position to their values in the previous position.

When constructing testers for an operator that has an expansion formula (such as all the LTL operators), one uses the expansion formula as the core for the transition relation of the tester. However, when developing testers for more complicated or simply "unknown" (new) operators, the expansion formula approach may not always be an option. In such cases, one may use the intuition that treats a tester as a non-deterministic guesser, the correctness of whose output needs to be confirmed at a later stage. That was the approach successfully applied for handling PSL and MITL operators. And, while the tester construction for PSL produced expansion formulas as a nice side effect, there is no such result for MITL, where reliance on "guessing" plays a crucial role. When comparing testers to an alternating automata, the main philosophical distinction is that an alternating automata is less structured than a non-deterministic acceptor, while testers, on the other hand, have more structure than classical acceptors.

The additional support provided by a transducer make them truly plug-and-play objects, which has several important practical implications. The most straightforward illustration of this phenomenon is application of tester towards CTL* model checking [14]. The paper shows how to reduce CTL* model checking problem to that of CTL . Essentially, each path-quantifier free sub-formula is replaced by the corresponding LTL transducer. We could have performed a similar reduction using acceptors. However, using testers we have a freedom for each such sub-formula to leave the outer-most temporal operator intact and construct the tester for the remaining part. This results in a true CTL* to CTL reduction, where we may still have temporal operators in the final CTL formula. The ability to decompose an LTL formula using testers is also crucial for deductive verification, which we will discuss in a great detail in Section 11.

Another benefit of the plug-and-play nature of testers is the possibility to use different algorithms for different parts of the formula. For example, a user can manually build a highly optimized tester for a sub-formula, and the rest of the formula can be handled automatically. We can also combine testers with other techniques as was done in [7], where PSL operators are handled using the tester approach, but the rest of the formula uses an existing LTL to NBA transformation which, according to the experimental data, results in the fastest available implementation for PSL to NBA conversion.

2   Accellera PSL

In this section we introduce the property specification language PSL [1]. The construction of testers for PSL formulas will be presented in Section 8.

In this paper, we only consider a subset of PSL. For brevity, we omit the discussions of OBE (Optional Branching Extension) formulas that are based on CTL . Note that using testers we can obtain a model checking algorithm even for CTL* branching formulas by combining PSL testers with the work in [14]. In addition, we do not consider clocked formulas and formulas with *abort* operator. This is not a severe limitation since none of the above add any expressive power to PSL. One can find a rewriting scheme for the @ operator (clock operator) in [10] and for the *abort* operator in [22]. The rewriting rules produce a semantically equivalent formula not containing the operators, which is linear in the size of the original formula.

2.1   Syntax

The logic Accellera PSL is defined with respect to a non-empty set of atomic propositions P. Let B be the set of boolean expressions over P. We assume that the expressions *true* and *false* belong to B.

Definition 1 (Sequential Extended Regular Expressions (SEREs)) .

- *Every boolean expression $b \in B$ is a SERE.*
- *If r, r_1, and r_2 are SEREs, then the following are SEREs:*
    - $\{r\}$
    - $[*0]$
    - $r_1 ; r_2$
    - $r_1 \,\&\&\, r_2$
    - $r_1 : r_2$
    - $r[*]$
    - $r_1 \mid r_2$

Definition 2 (Formulas of the Foundation Language (FL formulas)) .

- *If r is a SERE, then both r and $r!$ are FL formulas.*
- *If φ and ψ are FL formulas, r is a SERE, and b is a boolean expression, then the following are FL formulas:*

• (φ)	• $\neg\varphi$	• $\varphi \wedge \psi$	• $\langle r \rangle \varphi$
• $X!\varphi$	• $[\varphi \, \mathcal{U} \, \psi]$	• φ *abort* b	• $r \mapsto \varphi$

Definition 3 (Accellera PSL Formulas) .

- *Every FL formula is an Accellera* PSL *formula.*

2.2   Semantics

The semantics of FL is defined with respect to finite and infinite words over $\Sigma = 2^P \cup \{\top, \bot\}$. We denote a letter from Σ by l and an empty, finite, or infinite word from Σ by $u, v,$ or w (possibly with subscripts). We denote the length of word v as $|v|$. An empty word $v = \epsilon$ has length 0, a finite word $v = (l_0 l_1 l_2 \ldots l_k)$ has length $k+1$, and an infinite word has length ω. We use $i, j,$ and k to denote non-negative integers. We denote the ith letter of v by v^{i-1} (since counting of letters starts at zero). We denote by $v^{i\cdot\cdot}$ the suffix of v starting at v^i. That is, for every $i < |v|$, $v^{i\cdot\cdot} = v^i v^{i+1} \cdots v^n$ or $v^{i\cdot\cdot} = v^i v^{i+1} \cdots$. We denote by $v^{i\cdot\cdot j}$ the finite sequence of letters starting from v^i and ending in v^j. That is, for $j \geq i$, $v^{i\cdot\cdot j} = v^i v^{i+1} \cdots v^j$ and for $j < i$, $v^{i\cdot\cdot j} = \epsilon$. We use l^ω to denote an infinite-length word, each letter of which is l.

We use $\bar{v}$ to denote the word obtained by replacing every $\top$ with a $\bot$ and vice versa. We call $\bar{v}$ the *complement* of v.

The semantics of FL *formulas* over *words* is defined inductively, using as the base case the semantics of *boolean expressions* over *letters* in Σ. The semantics of a boolean expression is assumed to be given as a relation $\models \subseteq \Sigma \times B$ relating letters in Σ with boolean expressions in B. If $(l, b) \in \models$, we say that the letter l satisfies the boolean expression b and denote it by $l \models b$. We assume the two special letters $\top$ and $\bot$ behave as follows: for every boolean expression b, $\top \models b$ and $\bot \not\models b$. We assume that, otherwise, the boolean relation $\models$ behaves in the usual manner. In particular, that for every letter $l \in 2^P$, atomic proposition $p \in P$ and boolean expressions $b, b_1, b_2 \in B$, (i) $l \models p$ iff $p \in l$, (ii) $l \models \neg b$ iff $l \not\models b$, and (iii) $l \models true$ and $l \not\models false$. Finally, we assume that for every letter $l \in \Sigma$, $l \models b_1 \wedge b_2$ iff $l \models b_1$ and $l \models b_2$.

Semantics of SEREs. SEREs are defined over finite words from the alphabet Σ. The notation $v \models r$, where r is a SERE and v a finite word means that v *tightly models r.* The semantics of unclocked SEREs are defined as follows, where b denotes a boolean expression, and $r, r_1,$ and r_2 denote unclocked SEREs.

- $v \models \{r\} \Longleftrightarrow v \models r$
- $v \models b \Longleftrightarrow |v| = 1 \wedge v^0 \models b$
- $v \models r_1 \,;\, r_2 \Longleftrightarrow \exists v_1, v_2 \text{ s.t. } v = v_1 v_2, v_1 \models r_1 \text{ and } v_2 \models r_2$
- $v \models r_1 : r_2 \Longleftrightarrow \exists v_1, v_2, \text{ and } l \text{ s.t. } v = v_1 l v_2, v_1 l \models r_1 \text{ and } l v_2 \models r_2$
- $v \models r_1 \mid r_2 \Longleftrightarrow v \models r_1 \text{ or } v \models r_2$
- $v \models r_1 \,\&\&\, r_2 \Longleftrightarrow v \models r_1 \text{ and } v \models r_2$
- $v \models [*0] \Longleftrightarrow v = \epsilon$
- $v \models r[*] \Longleftrightarrow v = \epsilon \text{ or } \exists v_1, v_2 \text{ s.t. } v_1 \neq \epsilon, v = v_1 v_2 \text{ and } v_1 \models r \text{ and } v_2 \models r[*]$

Semantics of FL. Let v be a finite or infinite word, b be a boolean expression, r be a SERE, and φ, ψ be FL formulas. We use $\vDash$ to define the semantics of FL formulas. If $v \vDash \varphi$ we say that v models (or satisfies) φ.

- $v \vDash (\varphi) \Longleftrightarrow v \vDash \varphi$
- $v \vDash \neg\varphi \Longleftrightarrow \bar{v} \nvDash \varphi$
- $v \vDash \varphi \wedge \psi \Longleftrightarrow v \vDash \varphi$ and $v \vDash \psi$
- $v \vDash b! \Longleftrightarrow |v| > 0$ and $v^0 \Vmodels b$
- $v \vDash b \Longleftrightarrow |v| = 0$ or $v^0 \Vmodels b$
- $v \vDash r! \Longleftrightarrow \exists j < |v|$ s.t. $v^{0..j} \Vmodels r$
- $v \vDash r \Longleftrightarrow \forall j < |v|, v^{0..j} \top^\omega \vDash r!$
- $v \vDash X!\varphi \Longleftrightarrow |v| > 1$ and $v^{1..} \vDash \varphi$
- $v \vDash [\varphi \mathcal{U} \psi] \Longleftrightarrow \exists k < |v|$ s.t. $v^{k..} \vDash \psi$, and $\forall j < k, v^{j..} \vDash \varphi$
- $v \vDash [\varphi \mathcal{W} \psi] \Longleftrightarrow \exists k < |v|$ s.t. $v^{k..} \vDash \psi$, and $\forall j < min(k, |v|) \ v^{j..} \vDash \varphi$
- $v \vDash \varphi \ abort \ b \Longleftrightarrow v \vDash \varphi$ or $\exists j < |v|$ s.t. $v^j \Vmodels b$ and $v^{0..j-1} \top^\omega \vDash \varphi$
- $v \vDash \langle r \rangle \varphi \Longleftrightarrow \exists j < |v|$ s.t. $\bar{v}^{0..j} \Vmodels r, v^{j..} \vDash \varphi$
- $v \vDash r \mapsto \varphi \Longleftrightarrow \forall j < |v|$ s.t. $\bar{v}^{0..j} \Vmodels r, v^{j..} \vDash \varphi$

2.3 Associating a Regular Grammar with a SERE

Following [12], a grammar $\mathcal{G} = \langle \mathcal{V}, \mathcal{T}, \mathcal{P}, \mathcal{S} \rangle$ consists of the following components:

- $\mathcal{V}$: A finite set of *variables*.
- $\mathcal{T}$: A finite set of *terminals*. We assume that $\mathcal{V}$ and $\mathcal{T}$ are disjoint. In our framework, $\mathcal{T}$ consists of boolean expressions and a special terminal ϵ.
- $\mathcal{P}$: A finite set of *productions*. We only consider right-linear grammars, so all productions are of the form $V \to aW$ or $V \to a$, where a is a terminal, and V and W are variables.
- $\mathcal{S}$: A special variable called a *start symbol*.

We say that a grammar $\mathcal{G}$ is *associated* with a SERE r if, intuitively, they both define the same language. While this definition is not accurate, we show a precise construction of an associated grammar for a given SERE in Appendix A. For example, we associate the following grammar $\mathcal{G}$ with SERE $r = (a_1b_1)[*]$ && $(a_2b_2)[*]$

$$V_1 \to \epsilon \mid (a_1 \wedge a_2)V_2$$
$$V_2 \to \quad (b_1 \wedge b_2)V_1$$

Theorem 1. *For every SERE r of length n, there exists an associated grammar $\mathcal{G}$ with the number of productions $O(2^n)$. If we restrict SERE's to the three traditional operators: concatenation (;), union (|), and Kleene closure ([*]), the number of productions becomes linear in the size of r.*

3 Signals, Their Temporal Logic and Timed Automata

In this section we presented the real-time logic MITL, for which we will present testers in Section 9. Most of the material in this section and in Section 9 is taken from [16].

3.1 Signals

Two basic semantic domains can be used to describe timed behaviors. *Time-event sequences* consist of instantaneous events separated by time durations while discrete-valued *signals* are functions from time to some discrete domain. The reader may consult the introduction to [5] for more details on the algebraic characterization of these domains. In this work we use Boolean signals as the semantic domain, which is the natural choice for MITL.

Let the time domain $\mathbb{T}$ be the set $\mathbb{R}_{\geq 0}$ of non-negative real numbers. A Boolean signal is a function $\xi : \mathbb{T} \to \mathbb{B}^n$. We use $\xi[t]$ for the value of the signal at time t and the notation $\sigma_1^{t_1} \cdot \sigma_2^{t_2} \cdots$ for a signal whose value is σ_1 at the interval $[0, t_1)$, σ_2 in the interval $[t_1, t_1 + t_2)$, etc. For the sake of simplicity we restrict ourselves to such left-closed right-open signal segments and to timed modalities that use only closed intervals. As a consequence we prohibit signal with punctual intervals which are meaningless in the algebraic definition of signals in [5].

3.2 Real-Time Temporal Logic

The syntax of MITL is defined by the grammar

$$\varphi := p \mid \neg\varphi \mid \varphi_1 \vee \varphi_2 \mid \varphi_1 \mathcal{U}_{[a,b]}\varphi_2 \mid \varphi_1 \mathcal{U}\varphi_2$$

where p belongs to a set $P = \{p_1, \ldots, p_n\}$ of propositions and $b > a \geq 0$ are rational numbers (in fact, it is sufficient to consider integer constants). From the basic MITL operators one can derive other standard Boolean and temporal operators, in particular the time-constrained *eventually* and *always* operators:

$$\Diamond_{[a,b]} \varphi = \mathrm{T}\, \mathcal{U}_{[a,b]}\varphi \quad \text{and} \quad \Box_{[a,b]} \varphi = \neg \Diamond_{[a,b]} \neg\varphi$$

We interpret MITL$_{[a,b]}$ over n-dimensional Boolean signals and define the satisfiability relation similarly to LTL.

$$
\begin{aligned}
(\xi, t) &\models p & &\leftrightarrow p[t] = \mathrm{T} \\
(\xi, t) &\models \neg\varphi & &\leftrightarrow (\xi, t) \not\models \varphi \\
(\xi, t) &\models \varphi_1 \vee \varphi_2 & &\leftrightarrow (\xi, t) \models \varphi_1 \text{ or } (\xi, t) \models \varphi_2 \\
(\xi, t) &\models \varphi_1 \mathcal{U}\varphi_2 & &\leftrightarrow \exists t' \geq t\ (\xi, t') \models \varphi_2 \text{ and } \forall t'' \in [t, t'], (\xi, t'') \models \varphi_1 \\
(\xi, t) &\models \varphi_1 \mathcal{U}_{[a,b]}\varphi_2 & &\leftrightarrow \exists t' \in [t+a, t+b]\ (\xi, t') \models \varphi_2 \text{ and } \forall t'' \in [t, t'], (\xi, t'') \models \varphi_1
\end{aligned}
$$

Note that our definition of the semantics of the time-bounded *until* operator differs slightly from definition in [3] which requires φ_1 to hold in the open interval (t', t). Hence our definition can be expressed in their terms as $\varphi_1 \wedge (\varphi_1 \mathcal{U}_{[a,b]}(\varphi_1 \wedge \varphi_2))$. A signal ξ satisfies the formula φ iff $(\xi, 0) \models \varphi$.

3.3 Timed Automata

We use a variant of timed automata which differs slightly from the classical definitions [2], [23] as it reads multi-dimensional *dense-time* Boolean signals, hence the alphabet letters are associated with *states* rather than with *transitions*. We also extend the domain of clock values to include the special symbol $\perp$ indicating that the clock is currently *inactive*.[2]

The set of valuations of a set $C = \{c_1, \ldots, c_n\}$ of clock variables, each denoted as $v = (v_1, \ldots, v_n)$, defines the clock space $\mathcal{H} = (\mathbb{R}_{\geq 0} \cup \{\perp\})^n$. A *configuration* of a timed automaton is a pair of the form (q, v) with q being a discrete state. For a clock valuation $v = (v_1, \ldots, v_n)$, $v + t$ is the valuation $(v'_1, \ldots, v'_n)$ such that $v'_i = v_i$ if $v_i = \perp$ and $v'_i = v_i + t$ otherwise. A *clock constraint* is a Boolean combination of conditions of the forms $c \geq d$ or $c > d$ for some integer d.

Definition 1 (Timed Automaton). *A timed automaton over signals is a tuple $\mathcal{A} = (\Sigma, Q, C, \lambda, I, \Delta, q_0, F)$ where Σ is the input alphabet ($\mathbb{B}^n$ in this paper), Q is a finite set of discrete states and C is a set of clock variables. The labeling function $\lambda : Q \to 2^\Sigma$ associates a subset of the alphabet to every state while the staying condition (invariant) I assigns to every state q a subset I_q of $\mathcal{H}$ defined by a conjunction of inequalities of the form $x \leq d$, for some clock x and integer d. The transition relation Δ consists of elements of the form (q, g, ρ, q') where q and q' are discrete states, the transition guard g is a subset of $\mathcal{H}$ defined by a clock constraint and ρ is the update function, a transformation of $\mathcal{H}$ defined by a assignments of the form $c := 0$ or $c := \perp$. Finally q_0 is the initial state and $F \subseteq Q$ is the acceptance condition.*

The behavior of the automaton as it reads a signal ξ consists of an alternation between time progress periods where the automaton stays in a state q as long as $\xi[t] \in \lambda(q)$ and I_q holds, and discrete instantaneous transitions guarded by clock conditions. Formally, a *step* of the automaton is one of the following:

- A time step: $(q, v) \xrightarrow{\sigma^t} (q, v + t)$, $t \in \mathbb{R}_+$ such that $\sigma \in \lambda(q)$ and $v + t$ satisfies I_q (due to the structure of I_q this holds as well for every t', $0 \leq t' < t$).
- A discrete step: $(q, v) \xrightarrow{\delta} (q', v')$, for some transition $\delta = (q, g, \rho, q') \in \Delta$, such that v satisfies g and $v' = \rho(v)$.

A *run* of the automaton starting from a configuration (q_0, v_0) is a finite or infinite sequence of alternating time and discrete steps of the form

$$\xi : \quad (q_0, v_0) \xrightarrow{\sigma_1^{t_1}} (q_0, v_0 + t_1) \xrightarrow{\delta_1} (q_1, v_1) \xrightarrow{\sigma_2^{t_2}} (q_1, v_1 + t_2) \xrightarrow{\delta_2} \cdots ,$$

such the $\sum t_i$ diverges. A run is accepting if the set of time instants in which it visits states in F is unbounded. The signal carried by the run is $\sigma_1^{t_1} \cdot \sigma_2^{t_2} \cdots$ The language of the automaton consists of all signals carried by accepting runs.

4   Computational Model

In this section we present the computational model for describing software and hardware systems whose properties we wish to verify.

---

[2] This is a syntactic sugar since clock inactivity in a state can be encoded implicitly by the fact that in all paths emanating from the state, the clock is reset to zero before being tested [9].

4.1   Fair Discrete Systems with Finite Computations

As our computational model We take a *just discrete system* (JDS), which is a variant of *fair transition system* [19], and is a weaker version of the more general *fair discrete system* considered in [13]. Under this model, a system $\mathcal{D} : \langle V, \Theta, R, \mathcal{J}, F \rangle$ consists of the following components:

- V: A finite set of *system variables*. A *state* of the system $\mathcal{D}$ provides a type-consistent interpretation of the system variables V. For a state s and a system variable $v \in V$, we denote the value assigned to v by the state s by $s[v]$.
- Θ: The *initial condition*. This is an assertion (state formula) characterizing the initial states. A state is defined to be *initial* if it satisfies Θ.
- $R(V, V')$: The *transition relation*, which is an assertion that relates the values of the variables in V interpreted by a state s to the values of the variables V' in an R-*successor* state s'.
- $\mathcal{J}$: A set of *justice* (*weak fairness*) requirements. Each justice requirement is an assertion. An infinite computation must include infinitely many states satisfying the assertion.
- F: The *termination condition*, which is an assertion specifying the set of *final* states. Each finite computation must end in a final state.

A *computation* of a JDS $\mathcal{D}$ is a non-empty sequence of states $\sigma : s_0, s_1, s_2, ...$, satisfying the requirements:

- *Initiality*: s_0 is initial.
- *Consecution*: For each $i \in [0, |\sigma|)$, the state s_{i+1} is a R-successor of state s_i. That is, $\langle s_i, s_{i+1} \rangle \in R(V, V')$ where, for each $v \in V$, we interpret v as $s_i[v]$ and v' as $s_{i+1}[v]$.
- *Justice*: If σ is infinite, then for every $J \in \mathcal{J}$, σ contains infinitely many occurrences of J-states.
- *Termination*: If $\sigma = s_0, s_1, s_2, ..., s_k$ (i.e., σ is finite), then s_k must satisfy F.

Given two JDS's, $\mathcal{D}_1$ and $\mathcal{D}_2$, their *synchronous parallel composition*, $\mathcal{D}_1 \parallel \mathcal{D}_2$, is the JDS whose sets of variables and justice requirements are the unions of the corresponding sets in the two systems, whose initial and termination conditions are the conjunctions of the corresponding assertions, and whose transition relation is defined as the conjunction of the two transition relations. Thus, a step in an execution of the composed system is a joint step of the systems $\mathcal{D}_1$ and $\mathcal{D}_2$.

4.2   Interpretation of PSL Formulas over a JDS

We assume that the set of atomic propositions P is a subset of the variables V, so we can easily evaluate all the propositions at a given state of a JDS. We say that a letter $l \in 2^P$ *corresponds* to a state s if $p \in l$ iff $s[p] = 1$. Similarly, we define a correspondence between words and computations. We say, that a computation σ models (or satisfies) PSL formula φ, denoted $\sigma \vDash \varphi$, if the corresponding word v satisfies PSL formula φ.

5 Temporal Testers

One of the main problems in constructing a Büchi automaton for a PSL formula (or for that matter any ω-regular language) is that the conventional construction is not compositional. In particular, given Büchi automata $\mathcal{A}_\varphi$ and $\mathcal{A}_\psi$ for formulas φ and ψ, it is not trivial to build an automaton for $\varphi \, \mathcal{U} \, \psi$. Compositionality is an important consideration, especially in the context of PSL. It is expected that specifications are written in a modular way, and PSL has several language constructs to facilitate that. For example, any property can be given a name, and a more complex property can be built by simply using a named sub-property instead of an atomic proposition.

One way to achieve compositionality with Büchi automata is to use alternation [6]. Nothing special is required from the Büchi automata to be composed in such manner, but the presence of universal branching in the resulting automaton is undesirable. Though most model checkers can deal with existential non-determinism directly and efficiently, universal branching is usually preprocessed at exponential cost.

Our approach is based on the observation that while there is very little room to maneuver during the merging step of two Büchi automata, the construction process of the sub-components is wide open for a change. In particular, we suggest that each sub-component assumes the responsibility of being easily composed with other parts. The hope is that, by requiring that individual parts be more structured than the traditional Büchi automata, we can significantly simplify the composition process.

Recall that the main property of Büchi automata (as well as any other acceptor) is to correctly identify a language membership of a given sequence of letters, starting from the very first letter. It turns out that for composition it is also very useful to know whether a word is in the language starting from an arbitrary position i. We refer to this new class of objects as *testers*. Essentially, testers are transducers that at each step output whether the suffix of the input sequence is in the language. Of course, the suffix is not known by the time the decision has to be made, so the testers are inherently non-deterministic.

Formally, a *full tester* for a formula φ is a JDS T_φ, which has a distinguished boolean variable x_φ, such that:

- **Soundness:** For every computation $\sigma : s_0, s_1, s_2, \ldots$ of T_φ, $s_i[x_\varphi] = 1$ iff $(\sigma, i) \models \varphi$
- **Completeness:** For every sequence of states $\sigma : s_0, s_1, s_2, \ldots$, there is a corresponding computation of T_φ $\sigma' : s'_0, s'_1, s'_2, \ldots$ such that for each i, s_i and s'_i agree on the interpretation of φ-variables.

Intuitively, the second condition requires that a tester must be able to correctly interpret x_φ for an arbitrary input sequence. Otherwise, the first condition can be trivially satisfied by a JDS that has no computations.

5.1 Positive and Negative Testers

For many applications, such as model checking, a full tester can be too powerful. Indeed, everywhere where an acceptor suffices, we can use a full tester, but in such case we are really only interested in the very first output value and only when the value is *true*. While we still need intermediate output values for compositionality, we can relax the soundness condition to concentrate on the positive values of x_φ. Another way to look at the problem is the fact that a full tester for a formula φ not only implicitly defines an acceptor for φ itself, but also for $\neg\varphi$. An undesirable consequence of this fact is that a full tester for a safety property such as $\Box\, p$ will have a non trivial justice requirement since it is also a full tester for $\Diamond\, \neg p$. To address this issue, we define positive and negative testers. Formally, a *positive tester* for a formula φ is a JDS T_φ^+, which has a distinguished boolean variable x_φ, such that:

- **Soundness:** For every computation $\sigma : s_0, s_1, s_2, \ldots$ of T_φ^+, if $s_i[x_\varphi] = 1$ then $(\sigma, i) \models \varphi$

- **Completeness:** For every sequence of states $\sigma : s_0, s_1, s_2, \ldots$, there exists a corresponding T_φ^+-computation $\sigma' : s_0', s_1', s_2', \ldots$ such that for each i, s_i and s_i' agree on the interpretation of φ-variables, and $s_i[x_\varphi] = 1$ iff $(\sigma, i) \models \varphi$.

The definition of a *negative tester* is fully analogous.

Theorem 1. *A full tester is also a proper positive tester and a negative tester.*

Theorem 2. *If T_φ^+ a positive tester and T_φ^- is a negative tester for a formula φ that may only share φ-variables, then a full tester can be defined as the composition $T_\varphi^+ \,|||\, T_\varphi^-$, whose transition relation is augmented with the following conjunct that defines the output variable x_φ:*

$$(x_\varphi^+ \to x_\varphi) \wedge (x_\varphi \to x_\varphi^-)$$

From now on, we may refer to a full tester as simply a tester.

6 LTL **Testers**

We continue the presentation of testers by considering the two basic LTL operators $X!$ (next) and $\mathcal{U}$ (until), which are also part of the PSL logic (being an extension of LTL). First, we show how to build testers for the two *basic formulas* $X!\, b$ and $b_1\, \mathcal{U}\, b_2$, where b, b_1, and b_2 are boolean formulas. Then, we demonstrate the compositionality of the testers by easily extending the construction to cover full LTL. Note that our construction for LTL operators is very similar to the one presented in [13].

6.1 A Tester for $\varphi = X!\, b$

Let $T_\varphi = \langle V_\varphi, \Theta_\varphi, R_\varphi, \mathcal{J}_\varphi, F_\varphi \rangle$ be the tester we wish to construct. The components of T_φ are defined as follows:

$$T(X!\,b) : \begin{cases} V_\varphi : Vars(b) \cup \{x_\varphi\} \\ \Theta_\varphi : 1 \\ R_\varphi(V, V') : x_\varphi = b' \\ \mathcal{J}_\varphi : \emptyset \\ F_\varphi : \neg x_\varphi \end{cases}$$

The set $Vars(b)$ contains all the propositions on which the boolean formula b depends.

It almost immediately follows from the construction that $T(X!\,b)$ is indeed a good tester for $X!\,b$. The soundness of the $T(X!\,b)$ is guaranteed by the transition relation with the exception that we still have a freedom to incorrectly interpret x_φ at the very last state. This case is handled separately by insisting that every final state must interpret x_φ as *false*. The completeness follows from the fact that we do not restrict the $Vars(b)$ variables in any way by the transition relation, and we can always interpret x_φ properly, by either matching b' or setting it to *false* in the last state.

6.2 A Tester for $\varphi = b_1\,\mathcal{U}\,b_2$

The components of T_φ are defined as follows:

$$T(b_1\,\mathcal{U}\,b_2) : \begin{cases} V_\varphi : Vars(b_1, b_2) \cup \{x_\varphi\} \\ \Theta_\varphi : 1 \\ R_\varphi(V, V') : x_\varphi = [b_2 \vee (b_1 \wedge x'_\varphi)] \\ \mathcal{J}_\varphi : \neg x_\varphi \vee b_2 \\ F_\varphi : x_\varphi \leftrightarrow b_2 \end{cases}$$

Unlike the previous tester, $T(b_1\,\mathcal{U}\,b_2)$ has a non-empty justice set. A technical reason is that the transition relation allows x_φ to be continuously set to true without having a single state that actually satisfies b_2. The situation is ruled out by the justice requirement. Another way to look at the problem is that R_φ represents an expansion formula for the $\mathcal{U}$ (until) operator, namely $b_1\,\mathcal{U}\,b_2 \leftrightarrow b_2 \vee (b_1 \wedge X![b_1\,\mathcal{U}\,b_2])$. In general, starting with an expansion formula is a good first step when building a tester. However, the expansion formula alone is usually not sufficient for a proper tester. Indeed, consider the operator $\mathcal{W}$ (weak until, unless), which has exactly the same expansion formula, namely $b_1\,\mathcal{W}\,b_2 \leftrightarrow b_2 \vee (b_1 \wedge X![b_1\,\mathcal{W}\,b_2])$. We use justice to differentiate between the two operators. Note that the justice is only needed to confirm *true* output values. Therefore, a negative tester T_φ^- for $\varphi = b_1\,\mathcal{U}\,b_2$ is simpler (no justice) and can be formally defined as:

$$T^-(b_1\,\mathcal{U}\,b_2) : \begin{cases} V_\varphi : Vars(b_1, b_2) \cup \{x_\varphi\} \\ \Theta_\varphi : 1 \\ R_\varphi(V, V') : b_2 \vee (b_1 \wedge x'_\varphi) \to x_\varphi \\ \mathcal{J}_\varphi : \emptyset \\ F_\varphi : b_2 \to x_\varphi \end{cases}$$

7 Tester Composition

In Fig. 2, we present a recursive algorithm that builds a tester for an arbitrary LTL formula φ. In Example 1, we illustrate the algorithm by applying the tester construction for the formula $\varphi = true\,\mathcal{U}\big(X![b_1\,\mathcal{U}\,b_2] \vee (b_3\,\mathcal{U}[b_1\,\mathcal{U}\,b_2])\big)$.

- **Base Case**: If φ is a basic formula (i.e., $\varphi = X! \, b$ or $\varphi = b_1 \, \mathcal{U} \, b_2$), use construction from Section 6. For the trivial case, when the formula φ does not contain any temporal operators, we can use a tester for *false* $\mathcal{U} \, \varphi$.

- **Induction Step**: Let ψ be an innermost basic sub-formula of φ, then $T_\varphi = T_{\varphi[\psi/x_\psi]} \, ||| \, T_\psi$, where $\varphi[\psi/x_\psi]$ denotes the formula φ in which each occurrence of the sub-formula ψ is replaced with x_ψ.

Fig. 2. Tester construction for an arbitrary LTL formula φ

Example 1. *A tester for* $\varphi = true \, \mathcal{U} \big(X! [b_1 \, \mathcal{U} \, b_2] \vee \neg (b_3 \, \mathcal{U} [b_1 \, \mathcal{U} \, b_2]) \big)$

We start by identifying $b_1 \, \mathcal{U} \, b_2$ to be the innermost basic sub-formula and building the corresponding tester, $T_{b_1 \, \mathcal{U} \, b_2}$. Assume that z is the output variable of the tester $T_{b_1 \, \mathcal{U} \, b_2}$. Let $\alpha = \varphi[b_1 \, \mathcal{U} \, b_2/z]$; after the substitution $\alpha = true \, \mathcal{U} \big(X! \, z \vee \neg (b_3 \, \mathcal{U} \, z) \big)$. Note that we performed the substitution twice, but there is no need for two testers, which can result in significant savings. We proceed in similar fashion and build two more testers $T_{X! \, z}$ and $T_{b_3 \, \mathcal{U} \, z}$ with the output variables x and y. After the substitutions, we obtain $\beta = true \, \mathcal{U} [x \vee \neg y]$. Since $x \vee \neg y$ is just a boolean expression, the formula satisfies the condition of the base case, and we can finish the construction with one more step. The final result can be expressed as:

$$T_\varphi = T_\beta \, ||| \, T_{X! \, z} \, ||| \, T_{b_3 \, \mathcal{U} \, z} \, ||| \, T_{b_1 \, \mathcal{U} \, b_2}.$$

7.1   Composition Rules for Positive and Negative Testers

Definition 4 (Polarity of a sub-formula ψ) *Given a formula φ, the* polarity *of a sub-formula ψ with respect to φ is positive if the number of negations enclosing ψ in φ is even and negative otherwise.*

To build a positive tester T_φ^+, we optimize the induction step in Fig. 2 as follows:

- If sub-formula ψ has a positive polarity, then $T_\varphi^+ = T_{\varphi[\psi/x_\psi]}^+ \, ||| \, T_\psi^+$

- If sub-formula ψ has a negative polarity, then $T_\varphi^+ = T_{\varphi[\psi/x_\psi]}^+ \, ||| \, T_\psi^-$

- Otherwise, if sub-formula appears with both positive and negative polarity, then $T_\varphi^+ = T_{\varphi[\psi/x_\psi]}^+ \, ||| \, T_\psi$

The algorithm for building a negative tester is fully symmetric. To illustrate this construction consider the formula φ presented in Example 1. A positive tester is given by:

$$T_\varphi^+ = T_\beta^+ \, ||| \, T_{X! \, z}^+ \, ||| \, T_{b_3 \, \mathcal{U} \, z}^- \, ||| \, T_{b_1 \, \mathcal{U} \, b_2}.$$

A negative tester is given by:

$$T_\varphi^- = T_\beta^- \, ||| \, T_{X! \, z}^- \, ||| \, T_{b_3 \, \mathcal{U} \, z}^+ \, ||| \, T_{b_1 \, \mathcal{U} \, b_2}.$$

Also note that while we assumed that φ is an LTL formula, the algorithms described in this section are applicable for PSL and MITL as well. The only extension necessary is the ability to deal with additional basic formulas.

8 PSL Testers

As we have mentioned before, to handle the full PSL it is enough to handle all the basic PSL formulas. More complicated formulas can be handled via tester composition according to the algorithm in Fig. 2. There are only two additional PSL basic formulas that we need to consider, namely $\varphi = \langle r \rangle b$ and $\varphi = r$, where r is a SERE and b is a boolean expression. All other PSL temporal operators can be expressed using those two and the LTL operators, $X!$ and $\mathcal{U}$. For example, $r! \equiv \langle r \rangle true$, and $r \mapsto b \equiv \neg(\langle r \rangle \neg \varphi)$.

8.1 A Tester for $\varphi = \langle r \rangle b$

Let $T_\varphi = \langle V_\varphi, \Theta_\varphi, R_\varphi, \mathcal{J}_\varphi, F_\varphi \rangle$ be the tester we wish to construct. Assume that x_φ is the output variable. Let $\mathcal{G} = \langle \mathcal{V}, \mathcal{T}, \mathcal{P}, \mathcal{S} \rangle$ be a grammar associated with r. With no loss of generality, we assume that $\mathcal{G}$ has variables $V_1, \ldots, V_n$ with V_1 being the start symbol. In addition, each variable V_i, has derivations of the form:

$$V_i \rightarrow \alpha_1 \mid \cdots \mid \alpha_m \mid \beta_1 V_1 \mid \cdots \mid \beta_n V_n$$

where $\alpha_1, \ldots, \alpha_m, \beta_1, \ldots, \beta_n$ are boolean expressions. The case that variable V_i does not have a particular derivation $V_i \rightarrow \beta_j V_j$ or $V_i \rightarrow \alpha_k$, is covered by having $\beta_j = false$, and similarly, $\alpha_k = false$. Note that by insisting on this specific form, which does not allow ϵ productions, we cannot express whether an empty string is in the language. However since, by definition of the $\langle \cdot \rangle$ operator, a prefix that satisfies r must be non-empty, we do not need to consider this. The tester T_φ is given by:

$$T_\varphi : \begin{cases} V_\varphi : Vars(r, b) \cup \{x_\varphi\} \cup \{X_1, \ldots, X_n, Y_1, \ldots, Y_n\} \\ \Theta_\varphi : 1 \\ R_\varphi : \text{Each derivation } V_i \rightarrow \alpha_1 \mid \cdots \mid \alpha_m \mid \beta_1 V_1 \mid \cdots \mid \beta_n V_n \\ \quad \text{contributes to } \rho \text{ the conjunct} \\ \quad X_i = (\alpha_1 \wedge b) \vee \cdots \vee (\alpha_m \wedge b) \vee (\beta_1 \wedge X_1') \vee \cdots \vee (\beta_n \wedge X_n') \\ \quad \text{and the conjunct} \\ \quad Y_i \rightarrow (\alpha_1 \wedge b) \vee \cdots \vee (\alpha_m \wedge b) \vee (\beta_1 \wedge Y_1') \vee \cdots \vee (\beta_n \wedge Y_n') \\ \quad \text{the output variable is constrained by the conjunct} \\ \quad x_\varphi = X_1 \\ \mathcal{J}_\varphi : \{\neg Y_1 \wedge \cdots \wedge \neg Y_n, \quad X_1 = Y_1 \wedge \cdots \wedge X_n = Y_n\} \\ F_\varphi : \text{Each derivation } V_i \rightarrow \alpha_1 \mid \cdots \mid \alpha_m \mid \beta_1 V_1 \mid \cdots \mid \beta_n V_n \\ \quad \text{contributes to } F \text{ the conjunct} \\ \quad X_i = (\alpha_1 \wedge b) \vee \cdots \vee (\alpha_m \wedge b) \end{cases}$$

Example 2. *A Tester for* $\varphi = \langle \{pq\}[*] \rangle b$.

To illustrate the construction, consider the formula $\langle \{pq\}[*] \rangle b$. Following the algorithm from Appendix A and removing ϵ productions, the associated right-linear grammar for the SERE $\{pq\}[*]$ is given by

$$V_1 \rightarrow \quad pV_2$$
$$V_2 \rightarrow q \mid qV_1$$

Consequently, a tester for $\langle\{pq\}[*]\rangle b$ is given by

$$
T(\langle\{pq\}[*]\rangle b) : \left\{
\begin{array}{l}
V_\varphi : \{p, q, b, x_\varphi\} \cup \{X_1, X_2, Y_1, Y_2\} \\
\Theta_\varphi : 1 \\
R_\varphi(V, V') : \left(
\begin{array}{ll}
(X_1 = (p \wedge X_2')) & \wedge \\
(X_2 = (q \wedge b) \vee (q \wedge X_1')) \wedge \\
(Y_1 \rightarrow (p \wedge Y_2')) & \wedge \\
(Y_2 \rightarrow (q \wedge b) \vee (q \wedge Y_1')) \wedge \\
x_\varphi = X_1 &
\end{array}
\right) \\
\mathcal{J}_\varphi : \{\neg Y_1 \wedge \neg Y_2, \quad X_1 = Y_1 \wedge X_2 = Y_2\} \\
F_\varphi : (X_1 = false) \wedge (X_2 = q \wedge b)
\end{array}
\right.
$$

The variables $\{X_1, \ldots, X_n, Y_1, \ldots, Y_n\}$ are expected to check that the rest of the sequence from now on has a prefix satisfying the SERE r. Thus, the subsequence $s_j, \ldots, s_k, \ldots \models \langle r \rangle b$ iff there exists a generation sequence $V^j = V_1, V^{j+1}, \ldots, V^k$, such that for each $i, j \leq i < k$, there exists a grammar rule $V^i \rightarrow \beta V^{i+1}$, where $s_i \models \beta$, $V^k \rightarrow \alpha$, and $s_k \models (\alpha \wedge b)$.

The generation sequence is represented in a run of the tester by a sequence of true valuations for the variables $Z^j = Z_1, Z^{j+1}, \ldots, Z^k$ where $Z^i \in \{X^i, Y^i\}$ for each $i \in [j..k]$. An important element in this checking is to make sure that any such generation sequence is finite. This is accomplished through the double representation of each V_i by X_i and Y_i. The justice requirement $(X_1 = Y_1) \wedge \cdots \wedge (X_n = Y_n)$ guarantees that that any true X_i is eventually copied into Y_i. The justice requirement $\neg Y_1 \wedge \cdots \wedge \neg Y_n$ guarantees that all true Y_i's are eventually falsified. Together, they guarantee that there exists no infinite generation sequence. The double representation approach was first introduced in [20].

8.2   A Tester for $\varphi = r$

We start the construction exactly the same way as we did for $\varphi = \langle r \rangle b$, in Section 8.1. Let $T_\varphi = \langle V_\varphi, \Theta_\varphi, R_\varphi, \mathcal{J}_\varphi, F_\varphi \rangle$ be the tester we wish to construct. Assume that x_φ is the output variable. Let $\mathcal{G} = \langle \mathcal{V}, \mathcal{T}, \mathcal{P}, \mathcal{S} \rangle$ be a grammar associated with r.

The tester T_φ is given by:

$$
T(r) : \left\{
\begin{array}{l}
V_\varphi : \mathit{Vars}(r) \cup \{x_\varphi\} \cup \{X_1, \ldots, X_n, Y_1, \ldots, Y_n\} \\
\Theta_\varphi : 1 \\
R_\varphi(V, V') : \text{Each derivation } V_i \rightarrow \alpha_1 \mid \cdots \mid \alpha_m \mid \beta_1 V_1 \mid \cdots \mid \beta_n V_n \\
\qquad \text{contributes to } \rho \text{ the conjunct} \\
\qquad X_i = \alpha_1 \vee \cdots \vee \alpha_m \vee (\beta_1 \wedge X_1') \vee \cdots \vee (\beta_n \wedge X_n') \\
\qquad \text{and the conjunct} \\
\qquad \alpha_1 \vee \cdots \vee \alpha_m \vee (\beta_1 \wedge Y_1') \vee \cdots \vee (\beta_n \wedge Y_n') \rightarrow Y_i \\
\qquad \text{the output variable is constrained by the conjunct} \\
\qquad x_\varphi = X_1 \\
\mathcal{J}_\varphi : \{Y_1 \wedge \cdots \wedge Y_n, \quad X_1 = Y_1 \wedge \cdots \wedge X_n = Y_n\} \\
F_\varphi : \text{Each derivation } V_i \rightarrow \alpha_1 \mid \cdots \mid \alpha_m \mid \beta_1 V_1 \mid \cdots \mid \beta_n V_n \\
\qquad \text{contributes to } F \text{ the conjunct} \\
\qquad X_i = \alpha_1 \vee \cdots \vee \alpha_m \vee \beta_1 \vee \cdots \vee \beta_n
\end{array}
\right.
$$

The variables $\{X_1, \ldots, X_n, Y_1, \ldots, Y_n\}$ are expected to check that the rest of the sequence from now on has a prefix that does not violate SERE r. We follow a similar approach as for the tester $\varphi = \langle r \rangle b$. However, now we are more concerned with false values of the variables $X_1 \ldots X_n$. The duality comes from the fact that, now, we are trying to prevent postponing the violation of the formula r forever.

8.3   Complexity of the Construction

Theorem 2. *For every* PSL *formula φ of length n, there exists a tester with $O(2^n)$ variables. If we restrict SERE's to three traditional operators: concatenation (;), union (|), and Kleene closure ([∗]), the number of variables is linear in the size of φ.*

To justify the result, we can just count the fresh variables introduced at each step of the tester construction. There is only linear number of sub-formulas, so there is a linear number of output variables. The only other variables introduced are the ones that are used to handle SERE's. According to Theorem 1, the associated grammars contain at most $O(2^n)$ non-terminals ($O(n)$ - for the restricted case). We conclude by observing that testers for the formulas $\varphi = \langle r \rangle b$ and $\varphi = r$ introduce exactly two variables, X_i and Y_i, for each non-terminal V_i.

9   MITL **Testers**

In this section we show how to build for every MITL formula φ a *timed tester*, which is a timed automaton T_φ that accepts a language defined by the formula $\varphi \wedge \Box(x_\varphi \equiv \varphi)$. For untimed operators, we can use LTL testers defined in Section 5. In addition, we can use tester composition algorithm described in Section 7. Therefore, in order to handle an arbitrary MITL formula, we just need to build one additional tester for $\varphi = p\,\mathcal{U}_{[a,b]}\,q$. Much of the material in this section is taken from [16].

Our construction for timed until would follow the lines for the untimed case, based on generating predictions for x_φ and aborting when actual values of the signals p and q show they were wrong. However, working on dense time we have the problem that a-priori, the set of potential predictions even for a bounded period of time includes signals with an arbitrary number of switchings between true and false, and such predictions cannot be memorized by a finite-state timed device. An analogous problem exists with untimed case also, since, there, we also make an unbounded number of prediction that should be a checked sometime in the futures. We have resolved the problem for the untimed case based on the observation that our guesses essentially form a finite number of equivalence classes, so we only need to memorize finitely many things. For example, consider untimed until, $\varphi = p\,\mathcal{U}\,q$. Assume, that at the current state p is true and q is false, and we guess that x_φ is true, meaning φ holds at the current position. Moreover, at the next state again $p \wedge \neg q$ is true, and we again predict that x_φ is true. There is no need to distinguish the prediction done at the current and the previous state, and it is enough to remember and verify just one of them. The solution for the timed case is completely different and based on the observation that predictions that switch too frequently cannot be correct. The following lemma, taken from [16] formalizes this observation:

Lemma 1. *Let x be a boolean signal satisfying $\Box(x \equiv p\,\mathcal{U}_{[a,b]}\,q)$ for some arbitrary signals p and q. Then, for any factorization $x = v \cdot 1^{r_1} \cdot 0^{r_2} \cdot 1^{r_3} \cdot 0^{r_4} \cdot w$ we have $r_2 + r_3 > \min\{a, b-a\}$.*

Proof: The following observations concerning the constraints on the values of x, p and q at every t follow from the definitions:

1. If x holds at t, p must hold in all the interval $[t, t+a]$;
2. If q holds at $t+b$ and p holds throughout $[t, t+b]$ then x holds during $[t, t+b-a]$.

Let $[t_1, t_2)$ and $[t_2, t_3)$ be the corresponding intervals for 0^{r_2} and 1^{r_3}, respectively (see Fig. 3), and let us show that $(t_2 - t_1) < a$ implies that $(t_3, t_2) \geq b - a$. Since $(t_2 - t_1) < a$ and $x(t_1 - \epsilon) = 1$, observation 1 implies that $p = 1$ throughout the interval $[t_1, t_2]$. As $x(t) = 1$ for all $t \in [t_2, t_3)$, it follows that $p(t) = 1$ for all $t \in [t_1, t_3)$. This implies that q must start holding at $t_2 + b$ and not before that, because otherwise this will imply that x holds inside the interior of $[t_1, t_2]$ contrary to our assumptions. It follows by observation 2 that x holds continuously in $[t_2, t_2 + b - a]$. Consequently, $t_3 \geq t_2 + b - a$, implying that $(t_3 - t_2) \geq b - a$ ◢

The importance of this property is that it bounds the variability of any reasonable prediction and constrains the relation between the logical and metrical length of the candidate signals. Let $d = \min\{a, b-a\}$ and $m = b/d$. Each 01 part of x has metric length of at least d, and an acceptable prediction of the form $(01)^m \cdot 0$ has a metric length beyond b. Therefore, its initial part can be forgotten and the remaining part has at most $2m$ predictions left unverified.

In addition to the above lemma, we are going to use the following equivalence:

$$p\,\mathcal{U}_{[a,a+b]}\,q \quad \equiv \quad \Diamond_a\left[\boxminus_{[0,a]}\,p \wedge (p\,\mathcal{U}_{[0,b]}\,q)\right]$$

where $\Diamond_a$ is a "shift by a" operator, a shorthand for $\Diamond_{[a,a]}$, and $\boxminus_{[0,a]}\,p$ is a past analog of the $\Box_{[a,b]}$ operator. Note that $\Diamond_{[a,a]}p$ is not a proper MITL formula since operator $\Diamond_{[a,b]}$ requires that $a < b$. The formula $\boxminus_{[0,a]}\,p$ is also not in the language, but it can be added if needed. We define that the formula $\boxminus_{[0,a]}\,p$ is satisfied iff p has been continuously true for the last a time units.

Thus, assuming that we have constructed testers $T[\Diamond_a\,p]$, $T[\boxminus_{[0,a]}\,p]$, and $T[p\,\mathcal{U}_{[0,b]}\,q]$ for the corresponding formulas, then $T[p\,\mathcal{U}_{[a,a+b]}\,q]$ can be given by the three ways synchronous parallel composition:

$$T[p\,\mathcal{U}_{[0,b]}\,q] \quad ||| \quad T[\boxminus_{[0,a]}\,p] \quad ||| \quad T[\Diamond_a(x_{p\,\mathcal{U}_{[0,b]}\,q} \wedge x_{\boxminus_{[0,a]}\,p})].$$

Fig. 3. A signal u satisfying $\Box(x \equiv p\,\mathcal{U}_{[a,b]}\,q)$

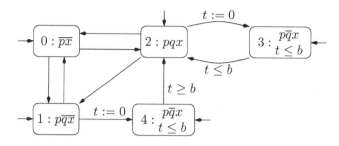

Fig. 4. A tester for $p\,\mathcal{U}_{[0,b]}\,q$

Next, we are going to present the three remaining testers. By convention, each node in Fig. 4, Fig. 5, and Fig. 6 has an implicit self-loop; the self-loops are omitted for sake of clarity. We also assume that all the clocks are initially set to 0. In addition, note that unlike the untimed case, for the timed testers shown in this paper the validity of predictions is always resolved in finite time. Therefore, we do not need any conditions at infinity.

9.1 A Tester for $p\,\mathcal{U}_{[0,b]}\,q$

In Fig. 4, we present a tester for this formula.

9.2 A Tester for $\square_{[0,a]}\,p$

In Fig. 5, we present a tester for the formula $\square_{[0,a]}\,p$.

9.3 A Tester for $\diamondsuit_a\,p$

In general, it is impossible to construct a tester for the formula $\diamondsuit_a\,p$ with a bounded number of clocks. However, if we know that the signal p has bounded variability, then such a construction is possible. We assume in the following that p has no more than k changes for each period of length a. This holds in our case since operator $\diamondsuit_a$ is only used as an auxiliary construct to handle $\mathcal{U}_{[a,a+b]}$ operator to which Lemma 1 applies. The tester for $\diamondsuit_a\,p$ can be given by the following parallel composition:

$$U \ ||| \ P \ ||| \ ON[0] \ ||| \ OFF[0] \ ||| \ \cdots \ ||| \ ON[k-1] \ ||| \ OFF[k-1]$$

In Fig. 6, we present the automata U, P, and generic $ON[i]$ and $OFF[i]$.

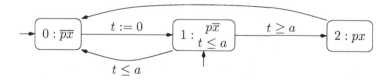

Fig. 5. A tester for $\square_{[0,a]}\,p$

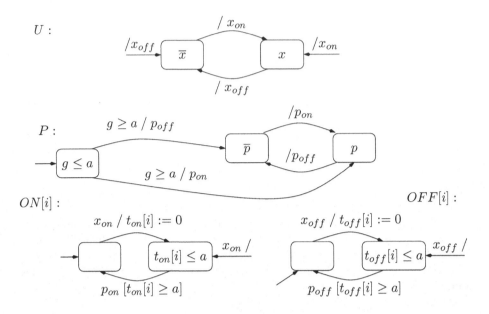

Fig. 6. The automata U, P, $ON[i]$, and $OFF[i]$

10   Using Testers for Model Checking

One of the main advantages of our construction is that all the steps, as well as the final result – the tester itself, can be represented symbolically. That is particularly handy if one is to use symbolic model checking [4]. Assume that the formula under consideration is φ, and $T_\varphi = \langle V_\varphi, \Theta_\varphi, R_\varphi, \mathcal{J}_\varphi, F_\varphi \rangle$ is the corresponding tester. Let JDS $\mathcal{D}$ represent the system we wish to model check.

We are going to use traditional automata theoretic approach based on synchronous composition, as in [4]. We perform the following steps:

- Compose $\mathcal{D}$ with T_φ^+ to obtain $\mathcal{D} \,|||\, T_\varphi^+$.
- Check if $\mathcal{D} \,|||\, T_\varphi^+$ has a (fair) computation, such that $s_0[x_\varphi] = 0$.
  $\mathcal{D} \,|||\, T_\varphi^+$ has such a computation iff $\mathcal{D}$ does not satisfy φ.

As can be seen, a tester can be used anywhere instead of an automaton. Indeed, we can always obtain an automaton from a tester by restricting the initial state to interpret x_φ as *true*.

11   LTL Deductive Verification

Another important application of testers is deductive verification, which is ultimately the only approach towards verification of infinite state systems. A complete deductive proof system for linear-time temporal logic (LTL) has been presented in [17] and further elaborated in [18] and [19]. The approach first defines deductive proof rules for special form formulas, the most important of which are formulas of the form $p \Rightarrow \Box\, q$, $p \Rightarrow \Diamond\, q$, and $\Box\, \Diamond\, p \Rightarrow \Box\, \Diamond\, q$, where p and q are arbitrary *past formulas*, where $\varphi \Rightarrow \psi$ is a shorthand for $\Box(\neg\varphi \vee \psi)$. To deal with arbitrary formulas, [17] invokes a general canonic-form theorem, according to which every (quantifier-free) LTL formula is equivalent to a conjunction of formulas of the form $\Box\, \Diamond\, p_i \Rightarrow \Box\, \Diamond\, q_i$, for some past formulas p_i and q_i. While this approach is theoretically adequate, it is not a practically acceptable solution to the verification of arbitrary LTL formulas. This is because the best known algorithms for converting an arbitrary LTL formula into canonic form are at least doubly exponential (e.g., [11] which is actually non-elementary).

The new tester-based approach which has been first introduced in [14], is based on a successive elimination of temporal operators from a given formula φ until we hit a special form, to which we can apply the predefined rules. Elimination of the temporal operators is based on the construction of temporal testers, as presented in Section 5. Let φ be a an arbitrary LTL or even PSL formula containing one or more occurrences of the sub-formula ψ. In Fig. 7, we present the rule that reduces the proof of φ with respect to some system $\mathcal{D}$ to the proof of $\varphi[\psi/x_\psi]$ over $\mathcal{D} \,|||\, T[\varphi]$, where $T[\varphi]$ is a temporal tester for φ, x_φ is the output variable of $T[\varphi]$, and $\varphi[\psi/x_\psi]$ denotes the formula φ in which each occurrence of the sub-formula ψ is replaced with x_ψ.

For an arbitrary PSL formula φ and FDS $\mathcal{D}$,

$$\frac{\mathcal{D} \,|||\, T_\varphi \models \varphi[\psi/x_\psi]}{\mathcal{D} \quad \models \varphi}$$

Fig. 7.

We are going to illustrate application of the rule from Fig. 7 on the following example:

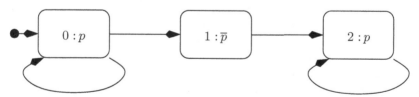

The property whose validity we wish to establish is $\Diamond\, \Box\, p$. First, we construct a tester for $\Box\, p$ and compose it with our system. The transition relation of the new system $\mathcal{D} \,|||\, T[\varphi]$ is presented in Fig. 8.

The justice requirement associated with $\mathcal{D} \,|||\, T[\varphi]$ is $x_\Box \vee \neg p$, and all just states are depicted using double ovals. The new property under consideration $\varphi[\Box\, p/x_\Box]$, which after the substitution is simply $\Diamond\, x_\Box$. This is one of the special form formulas, and we can apply the deductive proof from Fig. 9. Strictly speaking our original formula also has a specialized rule, but for the sake of example we ignored it. However, this is not totally artificial since the rule we are going to apply is simpler. Of course, our system after composition is more complex. Nevertheless, one can argue that the additional state

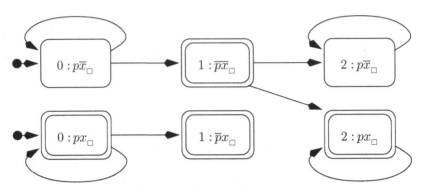

Fig. 8. System $\mathcal{D} \,\|\|\, T[\varphi]$

For an FDS $\mathcal{D}$ with transition relation ρ and justice set $\mathcal{J} = \{J_1, \ldots, J_m\}$,
assertions $p, q, \varphi_1, \ldots, \varphi_m$,
well-founded domain $(\mathcal{A}, \succ)$ and a ranking function $\delta : \Sigma \mapsto \mathcal{A}$

W1. $p \quad \Rightarrow q \vee \bigvee_{j=1}^{m} \varphi_j$

W2. For $i = 1, \ldots, m$

$$\varphi_i \wedge \rho \Rightarrow q' \vee (\neg J_i' \wedge \varphi_i' \wedge \delta = \delta') \vee \left(\bigvee_{j=1}^{m} \varphi_j' \wedge (\delta \succ \delta') \right)$$

$$p \Rightarrow \Diamond q$$

Fig. 9. Well-founded eventuality under justice

---

variable $x_\square$ makes thing easier since it essentially provides CTL like statification for the formula $\square p$, where all fair paths out of a state with $x_\square$ set to true must satisfy $\square p$.

To apply the rule from Fig. 9, we need to define a well-founded domain $(\mathcal{A}, \succ)$, a ranking function δ, and a set of intermediate assertions $\varphi_1, \ldots, \varphi_m$. The function δ is intended to measure the distance of the current state to a state satisfying the goal q. Premise W1 states that every p-state satisfies q or one of $\varphi_1, \ldots, \varphi_m$. Premise W2 states that for every i, $1 \le i \le m$, a φ_i-state with rank $\delta = u$ is followed by either a q-state or a φ_i-state that does not satisfy J_i and has the same rank u, or by a φ_j-state $(1 \le j \le m)$ with a smaller rank (i.e., $u \succ \delta$). The rule claims that if premise W1, and the set of m premises W2 are $\mathcal{D}$-valid, then for all (fair) computations a p-state is eventually followed by q-state. In our case, we take p to be true, $\delta = 2 -$ state id (e.g., δ for the state labeled with $[0 : px_\square]$ is $2 - 0 = 2$), $\varphi_1 = \overline{x}_\square$.

References

1. Accellera Organization, Inc. Property Specification Language Reference Manual, Version 1.01 (2003), http://www.accellera.org/
2. Alur, R., Dill, D.L.: A theory of timed automata. Theoretical Computer Science 126(2), 183–235 (1994)

3. Alur, R., Feder, T., Henzinger, T.A.: The benefits of relaxing punctuality. In: Symposium on Principles of Distributed Computing, pp. 139–152 (1991)
4. Clarke, E.M., Grumberg, O., Peled, D.A.: Model checking. MIT Press (2000)
5. Asarin, E., Caspi, P., Maler, O.: Timed regular expressions. Journal of the ACM 49(2), 172–206 (2002)
6. Chandra, A.K., Kozen, D.C., Stockmeyer, L.J.: Alternation. Journal of ACM 28(1), 114–133 (1981)
7. Cimatti, A., Roveri, M., Semprini, S., Tonetta, S.: From PSL to NBA: a modular symbolic encoding, pp. 125–133 (2006)
8. Bustan, D., Fisman, D., Havlicek, J.: Automata Construction for PSL (2005),
   `http://www.wisdom.weizmann.ac.il/~dana/publicat/`
   `automta_constructionTR.pdf`
9. Daws, C., Yovine, S.: Reducing the number of clock variables of timed automata, pp. 73–81
10. Eisner, C., Fisman, D., Havlicek, J., Gordon, M., McIsaac, A., Van Campenhout, D.: Formal Syntax and Semantics of PSL (2003),
    `http://www.wisdom.weizmann.ac.il/ dana/publicat/`
    `formal_semantics_standalone.pdf`
11. Gabbay, D.: The declarative past and imperative future. In: Banieqbal, B., Barringer, H., Pnueli, A. (eds.) Temporal Logic in Specification, vol. 398, pp. 407–448 (1987)
12. Hopcroft, J.E., Ullman, J.D.: Introduction to Automata Theory, Languages, and Computation. Addison Wesley, Reading (1979)
13. Kesten, Y., Pnueli, A., Raviv, L.: Algorithmic verification of linear temporal logic specifications. In: Larsen, K.G., Skyum, S., Winskel, G. (eds.) ICALP 1998. LNCS, vol. 1443, pp. 1–16. Springer, Heidelberg (1998)
14. Kesten, Y., Pnueli, A.: A compositional approach to CTL* verification. Theoretical Computer Science 331, 397–428 (2005)
15. Lichtenstein, O., Pnueli, A.: Checking that finite state concurrent programs satisfy their linear specification. In: POPL 1985: Proceedings of the 12th ACM SIGACT-SIGPLAN symposium on Principles of programming languages, pp. 97–107. ACM Press, New York (1985)
16. Maler, O., Nickovic, D., Pnueli, A.: From MITL to timed automata. In: Asarin, E., Bouyer, P. (eds.) FORMATS 2006. LNCS, vol. 4202, pp. 274–289. Springer, Heidelberg (2006)
17. Manna, Z., Pnueli, A.: Completing the temporal picture. Theoretical Computer Science 83(1), 97–130 (1991)
18. Manna, Z., Pnueli, A.: The Temporal Logic of Reactive and Concurrent Systems: Specification, New York (1991)
19. Manna, Z., Pnueli, A.: Temporal Verification of Reactive Systems: Safety. Springer, New York (1995)
20. Miyano, S., Hayashi, T.: Alternating finite automata on ω-words. Theoretical Computer Science 32, 321–330 (1984)
21. Pnueli, A., Zaks, A.: PSL model checking and run-time verification via testers. In: Misra, J., Nipkow, T., Sekerinski, E. (eds.) FM 2006. LNCS, vol. 4085, pp. 573–586. Springer, Heidelberg (2006)
22. Pnueli, A., Zaks, A.: PSL model checking and run-time verification via testers. Technical Report, Dept. of Computer Science, New York University (2006)
23. Henzinger, T.A., Nicollin, X., Sifakis, J., Yovine, S.: Symbolic Model Checking for Real-Time Systems. In: 7th. Symposium of Logics in Computer Science, Santa-Cruz, California, pp. 394–406. IEEE Computer Scienty Press (1992)
24. Vardi, M.Y., Wolper, P.: An automata-theoretic approach to automatic program verification. Proc. First IEEE Symp. Logic in Comp. Sci., 332–344 (1986)

A   Associating a Regular Grammar with a SERE

Let b be a boolean expression, r', r, r_1, r_2 be SEREs, and $\mathcal{G}', \mathcal{G}, \mathcal{G}_1, \mathcal{G}_2$ the corresponding grammars. Our algorithm is recursive and we assume that $\mathcal{G}, \mathcal{G}_1$, and $\mathcal{G}_2$ have already been properly constructed. Our goal is to build $\mathcal{G}' = \langle \mathcal{V}', \mathcal{T}', \mathcal{P}', \mathcal{S}' \rangle$ for the SERE r'.

- $r' = b$
  - $\mathcal{V}' = \{V\}$
  - $\mathcal{T}' = \{b\}$
  - $\mathcal{P}' = \{V \to b\}$
  - $\mathcal{S}' = V$

- $r' = r_1 \,;\, r_2$
  - $\mathcal{V}' = \mathcal{V}_1 \cup \mathcal{V}_2$
  - $\mathcal{T}' = \mathcal{T}_1 \cup \mathcal{T}_2$

  $$\mathcal{P}' = \begin{array}{ll} \{V \to aW \mid V \to aW \in \mathcal{P}_1\} & \cup \\ \{V \to a\mathcal{S}_2 \mid V \to a \in \mathcal{P}_1, a \neq \epsilon\} & \cup \\ \{V \to a\mathcal{S}_2 \mid V \to aW \in \mathcal{P}_1, W \to \epsilon \in \mathcal{P}_1\} \cup \\ \mathcal{P}_2 \end{array}$$

  - $\mathcal{S}' = \mathcal{S}_1$

- $r' = r_1 : r_2$
  - $\mathcal{V}' = \mathcal{V}_1 \cup \mathcal{V}_2$
  - $\mathcal{T}' = \mathcal{T}_1 \cup \mathcal{T}_2$

  $$\mathcal{P}' = \begin{array}{ll} \{V \to aW \mid V \to aW \in \mathcal{P}_1\} & \cup \\ \{V \to a \wedge b \mid V \to a \in \mathcal{P}_1, \mathcal{S}_2 \to b \in \mathcal{P}_2\} & \cup \\ \{V \to (a \wedge b)W \mid V \to a \in \mathcal{P}_1, \mathcal{S}_2 \to bW \in \mathcal{P}_2\} \cup \\ \mathcal{P}_2 \end{array}$$

  $$\text{where } a \wedge b = \begin{cases} \epsilon, & \text{if } a = b = \epsilon \\ a, & \text{if } b = \epsilon \\ b, & \text{if } a = \epsilon \\ a \wedge b, & \text{otherwise} \end{cases}$$

  - $\mathcal{S}' = \mathcal{S}_1$

- $r' = r_1 \mid r_2$
  - $\mathcal{V}' = \{\mathcal{S}'\} \cup \mathcal{V}_1 \cup \mathcal{V}_2$
  - $\mathcal{T}' = \mathcal{T}_1 \cup \mathcal{T}_2$

  $$\mathcal{P}' = \begin{array}{ll} \{\mathcal{S}' \to aW \mid \mathcal{S}_1 \to aW \in \mathcal{P}_1\} \cup \\ \{\mathcal{S}' \to aW \mid \mathcal{S}_2 \to aW \in \mathcal{P}_1\} \cup \\ \mathcal{P}_1 & \cup \\ \mathcal{P}_2 \end{array}$$

  - $\mathcal{S}' = \mathcal{S}'$

- $r' = r_1 \ \&\& \ r_2$
  - $\mathcal{V}' = \mathcal{V}_1 \times \mathcal{V}_2$
  - $\mathcal{T}' = \mathcal{T}_1 \cup \mathcal{T}_2$
  - $\mathcal{P}' = \begin{array}{l} \{(V,X) \to a \wedge b(W,Y) \mid V \to aW \in \mathcal{P}_1, X \to bY \in \mathcal{P}_2\} \ \cup \\ \{(V,X) \to a \wedge b \mid V \to a \in \mathcal{P}_1, X \to b \in \mathcal{P}_2\} \end{array}$
  - $\mathcal{S}' = (\mathcal{S}_1, \mathcal{S}_2)$

- $r' = [*0]$
  - $\mathcal{V}' = \{V\}$
  - $\mathcal{T}' = \{b\}$
  - $\mathcal{P}' = \{V \to \epsilon\}$
  - $\mathcal{S}' = V$

- $r' = r[*]$
  - $\mathcal{V}' = \mathcal{V}$
  - $\mathcal{T}' = \mathcal{T}$
  - $\mathcal{P}' = \begin{array}{ll} \{\mathcal{S} \to \epsilon\} & \cup \\ \{V \to a\mathcal{S} \mid V \to a \in \mathcal{P}, a \neq \epsilon\} & \cup \\ \{V \to a\mathcal{S} \mid V \to aW \in \mathcal{P}, W \to \epsilon \in \mathcal{P}\} \end{array}$
  - $\mathcal{S}' = \mathcal{S}$

DESIGN AND SYNTHESIS OF SYNCHRONIZATION SKELETONS
USING BRANCHING TIME TEMPORAL LOGIC*

Edmund M. Clarke
E. Allen Emerson
Aiken Computation Laboratory
Harvard University
Cambridge, Mass. 02138, USA

1. INTRODUCTION

We propose a method of constructing concurrent programs in which the *synchroni-zation skeleton* of the program is automatically synthesized from a high-level (branching time) Temporal Logic specification. The synchronization skeleton is an abstraction of the actual program where detail irrelevant to synchronization is suppressed. For example, in the synchronization skeleton for a solution to the critical section problem each process's critical section may be viewed as a single node since the internal structure of the critical section is unimportant. Most solutions to synchronization problems in the literature are in fact given as synchro-nization skeletons. Because synchronization skeletons are in general finite state, the propositional version of Temporal Logic can be used to specify their properties.

Our synthesis method exploits the (bounded) *finite model property* for an appro-priate propositional Temporal Logic which asserts that if a formula of the logic is satisfiable, it is satisfiable in a finite model (of size bounded by a function of the length of the formula). Decision procedures have been devised which, given a formula of Temporal Logic, f, will decide whether f is satisfiable or unsatisfiable. If f is satisfiable, a finite model of f is constructed. In our application, un-satisfiability of f means that the specification is inconsistent (and must be re-formulated). If the formula f is satisfiable, then the specification it expresses is consistent. A model for f with a finite number of states is constructed by the decision procedure. The synchronization skeleton of a program meeting the specifica-tion can be read from this model. The finite model property ensures that any program whose synchronization properties can be expressed in propositional Temporal Logic can be realized by a system of concurrently running processes, each of which is a finite state machine.

Initially, the synchronization skeletons we synthesize will be for concurrent programs running in a shared-memory environment and for monitors. However, we believe that it is also possible to extend these techniques to synthesize distributed programs. One such application would be the automatic synthesis of network communi-cation protocols from propositional Temporal Logic specifications.

Previous efforts toward parallel program synthesis can be found in the work of [LA78] and [RK80]. [LA78] uses a specification language that is essentially predicate

This work was partially supported by NSF Grant MCS-7908365.

---

* Originally published in: Kozen, D. (ed.) Logic of Programs. LNCS, vol. 131, pp. 52–71. Springer, Heidelberg (1982).

O. Grumberg and H. Veith (Eds.): 25MC Festschrift, LNCS 5000, pp. 196–215, 2008.
© Springer-Verlag Berlin Heidelberg 2008

calculus augmented with a special predicate to define the relative order of events
in time. [RK80] uses an applied linear time Temporal Logic. Both [LA80] and [RK80]
use *ad hoc* techniques to construct a monitor that meets the specification. We have
recently learned that [WO81] has independently developed model-theoretic synthesis
techniques similar to our own. However, he uses a linear time logic for specification and generates CSP-like programs.

We also discuss how a Model Checker for Temporal Logic formulae can be used to
verify the correctness of *a priori* existing programs. In the traditional approach
to concurrent program verification, the proof that a program meets its specification
is constructed using various axioms and rules of inference in a deductive system
such as Temporal Logic. The task of proof construction can be quite tedious, and a
good deal of ingenuity may be required. We believe that this task may be unnecessary
in the case of finite state concurrent systems, and can be replaced by a mechanical
check that the system meets a specification expressed in a propositional temporal
logic. The global system flowgraph of a finite state concurrent system may be
viewed as defining a finite structure. We describe an efficient algorithm (a model
checker) to decide whether a given finite structure is a model of a particular
formula. We also discuss extended logics for which it is not possible to construct
efficient model checkers.

The paper is organized as follows: Section 2 discusses the model of parallel
computation. Section 3 presents the branching time logic that is used to specify
synchronization skeletons. Sections 4 and 5 describe the model checker and the
decision procedure, respectively. Finally, Section 6 shows how the synthesis method
can be used to construct a solution to the starvation free mutual exclusion problem.

2.   MODEL OF PARALLEL COMPUTATION

We discuss concurrent systems consisting of a finite number of fixed processes
$P_1, \ldots, P_m$ running in parallel. The treatment of parallelism is the usual one: non-
deterministic interleaving of the sequential "atomic" actions of the individual
processes P_i. Each time an atomic action is executed, the system "execution" state
is updated. This state may be thought of as containing the location counters and
the data values for all processes. The behavior of a system starting in a particular
state may be described by a computation tree. Each node of the tree is labelled
with the state it represents, and each arc out of a node is labelled with a process
index indicating which nondeterministic choice is made, i.e., which process's atomic
action is executed next. The root is labelled with the start state. Thus, a path
from the root through the tree represents a possible computation sequence of the
system beginning in a given start state. Our temporal logic specifications may then
be thought of as making statements about patterns of behavior in the computation
trees.

Each process P_i is represented as a flowgraph. Each node represents a region or a block of code and is identified by a unique label. For example there may be a node labelled CS_i the i representing "the critical section of code of process P_i." Such a region of code is uninterpreted in that its internal structure and intended application are unspecified. While in CS_i, the process P_i may simply increment variable x or it may perform an extensive series of updates on a large database. The underlying semantics of the computation performed in the various code regions are irrelevant to the synchronization skeleton. The arcs between nodes represent possible transitions between code regions. The labels on the arcs indicate under what conditions P_i can make a transition to a neighboring node. Our job is to supply the enabling conditions on the arcs so that the global system of processes $P_1,\ldots,P_k$ meets a given Temporal Logic specification.

3.   THE SPECIFICATION LANGUAGE

Our specification language is a (propositional) branching time Temporal Logic called Computation Tree Logic (CTL) and is based on the language presented in [EC80]. Our current notation is inspired by the language of "Unified Branching Time" (UB) discussed in [BM81]. UB is roughly equivalent to that subset of the language presented in [EC80] obtained by deleting the infinitary quantifiers and the arc conditions and adding an explicit next-time operator. For example, in [EC80] we write $\forall$ path $\exists$ node P to express the inevitability of predicate P. The corresponding formula in our UB-like notation is AFP. The language presented in [EC80] is more expressive than UB as evidenced by the formula $\forall$ path $\overset{\infty}{\forall}$ node P (which is not equivalent to any formula in UB or in the language of [EC80] without infinitary quantifiers). However, the UB-like notation is more concise and is sufficiently expressive for the purposes of program synthesis.

We use the following syntax (where p denotes an atomic proposition and f_i denotes a (sub-)formula):

1. Each of p, $f_1 \wedge f_2$, and $\sim f_1$ is a formula (where the latter two constructs indicate conjunction and negation, respectively).

2. $EX_j f_1$ is a formula which intuitively means that there is an immediate successor state reachable by executing one step of process P_j in which formula f_1 holds.

3. $A[f_1 U f_2]$ is a formula which intuitively means that for every computation path, there exists an initial prefix of the path such that f_2 holds at the last state of the prefix and f_1 holds at all other states along the prefix.

4. $E[f_1 U f_2]$ is a formula which intuitively means that for some computation path, there exists an initial prefix of the path such that f_2 holds at the last state of the prefix and f_1 holds at all other states along the prefix.

Formally, we define the semantics of CTL formulae with respect to a structure $M = (S, A_1, \ldots, A_k, L)$ which consists of:

S - a countable set of states,

A_i- $\subseteq S \times S$, a binary relation on S giving the possible transitions by process i, and

L - an assignment of atomic propositions true in each state.

Let $A = A_1 \cup \ldots \cup A_k$. We require that A be total, i.e., that $\forall x \in S \; \exists y (x,y) \in A$. A *path* is an infinite sequence of states $(s_0, s_1, s_2 \ldots) \in S^\omega$ such that $\forall i (s_i, s_{i+1}) \in A$. To any structure M and state $s \in S$ of M, there corresponds a computation tree with root labelled s_0 such that $s \xrightarrow{i} t$ is an arc in the tree iff $(s,t) \in A_i$.

We use the usual notation to indicate truth in a structure: $M, s_0 \models f$ means that at state s_0 in structure M formula f holds true. When the structure M is understood, we write $s_0 \models f$. We define $\models$ inductively:

$s_0 \models p$ iff $p \in L(s_0)$

$s_0 \models \sim f$ iff not $(s_0 \models f)$

$s_0 \models f_1 \wedge f_2$ iff $s_0 \models f_1$ and $s_0 \models f_2$

$s_0 \models EX_j f$ iff for some state t such that $(s_0, t) \in A_j$, $t \models f$

$s_0 \models A[f_1 U f_2]$ iff for all paths $(s_0, s_1, \ldots)$, $\exists i [i \geqslant 0 \wedge s_i \models f_2$
$\wedge \forall j (0 \leqslant j \wedge j < i \rightarrow s_j \models f_1)]$

$s_0 \models E[f_1 U f_2]$ iff for some path $(s_0, s_1, \ldots)$, $\exists i [i \geqslant 0 \wedge s_i \models f_2$
$\wedge \forall j (0 \leqslant j \wedge j < i \rightarrow s_j \models f_1)]$

We write $\models f$ to indicate that f is universally valid, i.e., true at all states in all structures. Similarly, we write $\dashv f$ to indicate that f is satisfiable, i.e., f is true in some state of some structure.

We introduce some abbreviations:

$f_1 \vee f_2 \equiv \sim(\sim f_1 \wedge \sim f_2)$, $f_1 \rightarrow f_2 \equiv \sim f_1 \vee f_2$, and $f_1 \leftrightarrow f_2 \equiv (f_1 \rightarrow f_2) \wedge (f_2 \rightarrow f_1)$ for logical disjunction, implication, and equivalence, respectively.

$A[f_1 V f_2] \equiv \sim E[\sim f_1 U \sim f_2]$ which means for every path, for every state s on the path, if f_1 is false at all states on the path prior to s, then f_2 holds at s.

$E[f_1 V f_2] \equiv \sim A[\sim f_1 U \sim f_2]$ which means for some path, for every state s on the path, if f_1 is false at all states on the path prior to s, then f_2 holds at s.

$AFf_1 \equiv A[\text{true } U f_1]$ which means for every path, there exists a state on the path at which f_1 holds.

$EFf_1 \equiv E[\text{true } U f_1]$ which means for some path, there exists a state on the path at which f_1 holds.

$AGf_1 \equiv \sim EF \sim f_1$ which means for every path, at every node on the path f_1 holds.

$EGf_1 \equiv \sim AF \sim f_1$ which means for some path, at every node on the path f_1 holds.

$AX_i f \equiv \sim EX_i \sim f$ which means at all successor states reachable by an atomic step of process P_i, f holds.

$EXF \equiv EX_1 f \vee \ldots \vee EX_k f$ which means at some successor state f holds.

$AXf \equiv \sim EX \sim f$ which means at all successor states f holds.

4. MODEL CHECKER

Assume that we wish to determine whether formula f is true in the finite structure $M = (S, A_1, \ldots, A_k, L)$. Let $sub^+(f_0)$ denote the set subformulae of f_0 with main connective other than $\sim$. We label each state $s \in S$ with the set of positive/negative formulae f in $sub^+(f_0)$ so that

$$f \in label(s) \quad iff \quad M, s \models f$$
$$\sim f \in label(s) \quad iff \quad M, s \models \sim f \quad .$$

The algorithm makes $n + 1$ passes where $n = length(f_0)$. On pass i every state $s \in S$ is labelled with f or $\sim f$ for each formula $f \in sub^+(f_0)$ of length i. Information gathered in earlier passes about formulae of length less than i is used to perform the labelling. For example, if $f = f_1 \wedge f_2$, then f should be placed in the set for s precisely when f_1 and f_2 are already present in the set for s. For modalities such as $A[f_1 U f_2]$ information from the successor states of s (as well as from s itself) is used. Since $A[f_1 U f_2] = f_2 \vee (f_1 \wedge AXA[f_1 U f_2])$, $A[f_1 U f_2]$ should be placed in the set for s when f_2 is already in the set for s or when f_1 is in the set for s and $A[f_1 U f_2]$ is in the set of each immediate successor state of s.

Satisfaction of $A[f_1 U f_2]$ may be seen to "radiate" outward from states where it holds immediately by virtue of f_2 holding:

Let

$$(A[f_1 U f_2])^0 \quad = \quad f_2$$
$$(A[f_1 U f_2])^{k+1} \quad = \quad f_2 \vee AX(A[f_1 U f_2])^k \quad .$$

It can be shown that $M, s \models (A[f_1 U f_2])^k$ iff $M, s \models A[f_1 U f_2]$ and along every path starting at s, f_2 holds by the k-th state following s. Thus, states where $(A[f_1 U f_2])^0$ holds are found first, then states where $(A[f_1 U f_2])^1$ holds, etc. If $A[f_1 U f_2]$ holds, then $(A[f_1 U f_2])^{card(S)}$ must hold since all loop-free paths in M are of length $\leq card(S)$: Thus, if after $card(S)$ steps of radiating outward, $A[f_1 U f_2]$ has still not been found to hold at state s, then put $\sim A[f_1 U f_2]$ in the set for s.

The algorithm for pass i is listed below in an Algol-like syntax:

```
    for every state s ∈ S do
      for every f ∈ sub⁺(f₀) of length i do
        if  f = A[f₁Uf₂]  and  f₂ ∈ set(s)  or
            f = E[f₁Uf₂]  and  f₂ ∈ set(s)  or
            f = EXⱼf₁  and  ∃t((s,t) ∈ Aⱼ  and  f₁ ∈ set(t))  or
            f = f₁ ∧ f₂  and  f₁ ∈ set(s)  and  f₂ ∈ set(s)
        then add  f  to  set(s)
      end
    end;
  A: for  j = 1  to  card(S)  do
      for every state s ∈ S do
        for every f ∈ sub⁺(f₀) of length i do
          if  f = A[f₁Uf₂]  and  f₁ ∈ set(s)  and  ∀t((s,t) ∈ A → f ∈ set(t))  or
              f = E[f₁Uf₂]  and  f₁ ∈ set(s)  and  ∃t((s,t) ∈ A ∧ f ∈ set(t))
          then add  f  to  set(s)
        end
    B: end
    end;
    for every state s ∈ S do
      for every f ∈ sub⁺(f₀) of length i do
        then add  ~f  to  set(s)
      end
  C: end
```

Figures 4.1-4.4 give snapshots of the algorithm in operation on the structure shown for the formula AFb ∧ EGa (which abbreviates AFb ∧ ~AF~a).

Suppose we extend the logic to permit ∀path ∀̆ node p or, equivalently, its dual ∃path ∃̆ node p which we write $\overset{\infty}{EF}p$. We can generalize the model checker to handle this case by using the following proposition:

PROPOSITION 4.1. *Let $M = (S, A_1, \ldots, A_k, L)$ be a structure and $s \in S$. Then $M, s \models \overset{\infty}{EF}p$ iff there exists a path from s to a node s' such that $M, s' \models p$ and either s' is a successor of itself or the strongly connected component of M containing s' has cardinality greater than 1.* ∎

Proof. (Only if:) Suppose $M, s \models \overset{\infty}{EF}p$. Then there is an infinite path $(s_0, s_1, s_2, \ldots)$ through M and a state $s' \in S$ such that

(1) $s_0 = s$,

(2) $s' = s_i$ for infinitely many distinct i, and

(3) $M, s' \models p$.

If s' is a successor of itself, we are done. Otherwise, there is a finite path $(s', \ldots, s'', \ldots s')$ from s' back to itself (because of (2)) which contains a state $s'' \neq s$. So, s'' is reachable from s' and s' is reachable from s'', and s' is in a strongly connected component of M of cardinality greater than 1.

(If:) If s' is a successor of itself, then p is true infinitely often along the path $(s', s', \ldots)$. Since s' is reachable from s, $M, s \models \overset{\infty}{EF}p$. If the

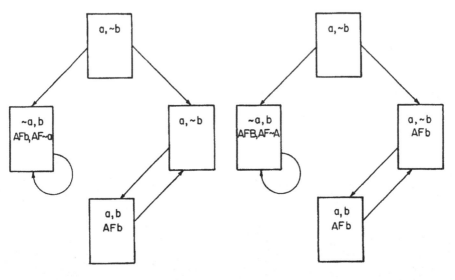

1st time at label A in pass 1

Figure 4.1

1st time at label B in pass 1

Figure 4.2

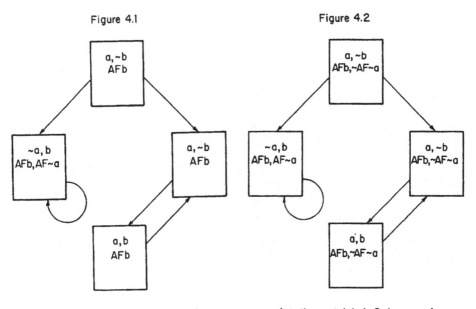

2nd time at label B in pass 1

Figure 4.3

1st time at label C in pass 1

Figure 4.4

strongly connected component of M containing s' is of cardinality greater than 1, then there is a state $s'' \neq s'$ such that s' is reachable from s'' and s'' is reachable from s''. Hence there is a finite path from s' back to itself, and an infinite path starting at s' which goes through s' infinitely often. Since s' is reachable from s, $M,s \models E\overset{\infty}{F}p$. ∎

Notice that all algorithms discussed so far run in time polynomial in the size of the candidate model and formula. The algorithm for basic CTL presented above runs in time $length(f) \cdot (card(S))^2$. Since there is a linear time algorithm for finding the strongly connected components of a graph [TA72], we can also achieve the $length(f) \cdot (card(S))^2$ time bound when we include the infinitary quantifiers.

Finally, we show that it is not always possible to obtain polynomial time algorithms for model checking. Suppose we extend our language to allow either an existential or a universal path quantifier to prefix an arbitrary assertion from linear time logic as in [LA80] and [GP80]. Thus, we can write assertions such as

$$E[Fg_1 \wedge \ldots \wedge Fg_n \wedge Gh_1 \wedge \ldots \wedge Gh_n]$$

meaning

"there exists a computation path ρ such that, along ρ
sometimes g_1 and ... and sometimes g_n and
always h_1 and ... and always h_n."

We claim that the problem of determining whether a given formula f holds in a given finite structure M is NP-hard.

PROPOSITION 4.2. *Directed Hamiltonian Path is reducible to the problem of determining whether $M,s \models f$ where*

M *is a finite structure,*

s *is a state in M and*

f *is the assertion (using atomic propositions $p_1, \ldots, p_n$):*

$E[Fp_1 \wedge \ldots \wedge Fp_n \wedge G(p_1 \rightarrow XG \sim p_1) \wedge \ldots \wedge G(p_n \rightarrow XG \sim p_n))$. ∎

Proof. Consider an arbitrary directed graph $G = (V,A)$ where $V = \{v_1, \ldots, v_n\}$. We obtain a structure from G by making proposition p_i hold at node v_i and false at all other nodes (for $1 \leqslant i \leqslant n$), and by adding a source node u_1 from which all v_i are accessible (but not *vice versa*) and a sink node u_2 which is accessible from all v_i (but not *vice versa*).

Formally, let the structure $M = (U,B,L)$ consist of

$U = V \cup \{u_1,u_2\}$ where $u_1,u_2 \notin V$

L, on assignment of states to propositions such that

$v_i \models p_i$, $v_i \not\models p_j$, $(1 \leqslant i, j \leqslant n, i \neq j)$

$u_1 \not\models p_i$, $u_2 \not\models p_i$ $(1 \leqslant i \leqslant n)$ and

$$B = A \cup \{(u_1, v_i) : v_i \in V\} \cup \{(v_i, u_2) : v_i \in V\} \cup \{(u_2, u_2)\} .$$

It follows that

> $M, u_1 \not\models f$ $\underline{iff}$ there is a directed infinite path in M starting at u_1
> which goes through all $v_i \in V$ exactly once and ends in the
> self-loop through u_2;
> $\underline{iff}$ there is a directed Hamiltonian path in G. ∎

We believe that the model checker may turn out to be of considerable value in
the verification of certain finite state concurrent systems such as network protocols.
We have developed an experimental implementation of the model checker at Harvard
which is written in C and runs on the DEC 11-70.

5.   THE DECISION PROCEDURE

In this section we outline a tableau-based decision procedure for satisfiability
of CTL formulae. Our algorithm is similar to one proposed for UB in [BM81].[*]
Tableau-based decision procedures for simpler program logics such as PDL and DPDL are
given in [PR77] and [BH81]. The reader should consult [HC68] for a discussion of
tableau-based decision procedures for classical modal logics and [SM68] for a discussion of tableau-based decision procedures for propositional logic.

We now briefly describe our decision procedure for CTL and illustrate
it with a simple example. The decision procedure is described in detail in the
full paper. To simplify the notation in the present discussion, we omit the
labels on arcs which are normally used to distinguish between transitions by
different processes.

The decision procedure takes as input a formula f_0 and returns either "YES,
f_0 is satisfiable," or "NO, f_0 is unsatisfiable." If f_0 is satisfiable, a finite
model is constructed. The decision procedure performs the following steps:

1. Build the initial tableau T which encodes potential models of f_0. If
f_0 is satisfiable, it has a finite model that can be "embedded" in T.

2. Test the tableau for consistency by deleting inconsistent portions. If the
"root" of the tableau is deleted, f_0 is unsatisfiable. Otherwise, f_0 is satisfiable.

3. Unravel the tableau into a model of f_0.

The decision procedure begins by building a tableau T which is a finite
directed AND/OR graph. Each node of T is either an AND-node or an OR-node and is
labelled by a set of formulae. We use $G_1, G_2, \ldots$ to denote the labels of OR-nodes,
$H_1, H_2, \ldots$ to denote the labels of AND-nodes, and $F_1, F_2, \ldots$ to denote the labels
of arbitrary nodes of either type. No two AND-nodes have the same label, and no two

---

[*]The [BM81] algorithm is incorrect and will erroneously claim that certain satisfiable formulae are unsatisfiable. Correct tableau-based and filtration-based
decision procedures for UB are given in [EH81]. In addition, Ben-Ari [BA81] states
that a corrected version of [BM81] based on different techniques is forthcoming.

OR-nodes have the same label. The intended meaning is that, when node F is considered as a state in an appropriate structure, $F \models f$ for all $f \in F$. The tableau T has a "root" node $G_0 = \{f_0\}$ from which all other nodes in T are accessible.

The set of successors of an OR-node G, Blocks$(G) = \{H_1, H_2, \ldots, H_k\}$ has the property that

$$\dashv G \text{ iff } \dashv H_1 \text{ or } \ldots \text{ or } \dashv H_k \ .$$

We can explain the construction of Blocks(G) as follows: Each formula in G may be viewed as a conjunctive formula $\alpha \equiv \alpha_1 \wedge \alpha_2$ or a disjunctive formula $\beta \equiv \beta_1 \vee \beta_2$. Clearly, $f \wedge g$ is an α formula and $f \vee g$ is a β formula. A modal formula may be classified as α or β based on its fixpoint characterization; thus, $EFp = p \vee EXEFp$ is a β formula and $AGp = p \wedge AXAGp$ is an α formula. A formula that involves no modalities or has main connective one of EX or AX is both α and β and is called an *elementary* formula. Any other formula is *nonelementary*. We say that a set of formulae F is *downward closed* provided that (i) if $\alpha \in F$ then $\alpha_1, \alpha_2 \in F$, and (ii) if $\beta \in F$ then $\beta_1 \in F$ or $\beta_2 \in F$. We construct the members H_i of Blocks(G) by repeatedly expanding each nonelementary formula in G into its α or β components. Each β expansion yields two blocks, one with β_1 and one with β_2. Expansion stops when all H_i are downward closed.

The set of successors of an AND-node H, Tiles$(H) = \{G_1, G_2, \ldots, G_k\}$ has the property that, if H contains no propositional inconsistencies, then

$$\dashv H \text{ iff } \dashv G_1 \text{ and } \ldots \text{ and } \dashv G_k \ .$$

To construct Tiles(H) we use the information supplied by the elementary formulae in H. For example, if $\{AXh_1, AXh_2, EXg_1, EXg_2, EXg_3\}$ is the set of all elementary formulae in H, then Tiles$(H) = \{\{h_1, h_2, g_1\}, \{h_1, h_2, g_2\}, \{h_1, h_2, g_3\}\}$.

To build T, we start out by letting $G_0 = \{f_0\}$ be the root node. Then we create Blocks$(G_0) = \{H_1, H_2, \ldots, H_k\}$ and attach each H_i as a successor of G_0. For each H_i we create Tiles(H_i) and attach its members as the successors of H_i. For each $G_j \in$ Tiles(H_i) we create Blocks(G_j), etc. Whenever we encounter two nodes of the same type with identical labels we identify them. This ensures that no two AND-nodes will have the same label and that no two OR-nodes will have the same label. The tableau construction will eventually terminate since there are only $2^{\text{length}(f_0)}$ possible labels, each of which can occur at most twice.

Suppose, for example, that we want to determine whether $EFp \wedge EF{\sim}p$ is satisfiable. We build the tableau T starting with root node $G_0 = \{EFp \wedge EF{\sim}p\}$. We construct Blocks$(G_0) = \{H_0, H_1, H_2, H_3\}$. Each H_i is attached as a successor of G_0. Next, Tiles(H_i) is determined for each H_i (except H_1 which is immediately seen to contain a propositional inconsistency) and its members are attached as successors of H_i. (Note that two copies of $G_1 = \{EF{\sim}p\}$ are created, one in Tiles(H_0) and the other in Tiles(H_2); but they are then merged into a single node.) Similarly, $G_2 \in$ Tiles$(H_2) \cap$ Tiles(H_3). Continuing in this fashion we obtain the complete tableau shown in Fig. 5.1.

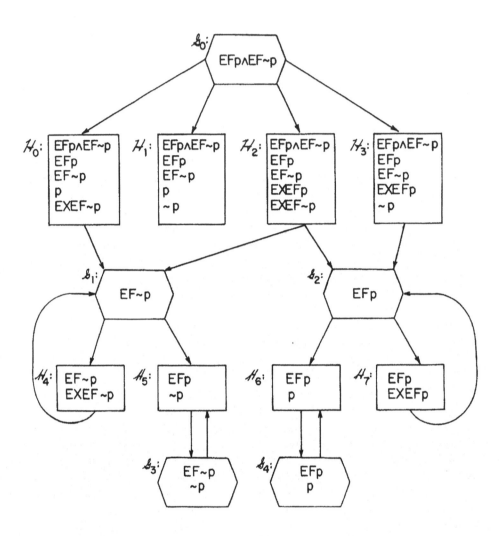

Figure 5.1

Next we must test the tableau for consistency. Note that H_1 is inconsistent because it contains both p and ~p. We must also check that is possible for eventuality formulae such as AFh or EFh to be *fulfilled*: e.g., if $EFh \in F$, then there must be some node F' reachable from F such that $h \in F'$. If any node fails to pass this test, it is marked inconsistent. In this example, all nodes pass the test. Since the root is not marked inconsistent, $EFp \wedge EF\sim p$ is satisfiable.

Finally, we construct a model M of $EFp \wedge EF\sim p$. The states in M will be (copies of) the AND-nodes in the tableau. The model will have the property that for each state H, $M,H \models f$ for all $f \in H$. The root of M can be any consistent state $H_1 \in Blocks(G_0)$. We choose H_0. Now H_0 contains the eventualities EFp and $EF\sim p$. We must ensure that they are actually fulfilled in M. EFp is immediately fulfilled in H_0, but $EF\sim p$ is not. So when we choose a successor state to H_0, which must be one of H_4 or H_5, we want to ensure that $EF\sim p$ is fulfilled. Thus, we choose H_5. Finally, the only possible successor state of H_5 is H_5 itself.

6. SYNTHESIS ALGORITHM

We now present our method of synthesizing synchronization skeletons from a CTL description of their intended behavior. We identify the following steps:

1. Specify the desired behavior of the concurrent system using CTL.
2. Apply the decision procedure to the resulting CTL formula in order to obtain a finite model of the formula.
3. Factor out the synchronization skeletons of the individual processes from the global system flowgraph defined by the model.

We illustrate the method by solving a mutual exclusion problem for processes P_1 and P_2. Each process is always in one of three regions of code:

NCS$_i$ the NonCritical Section
TRY$_i$ the TRYing Section
CS$_i$ the Critical Section

which it moves through as suggested in Fig. 6.1.

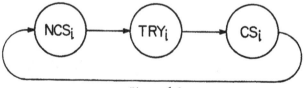

Figure 6.1

When it is in region NCS$_i$, process P_i performs "noncritical" computations which can proceed in parallel with computations by the other process P_j. At certain times, however, P_i may need to perform certain "critical" computations in the region CS$_i$. Thus, P_i remains in NCS$_i$ as long as it has not yet decided to attempt

critical section entry. When and if it decides to make this attempt, it moves into
the region TRY_i. From there it enters CS_i as soon as possible, provided that the
mutual exclusion constraint $\sim(CS_1 \wedge CS_2)$ is not violated. It remains in CS_i as long as
necessary to perform its "critical" computations and then re-enters NCS_i. Note
that in the synchronization skeleton described, we only record transitions between
different regions of code. Moves entirely within the same region are not considered
in specifying synchronization. Listed below are the CTL formulae whose conjunction
specifies the mutual exclusion system:

1.   start state
$$NCS_1 \wedge NCS_2$$

2.   mutual exclusion
$$AG(\sim(CS_1 \wedge CS_2))$$

3.   absence of starvation for P_i
$$AG(TRY_i \rightarrow AF\ CS_i)$$

4.   each process P_i is always in exactly one of the three code regions
$$AG(NCS_i \vee TRY_i \vee CS_i)$$
$$AG(NCS_i \rightarrow \sim(TRY_i \vee CS_i))$$
$$AG(TRY_i \rightarrow \sim(NCS_i \vee CS_i))$$
$$AG(CS_i \rightarrow \sim(NCS_i \vee TRY_i))$$

5.   it is always possible for P_i to enter its trying region from its noncritical region
$$AG(NCS_i \rightarrow EX_i TRY_i)$$

6.   it is always the case that any move P_i makes from its trying region is
into the critical region
$$AG(TRY_i \wedge EX_i True \rightarrow AX_i CS_i)$$

7.   it is always possible for P_i to re-enter its noncritical region from
its critical region
$$AG(CS_i \rightarrow EX_i NCS_i)$$

8.   a transition by one process cannot cause a move by the other
$$AG(NCS_i \rightarrow AX_j NCS_i)$$
$$AG(TRY_i \rightarrow AX_j TRY_i)$$
$$AG(CS_i \rightarrow AX_j CS_i)$$

9.   some process can always move
$$AG(EX\ true)$$

We must now construct the initial AND/OR graph tableau. In order to reduce the
recording of inessential or redundant information in the node labels we observe the
following rules:

(1) Automatically convert a formula of the form $f_1 \wedge \ldots \wedge f_n$ to the set of
formulae $\{f_1, \ldots, f_n\}$. (Recall that the set of formulae $\{f_1, \ldots, f_n\}$ is satisfiable iff $f_1 \wedge \ldots \wedge f_n$ is satisfiable.)

(2) Do not physically write down an invariance assertion of the form AGf
because it holds everywhere as do its consequences f and $AXAGf$ (obtained by

α-expansion). The consequence AXAGf serves only to propagate forward the truth of AGf to any "descendent" nodes in the tableau. Do that propagation automatically but without writing down AGf in any of the descendent nodes. The consequence f may be written down if needed.

(3) An assertion of the form f v g need not be recorded when f is already present. Since any state which satisfies f must also satisfy f v g, f v g is redundant.

(4) If we have TRY_i present, there is no need to record $\sim NCS_i$ and $\sim CS_i$. If we have NCS_i present, there is no need to record $\sim TRY_i$ and $\sim CS_i$. If we have CS_i present, there is no need to record $\sim NCS_i$ and $\sim TRY_i$.

By the above conventions, the root node of the tableau will have the two formulae NCS_1 and NCS_2 recorded in its label which we now write as $\langle NCS_1 \ NCS_2 \rangle$. In building the tableau, it will be helpful to have constructed Blocks(G) for the following OR-nodes: $\langle NCS_1 \ NCS_2 \rangle$, $\langle TRY_1 \ NCS_2 \rangle$, $\langle CS_1 \ NCS_2 \rangle$, $\langle TRY_1 \ TRY_2 \rangle$, and $\langle CS_1 \ TRY_2 \rangle$. For all other OR-nodes G' appearing in the tableau, Blocks(G') will be identical to or can be obtained by symmetry from Blocks(G) for some G in the above list. We then build the tableau using the information about Blocks and Tiles contained in the list. Next we apply the marking rules to delete inconsistent nodes. Note that the OR-node $\langle CS_1 \ CS_2 \ AFCS_2 \rangle$ is marked as deleted because of a propositional inconsistency (with $\sim(CS_1 \wedge CS_2)$, a consequence of the unwritten invariance $AG(\sim(CS_1 \ CS_2))$. This, in turn, causes the AND-node that is the predecessor of $\langle CS_1 \ CS_2 \ AFCS_2 \rangle$ to be marked. The resulting tableau is shown in Fig. 6.2. Each node in Fig. 6.2 is labelled with a minimal set of formulae sufficient to distinguish it from any other node.

We construct a model M from T by pasting together model fragments for the AND-nodes using local structure information provided by T. Intuitively, a fragment is a rooted dag of AND-nodes embeddable in T such that all eventuality formulae in the label of the root node are fulfilled in the fragment.

The root node of the model is H_0, the unique successor of G_0. From the tableau we see that H_0 must have two successors, one of H_1 or H_2 and one of H_3 or H_4. Each candidate successor state contains an eventuality to fulfill, so we must construct and attach its fragment. Using the method described, we choose the fragement rooted at H_1 to be the left successor and the fragment rooted at H_4 to be the right successor (see Fig. 6.3). This yields the portion of the model shown in Fig. 6.4.

We continue the construction by finding successors for each of the leaves: H_5, H_9, H_{10} and H_8. We start with H_5. By inspection of T, we see that the only successors H_5 can have are H_0 and H_9. Since H_0 and H_9 already occur in the structure built so far, we add the arcs $H_5 \overset{1}{\to} H_0$ and $H_5 \overset{2}{\to} H_9$ to the structure. Note that this introduces a cycle $(H_0 \overset{1}{\to} H_1 \overset{1}{\to} H_5 \overset{1}{\to} H_0)$. In general, a cycle can be dangerous because it might form a path along which some eventuality is never fulfilled; however, there is no problem this time because the root of a

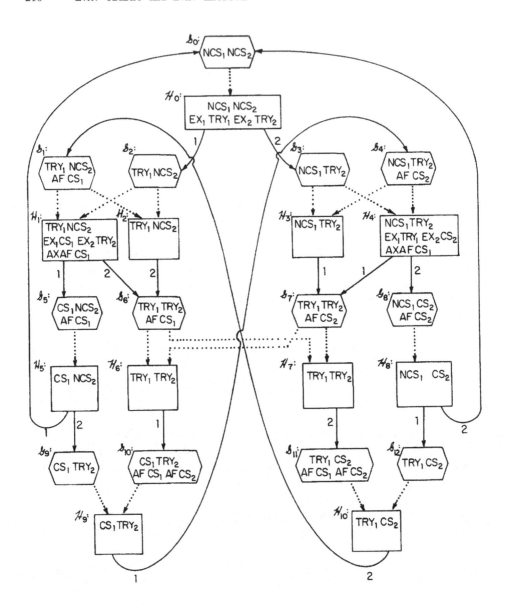

Figure 6.2

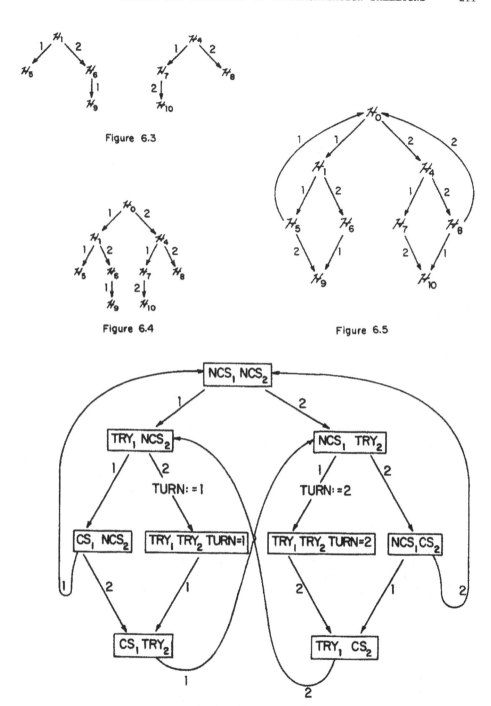

Figure 6.3

Figure 6.4

Figure 6.5

Figure 6.6

fragment, H_1, occurs along the cycle. A fragment root serves as a checkpoint to ensure that all eventualities are fulfilled. By symmetry between the roles of 1 and 2, we add in the arcs $H_8 \xrightarrow{1} H_{10}$ and $H_8 \xrightarrow{2} H_0$. The structure now has the form shown in Fig. 6.5.

We now have two leaves remaining: H_9 and H_{10}. We see from the tableau that H_4 is a possible successor to H_9. We add in the arc $H_9 \xrightarrow{1} H_4$. Again a cycle is formed but since H_4 is a fragment root no problems arise. Similarly, we add in the arc $H_{10} \xrightarrow{2} H_1$. The decision procedure thus yields a model M such that $M, s_0 \models f_0$ where f_0 is the conjunction of the mutual exclusion system specifications.

We may view the model as a flowgraph of global system behavior. For example, when the system is in state H_1, process P_1 is in its trying region and process P_2 is in its noncritical section. P_1 may enter its critical section or P_2 may enter its trying region. No other moves are possible in state H_1. Note that all states except H_6 and H_7 are distinguished by their propositional labels. In order to distinguish H_6 from H_7, we introduce a variable TURN which is set to 1 upon entry to H_6 and to 2 upon entry to H_7. If we introduce TURN's value into the labels of H_6 and H_7 then, the labels uniquely identify each node in the global system flowgraph. See Fig. 6.6.

We describe how to obtain the synchronization skeletons of the individual processes from the global system flowgraph. In the sequel we will refer to these global system states by the propositional labels.

When P_1 is in NCS_1, there are three possible global states $[NCS_1 \ NCS_2]$, $[NCS_1 \ TRY_2]$, and $[NCS_1 \ CS_2]$. In each case it is always possible for P_1 to make a transition into TRY_1 by the global transitions $[NCS_1 \ NCS_2] \xrightarrow{1} [TRY_1 \ NCS_2]$, $[NCS_1 \ TRY_2] \xrightarrow{1, TURN:=2} [TRY_1 \ TRY_2]$, and $[NCS_1 \ CS_2] \xrightarrow{1} [TRY_1 \ CS_2]$. From each global transition by P_1, we obtain a transition in the synchronization skeleton of P_1. The P_2 component of the global state provides enabling conditions for the transitions in the skeleton of P_1. If along a global transition, there is an assignment to TURN, the assignment is copied into the corresponding transition of the synchronization skeleton.

Now when P_1 is in TRY_1, there are four possible global states: $[TRY_1 \ NCS_2]$, $[TRY_1 \ NCS_2]$, $[TRY_1 \ TRY_2 \ TURN = 1]$, $[TRY_1 \ TRY_2 \ TURN = 2]$, and $[TRY_1 \ CS_2]$ and their associated global transitions by P_1: $[TRY_1 \ NCS_2] \xrightarrow{1} [CS_1 \ NCS_2]$ and $[TRY_1 \ TRY_2 \ TURN = 1] \xrightarrow{1} [CS_1 \ TRY_2]$. (No transitions by P_1 are possible in $[TRY_1 \ TRY_2 \ TURN = 2]$ or $[TRY_1 \ CS_2]$.) When P_1 is in CS_1 the associated global states and transitions are: $[CS_1 \ NCS_2]$, $[CS_1 \ TRY_2]$, $[CS_1 \ NCS_2] \xrightarrow{1} [NCS_1 \ NCS_2]$, and $[CS_1 \ TRY_2] \xrightarrow{1} [NCS_1 \ TRY_2]$. Altogether, the synchronization skeleton for P_1 is shown in Fig. 6.7(a). By symmetry in the global state diagram we obtain the synchronization skeleton for P_2 as shown in Fig. 6.7(b).

The general method of factoring out the synchronization skeletons of the individual processes may be described as follows: Take the model of the specification formula and retain only the propositional formulae in the labels of each node.

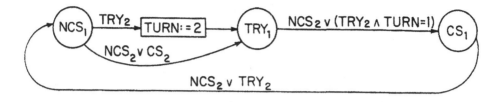

Figure 6.7 (a)

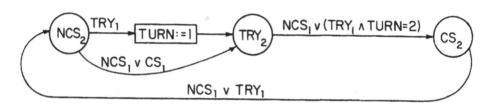

Figure 6.7 (b)

There may now be distinct nodes with the same label. Auxiliary variables are introduced to ensure that each node gets a distinct label: if label L occurs at $n > 1$ distinct nodes $v_1, \ldots, v_n$, then for each v_i, set $L := i$ on all arcs coming into v_i and add $L = i$ as an additional component to the label of v_i. The resulting newly labelled graph is the global system flowgraph.

We now construct the synchronization skeleton for process P_i which has m distinct code regions $R_1, \ldots, R_m$. Initially, the synchronization skeleton for P_i is a graph with m distinct nodes $R_1, \ldots, R_m$ and no arcs. Draw an arc from R_j to R_k if there is at least one arc of the form $L_j \rightarrow L_k$ in the global system flowgraph where R_j is a component of the label L_j and R_k is a component of the label L_k. The arc $R_j \rightarrow R_k$ is a transition in the synchronization skeleton and is labelled with the enabling condition

$$v\{(S_1 \wedge \ldots \wedge S_p) : [R_j \ S_1 \ldots S_p] \downarrow [R_k \ S_1 \ldots S_p] \text{ is an arc in the global system flowgraph}\}.$$

Add $L := n$ to the label of $R_j \rightarrow R_k$ if some arc $[R_j \ S_1 \ldots S_p] \xrightarrow{i, L := n} [R_k \ S_1 \ldots S_p]$ also occurs in the flowgraph.

7. CONCLUSION

We have shown that it is possible to automatically synthesize the synchronization skeleton of a concurrent program from a Temporal Logic specification. We believe that this approach may in the long run turn out to be quite practical. Since synchronization skeletons are, in general, quite small, the potentially exponential behavior of our algorithm need not be an insurmountable obstacle. Much additional research will be needed, however, to make the approach feasible in practice.

We have also described a model checking algorithm which can be applied to mechanically verify that a finite state concurrent program meets a particular Temporal Logic specification. We believe that practical software tools based on this technique could be developed in the near future. Indeed, we have already programmed an experimental implementation of the model checker on the DEC 11/70 at Harvard.* Certain applications seem particularly suited to the model checker approach to verification: One example is the problem of verifying the correctness of existing network protocols many of which are coded as finite state machines. We encourage additional work in this area.

---

*We would like to acknowledge Marshall Brinn who did the actual programming for our implementation of the model checker.

8. BIBLIOGRAPHY

[BA81]   Ben-Ari, M., personal communication, 1981.

[BH81]   Ben-Ari, M., Halpern, J., and Pnueli, A., Finite Models for Deterministic
          Propositional Logic. Proceedings 8th Int. Colloquium on Automata,
          Languages, and Programming, to appear, 1981.

[BM81]   Ben-Ari, M., Manna, Z., and Pnueli, A., The Temporal Logic of Branching
          Time. 8th Annual ACM Symp. on Principles of Programming Languages, 1981.

[CL77]   Clarke, E.M., Program Invariants as Fixpoints. 18th Annual Symp. on
          Foundations of Computer Science, 1977.

[EC80]   Emerson, E.A., and Clarke, E.M., Characterizing Correctness Properties of
          Parallel Programs as Fixpoints. Proceedings 7th Int. Colloquium on Automata,
          Languages, and Programming, Lecture Notes in Computer Science #85,
          Springer-Verlag, 1981.

[EH81]   Emerson, E.A., and Halpern, J., A New Decision Procedure for the Temporal
          Logic of Branching Time, unpublished manuscript, Harvard Univ., 1981.

[FS81]   Flon, L., and Suzuki, N., The Total Correctness of Parallel Programs.
          SIAM J. Comp., to appear, 1981.

[GP80]   Gabbay, D., Pnueli, A., et al., The Temporal Analysis of Fairness. 7th
          Annual ACM Symp. on Principles of Programming Languages, 1980.

[HC68]   Hughes, G., and Cresswell, M., An Introduction to Modal Logic. Methuen,
          London, 1968.

[LA80]   Lamport, L., "Sometime" is Sometimes "Not Never." 7th Annual ACM Symp. on
          Principles of Prgramming Languages, 1980.

[LA78]   Laventhal, M., Synthesis of Synchronization Code for Data Abstractions,
          Ph.D. Thesis, M.I.T., June 1978.

[PA69]   Park, D., Fixpoint Induction and Proofs of Program Properties, in Machine
          Intelligence 5 (D. Mitchie, ed.), Edinburgh University Press, 1970.

[PR77]   Pratt, V., A Practical Decision Method for Propositional Dynamic Logic.
          10th ACM Symp. on Theory of Computing, 1977.

[RK80]   Ramamritham, K., and Keller, R., Specification and Synthesis of Synchronizers.
          9th International Conference on Parallel Processing, 1980.

[SM68]   Smullyan, R.M., First Order Logic. Springer-Verlag, Berlin, 1968.

[TA55]   Tarski, A., A Lattice-Theoretical Fixpoint Theorem and Its Applications.
          Pacific J. Math., 5, pp. 285-309 (1955).

[TA72]   Tarjan, R., Depth First Search and Linear Graph Algorithms. SIAM J. Comp.
          1:2, pp. 146-160, 1972.

[WO81]   Wolper, P. Synthesis of Communicating Processes From Temporal Logic
          Specifications, unpublished manuscript, Stanford Univ., 1981.

SPECIFICATION AND VERIFICATION OF
CONCURRENT SYSTEMS IN CESAR*

J.P. Queille and J. Sifakis
Laboratoire IMAG, BP 53X
38041 Grenoble Cedex, France

Abstract :

The aim of this paper is to illustrate by an example, the alternating bit protocol,
the use of CESAR, an interactive system for aiding the design of distributed applications.
CESAR allows the progressive validation of the algorithmic description of a, system
of communicating sequential processes with respect to a given set of specifications.
The algorithmic description is done in a high level language inspired from CSP and
specifications are a set of formulas of a branching time logic, the temporal operators of which can be computed iteratively as fixed points of monotonic predicate
transformers. The verification of a system consists in obtaining by automatic translation of its description program an Interpreted Petri Net representing it and
evaluating each formula of the specifications.

1. INTRODUCTION

The aim of this paper is to illustrate by an example the use of the system CESAR for
the analysis of the properties of parallel systems.
CESAR is a system for aiding the design and integration of distributed applications.
Its input language is a high level language, inspired from CSP [Hoare 78], for the
algorithmic description of systems of communicating sequential processes. CESAR
allows a progressive validation during the design process by considering two comple-
mentary aspects in a description :
- coherence in data manipulation (static characteristics of data and exchanged
  variables, visibility and access rights...)
- validation of the dynamic behaviour of a description with respect to its specifications.
Behavioural analysis of a system described by a program in the input language is
based on the study of a representation of it in terms of Interpreted Petri Nets
(IPN). Figure 1 illustrates the general principle of the system CESAR : given an
algorithmic description of a system by a program in a high level language, a model
representing some aspects of the described functioning is obtained by automatic

* Originally published in: Dezani-Ciancaglini, M., Montanari, U. (eds.)
  International Symposium on Programming. LNCS, vol. 137, pp. 337-351.
  Springer, Heidelberg (1982).

O. Grumberg and H. Veith (Eds.): 25MC Festschrift, LNCS 5000, pp. 216–230, 2008.
© Springer-Verlag Berlin Heidelberg 2008

translation. This model (an IPN) is treated by an analyzer in order to verify the conformity of the described system to given specifications. Specifications are a set of formulas of a branching time logic and express correctness properties which must be satisfied by the system. Using branching time logic instead of linear time logic as it has often been done [Gabbay 80] [Lamport 80] [Manna 81], is one of the peculiarities of our approach. It is shown that in this logic it is possible to compute

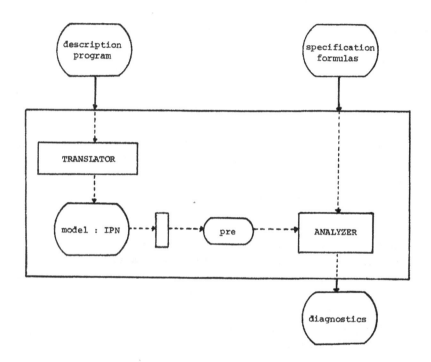

Figure 1

iteratively the interpretation of temporal operators as fixed points of monotonic predicate transformers.

Our approach presents some similarities to these followed in [Jensen 79] [Lauer 75] as far as the use of Petri nets as a model for the semantical analysis is concerned. The example considered throughout this paper is the alternating bit protocol. We have chosen this example because protocol modelling and verification is one of the principal application domains for CESAR. Furthemore, as protocols have been the object of many studies and especially the alternating bit protocol [Bartlett 69] [Bremer 79]

[Schwartz 81] [SIGPN 81], a rather precise comparison between the different approaches can be done.

This paper is organized in four parts. In part 2, the features of the description language are given and an illustration of its use for the description of the AB-protocol. After presenting the specification language, a part of the specifications of this protocol is given (part 3). In part 4 are exposed the analysis principle applied in CESAR and the theoretical results on which it is based.

2. DESCRIPTION IN CESAR

2.1. The description language

A system is described as a set of communicating sequential processes. Communications are declared as names of "exchanged variables". Exchange is done by rendez-vous between two processes, the one executing an output operation $!V:=exp$ and the other an input operation $?V$ where V is the exchanged variable. The process executing the input operation has a local copy of the exchanged variable also denoted by V (not preceded by $?$).

In addition to exchanged variables, processes have internal variables (which cannot be used for communication). Internal and exchanged variables are typed. Usual standard types and type constructors are available but the user can also introduce non-specified types for which it is not necessary to make manipulation rules explicit.

The basic statement of the language is the vectorial assignment. An input or output operation can be executed simultaneously with a vectorial assignment. We denote by nop the assignment.whose right member is the identity function.

Besides the usual control structures, the CESAR description language provides the two following non-deterministic composed statements :

$$\underline{if} \ b_1 \rightarrow s_1 \ // \ b_2 \rightarrow s_2 \ // \ \ldots \ \underline{fi}$$

$$\underline{do} \ b_1 \rightarrow s_1 \ // \ b_2 \rightarrow s_2 \ // \ \ldots \ \underline{od}$$

where the b_i's are boolean conditions (guards) and the s_i's are sequences of statements. Their meaning is the following.

- IF : wait until one of the conditions is true and execute the corresponding sequence of statements.
- DO : repetition of an IF statement until a statement EXIT is encountered during the execution of some s_i.

For both of these constructs, if more than one conditions are true, the choice is non-deterministic. If a statement s_i begins with an input or output operation, the condition "the exchange can be executed" (i.e. the rendez-vous is possible) implicitely strengthens the guard b_i. The interpretation of the IF and DO constructs are the same as the interpretation of the WHEN and CYCLE statements in [Brinch Hansen 78].

2.2. Translation of description programs into interpreted Petri nets

Given a program in the input language, the translator generates an Interpreted Petri
Net (IPN) representing the main aspects of its behaviour. It performs also the type
verification and deletes the internal variables of non-specified types.
The IPN corresponding to a program is obtained by composing the IPN's representing
its sequential processes. The translation method of the process uses a graph grammar,
every rule of which is associated with a rule of the grammar of the description language [Queille 81].
An IPN is a Petri net with :
- a vector of variables X,
- a mapping associating with each transition of the net a guarded command $c_i \rightarrow a_i$
  where c_i is a condition on X and a_i is a vectorial assignment $a_i = (X := \alpha_i(X))$.
Functioning rules of an IPN are those of standard Petri nets, with the addition of
the following rules :
- a transition can fire only when its associated condition is true,
- when a transition fires, its associated action is executed.
IPN's are a useful tool for representing parallel programs in a non-deterministic way
[Keller 76]. They can be graphically represented by the corresponding Petri net, the
transitions of which are inscribed by the associated guarded commands. By convention,
the always true condition and the identity assignment can be omitted. Thus, if a transition has no inscription its firing rule is the same as in a standard Petri net.
The translation method is such that each net representing a sequential process is a
safe state graph. The composition rule expresses the rendez-vous by merging transitions and so, it preserves safety of each process. This property is used by the analyzer in order to simplify predicate manipulations.

2.3 Example : The Alternating Bit Protocol

2.3.1 Presentation of the protocol

The Alternating Bit Protocol (AB-Protocol) introduced in [Barlett 69] to provide a
reliable full-duplex transmission over half-duplex links, is a protocol where the
control information of each transmitted message or acknowledgement is a single control bit which can be used to detect loss of messages or acknowledgements and recover
from them. In this paper, we are not interested in transmission errors which at the
protocol level are not distinguished from losses. Since this protocol is completely
symmetrical we suppose transmission of data in a single direction and describe it by
considering a Sender and a Receiver as follows :

The Sender sends messages to the Receiver, which answers by sending acknowledgements. The Sender associates with each message a control bit which takes alternating values. After sending a message, the Sender does not change the control bit and does not send the next message before the reception of the corresponding acknowledgement (an acknowledgement with the same control bit). To recover from loss of messages or of acknowledgements, the Sender awaits the acknowledgement during a finite delay (measured by an arbitrary local clock) and then repeats the same message (without changing the control bit).

The Receiver behaves symmetrically. After receiving a message, it sends an acknowledgement with the same control bit and then awaits the next message (with a control bit of alternate value). If the next message does not arrive within an arbitrary local delay, the Receiver repeats the previous acknowledgement.

If we assume that the line cannot loose all the messages and acknowledgements (i.e. the line is not cut), this protocol ensures the correct transmission of each message after a sufficient number of repetitions. Message duplication does not cause any problem because the protocol guarantees that any sequence of received messages with the same control bit are duplications of the same message and the bit is changed by the Sender for all new messages. Thus, the Receiver has just to skip all the messages of such sequences except the first one. Symmetrically, the Sender has to skip duplications of acknowledgements in the same way.

2.3.2 Description programs and IPN's for the AB-protocol

We introduce two non-specified types :
- data to represent the data part of the messages
- pattern to represent the pattern of bits which is recognized as an acknowledgement.

Using the standard type boolean, we can define both the type msg for the messages and the type ack for the acknowledgements as two structures :

```
type msg = ( MESSAGE : data ;
             B : boolean ) ;
type ack = ( ACKNOWLEDGEMENT : pattern ;
             B : boolean ) ;
```

The program for the sender is given in the following page ($\top$ means true ; $\hat{}$ is the complementation operator).

```
process SENDER
   ( output M : msg ;
     input A : ack ) ;

X : data ;
Y : boolean := 0 ;                                     -- initial value

begin

                     loop
send:                  !M := (X, Y) ;                  -- send the message
                       do
receiveack:              T -> ?A ;                     -- receive acknowledgement
                           if
acceptack:                   A.B = Y -> Y := ^Y ;        -- expected acknowledgment
                                   exit //
skipack:                     A.B ≠ Y -> nop              -- else skip
                           fi //
repeat:                  T -> !M := (X, Y)             -- repeat the message
                       od
                     end loop

end SENDER ;
```

The program for the Receiver is the following :

```
process RECEIVER
   ( input MM : msg ;
     output AA : ack ) ;

Z : boolean := 0 ;                                     -- initial value

begin

                     loop
                       do
receive:                 T -> ?MM ;                     -- receive message
                           if
accept:                      MM.B = Z -> exit //          -- expected message
skip:                        MM.B ≠ Z -> nop              -- else skip
                           fi //
repeatack:               T -> !AA := ("ack", ^Z) -- repeat previous acknowledgement
                       od;
sendack:                 !AA := ("ack", Z), Z := ^Z -- send acknowledgement
                     end loop

end RECEIVER ;
```

The transmission line is described by the two following processes :

```
process SENDTORECEIVE
   ( input M : msg ;
     output MM : msg ) ;

begin

                     loop
get:                   ?M ;                            -- message is sent
                           if
transmit:                  T -> !MM := M //            -- message is transmitted
loose:                     T -> nop                    -- message is lost
                           fi
                     end loop

end SENDTORECEIVE ;
```

```
process RECEIVETOSEND
   ( input AA : ack ;
     output A : ack ) ;

begin

                     loop
getack:                 ?AA ;                      -- acknowledgement is sent
                        if
transmitack:               T -> !A := AA //        -- acknowledgement is transmitted
looseack:                  T -> nop               -- acknowledgement is lost
                        fi
                     end loop

end RECEIVETOSEND ;
```

Figure 2 presents the IPN obtained by translation of the description program.

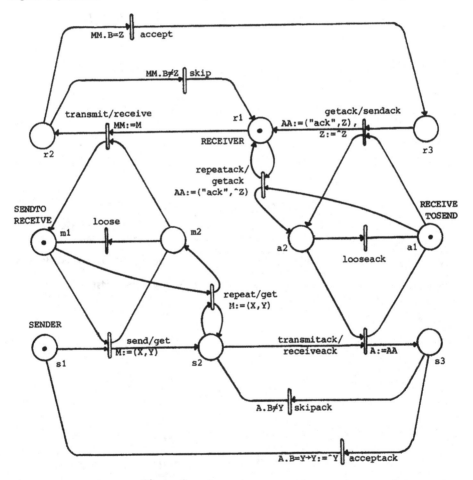

Figure 2

3. SPECIFICATION IN CESAR

3.1 The specification language

The specification language of CESAR is a branching time logic L [Lamport 80]
[Rescher 71] constructed from a set of propositional variables F and the constants
true, false, by using the logical connectives, $\neg$, $\wedge$, $\vee$, $\Longrightarrow$ and the unary temporal
operators POT and INEV. The abbreviations ALL(f) and SOME(f) are used for respectively
$\neg$POT($\neg$f) and $\neg$INEV($\neg$f).

The formulas of L represent assertions about the functioning of a given system if we
consider that propositional variables represent predicates on its state and give a
precise meaning to the operators POT and INEV. In order to do this, we consider transition systems as a model for L since IPN's can be given a semantics in terms of
them [Keller 76].

A transition system is defined as a doublet $S = (Q, \rightarrow)$ where Q is a set of states and
$\rightarrow$ is a binary relation on Q ($\rightarrow \subseteq Q \times Q$). The relation $\rightarrow$ represents the actions or transitions of the system : $q \rightarrow q'$ means that there is an action executable from q which
after its execution leads to a state q'. An execution sequence from a given state q_0
is a sequence s of states such that if s is finite then its last element q_t is a sink
state (i.e. $\neg q''(q_t \rightarrow q'')$). In order to simplify the notations we take s(k) to be equal
to the k-th element of s if it is defined ; if not, we take s(k)=ω where ω represents
some ficticious non accessible state adjoined to Q such that $\neg q \in Q(q \rightarrow \omega)$. Thus, relation s(0) $\overset{k}{\twoheadrightarrow}$ s(k) is satisfied iff s(k)$\neq \omega$. The set of all the execution sequences from
a state q will be denoted by EXq.

Given L and a transition system S=(Q,$\rightarrow$) we define an interpretation of L as a function
$| |$ associating to each formula of L a truth-valued function of the system state in
the following manner :

- $\forall f \in F$ $|f| \in [Q \rightarrow \{tt, ff\}]$ where $[Q \rightarrow \{tt, ff\}]$ is the set of the unary predicates on Q
- $\forall q \in Q$ $|\underline{true}|$ (q) = tt
- $\forall f \in L$ $|\neg f|$ (q) = tt iff $|f|$ (q) = ff
- $\forall f_1, f_2 \in L$ $|f_1 \wedge f_2|$ (q) = tt iff $|f_1|$ (q) = tt $\underline{and}$ $|f_2|$ (q) = tt
- $\forall f \in L$ $|POT(f)|$ (q) $\equiv \exists s \in EXq \; \exists k \in \mathbb{N} \; [q \overset{k}{\twoheadrightarrow} s(k) \; \underline{and} \; |f| \; (s(k))]$
- $\forall f \in L$ $|INEV(f)|$ (q) $\equiv \forall s \in EXq \; \exists k \in \mathbb{N} \; [q \overset{k}{\twoheadrightarrow} s(k) \; \underline{and} \; |f| \; (s(k))]$

Obviously, $|POT(f)|$ represents the set of the states q of S such that there exists an
execution sequence starting from q containing a state satisfying $|f|$. We say that
$|POT(f)|$ is the set of the states from which some state of $|f|$ is potentially reacha-
ble. In the same way, $|INEV(f)|$ is the set of the states from which $|f|$ is inevitably
reachable in the sense that every execution sequence starting from a state of this
set contains a state satisfying $|f|$.

The interpretation of the dual operators ALL and SOME is,

$$|ALL(f)|(q) \equiv \forall s \epsilon EXq \; \forall k \epsilon \mathbb{N} \; [q \overset{k}{\to} s(k) \; \underline{implies} \; |f| \; (s(k))]$$

$$|SOME(f)|(q) \equiv \exists s \epsilon EXq \; \forall k \epsilon \mathbb{N}[q \overset{k}{\to} s(k) \; \underline{implies} \; |f| \; (s(k))]$$

Remark that if the state q of a transition system satisfies $|ALL(f)|$ then all the states of <u>all</u> the execution sequences from q verify $|f|$. Also, if a state q satisfies $|SOME(f)|$ then there exists <u>some</u> execution sequence from q such that all its states verify $|f|$.

The properties of a branching time logic similar to L have been studied in [Ben-Ari 81] where a decision procedure and a complete deduction system are given.

3.2 Example

In this section we give examples illustrating the use of the specification language for expressing system properties. The formulas of this languages are constructed from the following set of propositional variables :

- propositional variables representing predicates on the variables of the description program (only program variables of specified types are considered),

- the propositional variable <u>Init</u> which characterizes the set of all the possible initial (control and data) states,

- propositional variables on the control of the system referring to names of actions (labels) defined in the description program ; for each labelled action a, the propositional variables <u>enable</u> a and <u>after</u> a are introduced such that $|\underline{enable} \; a|$ and $|\underline{after} \; a|$ characterize respectively the set of the states from which this action can be executed and the set of the states reached just after the termination of this action. The following abbreviations are used :

  . $\underline{enable} \; (a_1,\ldots,a_k) = \overset{k}{\underset{i=1}{\vee}} \; \underline{enable} \; a_i$, where $\{a_1,\ldots,a_k\}$ is a set of actions,

  . $\underline{enable} \; P = \underline{enable} \; A(P)$ where P is a process the set of the actions of which is $A(P)$,

  . $\underline{after} \; (a_1,\ldots,a_k) = \overset{k}{\underset{i=1}{\vee}} \; \underline{after} \; a_i$, where $\{a_1,\ldots,a_k\}$ is a set of actions.

Obviously, a large number of properties can be formulated concerning the behaviour of a system. For methodological reasons, it is interesting to classify the most important of them as this has already been done for linear time logic in [Gabbay 80] [Lamport 80] and [Manna 81]. Hereafter we introduce three families of properties and give specifications of the AB-protocol in terms of them.

Invariant properties

Invariant properties express the fact that a predicate P, constructed by using only logical operators, is always true.

They are formulas of the type : <u>Init</u> ⟹ ALL(P)

In the case of the AB-protocol such formulas can be used to express :

* Init ⟹ ALL(<u>after</u>(send,repeat) ⟹ (M.B=Y))

  i.e. after the emission of a message the value of the control bit emitted M.B is equal to the control bit Y of the SENDER.

* Init ⟹ ALL(<u>after</u> receive ⟹ (MM=M))

  i.e. after the reception of a message the value of the received message MM is equal to the value of the emitted message M, i.e. the line does not modify the transmitted information.

* Init ⟹ ALL(<u>after</u> receive ⟹ (MM.B=Y))

  i.e. after reception of a message the value of the received control bit MM.B is equal to the value of the control bit of the SENDER at the same time.

Liveness properties

These properties express the fact that an action can always be executed.

- <u>Liveness of an action a</u> : from every state q, successor of a state satisfying <u>Init</u>, there exists an execution sequence of EXq containing a state which enables a. This is expressed by the formula : <u>Init</u> ⟹ ALL POT <u>enable</u> a

- <u>Liveness of a set of actions</u> $\{a_1,\ldots,a_k\}$: each one of the actions a_i is live. This can be expressed by the formula : <u>Init</u> ⟹ $\overset{k}{\underset{i=1}{\wedge}}$(ALL POT <u>enable</u> a_i).

Or, by distributivity of ALL with respect to ∧ : <u>Init</u> ⟹ ALL($\overset{k}{\underset{i=1}{\wedge}}$ POT <u>enable</u> a_i).

- <u>Absence of deadlock for a set of actions</u> $\{a_1,\ldots,a_k\}$: from every state q, successor of a state satisfying <u>Init</u>, there exists an execution sequence of EXq which contains a state enabling at least one of the actions a_i. This is expressed by :

<u>Init</u> ⟹ ALL POT <u>enable</u> $(a_1,\ldots,a_k)$.

Some interesting liveness properties of the given example are (starting from the weakest ones) :

* <u>Init</u> ⟹ ALL POT <u>enable</u> (SENDER), i.e. absence of deadlock for the SENDER

* <u>Init</u> ⟹ ALL POT <u>enable</u> (RECEIVER), i.e. absence of deadlock for the RÉCEIVER

* <u>Init</u> ⟹ ALL POT <u>enable</u> send, i.e. the action of emitting a new message is live

* <u>Init</u> ⟹ ALL POT <u>enable</u> accept, i.e. the action of receiving a new message is live.

Properties of response to an action

They are properties expressing the fact that an action b is a consequence of an action a.

- <u>Possible response</u> : if an action a is executed then it is possible that an action b becomes executable. This is expressed by the formula :

  Init ⟹ ALL(<u>after</u> a ⟹ POT <u>enable</u> b)

- <u>Inevitably possible response</u> : if an action a is executed then necessarily b becomes executable. This is expressed by the formula :

  Init ⟹ ALL(<u>after</u> a ⟹ INEV <u>enable</u> b)

Some interesting properties of this family for the given example are :

* <u>Init</u> ==> ALL (<u>after</u> (send,repeat) ==> POT <u>enable</u> receive)

    i.e. the line from the SENDER to the RECEIVER is able to transmit messages.

* <u>Init</u> ==> ALL (<u>after</u>(sendack,repeatack) ==> POT <u>enable</u> receivack)

    i.e. the line from the RECEIVER to the SENDER is able to transmit acknowledgements.

* <u>Init</u> ==> ALL(<u>after</u>(send,repeat) ==> INEV <u>enable</u> receivack)

    i.e. after sending a message the SENDER waits for an acknowledgement.

* <u>Init</u> ==> ALL[(<u>after</u> accept ==> INEV(<u>enable</u> sendack)) ∧
    (<u>after</u> sendack ==> AA.B=MM.B)]

    i.e. when the RECEIVER receives a new message, it will send the corresponding acknowledgement.

4. PROVING SPECIFICATIONS IN CESAR

4.1. The results used by the analyser

In this paragraph we present the basic theoretical results used by the analyser. The method consists in iteratively computing fixed points of predicate transformers obtained from the IPN under study. Fixed points are precisely the interpretations of temporal operators as it is shown by the following results proved in detail in [Sifakis 79].

Let $S = (Q, \rightarrow)$ be a transition system. It is convenient to identify any unary predicate on Q with its characteristic set. $(2^Q, \cup, \cap, ^-)$ represents the lattice of predicates and $[2^Q \rightarrow 2^Q]$ the set of the internal mappings of 2^Q (predicate transformers). For $f, g \in [2^Q \rightarrow 2^Q]$, $f \cup g$, $f \cap g$, $\bar{f}$, $\tilde{f}$ and Id denote the functions $f \cup g = \lambda p. \ f(P) \cup g(P)$, $f \cap g = \lambda P. \ f(P) \cap g(P)$, $\bar{f} = \lambda P. \ \overline{f(P)}$, $\tilde{f} = \lambda P. \ \bar{f}(\bar{P})$, Id $= \lambda P. \ P$.

We also introduce the notations :

$$f^* = Id \cup f \cup f^2 \cup \ldots \ f^k \cup \ldots = \bigcup_{i \in \mathbb{N}} f^i$$

$$f^x = Id \cap f \cap f^2 \cap \ldots \ f^k \cap \ldots = \bigcap_{i \in \mathbb{N}} f^i$$

<u>Definition 1</u> : Given $S = (Q, \rightarrow)$ a transition system, $P \in 2^Q$ and $q \in Q$, we define the predicate transformer pre : pre $P(q) \equiv \exists q'(q \rightarrow q' \ \underline{and} \ P(q'))$.

<u>Proposition 1</u> :

Let f be a formula of L, $S = (Q, \rightarrow)$ a transition system such that $\rightarrow$ be image-finite and $|\ |$ an interpretation of L in S.

a) $|ALL(f)| = \tilde{pre}^x |f|$

b) $|SOME(f)| = (Id \cap (pre \cup \tilde{pre}))^x |f|$

<u>Proposition 2</u> :

Let f be a formula of L, $S = (Q, \rightarrow)$ a transition system such that $\rightarrow$ be image-finite and $|\ |$ an interpretation of L in S.

a) $|POT(f)| = pre^*|f|$

b) $|INEV(f)| = (Id \cup pre\widetilde{npre})^* |f|$

4.2 The principle of the verification method

According to the results of the preceding section, it is possible to compute iteratively the interpretation of the temporal operators. We present hereafter the principle of the verification method applied by the analyzer :

Let f be a formula to be verified on a given program PROG and N the IPN obtained by
translation from PROG. Denote by $F = \{f_1,\ldots,f_n\}$ the set of the propositional variables
occuring in f.

- Associate a boolean variable with each place of N.

- For each <u>after</u> aϵF, express $|after\ a|$ as a predicate on these variables (if necessa-
  ry, N is transformed by adding new places).

- For each <u>enable</u> aϵF, express $|enable\ a|$ as a predicate on the boolean control va-
  riables and program variables.

- Express <u>Init</u> as a predicate representing the set of all possible initial states
  (knowing the initial marking of the net and the initial values of program variables).

- Reduce N without transforming the places which are involved in the expression of
  the predicates of $|F| = \{|f_1|,\ldots,|f_n|\}$. Reducing N consists in applying transforma-
  tion rules preserving the property expressed by f in order to obtain an IPN of
  less complexity.

- Compute the predicate transformer pre associated to the reduced IPN and then, the
  interpretation of temporal operators following the evaluation order imposed by the
  formula f. During these computations simplification rules are applied, taking advantage of the fact that sequential processes correspond to state graphs. Given that
  there is no criterion on the speed of the convergence of these iterations, the user
  can impose a maximum number of iterations.

- If some iterative computation yields no result within the acceptable number of ite-
  rations then the analyzer fails to give an answer. If not, it evaluates $|f|$: the
  property described by f is verified iff $|f|$ (q) = tt for every state q.

4.3 Example

For the AB-protocol, the liveness property <u>Init</u> $\Longrightarrow$ ALL POT <u>enable</u> (SENDER) is verified by computing successively :

1) $\underline{Init} = s_1 m_1 a_1 r_1 \bar{y} \bar{z}$. Intersection operators are omitted. The boolean variables s_i, m_i,
   a_i, r_i, represent the fact that the places with the same name have a token
   (see figure 2).

2) $\underline{enable}(SENDER) = s_1 m_1 \cup s_2 m_1 \cup s_2 a_2 \cup s_3$

3) the interpretation of POT <u>enable</u> (SENDER) as the limit of : $P_{k+1} = P_k \cup pre(P_k)$ with

P_0 = <u>enable</u> (SENDER).

The following relations are invariants generated by the translator expressing the fact that each process is a safe state graph and they are used to simplify the boolean expressions computed by the analyzer :

$s_1 \bar{s}_2 \bar{s}_3 \cup \bar{s}_1 s_2 \bar{s}_3 \cup \bar{s}_1 \bar{s}_2 s_3 = \top$ ($\top$ is the always true predicate)

$r_1 \bar{r}_2 \bar{r}_3 \cup \bar{r}_1 r_2 \bar{r}_3 \cup \bar{r}_1 \bar{r}_2 r_3 = \top$

$\qquad m_1 \bar{m}_2 \cup \bar{m}_1 m_2 = \top$

$\qquad a_1 \bar{a}_2 \cup \bar{a}_1 a_2 = \top$

The first step of the computation gives, $\mathrm{pre}(P_0) = s_3 \cup r_2 \cup r_3 \cup a_2 \cup m_2$. Thus,

$P_1 = P_0 \cup \mathrm{pre}(P_0) = \top$ and POT <u>enable</u> (SENDER) = $\top$.

4) ALL POT <u>enable</u> (SENDER) = $\top$

5) [<u>Init</u> ==> ALL POT <u>enable</u> (SENDER)] = $\top$ (the property is verified).

5. CONCLUSION

We have tried to illustrate with an example, the AB-protocol, the analysis method applied in CESAR.

This method is based on the idea of translating the description of a system, given in some high-level formalism, into a model for which there exists a verification theory. This approach presents the advantage, on the one hand of abstracting from all the details which are not relevant to the verification of the behaviour (for example, data represented by variables of non-specified types), on the other hand, of displaying the control structure (invariants, for instance). In particular, the translation into a Petri net gives the possibility of naming control points which makes the expression of the properties easier.

The language of the formulas allows the expression of a great number of foundamental properties (invariant properties, liveness properties, properties of response to an action). The use of such a language is interesting from a methodological point of view as it provides the possibility of classification and comparison of the properties according to various criteria. Also, the representation of properties by formulas using temporal operators leads to mechanizable proofs provided that a method for obtaining from a given description the associated predicate transformer pre be given. Computing fixed points of monotonic functions is, from a practical point of view, a central problem and it determines the limitations of our approach. Appart from the limitations of theoretical nature (non-decidability of the "interesting" system properties) serious problems appear when applying iterative methods which require the manipulation, simplification and comparison of predicates on many variables. For this reason, the current version of CESAR can verify formulas with variables of type <u>boolean</u>, <u>enumerated</u> and <u>integer</u> with known bounds, only.In order to simplify computations, the analyzer encodes the enumerated and bounded integer variables so that it manipulates only boolean variables ; this coding is completely transparent to the user.

However, in spite of these simplifications the problems due to the complexity of the analyzed system remain crucial. We intend to increase the efficiency of the applied method by working in the following directions :

- Use of methods for approximating fixed points of monotonic operators in a lattice [Cousot 78] [Clarke 80],

- Reduction of the complexity of the iterative computations by decomposing global assertions into a set of local assertions,

- Study of a methodology of description since the possibility of proving a property greatly depends on the way the description is built.

REFERENCES

[Bartlett 69]   K.A. BARTLETT, R.A. SCANTLEBURY and P.T. WILKINSON "A note on reliable full-duplex transmission over half-duplex links" CACM, Vol. 12, N°5, May 1969, pp. 260-261.

[Ben-Ari 81]   M. BEN-ARI, Z. MANNA and A. PNUELI "The temporal logic of branching time" Proc. 8th Annual ACM Symp. on Principles of Programming Languages, Jan. 1981, pp. 164-176.

[Bremer 79]   J. BREMER and O. DROBNIK "A new approach to protocol design and validation" IBM research report RC 8018, IBM Yorktown Heights, Dec. 1979

[Brinch Hansen 78] P. BRINCH HANSEN "Distributed Processes : A concurrent programming concept" CACM, Vol. 21, N°5, Nov. 1978, pp. 934-941.

[Clarke 80]   E.M. CLARKE Jr. "Synthesis of resource invariants for concurrent programs" ACM Trans. on Progr. Languages and Systems, Vol. 2, N°3, July 1980, pp. 338-358.

[Cousot 78]   P. COUSOT and N. HALBWACHS "Automatic discovery of linear restraints among variables of a program" Proc. 5th ACM. Symp. on Principles of Programming Languages, Tucson, Ariz., 1978, pp. 84-96.

[Gabbay 80]   D. GABBAY, A. PNUELLI, S. SHELAH and J. STAVI "On the temporal analysis of fairness" Conference Record of the 7th Annual ACM Symposium on Principles of Programming Languages, Jan. 1980, pp. 163-173.

[Hoare 78]   C.A.R. HOARE "Communicating Sequential Processes" Comm. ACM 21-8, August 1978, pp. 666-667.

[Jensen 79]   K. JENSEN, M. KYNG and O.L. MADSEN "A Petri net definition of a system description language" Semantics of Concurrent Computation in LNCS, Springer Verlag, July 1979, pp. 348-368.

[Keller 76]   R.M. KELLER "Formal verification of parallel programs" Comm. ACM 19, 7 (July 1976), pp. 371-384.

[Lamport 80]   L. LAMPORT ""Sometime" is sometimes "not never" - On the temporal logic of programs" Proc. of the 7th Annual ACM Symp. on Principles of Programming Languages, Las Vegas, Janv. 1980, pp. 174-185.

[Lauer 75]   P.E. LAUER and R.H. CAMPBELL "Formal semantics of a class of high level primitives for coordinating concurrent processes" Acta Informatica 5, pp. 297-332 (1975).

[Manna 81]   Z. MANNA and A. PNUELI "Verification of concurrent programs : The temporal framework" Intern. Summer School, Theoretical Foundations of Programming Methodology, Munich, July 1981.

[Queille 81]   J.P. QUEILLE "The CESAR system : An aided design and certification system for distributed applications" Proc. 2nd Int. Conf. on Distributed Computing Systems, April 1981, pp. 149-161.

[Rescher 71]   N. RESCHER and A. URQUHART "Temporal Logic" Springer Verlag, Vienna, 1971.

[Schwartz 81]   R.L. SCHWARTZ and P.M. MELLIAR-SMITH "Temporal logic specification of distributed systems" Proc. 2nd Int. Conf. on Distributed Computing Systems, April 1981, pp. 46-454.

[Sifakis 79]   J. SIFAKIS "A unified approach for studying the properties of transition systems" Research Report RR N° 179, IMAG December 1979 (Revised December 1980), to appear in TCS January 1982.

[SIGPN 81]   Special Interest Group : Petri nets and related system models. Newsletter N° 7, Feb. 1981, p-. 17-20.

Author Index

Lecture Notes in Computer Science

Sublibrary 1: Theoretical Computer Science and General Issues

For information about Vols. 1– 4750
please contact your bookseller or Springer